PHILOSOPHER AT

PHILOSOPHER AT LARGE

An Intellectual Autobiography

BY

MORTIMER J. ADLER

COLLIER BOOKS
Macmillan Publishing Company
New York

Maxwell Macmillan Canada
Toronto

Maxwell Macmillan International
New York   Oxford   Singapore   Sydney

Hoff cartoon reprinted by permission of *Esquire* magazine © 1934
by Esquire Magazine, Inc.
Copr. © 1945 James Thurber, Copr. © 1971 Helen W. Thurber Sauers.
From *Men, Women and Dogs*, published by Harcourt Brace and Jovanovich,
New York. Originally printed in *The New Yorker*.

Collier Books	Maxwell Macmillan Canada, Inc.
Macmillan Publishing Company	1200 Eglinton Avenue East
866 Third Avenue	Suite 200
New York, NY 10022	Don Mills, Ontario M3C 3N1

Macmillan Publishing Company is part of the Maxwell Communication
Group of Companies.

Library of Congress Cataloging-in-Publication Data
Adler, Mortimer Jerome, 1902–
    Philosopher at large: an intellectual autobiography/by Mortimer J.
Adler.
        p. cm.
    Originally published: New York: Macmillan, c1977.
    Includes bibliographical references and index.
    ISBN 0-02-001011-7
    1. Adler, Mortimer Jerome, 1902–   . 2. Philosophers—United
States—Biography. I. Title.
[B945.A2864A35 1992]   92–6299   CIP
191—dc20
[B]

Macmillan books are available at special discounts for bulk purchases for
sales promotions, premiums, fund-raising, or educational use. For details,
contact:

Special Sales Director
Macmillan Publishing Company
866 Third Avenue
New York, NY 10022

First Collier Books Edition 1992

10 9 8 7 6 5 4 3 2 1

Printed in the United States of America

To My Family

Contents

Acknowledgments

THE AUTHOR WISHES to express his gratitude for permission to reprint material from the following sources:

The Estate of Franklin P. Adams (Jacob I. Charney, Attorney) and Bell & Howell—Micro Photo Division for "To a Class Room Metaphysician," by Henry Morton Robinson, from Franklin P. Adams's column, "The Conning Tower," in *New York World*, May 31, 1927.

Harper's Magazine for excerpt from "Hutchins of Chicago, Part II," by Milton S. Mayer, in *Harper's Magazine*, April 1939; for excerpts from "This Pre-War Generation," by Mortimer J. Adler, in *Harper's Magazine*, October 1940. Copyright © 1940 by *Harper's Magazine*. Copyright © renewed 1967 by *Harper's Magazine*. All rights reserved; for excerpts from "The Chicago School," by Mortimer J. Adler, in *Harper's Magazine*, September 1941. Copyright © 1941 by *Harper's Magazine*. Copyright © renewed 1968 by *Harper's Magazine*. All rights reserved.

Used with permission of President and Fellows of Harvard College for excerpts from "The St. John's Program," by Walter Lippmann, in New York *Herald Tribune*, December 1938.

By permission of Hawthorn Books, Inc. from *A POCKETFUL OF WRY*, by Phyllis McGinley. Copyright © 1959 by Phyllis McGinley. All rights reserved.

Henry Holt and Co. and The Beacon Press for excerpts from *Reconstruction in Philosophy*, by John Dewey. Copyright © 1920 by Henry Holt and Co., Copyright © 1948 by The Beacon Press.

Humanities Press Inc. and Routledge & Kegan Paul Ltd. for excerpts from *Tractatus Logico-Philosophicus*, by Ludwig Wittgenstein. Copyright © 1947 by Humanities Press Inc., New Jersey, and Routledge & Kegan Paul Ltd., London.

The Nation for excerpts from "Slight of Hand" (Will Durant's *The Story of Philosophy*), by Mortimer J. Adler, in *The Nation*, September 29, 1926; for excerpts from "The Outlining of Knowledge: A Debate on Popularization," by John Haynes Holmes and Mortimer J. Adler, in *The Nation,* October 12, 1927; for excerpts in *The Nation,* May 8, 1929. Reprinted by permission.

The New York Times for excerpt from "Letter to the Editor," by Bertrand Russell, in *The New York Times,* February 16, 1941. © 1941 by The New York Times Company. Reprinted by permission; for excerpt from "What Makes Man Free?" (Mortimer J. Adler's *The Idea of Freedom*), by Brand Blanshard, in *The New York Times,* September 14, 1958. © 1958 by The New York Times Company. Reprinted by permission.

The New Yorker and William W. Watt for "On the Gospel According to St. John's," by William W. Watt, in *The New Yorker,* April 29, 1944. Reprinted by permission; © 1944, 1972, The New Yorker Magazine, Inc.

The Philosophical Quarterly and Ruth S. Campbell for excerpt of Book Review (Mortimer J. Adler's *The Idea of Freedom, Vol. II*), by C. A. Campbell, in *The Philosophical Quarterly,* April 1963.

Simon and Schuster, Inc. for excerpts from *How To Read A Book,* by Mortimer J. Adler. Copyright © 1940 by Mortimer J. Adler. Copyright © renewed 1967 by Mortimer J. Adler. All rights reserved.

Time Inc. for excerpts from "The University of Chicago," by John Chamberland, in *Fortune,* December 1937.

Diana Trilling for excerpt from "The Uncertain Future of the Humanistic Educational Ideal," by Lionel Trilling, in *The American Scholar,* Winter 1974–1975.

Dorothy Van Doren for "Philosopher at Large," by Mark Van Doren, in *Morning Worship and Other Poems.*

Yale University Press and Robert M. Hutchins for excerpts from *The Higher Learning in America, by* Robert M. Hutchins. Copyright © 1936 by Yale University Press.

Preface

As THE SUBTITLE indicates, this autobiography is far from being the whole story of my life. Much has been omitted that is not germane to the narrower scope of the events, undertakings, and engagements I have chosen to write about. This has resulted in some limitation on the degree to which self-understanding or self-revelation has been achieved. It has also resulted in narrowing the focus on institutions and persons to those which bear directly on the main themes of the narrative.

If, ideally, the writing of an autobiography should be an occasion for knowing one's self better, or if the reading of an autobiography by others should afford them insights into the character or personality of the author, I must disclaim any pretension to having even approximated that ideal. The only claim I would make is that I have described the development of my mind, portrayed its lineaments, and exhibited its controlling motives as clearly and as honestly as I could.

It seems appropriate to add by way of comment on my life as a whole, that what impressed me most as I wrote these pages was the frequent intercession of good fortune in ways that facilitated my staying on the path I wished to pursue almost from the very beginning. Beneficent external circumstances encouraged and impelled me to apply my energies to intellectual objectives that have been constant goals for the greater part of my life. I can take credit only for loyalty to those goals and strenuous effort to achieve them in some measure. Anything beyond that I owe to my guardian angel.

The other debts of gratitude I hasten to acknowledge are to the many friends who have helped me by reading and criticizing the manuscript of this book: Robert Hutchins, Clifton Fadiman, Jacques Barzun, William Gorman, Otto Bird, Hannah Kaiser, Elizabeth Paepcke, Arthur Houghton, Jr., John Van Doren, Charles and Geraldine Van Doren. For the typing and re-typing of the manuscript many times, and for their amused reaction to it in the process, I am most grateful to Rose-mary Barnes and Marlys Allen. I am indebted to Marlys and also Otto Bird for the construction of the bibliography of my writings that is appended to this book; and to Wayne Moquin for preparing the index.

I could not let this work go from my hands without the assurance I was able to draw from the sympathetic and critical reading given it by my wife Caroline.

MORTIMER J. ADLER

Chicago
January 1977

PHILOSOPHER AT LARGE

Chapter 1

Dropout

R EADING THE *Autobiography* of John Stuart Mill at the age of fifteen
while in the editorial office of the old New York *Sun* led me to
the discovery of Socrates; and this, in turn, formed my early resolution
to try to become a philosopher. Though I had not completed high
school, I managed to get into Columbia College, where, a year after I
entered, John Erskine introduced a course of readings in the great
books of Western civilization. That series of fortuitous circumstances,
with the addition of one more accident, equally benign, set the stage
and pointed the direction for all that subsequently happened in my life.
Not quite all, perhaps, but all that belongs to the record of work done
and things accomplished.

More than fifty years after my reading of Mill's *Autobiography*, I
spent a year in London with my wife, Caroline, and our two boys,
Douglas and Philip, aged eleven and nine. The house we lived in during that year was only a few blocks away from Kensington Square, tree-
lined, with a fenced garden in the center, and with rows of modest
houses on three of its four sides. On the front wall of one of these
houses was a plaque bearing the following inscription:

JOHN STUART MILL,
1806–1873
Philosopher, Lived Here

I do not know whether Mill wrote his *Autobiography* in that house,
but if I were to pick out a single book which changed the direction of
my life, that would be it. The account Mill gives of his own education
—an education that involved no schooling at all—sent me back to
school; or rather, made me want to go to college, although I was ill

prepared to do so. Since I had dropped out of high school, after only two and a half years, at the age of fourteen, I could hardly satisfy the entrance requirements for college.

Until I read Mill, working on the *Sun* fulfilled the only ambition of my youth. As far back as I can remember, I wanted to be a journalist, not a teacher, scholar, or philosopher. It was that drive which, by a circuitous route, brought me to Mill, and it was Mill who put an end to that drive.

At the beginning of this century, the New York public schools were already becoming overcrowded. To relieve the congestion, the authorities allowed bright children to skip grades. Benefiting from this policy on three occasions, I was graduated from P.S. 186 in upper Manhattan at the age of twelve and a half, and I elected to go to De Witt Clinton High School, one of Manhattan's liberal arts secondary schools.

Only one teacher really held my attention during my first year there —Garibaldi M. Lapolla, who taught freshman composition. Perceiving my fledgling aspirations to become a writer, he volunteered to help me learn how to write. He told me how Flaubert had trained de Maupassant by making him write the same story over and over again until, in Flaubert's judgment, it was stylistically perfect. He proposed that we try the same procedure. My task was to write a single-page description of any object I thought worthy of the effort; he would blue-pencil it; I would do it over and over again until the Maestro said, "Well done." I chose a city fire hydrant as the object to describe, and describe it I did, at least twenty times before Mr. Lapolla laid his blue pencil down.

Among the extracurricular activities at De Witt Clinton High School were two student publications, the *Magpie,* a monthly magazine, and a weekly newspaper, the *De Witt Clinton News.* I had been editor of the school paper at P.S. 186; so, early in my first year at high school, I submitted short stories for the magazine and tried out for the staff of the newspaper. Success in these ventures diverted my attention from studies and schoolwork, even to my cutting classes to spend more time on journalism. I wanted to be a journalist, not a scholar, and here was my opportunity to get ahead fast. Before the end of my second year, I became editor of the *Magpie,* and by the beginning of my third year, editor of the *News.* I probably did enough schoolwork to maintain the requisite grades, but my memory of those days is vague on the classroom side, while rich and vivid about my journalistic efforts.

With this division of my attention and energies, I might never have finished high school anyway, but my demise as a student came about for a different reason. The principal, an old-time martinet by the name of Francis H. J. Paul, ordered me to suspend a student from the staff of the *De Witt Clinton News* because his grades were below par. My overblown opinion of my importance in the local scheme of things blinded me to the fact that I was running only the school newspaper, and that he, not I, was running the school. I disobeyed his order and kept the failing student on my staff, continuing to publish his pieces in the paper; but I didn't cover my tracks to prevent the faculty supervisor, Mr. Biggs, from rummaging through my desk and uncovering plain evidence that I had disregarded the principal's command. I didn't know that Mr. Biggs had given the principal the *corpus delicti* when I was called into his office. I lied brazenly and then, when presented with the evidence, sheepishly confessed my guilt. The punishment—suspension from all extracurricular activities. No more work on the *News* and the *Magpie,* just studying and going to classes, which I had been doing less and less. I couldn't face it. I persuaded my parents to let me drop out of school and go to work. They were hard-pressed enough financially to agree to let me take out working papers (I was under sixteen) and find a job.

Going to work meant only one thing for me—a return to journalism. To do this I was quite willing to forgo finishing high school. But how? On a newspaper as a copyboy, of course. Which newspaper? That was determined by an earlier event in my life.

While still at P.S. 186, I had entered an essay competition sponsored by the New York *Sun* for students in the city schools. Napoleon was the subject. My delight in winning the second prize in my age group—a silver medal with Napoleon on one face and the colophon of the New York *Sun* on the other—turned a little sour when I learned that my closest friend, Malcolm Sanger, also aged eleven, had won first prize and a gold medal. But when it came to getting a job as copyboy on the New York *Sun,* the silver medal, which I exhibited to the personnel manager of the newspaper, had the charm of gold. I got the job, and it was better than I might have hoped for, because it was not in the City Room where my hours would have been four to midnight, but in the editorial rooms on the daytime shift.

Taking handwritten copy from the desks of the editors and sending it by rope-controlled dumbwaiter down to the composing room, and then, when the bell rang, taking galley proofs from the dumbwaiter to the desk of the editor in chief, Edward Page Mitchell, hardly satisfied my desire to become a big-time journalist. After all, I had been editor in chief of my own newspaper at De Witt Clinton. Since my copy-running duties did not consume much time, I filled my idle hours by writing an editorial each day and boldly laying it on Mr. Mitchell's desk, as I did those written by the three editorial page writers. For some strange and lucky reason, my desk in the outer office had the only typewriter in the editorial department; so Mr. Mitchell did not have to decipher my scrawl.

Day after day, editorial after editorial, I waited for Mr. Mitchell's buzzer to summon me to his desk to take my typewritten copy to the composing room. Each night, after he went home, I rummaged in his wastebasket to see if he had deposited my contribution there, but no typescript of mine was in the basket, either crumpled or torn up. Much later I discovered all of them banded together in a bottom drawer of his desk, but at the time I could not imagine what became of them. I therefore kept on persistently, since I felt that my whole future was at stake. On about the twenty-fifth day, the heavens opened up and the highroad to success was bathed in sunlight. There on the edge of Mr. Mitchell's desk lay an editorial of mine, copy-edited and initialed by Mr. Mitchell for typesetting. My hand trembled as I picked it up, my legs felt watery, yet instead of taking the easy way of sending the copy down to the composing room by dumbwaiter, I walked down the stairs cradling it in my hands all the way. The editorial, entitled "In 99 Years," celebrating the ninety-ninth anniversary of the crossing of the Atlantic by the S.S. *Savannah,* argued for the renewal of subsidies for the merchant marine, a subject about which I knew little and cared less. All that I knew about the matter had been learned by an hour's diligence in the library of the editorial department.

Shortly thereafter, Mr. Mitchell's secretary was drafted for the American Expeditionary Force to France. Having discovered that I could typewrite and that I had read proof on my high school newspaper, he moved me from the outer to the inner office as his secretary, in which post I typed the letters he wrote out in longhand, read the galley proofs for the editorial page, and did other odd jobs, such as getting his lunch every day, which consisted without variation of one bottle of milk and one Swiss cheese sandwich bought at the Automat across the street, together with five Bock panatela cigars, his daily quota. Not content with performing these secretarial duties, I undertook to write verse for the editorial page, and also the little paragraphs that filled up the third column when the last of the editorials fell short of the bottom of the page.

My pay as secretary to the editor in chief of the *Sun* was five dollars a week, a raise from the four a week I had been paid as copyboy; but at the rate of fifty cents for each editorial paragraph, twenty-five cents a line for verse, and at space rates of seven and a half dollars a column length for other editorial matter and for book reviews for the Sunday literary supplement, I managed to average, at age fifteen, thirty to thirty-five dollars a week—an enormous sum in those days. My parents felt that my weekly contribution to the family income more than justified their decision to let me drop out of school and go to work. What was left of my earnings each week I spent on gallery tickets for Broadway shows and on books I bought at Brentano's—mainly plays by G. B. Shaw, Lord Dunsany, and John Galsworthy, my heroes at that time.

Clearly, I was moving up the ladder of big-time journalism, with no obstacles that I could see to an early realization of my fondest hopes; but, with an overdose of ambition and an absurd degree of impatience (Mr. Mitchell once told me that I should not try to strike all twelve numbers on the clock at once), I decided to accelerate my advancement by attending night classes in the Extension Division of Columbia University—not because I wanted to remedy my deficiencies in schooling, but solely to improve the tools of my trade as a writer. I chose a course given by Prof. Frank Allen Patterson in Victorian literature, and that was the start of my undoing as a journalist.

We read the poetry of Browning, Tennyson, Dante Gabriel Rossetti, and Walter Savage Landor, the essays of Hazlitt and Lamb, and the *Autobiography* of John Stuart Mill. I read that book as I had never read any book before. The infant Mill had been tutored by his father, James Mill, and his father's friend Jeremy Bentham almost as soon as he was out of the cradle. When he was only three, he could read Greek, and by the time he reached five he had read the dialogues of Plato and could distinguish, so he said, between the tricks of the Socratic method and the substance of the Platonic philosophy. At five! Here I was fifteen, almost sixteen, and I had never heard of Plato before, or Socrates for that matter, and I certainly could not make their acquaintance in Greek. The list of books that young Mill read under his father's tutelage between the ages of seven and eleven included many of the books that John Erskine had assembled for a special honors seminar that I was to participate in four years later when I reached my junior year in Columbia College. But not only had Mill read many of the great books in the Western tradition before the age of eleven; he had, from that point on, over the next two or three years, edited his father's *History of India* and Jeremy Bentham's *Rationale of Judicial Evidence*.

At one point in my life I knew Mill's story almost by heart; for I had to read it with maximum attention to details when, as a young instructor at Columbia College, I was asked by the University Press to prepare an index for a new edition. Indexing, I discovered early on (and have found it amply confirmed ever since), raises the skill of reading to the highest level.

Reading Mill's *Autobiography* sent me in search of Plato. Luckily, I did not have far to go to find him. He was right next door, in the apartment adjoining the one in which I lived with my parents on Washington Heights. Next door to the Adlers lived the Feldmans. Sam Feldman, an immigrant Russian Jewish lawyer who held the office of Public Defender in the Borough of Manhattan, was an inveterate book buyer and had educated himself by reading a wide variety of the many books he bought. Some he just liked to look at and admire—even, as I know from my own experience, to feel a certain power over, just by having them in his possession. On his overloaded shelves stood a set of President Eliot's *Harvard Classics,* which included some of the dialogues of Plato. I borrowed the volume and turned first to the *Euthyphro,* a short dialogue on piety. Within a few days I had read several more— the *Apology,* the *Phaedo,* and the *Crito.* By that time I had become so fascinated by the Socratic method of questioning that I persuaded my friends to engage in mock dialogues that would allow me to exercise my skill as their Socratic interrogator.

This I found to be much more fun than writing editorial paragraphs for the *Sun* or correcting galley proofs. As the intellectual excitement in this new vocation grew, my interest in the old one waned.

Dissatisfied with the incompleteness of the selections from Plato in the *Harvard Classics,* I bought a secondhand set of the Jowett translation in five volumes and began to spend time at my desk at the *Sun* reading the dialogues of Plato instead of doing the work that earned my weekly paycheck. This could not go on for long unnoticed. One thing or another, which I no longer remember, precipitated my decision to abandon journalism and try to go to college—perhaps to become a philosopher, but certainly to read more books that might move my mind the way reading Plato had.

At the time I made my decision to leave the *Sun* and try to prepare myself for entrance to college, Mr. Mitchell was on vacation. I wrote a letter to Harold Anderson, chief editorial writer under Mr. Mitchell, explaining my intentions. "You have acted wisely," he replied; "you were undertaking to do too much with your work in this office and your studies. Anybody who can give all his time to study should do so. . . . You will, of course, call on Mr. Mitchell on his return and explain the situation to him, for I know he will want to see you."

The two years or more that I spent on the *Sun* did more for me, I am sure, than completing high school and going on directly to college could have done. If it did nothing else, it broke the routine of uninterrupted classroom attendance year after year, with the likely consequence of disinterest and boredom. But it did more than that. After being out of school, I looked forward with eager anticipation to serious study at college. I wanted to go to college for the only reason which, in my judgment, justifies embarking on that venture—to study just for the sake of learning and for no utilitarian or adventitious purpose to which the learning might be put to use. I had had my fill of extracurricular activities in high school and had experienced the drudgery of daily chores on the several jobs I held between high school and college. Getting into college meant being able to devote all my time and all my energy to study.

In addition, I learned on the *Sun* how to do not only a full day's work, but also a full week's work. I found that the task of writing came easier if performed every day of the week. Taking Sunday off—everyone worked six full days in those benighted times—made it more difficult to get back into the swing on Monday; so I formed the habit of going down to the office on Sunday and doing a full day's stint even though I was not paid for doing it. The habit of working seven days a week served me well in the short time I had to get ready for the college entrance examinations as well as during my three years at Columbia. The night courses I had taken in Columbia Extension made it possible for me to enter college with advanced standing, skipping the freshman year entirely and starting as a sophomore.

I wish I could say that the academic hiatus—the years of earning a living between high school and college—had also helped me to achieve a maturity that I have recently claimed would be achieved. I may have matured in certain respects as a result of going to work, but the evidence is depressingly ample that I had not become emotionally mature by the time I entered college. The fact that, during three years as an undergraduate, I devoted *all* my energies to study would, I suspect, in anybody's mind, be evidence enough that I remained emotionally immature. And emotionally immature I remained for many years thereafter—not only during the years that I was a member of the faculty of Columbia University, from 1923 to 1930, but also to a serious extent during the greater part of the twenty-two years I held a professorship at the University of Chicago. That, however, indicates a defect in my own makeup rather than in the educational theory I have gradually developed.

"The child is father of the man," wrote Wordsworth. True, but the child, like any father, propagates blindly, with no foreknowledge of the ultimate issue. When, in a lecture at the University of Denver in 1972, I first advocated two or four years of compulsory nonattendance at school as a break before going on to the university, I could not resist the temptation of referring to my years of work on the *Sun,* as if my thesis had grown out of that experience. It could have been cited as a slight bit of evidence in support of the thesis, but hardly more than that. The idea of interrupted schooling was born out of thinking about the student turmoil of the sixties. It was conceived in the context of other educational ideas which may have had some roots in my own experiences as a student and teacher; but these related ideas did not coalesce into a coherent educational theory until some years after I had retired from teaching.

Of the many years that I have spent since 1930 in theorizing and arguing about education, it is only since the early fifties, when I prepared an elaborate series of papers for a three-day conference held under the auspices of the Ford Foundation, that I have fully appreciated how novel and difficult is the problem of educating a whole people, not just an upper crust of ten percent. Yet this is the task which confronts our society and which has confronted no other before this century. The recognition of it is even more recent than that.

As late as 1941 I had no hesitation in talking about education in terms that would have been congenial to Aristotle in the fourth century B.C. I mention that year because I can vividly remember a debate that I had in Chicago that January with Bertrand Russell (who had just become Lord Russell). The subject in dispute was stated as follows: Resolved that the objectives of education are always and everywhere the same. I took the affirmative side, arguing that since human beings are always and everywhere the same in the specific properties they all possess as members of the same species, it must follow that the goal to be achieved by the educational process should be the same for all.

How Aristotelian and repugnant to Lord Russell my argument must have sounded! I summarized it in the following words: "*If* education must aim at the betterment of men by forming good habits in them, and *if* the virtues, or good habits, are the same for all men because their natural capacities are the same and tend naturally toward the same developments, *then* it follows that the virtues, or good habits, as the ends of education, are absolute and universal principles on which education should be founded."

The conclusion follows logically, I conceded, only if the premises— the two *ifs*—are true, but I immediately went on to assert that they were. "If my premises are in fact true, and if my reasoning is valid," I told Lord Russell and the audience, "then the conclusion is inescapable."

I will never forget Bertrand Russell's opening rejoinder. We had been asked to wear dinner jackets, I suppose to ensure the formality of the proceedings. It was to be a formal debate—in dress if not in thought. Respecting Lord Russell as my senior by many years, and also as immeasurably more eminent, I had carefully prepared my initial presentation of the affirmative position. It was all written out. Lord Russell came to the platform without a shred of paper and, I suspect, without a jot or tittle of preparatory thought on the subject. But he did have a clean stiff white cuff on his boiled shirt, and on it, I observed as I looked back at him from the podium in the course of reading my speech, he jotted down notes from time to time. When he arose to present the negative position, his opening sally was "I greatly admire Dr. Adler's rugged simplicity."

From that point on, with one off-the-cuff remark after another, Lord Russell provoked outbursts of laughter. At the end, the applause, won easily by his witticisms, appeared to indicate that he had triumphed. I felt that I should have been adjudged the victor at the bar of reason, though not in the court of laughter. But I now know that Lord Russell had the better side of the question, though not for any reason he gave at the time.

In the summers of 1973 and 1974, the Aspen Institute for Humanistic Studies held conferences on the changing concept of the educated person. It was generally agreed that traditional ideas of what it means to be educated, in the fullest sense of that term, can no longer be applied in the contemporary world, especially not in the technologically advanced industrial societies which are committed to political democracy and, consequently, to equality of educational opportunity. When such a society undertakes to educate its whole population, it must acknowledge the principle that every human being, with the possible exception of those in asylums, should aspire to become an educated person.

In view of individual differences in talent, aptitude, and temperament, the way in which the educational ideal is realized cannot be the same for everyone. On that score, Russell was right. However, if we conceive the educated person as any human being who, having acquired the tools of learning in school, goes on in the rest of life to use them for the fullest possible development of his or her capacities, then the ideal is realizable, at least to some degree, by every member of the population.

If this is accepted, we must consider how everyone should be schooled to fulfill such aspirations; and, beyond compulsory schooling, what educational facilities should be provided. Should the schooling of all children who are destined to become citizens and to have free time for the pursuits of leisure be differentiated or undifferentiated? Should some be liberally schooled and the rest vocationally trained? My answer to these questions, in favor of undifferentiated schooling, involves a number of points, none of which I would have understood or agreed to when I decided to go to college, or for that matter many years thereafter.

Beginning as early as possible, in order to take advantage of the child's capacity for early learning, all normal human beings should have the same basic schooling for twelve years. That basic schooling should be the same in its general direction, aiming to make all the children competent as learners, with the hope that they will become learned after they leave school, aiming to acquaint them superficially with the world of learning, and aiming to motivate them to go on learning for the rest of their lives. The schools are certainly not doing these three things for all the children, and probably they are not doing them very effectively even for a few.

If formal, compulsory schooling were to begin at age four, its twelve years could be terminated with the award at age sixteen of the bachelor's degree, signifying competence in the liberal arts or skills of learning—the ability to read and write, speak and listen, observe, measure, and calculate. Such competence defines the end result of the schooling that an industrial democracy owes all its children.

That, however, is only the beginning of education. In order that continued learning for all, and more formal schooling for some, should take place under the most auspicious circumstances, no one should be allowed to continue in school immediately after basic schooling has been completed at age sixteen. There should be a hiatus of at least two years—I would prefer four—during which time the young become mature by engaging in the world's work, either in the public or the private sector of the economy. They certainly cannot become mature as long as they remain in school; on the contrary, they suffer from prolonged adolescence. That is a pathological condition which can be prevented only by getting the young out of school as soon after the onset of puberty as possible.

After the academic hiatus, the skills of learning can be applied in studies at advanced schools (however they be named—college or university) which should be open only to those who have demonstrated both competence and inclination for specialized learning of a scholarly or professional kind. Those who do not seek advanced degrees should be provided with informal educational facilities for the continued learning in which all adults should engage for a lifetime if they are to become educated men and women. No one can become an educated person in school, even in the best of schools or with the most complete schooling. Schooling is only the first phase in the process of becoming educated, not the termination of it. Of course, that is a truth which no schoolboy is ever likely to understand or acknowledge. I certainly did not understand it when I decided to give up being a workingman on the *Sun* and become a schoolboy again; and I would have agreed to it even less when I had completed my undergraduate studies in the college at Columbia University. At that moment I was probably more firmly convinced than I have ever felt since that I had become an educated person.

But I have got ahead of myself, or at least of where I was that early spring of 1920, when I left the *Sun* with some regrets. For some time after, I missed the excitement of working on a daily newspaper, especially during the years of America's involvement in the First World War and the political turbulence that followed in its wake. I can still remember the sequence of events on the false armistice day—November 7, 1918. Fairly early that morning, I happened to go down to the composing room and saw the front page of the first edition of the *Evening Sun* locked up and ready to be matted, with the banner headline in the largest possible type announcing the war's end. The news that an armistice was about to be signed had leaked from France, but confirmation of it was not yet forthcoming from Washington. From

9:30 that morning until well past eleven, long-distance telephones buzzed back and forth, but the minutes passed without a green light to the pressroom to rush out an "extra." Suddenly, we heard one of the *Evening Sun*'s competitors—I think it was the *Telegraph*—hawking an "extra" on the street outside our building. At that moment the green light flashed; editorial restraint had been overcome, even though there had been no official confirmation of the news. Five of the six evening newspapers came out with an "extra." Only the old *New York Globe* kept on publishing a denial that an armistice had been or was about to be signed, and it sold as many copies as all the other papers combined. Everyone bought the cautiously negative *Globe* along with one or another of the wildly enthusiastic affirmative sheets. The excitement on the streets of New York exploded in wave after wave all afternoon and evening, exceeding the jubilation and hysteria that celebrated the genuine Armistice Day four days later.

In the interval between my leaving the *Sun* and entering Columbia College in September 1920, I had to grapple with two necessities. One was the necessity of finding a job that would enable me to support myself, and the other was the necessity of preparing myself to take the New York State Regents examinations for college entrance. How I managed both things at once I cannot now fully recall or clearly understand, but some of the incidents of that interval still remain vivid in my memory.

I remember the dislike I felt for job-hunting. I would leave home in the morning with a copy of the want ads, but instead of going through the painful process of knocking on doors and applying for jobs, I would go to the public library and spend the day, returning home in the late afternoon with the tale that I had searched all day and found nothing. Every now and then I would vary this procedure and line up with other applicants to be interviewed by a prospective employer, but I seldom did this more than once in any day. However, I did it frequently enough to have lightning strike once. I found a job with a small advertising agency. Weighing my experience on the *Sun* against my all-too-apparent youthfulness (I was just sixteen), they hired me as a copywriter. My first assignment was to write an advertisement for a chain of nut and candy stores.

My lack of aptitude for this task should have been enough to get me fired right off the bat; but I gave my employers additional grounds. At that time I was still taking evening courses at Columbia University. Among them was one in the literature of the Romantic period, given by Prof. Frank Allen Patterson, under whom I had previously studied the literature of the Victorian period and became acquainted with Mill's *Autobiography*. Professor Patterson cared little about philosophy; lyric poetry was his main interest. He countered my fledgling aspirations to become a philosopher by encouraging me to write poetry. I must have had a strong imitative bent, for just as reading the dialogues of Plato had sent me off trying to imitate Socrates, so reading Tennyson and Browning, Wordsworth, Shelley, and Keats set me to imitating them. I wrote reams of verse. Professor Patterson, who should have known better, smiled upon these efforts and misled me into thinking that maybe it was the poet in me, not the philosopher, that I should try to develop.

During my brief employment as an advertising copywriter, I happened to be struggling with a poem for Professor Patterson's special approval. Being of an ultraconservative temper, he favored Wordsworth, especially the Wordsworth of the "Ode: Intimations of Immortality," "Tintern Abbey," and the "Ode to Duty," and he shied away from the rebellious Shelley. To please him, I undertook to write a longish "poem" imitating Wordsworth's later style, entitled "On Placing Shelley next to Wordsworth on the Bookshelf." The bookshelf, it seemed to my bookish mind, was exactly the spot where that confrontation of antagonistic spirits should take place. Under Professor Patterson's direction, the poem went through many drafts. I became so caught up in the effort that, instead of writing copy for Cash's Meatee Nuts, I occupied my time revising my masterpiece. When this was observed, I was given my walking papers.

If that verse cost me my job, it also gained me entrance to college and a full-tuition scholarship to boot. Professor Patterson happened to be the director of the Extension Division at Columbia. His recommending me to the director of admissions probably turned the scales in my favor on both counts; but, as I recall from one long conversation, he had some misgivings about helping me. He had the feeling, he said, that I might turn out to be a better poet if I didn't go to college. Studying might turn me in other directions—toward philosophy or science. The budding Socrates might bloom, the budding Wordsworth wilt and die.

At the time I could not understand his premonition, nor for that matter did the resolution of this conflict occur until the very end of my three years in college. I can remember another longish piece of verse that I wrote, during my junior year, in the style of Browning's dramatic monologues, in which I had Skelton, a little-known pre-Elizabethan poet, soliloquize about the comparative merits of being a poet and a philosopher, with the issue left unresolved. I can also remember being a member of the Boar's Head Society, the members of which brought their literary efforts to be criticized by Prof. John Erskine. On one occasion I submitted a poem with the title "Lines Written toward the End of Winter," and Erskine's only comment was to ask why I had not called it "Ode to Spring." That and similar slaps by Erskine, who was much more discerning than Patterson, should have stopped me from further versifying, but it was other circumstances that put an end to it.

After losing my job with the advertising agency, I walked the streets in halfhearted pursuit of another. After a few weeks of this, an uncle of mine who worked for the Worthington Pump and Machinery Corporation came to my rescue. On his recommendation, I was hired as an office boy at four dollars a week. Carfare on the subway from upper Manhattan, where I lived, down to 115 Broadway came to sixty cents a week; and lunches at the Exchange Buffet or the Automat—one sandwich, a glass of milk, and a piece of pie—came to ninety cents a week more. That left little for book purchases or anything else. Nevertheless, it turned out to be a job that served my particular needs at the time, for shortly after I started at Worthington, I was assigned to the outer office of the president of the corporation. Since he sent me on errands only infrequently, most of the time I sat in a very comfortable office at a large receptionist's desk preparing for the New York State Regents examinations, which I had to take to make up for my lack of high school credits.

In addition to boning up for these exams, I even had time for a little extracurricular reading. Someone had suggested Hart's *Psychology of Insanity,* and the reading of that extraordinary little book—extraordinary in 1920—served as my introduction to the study of the mind and its quirks. Another book picked up at Brentano's was in the Modern Library, *Evolution in Modern Thought,* a collection of essays by Weismann, Bateson, Morgan, Driesch, and Bergson. I can remember how puzzled I was by the conflicting points of view. Try as I might, I simply could not figure out how evolution was supposed to work. I spent hours writing notes to myself and making diagrams in an effort to put down the steps by which a new species came into being. That puzzlement remained with me for many years—until I read Darwin's *Origin of Species* for the third time and found the clue in what he had to say about the extinction of intermediate varieties.

The third book I remember reading during those months at Worthington caught my attention by its title. The elder brother of my friend Malcolm Sanger was a junior in Columbia College. He had taken a philosophy course in which he had been assigned William James's lectures on pragmatism. I found the book on his desk, had never seen the word *pragmatism* before, became curious about its meaning, looked it up in a dictionary, and, still unsatisfied, went to Brentano's and bought the book. I read it very, very slowly, becoming more and more fascinated by the theory of truth, of knowledge, and of experience that William James had propounded in his lectures at Columbia University in 1907. I did not realize that the controversy about the pragmatic theory of truth was still raging in 1920; nor had I ever heard of the pragmatic school of philosophy, or of John Dewey, C. S. Peirce, or

F. C. S. Schiller. But one thing did ring a bell with me at once—the inscription on the dedication page of the book. It read: "To John Stuart Mill who would have been our leader had he been alive."

Mill had sent me to Plato and to Socrates, and now here was William James reminding me of Mill. It took me many years to understand the affinity between the American pragmatism of James and Dewey and the English utilitarianism of Bentham and Mill, but the reading of *Pragmatism* inducted me at once into the twists and turns of epistemologizing. That became one of the main preoccupations of my college years. I still have a term essay I wrote—this time in imitation of Immanuel Kant—entitled "Prolegomena to Any Future Epistemology." Luckily, while at Worthington, my early ponderings about truth and knowledge did not interfere with my efforts to pass the Regents examinations; if they had, I might never have gotten into college.

Chapter 2

General Honors

THE YEARS IMMEDIATELY following the end of the First World War were anything but boom times for the kind of small business in which my father was employed. The economy of the early twenties would now be described as in a marked recession; *slump* was the starker word then current for such conditions. My father earned less than five thousand dollars a year, and after he had given my mother twenty-five dollars a week to run the household and paid the rent and his insurance premiums, little remained for other expenses. My mother, who had taught school before she married, returned to part-time teaching to increase the family income, but even so the stringency called for the counting of pennies, nickels, and dimes.

My full-tuition scholarship at Columbia University (tuition then was two hundred fifty dollars a year), far from being a bonanza, posed a financial problem that my parents found extremely difficult, if not impossible, to solve. By 1920 I had been earning a weekly stipend for over two years, and though what I earned did not make me self-supporting, I would certainly be less of a drain on the family resources if I continued to hold a paying job than I would be if I went to college. Even with my tuition paid, I would need carfare, lunch money, and money for books and other perquisites, and I would have to be clothed and shod.

I don't think my parents were enamored of the idea of my getting a college degree; in fact, I don't think in their plans for me they had ever contemplated my going on to college if I finished high school in the normal course of events. High school would have been enough schooling; after that, work. On the other hand, my mother's career as a schoolteacher and my father's respect, both German and Jewish, for the *gelerhter,* made them reluctant to say no to my going to college. I think their consciences would have been sorely troubled if they had flatly rejected that option. But still they could not see how it could be managed.

Whether it was my suggestion or theirs I cannot now remember, but the problem seemed to be solved by the proposal that I should combine going to college with some form of part-time employment so as to be at least partly self-supporting. During the summer of 1920, I continued as an office boy at the Worthington Pump and Machinery Corporation and at the same time studied for the examinations I had to take in early September. Furthermore, had I not gone to night classes at Columbia Extension during the two years that I worked during the day at the New York *Sun?* This helped to persuade my parents that I could go on in the same way after I entered college, only reversing the mixture —studying during the day and working at night. I was so anxious at the time to get them to agree to what I desperately wanted to do that I did not permit my imagination to foresee or foretaste the irksomeness and irritation of "working one's way through college," not to mention the frustrations inherent in a plan that might help to pay the way but that also prevented one from making the most of the opportunity to study that college afforded.

September came to an end; college opened; I registered for courses adding up to fifteen points of credit, which was the normal academic load for a semester. In the line at the bursar's window in University Hall, I stood behind a thin, pale-faced, sandy-haired, sharp-featured young man who, I learned from the conversation we had while waiting in line, also had a scholarship voucher plus ten dollars for matriculation to turn in at the window. His name was Bill Douglas; he had just hitch-hiked across the country from Oregon; his scholarship covered his tuition in the Law School, but like me, he was planning to find work to defray other costs. Whether his plans fell out as mine did, I do not know; but I do know that the way in which he used his time at Columbia Law School determined his career, much in the same way that mine was to be determined by what I did with my time in Columbia College. As we stood in that line, I could not possibly have foreseen the number of times our paths would cross in the future—not at Columbia where Bill Douglas made the Law Review, but at Yale after I had come to know Bob Hutchins, then again with Hutchins at the University of Chicago, and much later, when Bill had become an associate justice of the Supreme Court, at the Center for the Study of Democratic Institutions in Santa Barbara, California.

Of the courses I registered for, only two—one in experimental psychology and one in logic—fired my interest and drew my mind further in the direction in which the reading I had been doing had already inclined it. Within the first week or two after classes started, I found myself so absorbed, and my time so engaged, that the thought of looking for a job became repugnant. Any job I might find—running an elevator or operating a switchboard—would take six or eight hours out of every day, six days a week. That would leave precious little time for studying. What was the point of going to college, I asked myself, if that consisted only in attending classes and did not include the much more important learning that might be gained by doing the exercises and reading required and, beyond that, getting a look into the books recommended as supplementary? Yet I had promised my parents that I would get a job and earn some money.

The problem was solved by procrastination and deception. I dragged my heels and reported failure to find employment I had not even looked for. At the same time, I spent every afternoon, and every evening until midnight or later, working at my books or papers in the little four-by-eight-foot cubicle that was my bedroom and study in my parents' apartment on Washington Heights in upper Manhattan. On Saturday mornings I would go to the Psychology Library in Schermerhorn Hall and bring home a load of a dozen books or more to consult and quote in writing up reports on the laboratory work completed the preceding week. The rest of the weekend found me at my desk reading or at my little Blickensderfer typewriter writing reports that were many times longer, more detailed, and more generously footnoted than the reports turned in by other students, who did no more, and often much less, than was expected of them by the instructors. Observing this performance on my part, my parents asked whether college work had to be so effortful and time-consuming. When I lied to them, assuring them that nothing less would do and enable me to retain my scholarship, they were naive or innocent enough to be deceived; and, being deceived, they were persuaded of what I wanted them to believe—that I could not possibly combine going to college and studying with part-time work.

Nevertheless, some money, however little, was needed. At that point, my mother's aunt and her brother, my favorite uncle, came to the rescue. Each volunteered to give me a dollar a week for pocket money. That, together with some promises I made, did the trick. I promised to walk the mile or so up and down Broadway between 145th Street, where we lived, and 120th Street, where Columbia stood, thus saving sixty cents a week in carfare, and in addition I said I would take my lunch from home in a paper bag. That left two dollars a week, carefully doled out, for books and other incidentals. Not without strain, my parents came through with the rest, mainly the money for new clothes, when needed, and for an occasional, very infrequent, minor indulgence.

The consequences of this arrangement, as well as the deceptions that led to them, were far-reaching. Carrying my lunch to school—to be eaten on the campus grass in good weather or in some vacant classroom when the weather was bad—brought me into association with two other students who were also in strained circumstances, one a classmate of mine by the name of Isadore Kaplan, the other John Storck, a young, married assistant in the Philosophy Department who had to scrimp to get by on the thousand dollars a year he earned. Lunching together day after day for several years, we carried on a three-sided conversation that ranged over and far beyond the things we were working on or studying. We argued interminably, often being late for a class or even missing it entirely after a lunch that was protracted by an argument we were unwilling to conclude because we had not been able to reach any conclusion on which all three of us could agree. If I were now to estimate the contribution made by the ways in which I spent my time at Columbia, and the influences that different elements in that environment had on me, I think I would give great, if not predominant, weight to these informal sessions at lunchtime.

The deception I practiced by putting so much effort and time on homework in the evening and on the weekend, in order to persuade my parents that I could not combine studying with earning money, also had its good effect. The working habits I had formed on the New York *Sun* made it relatively easy for me to sustain a seven-day schedule of attending classes, working in laboratories, exploring libraries, and reading and writing in my little cubicle at home. My parents continued to believe that going to college required this much work; and as my habit of doing it made it feel like the natural thing to do, I suspect that I came to believe it myself. It never occurred to me that I had become a specimen of the objectionable type known as a grind; and I am not sure that if it had occurred to me, I would have minded or altered my ways. So addicted had I become to studying, and so resentful of any invasions of my time, that I made few friends at college other than my two lunchtime companions. I was totally oblivious of the extracurricular activities that occupied considerable portions of the time of my classmates. I cannot remember having had to resist—during my first two years at college —the usual enticements of wine, women, and song; they simply did not exist for me. Like an overcautious turtle, I seldom stuck my head out of the protective shell formed by my preoccupation with psychology and philosophy. When forced to do so by college requirements, I twisted and turned evasively until I managed to get back in the groove.

One such infringement on my time that I tried to avoid came from a postwar New York statute requiring all college students to enroll in the S.A.T.C., the Students Army Training Corps. (Another was the college requirement of compulsory attendance at the gymnasium for physical training.) Five weeks after term began, I received a note from the dean's office warning me that I was failing to comply with the law about attendance at sessions of the S.A.T.C and demanding that I report to the armory next Friday afternoon for drill, after first collecting the G.I. equipment I would need. I brought home a bundle of it and threw it all wrapped up in the bottom of my closet. Friday came. I usually spent Friday afternoon working out the logic problems assigned for my philosophy class on Saturday morning, and it was with rising resentment that I put down my logic book and picked up the G.I. bundle. Starting to get dressed in the doughboy uniform of the First World War, I soon found that I did not know how to complete the process—whether to put the shirt collar inside or outside the tunic, how to wind the khaki puttees, inside or outside the boot tops, or what to do with the chin strap of the campaign hat that had been issued me. Baffled, I called my mother in to help, but she was as ignorant as I of military attire. Somehow we managed to put it all on me, though one look in the mirror left me in some doubt about the authenticity of my appearance. No matter; I boarded a bus to go up to the armory at 165th Street and Broadway with my logic book in hand and a pad to continue doing my logic exercises, which I much preferred to military ones.

As I entered the main hall of the armory, I came into full view of the major commanding the S.A.T.C. unit. One look at me brought forth a bellow of despair and rage. "Sergeant," he cried, "take that man inside and show him how to dress. He's wearing his hat like a sunbonnet. And take that damn book out of his hands and put a gun in them instead." The sergeant was only too glad to carry out this order, the execution of which I suffered with mounting humiliation and to the tune of the most eloquent profanity I had ever heard. What followed was even more humiliating. Either because I was preternaturally dense about such matters or because my mind was in a state of confusion caused by the ribbing I had just received, I repeatedly fouled up the squad I was placed in by turning left when I should have turned right or in some other way failing to maneuver as commanded. In the succeeding weeks, I remained in the awkward squad, and there I might have stayed for the rest of the year, had it not been for the fact that I became a menace to life and limb when we were issued bayonets for close-order drill. Lawfully or not, the authorities excused me from further attendance at the Friday afternoon sessions at the armory, and I went back to the logic drill, which I could perform with pleasure and without harm to anyone else.

That short skirmish with the army constituted my only military experience in a life that has spanned two world wars and several other extended military engagements that have wrenched young men from their normal pursuits, twisted the lives of all who became involved, maimed some, and brought death to others. The undeserved blessings of good fortune, I have had reason to reflect, should not be underestimated in calculating the factors that affect the way one's life turns out—though in this case it is a moot point whether I or the country that did not call upon my doubtful military competence was luckier.

A second regulation that I violated had what at first might appear to be more serious consequences for my academic career, but in fact it became a mark of distinction. At Columbia in my day, four years of physical education were required for graduation and, in addition, everyone had to pass a swimming test which called for two lengths in the pool and a high dive. Being a city boy who had never seen a swimming pool, and whose only experience with aquatics had been wading into the Atlantic Ocean on the Coney Island beach, I had reached seventeen without having learned to swim. I therefore reported for swimming instruction. The coach, like the drill sergeant, found me stubbornly negative about following instructions. He told me to stand at the edge of the pool and dive headfirst into about five feet of water, where I could not possibly drown. Again and again I jumped in feet-first instead, fearing the dire consequences of getting my head under water. Incensed by my performance, he stood behind me and, planting a solid kick on my behind, propelled me into a belly flop, which did submerge my head and caused me to come up choking and gasping for air. Barely suppressing tears of shame and indignation, I left the pool and never returned.

My gym attendance is another part of the same story. My gym class came at ten, three days a week, in between mathematics and French. Crossing the campus, undressing, putting on gym clothes, exercising, showering, getting dressed again, and getting back to Hamilton Hall for the next class, all in one hour, seemed to me a lot of bother, as well as a distraction from more important concerns, to no good purpose. For a while I put up with it, even enjoying just a little the one success I had —in rope climbing. But I was incredibly awkward in my efforts to jump the horse and totally incompetent on the horizontal and the parallel bars. As for running a mile around the track, that exertion seemed to me beyond the call of duty. I was not excused from further gym attendance because of my poor performance as I had been excused from military drill. I simply quit. Instead of acknowledging that I was poorly coordinated and nonathletic and, therefore, probably more in need of physical training than of mental discipline, I justified cutting gym from that point forward on the grounds that it was unreasonable to waste time getting dressed and undressed more than once a day.

Nonattendance resulted in a series of F's on my record. At the end of my senior year in 1923, after I had already been awarded a Phi Beta Kappa key and had paid twenty dollars for my diploma, I received a note from Dean Hawkes saying that I might attend the commencement exercises but that I would not get my bachelor's degree because I had neither passed my swimming test nor fulfilled the physical education requirement for graduation. Having earned 135 points of credit (120 points sufficed for graduation), I was, however, permitted to enter the graduate school without a B.A. degree. Six years later, without having bothered to stop for an M.A. on the way, I received a Ph.D.—I say "received" rather than "earned" because the doctorate fell on me in spite of myself and what I did or failed to do. How that happened is a story to be reserved until later, but that it happened gives me the rare distinction, I believe, of being possibly the only Ph.D. in the country without a master's degree, a bachelor's degree, or even a high school diploma.

This academic irregularity has had a number of sequelae. Many years later, long after I had become a full professor at the University of Chicago, friendly college or university presidents persuaded their boards of trustees to approve the granting of an honorary bachelor's or master's degree. I thus became academically respectable, *honoris causa*. I even learned to swim in spite of myself. It happened in 1934 on a Grace Line cruise ship sailing from New York through the Panama Canal to California. The ship had an attractive pool on the rear deck, which I avoided during the crowded hours before and after lunch. Instead, I went out there at cocktail hour, when I thought I could paddle around in the shallow end without shame or notice. The second time I did that, I was observed by a solitary gentleman at the deep end of the pool who came around to where I was splashing myself and said, "You can't swim? Would you like me to show you how?" Curtly, I shouted back, "No, I can't swim, and I don't want to learn how either." Before I could get out of the pool and away from him, he said, "But it really is very easy; let me show you." Exasperated, I told him a lie—that I had the best swimming coaches in the world try to teach me, and all had failed, so what made him think he had some special knack or trick up his sleeve. Unruffled by my rude response, he quietly asked, "Can you hum?" I replied that of course I could hum; who couldn't? "That's all you need to be able to do," he then astonished me by saying, "because if you can hum, you can swim."

That floored me. Anyone with even the most elementary grasp of logic would recognize that as a non sequitur. If you can hum, you can swim—sheer nonsense! Such an arrant disregard for both cogency and truth won my attention, and so I asked him what he could have meant by so preposterous a statement. "Will you let me show you?" he asked. My resistance was down and I could no longer refuse his request. He asked me what I could hum, and after some soul-searching, I came up with "My Country 'Tis of Thee." He then told me to go down to the deep end of the pool, walk down the ladder, keep my eyes open when my head went underwater, and at that moment begin to hum. "Hold on to the ladder as you go down to the bottom," he said, "and stay down until you have finished humming. Then let go and see what happens." Still thinking that he was making a fool of me, I reluctantly followed his directions. When I finished humming, I let go of the rails of the ladder and quickly popped up to the surface, where I managed to stay by holding on to the side of the pool.

"See," my preceptor said with unconcealed triumph in his voice and on his face, "you didn't drown by going underwater; in fact, you couldn't keep yourself down at the bottom; you popped up the moment you took your hands off the ladder. You can't swim yet, but now you will be able to learn, because the only obstacle to your learning is your fear of drowning when you put your head underwater, and no one can learn to swim without getting his head and face under, at least part of the time." I had to admit that while "if you can hum, you can swim" still remained a non sequitur, it had led me to a valid if-then—"if you can hum, you can learn how to swim." Shortly thereafter I did learn how to swim—not well, not even effectively, because kicking my legs has always slowed me down instead of propelling me through the water; nevertheless, I can swim well enough to venture out a little over my head, though not for long.

I should add that in 1941, at a beach party one evening on Cape Cod, I told one of my neighbors the story of my not getting my degree from Columbia College because I couldn't swim, as well as the rest of the tale about how I learned. Amused by this, Mrs. Weld revealed that she was the daughter of General Parsons, then chairman of the board of trustees of Columbia University. If I didn't object, she was going to write to him about rectifying this delinquency on the university's part now that I had learned to swim. Without giving it much thought, I told her to go ahead. That autumn I received a brief note from her. "Sorry— but I did try—at least they knew your eyes were open. Yours empty-handed, Sylvia P. Weld." Enclosed was a letter to her from Dean Hawkes, which I cannot resist quoting in full.

My dear Mrs. Weld,

Mr. Fackenthal has handed me your letter of November 13 concerning Mortimer Adler, who was a student of Columbia College some years ago.

If Mr. Adler states that he did not receive his degree merely because of failure to swim, he is mistaken. The requirement for our degree involves four sessions of Physical Education, of which Mr. Adler completed one. He scarcely attended any of the other prescribed sessions of the work.

I think that I recall speaking with Mr. Adler while he was still an undergraduate, making it clear to him that in absenting himself from the work in Physical Education he was really making a choice. If he preferred to go without the degree rather than to attend the classes in Physical

Education it was his privilege to do so. As I understood the matter he made this decision with his eyes open.

I have since spoken with Adler concerning the possibility of our doing something about his degree. So far as I can judge he is quite uninterested in the matter. Perhaps I have misinterpreted Mr. Adler's attitude, but I know him with sufficient intimacy to be quite certain of my ground.

Very truly yours,
H. E. Hawkes, Dean

I could not let the matter pass without sending Dean Hawkes a few not quite contrite words of explanation.

Dear Dean Hawkes,

Mrs. Weld forwarded me the letter you wrote her. You were quite right in all the statements you made therein. My eyes were certainly open.

Mrs. Weld and I were summer neighbors on Cape Cod this summer. I discovered that she was the daughter of General Parsons. When she asked me whether I knew her father, I said that my most intimate contact with him was sitting in the Columbia gymnasium the day he presented the graduates with their degrees, one of which I didn't get because I couldn't swim. In the heat of the summer I had completely forgotten that I didn't like climbing ropes, jumping horses, or any of those other manly activities. Mrs. Weld jocularly said that she was going to make it her mission in life to get my Bachelor of Arts degree. It never occurred to me that she would actually make the attempt. I would much rather have had her try to get the twenty dollars back that I paid for the diploma I didn't get. If you could help me do that I would split the money with you.

During my first year at Columbia, the exploration of the library opened my eyes and stretched my mind in ways not achievable by ordinary classroom instruction. Hamilton Hall, the university building that housed the college faculty and some of their classrooms, contained a capacious book-lined room called the College Study. The library rooms I had used before—at De Witt Clinton High School, at the *Sun,* and at the local public library—were all small and unattractive in comparison with the College Study. The books were arranged in alphabetical order clockwise around the room. I decided to circumnavigate the room, making a list of exciting titles for future reference, if not in every case for future reading. And exciting titles there were in a wide variety, by authors I had never heard of, yet they somehow left me with the impression that I should become acquainted with them and should look into the subjects they were treating.

The first book I put on my list was *Appearance and Reality,* by F. H. Bradley. His name rang a bell. At the time I did not fully appreciate that this Bradley was the same fellow with whom William James had argued about the theory of truth; nor did I know that Bradley,

Fellow of Balliol, was one of Oxford's most famous philosophers and dons. Yet somehow that book seemed to have great weight, an impression that was confirmed when I examined the analytical table of contents that set forth the argument, sometimes plainly, sometimes elliptically. It took willpower to restrain myself from dipping into the book and reading chapters that touched on logical or epistemological problems with which I had some superficial acquaintance. But I realized that if I allowed myself to do that, I would never complete my Magellan-like voyage of discovery; so I listed the author and title with a very brief comment on the scope of the book as far as I could conjecture it from an examination of its table of contents.

It took me months to get around from A to Z. I went to the College Study at every opportunity, after classes and between classes, especially in those hours I had free by cutting physical education. My list grew from week to week and included such discoveries in the B section as Bernard Bosanquet's *Principles of Logic* (as well as a work of Bradley's with a similar title) and Bergson's *Matter and Memory* and *Time and Free Will* (here again, the titles fascinated me; it had never occurred to me that these words in Bergson's titles could be placed in meaningful juxtaposition to one another). Then—to recall only the startling titles— there were Benedetto Croce's *Aesthetics as Science of Expression and General Linguistic* and *History as the Story of Liberty;* Leibniz's *Monadology* and *Theodicy;* Nietzsche's *Thus Spake Zarathustra, Beyond Good and Evil,* and *The Birth of Tragedy;* a book by Giovanni Papini (whose name I remember from having seen it mentioned in William James's *Pragmatism*) entitled *The Twilight of the Philosophers;* Schopenhauer's *World As Will and Idea* in three large volumes; and so on down to Zeller's *Pre-Socratic Philosophers.*

I had not yet taken a course in the history of philosophy. Many of the great names in that history were totally unfamiliar. I did not know that Leibniz and Schopenhauer were major figures and that Croce and Papini were relatively minor ones. However, among my book purchases on early Saturday morning visits to Brentano's while I was still working on the *Sun* had been Frank Thilly's one-volume *History of Philosophy* —a much less voluminous and overpowering work than Windelband's. I had never finished it, but several times I had read the opening sections dealing with the pre-Socratic physicists, or natural philosophers—from Thales, Anaxagoras, and Anaximenes down to Pythagoras, Democritus, and Empedocles, with those two most enigmatic fellows, Heraclitus and Parmenides, in between. Their names still ring in my memory, for I memorized them in chronological order and, in addition, attached to each the word that served as a mnemonic clue to his theory; thus, Thales-water, Anaxagoras-air, Heraclitus-change, Parmenides-permanence, Pythagoras-numbers, Democritus-atoms.

At the time, I am sure that I did not understand the importance of making annotated bibliographies before one undertakes the serious study of a body of literature; nor had I any theory about the value of memorizing a set of related facts. It was twenty years later, when I came to write *How To Read A Book,* that I found myself laying great stress on the importance of becoming acquainted with a book, of paying attention to the title and scanning the table of contents in an initial effort to find out what the book is all about. The habit of cataloguing and memorizing, which became perhaps the least unattractive of my analerotic compulsions—the need to order and arrange things and keep them rigidly fixed in the order I have imposed on them—had some virtue in it, as I realized later when I gradually came to understand the function that memory can perform in the service of thought. During those early years, some of the related items I memorized were lists of names I had constructed for myself; but some were numbered, orderly sequences found in the subject matter itself, which on frequent repetition acquired a certain liturgical quality—such, for example, as the names of the twelve cranial nerves in order from the twelfth to the first, or the names of the four cardinal virtues, the five intellectual virtues, and the three theological virtues, as well as the seven deadly sins and the nine ranks in the hierarchy of angels.

The pain of learning can be eased or compensated by the joy of remembering what one has learned; therefore, substituting rote memory for intellection—becoming satisfied with the mere memory of that which one does not fully understand—can be a great temptation. Like the sin of Lucifer is the false pride one may take in a spurious omniscience. *Peccavi!* My compulsion to catalogue, order, and then recite it all from memory reached its most laughable extreme in a contest I concocted toward the end of my senior year. One of my classmates, Edward Roche Hardy, was an infant prodigy. He was twelve or thirteen, and I was twenty. This irritated me, and on one occasion, in the presence of fellow students, I challenged him to summarize the intellectual history of Western civilization while we walked up Riverside Drive from 110th Street to Grant's Tomb. The report of the competition in the college newspaper awarded me the victory. It said, and I suppose at the time I almost believed, that I had succeeded in outlining the intellectual history of the West—from the Egyptians, Chaldeans, and Greeks down to American pragmatism with William James and John Dewey—in twenty-two minutes flat!

I was an objectionable student, in some respects perhaps repulsive. I had elected to major in psychology and philosophy, and Professor A. T. Poffenberger, Jr., of the Psychology Department was made my faculty advisor. He taught Experimental Psychology, which I took in my first year, having taken Elementary Psychology in Columbia Extension before entering college. The textbook for that course, written by Professor Poffenberger in collaboration with Prof. Robert Sessions Woodworth, the head of the department, had not yet been published. We used a mimeographed and unedited version, which I felt privileged to criticize as if I had been asked to comment on it by a prospective publisher. The class in Experimental Psychology met at 1:30 on Tuesday and Thursday afternoons. Every Tuesday and Thursday I would knock on Professor Poffenberger's door at around 1:00 P.M. Poor Poff! When he was in, he was probably taking a little postprandial siesta before his lecture, or if not that, then at least enjoying a few moments of quiet reflection. If he responded to my knock, I would barge in with a list of questions for him to answer or a list of criticisms for him to comment on, based on my reading of the chapter assigned for that day, in which I thought I had found ungrounded inferences, verbal ambiguities, unexplained data, or untested hypotheses. Poff, gentle soul that he was, bore up under this assault, patiently answering questions, explaining matters I had not understood, or challenging points I had raised. This went on until one day when I arrived with thirty-eight items for discussion. He may have been indisposed that day; or it may have been the massiveness of my agenda or the fierce pertinacity of my probing; but whatever it was, Poff gently suggested that we desist from sessions of this sort on the ground that the time before class was not only too short but also inappropriate for the enterprise I seemed to have in mind. I should add that in the subsequent eight years in which I continued my undergraduate and graduate studies in psychology, became a junior instructor in his department, taught that course in Experimental Psychology in which his book was still used as the text, and received—I repeat, *received*—the Ph.D. through his good offices, Poff and I became close friends.

My ferocious pertinacity as a student did not always turn out well. One of the very bright young men in the Philosophy Department was Professor Irwin Edman, a facile writer (he had just completed a text for Contemporary Civilization, a course that was required of all freshmen) and a gifted teacher, but one whom I regarded as more eloquent than logical. I felt about his lectures the same way I felt about the prose of George Santayana, the contemporary philosopher admired by Professor Edman because of his style. Style was precisely the trouble with Santayana and Edman in my opinion—too much style and gloss and too little unvarnished statement of an analysis or an argument. Edman offered a course in Idealism, which began with a study of the *Enneads* of Plotinus, spent considerable time on the *Divine Comedy* of Dante (why, in that context, I cannot remember), and was to conclude with Josiah Royce's *The World and the Individual.* I say "was to conclude" because I never finished the course.

Edman would lecture for fifty minutes, lulling the students with a flow of words including such beauties as *ineluctable* and *quintessential* and interrupting himself from time to time to put diagrams on the board, which left visible traces of chalk on his jacket and on his lips, for he would put the chalk to his mouth as if to moisten it, as one would a pencil tip. His "style" did not contemplate questions from students, nor could it easily accommodate such interruptions. My "style"—the very opposite—could not possibly forgo questioning what seemed unintelligible to me at best and downright illogical at worst; nor was I willing to accommodate myself to Edman's temperament. I broke into the pellucid flow of his words whenever it became unbearable not to challenge what he was saying. As the class went on from Plotinus to Dante, my interruptions became more frequent, more insistent, and more unmannerly, even to the point of rudeness. For a while, Edman tried to wrap cotton wool around my interjections so that they didn't scratch or mar the smooth flow of his discourse; but this infuriated me still further, and one or two sessions ended with our shouting at one another. The upshot came one day when I mounted the steps to the seventh floor of Philosophy Hall, where the class was held. I found Edman standing outside the door of the classroom waiting for me. "Mortimer," he said in a tone as solicitous of my welfare as he could manage, "I suggest that you take the afternoon off and do something else. You get much too excited in class, and the strain on your nerves is not good for you." I did as suggested and followed a similar course on many occasions thereafter. I must have cut a great many classes, for I cannot remember Edman's lectures on Josiah Royce, but I did read *The World and the Individual* on my own in order to pass the final examination and get a grade for that course.

My experience with John Dewey took a slightly different turn. I had learned, from William James's *Pragmatism,* about his founding of the "Chicago School," whose theories James found so congenial. In my exploration of the College Study, I had come upon two books by Dewey—*Studies in Logical Theory* and *Reconstruction in Philosophy*—in each of which the table of contents referred to matters that demanded my attention. Beyond that, I sensed, in the general atmosphere of Columbia, the importance attached to his name and role in the university. There was much talk about his returning from China, where he had been attempting to institute reforms in the educational system. He came back to Columbia during the academic year 1920–1921 and offered a course of lectures on Types of Philosophical Thought in the fall of 1921. I registered for it. In what ensued, I had not the slightest premonition of my future confrontations with Professor Dewey at Columbia or with his educational disciples at Teachers College; even less had I any anticipation of the accidents which would put me ten

years later in a position at the University of Chicago to challenge the
school which had continued to be regnant there in the hands of Dewey's
associates, James Tufts and George Herbert Mead.

The very opposite of a spellbinder, Dewey delivered his lectures in a
low, barely audible voice, with long pauses, some stumblings, and
frequent groping for words. His style either encouraged one's attention
to wander or demanded the most intense concentration on what he
said. I not only paid close attention but also, because of the slowness of
his delivery, took down in my notebook the entire lecture, almost word
for word. After class I went immediately home, while my memory was
still fresh, and typed up my notes. A single lecture would produce six
or eight single-spaced typewritten pages and would have more analytical
and argumentative coherence than it appeared to have as one listened
to it being haltingly delivered. Rummaging through my files recently, I
turned up a dusty loose-leaf binder containing my typewritten transcript
of that whole series of lectures. Apparently, it constitutes a philosophical
work that John Dewey himself never wrote or published.

After typing up the lecture delivered, let us say, on a Tuesday, I
would read it over and exercise my nit-picking skills to note inconsistencies of statement, ambiguities in terminology, or questionable points
in the argument. I would then type a letter which ran something like
this: "Dear Professor Dewey: In your lecture on Tuesday, you said, on
the one hand, that such-and-such is the case; and, on the other hand,
that so-and-so is the case. This seems to me to involve a contradiction.
Will you please explain?" Or like this: "At the beginning of your
lecture, you used the word *experience* in a very broad sense to cover
. . . whereas later in the lecture you used it in a much more restricted
sense to designate. . . . How do you reconcile these two uses of the
word?" I would then put the letter under Professor Dewey's office door
sometime on Wednesday so that he might take notice of it before the
class met again on Thursday afternoon. To my surprise and delight, at
the opening of the hour on the first such Thursday, Professor Dewey
waved an envelope which he held in his hand and, saying that he had
received a letter from a student in the class, read it, and either answered
the question or commented on the matter which had bothered me. I,
of course, took down his reply in my notes and typed it up along with
the rest of the lecture delivered that day.

This went on for a number of weeks during which I wrote a dozen or
more letters that grew longer and more intricate as I went back over my
notes and thought that I had discovered a multiplication, rather than a
reduction, of the inconsistencies and ambiguities. The climax came in
an unduly long letter that pointed out inconsistencies not only between
what Professor Dewey had said in his lectures and what he had said in
his replies to my letters, but also between earlier responses and later

ones. Dewey was long-suffering and patient, but this was too much even for him. On the receipt of that long letter, he asked his young assistant, Herbert Schneider, to call me into his office and enjoin me to desist from further correspondence. Schneider, who had been observing the whole affair with some amusement, performed that duty with a smile that did not weaken the firmness of the injunction. From then on, I continued to underline or encircle troublesome points in the lectures as I was typing them, but I kept such observations to myself.

During the same year that I attended Dewey's lectures, I also took a course in the history of philosophy given by F. J. E. Woodbridge, the Johnsonian Professor, a chair once held by Nicholas Murray Butler when he was still a very young man and before he became president of the university. Apart from the reading that I had done on my own, the only formal instruction in philosophy that I had experienced before this came in the second semester of the preceding year, with the study of Friedrich Paulsen's *Introduction to Philosophy,* a book that I shall never forget because of the way it diagrammed the various solutions of the "mind-body problem." Professor Woodbridge was a superb lecturer, as slow in delivery as Dewey but without any hesitation; more eloquent than Edman but with an eloquence that derived from the flow of his thought rather than from the flow of his words. Once again I was able to take his lectures down almost verbatim, but this time I did not type them up (I still have a thick notebook of the whole course, written in red ink and in a relatively legible script). So enchanted was I by the insights that graced every hour, I had no inclination to bedevil Professor Woodbridge with questions or comments.

The course consisted of three lectures a week and one discussion section conducted by young instructors in the Philosophy Department, among whom were at that time John Herman Randall, Horace Friess, and Herbert Schneider. I had read some of the dialogues of Plato before, but I had never cast my eye on a page of Aristotle. In addition to the *Nicomachean Ethics,* we were assigned the reading of the *Metaphysics,* Book Lambda, in which Aristotle expounds his argument for the existence of a prime mover. Woodbridge's lectures on Aristotle filled many hours toward the end of the first semester. After spending some time on the pre-Socratic philosophers, he dwelt lovingly and at length on the dialogues of Plato, interpreting them not merely as philosophical discourses but as skillfully dramatized intellectual comedies; and then, in lecture after lecture, he covered the major works of Aristotle, with special attention to the theory of the four causes, of form and matter, and of entelechy in a view of nature and of the cosmos that Woodbridge expounded as if it were his very own.

The final examination toward the end of the first semester contained a question about Book Lambda in Aristotle's *Metaphysics.* Most of my classmates were stumped by it. Beguiled by the imagery of Wood-bridge's exposition of its doctrine, I must have turned in a creditable answer, because, just before the holiday recess, I received, as a Christmas gift, a copy of the Oxford translation of the *Metaphysics* inscribed by F. J. E. Woodbridge and H. L. Friess "To Mortimer J. Adler, who has already begun to make good use of this book." It still stands on a book-shelf in my library as a visible reminder of the long-lasting influence that Woodbridge's teaching of Aristotle had on my mind.

The year that I entered Columbia, a new program of General and Special Honors was announced. I remember attending a meeting at which John Erskine, professor of English, outlined the program and invited students to apply for admission. The Special Honors part of the program embodied the standing requirements for graduation with honors in the field of one's major interest—concentrated reading in that field and the writing of term papers; but the General Honors part was genuinely novel. As outlined by Erskine, it consisted in reading what he called "the classics of Western civilization"—Homer, Herodotus, and Thucydides down to Darwin, Marx, and Freud—a book a week, for approximately the sixty weeks of termtime during the junior and senior years. It also involved one two-hour evening seminar each week on the book assigned. I did not know then that John Erskine had been trying for more than four years to get this program approved by the college faculty; that after the First World War, he had used something like it to engage the minds and to fill the otherwise idle hours of soldiers in the American army of occupation on the Rhine; and that, after his tour of duty in Germany, nothing less than the intervention of Presi-dent Butler had been required to get the General Honors course adopted. The first offering of the General Honors course was scheduled for the fall semester of 1921, and since I would be a member of the junior class at that time, I applied for admission, was accepted, and enrolled.

Among the fortunate coincidences to which I am immeasurably in-debted for the far-reaching effects they have had upon the course of my life, I would give top place to the good luck of having John Erskine as my preceptor in General Honors. Like the happy accident of reading Mill's *Autobiography* while working on the New York *Sun,* or the equally fortunate circumstance of imbibing from Woodbridge some grasp of how to philosophize in the manner of Aristotle, the impact on my mind of the books read in General Honors, and of Erskine's method of conducting the discussion of them, was momentous. That one course, as I told Bob Hutchins in 1929 when he became president of the University of Chicago, was a college in itself—the whole of a liberal education or certainly the core of it. Not just the books we read, though each one was an eye-opener, but the discussions which Erskine conducted in the manner of highly civil conversations about important themes and in a spirit of inquiry that he had celebrated in his famous essay "The Moral Obligation To Be Intelligent"; and still further, the conversations that the students themselves had with one another in between times, both about the books being read and about matters touched on in the seminars—all of these related aspects of General Honors gave it preeminence among all the educative influences that good fortune has conferred on me.

Many years later I had an experience that amply confirmed the soundness of Erskine's reason for introducing the General Honors program at Columbia. When he began teaching at Columbia in the first decade of this century, the elective system had not yet run riot and made havoc of the liberal arts curriculum. A large part of the curriculum still consisted of required courses, and in consequence of that, all students shared many classes and read many of the same books and so had a great deal of common subject-matter to talk about. But by the end of the second decade, Erskine told his colleagues, the elective system had scattered the student body into a wide variety of courses and left few, if any, books that the whole student body had read and could talk to one another about. Lacking common intellectual themes, student conversation had degenerated into small talk. Erskine proposed General Honors as the needed corrective.

How right he was I learned in 1952, when I lectured at the University of Wisconsin under the auspices of the senior honor students in the university. They asked me to dine with them before the lecture, and in order to generate a conversation in which everyone around the table might become engaged, I asked them to name the books that all of them had read during their four years at the school. To my astonishment, there was not a single title that all of them had read, not even a play by Shakespeare or a book of the Bible. My astonishment was surpassed by theirs when I told them about St. John's College in Annapolis, Maryland, where the required curriculum revolved around four years of reading and discussing the great books—the lineal descendant of Erskine's list of Western classics.

My intense preoccupation with books, lectures, note taking, and the nit-picking of professors tapered off a little in my senior year. The wedge that opened the door to other avenues of experience was James Waterman Wise, son of the famous rabbi, Stephen Wise. Jim had been my fellow student in Professor Poffenberger's class in Experimental Psychology. "Fellow *student*" is a misnomer, for he was not at all a student. Jim spent most of his time during the laboratory hours, and sometimes even during the lectures, shooting craps in the back of the room with another member of the class. I suspect he never cracked a book that whole year. The night before the final examination in late

May, Jim pressed the panic button, asking me to do what I could to help him get by. I spent the evening with him, made up a list of fifteen questions of which I guessed about ten would occur on the examination, and for each question gave Jim the answer in a nutshell, with some instruction on how to embroider it a little. Jim had a phenomenal memory; he could recite whole scenes from many of the plays of Shakespeare; he was widely literate and had his father's passion for eloquence as well as his gift for it; he just was not inclined to study, at least not in experimental psychology. It was Jim's memory and my knowledge of the subject that saved him on this occasion. Most of the questions on the examination the next morning closely resembled the ones I had prepared Jim for the night before, and having memorized the answers to them, he made an A minus on the exam.

I played similar games with Jim at the end of his junior year, which he spent at Harvard. My first reading of the four Gospels was occasioned by the need to help him pass an examination on the literature of the New Testament, which, unlike experimental psychology, genuinely interested him; but he had spent a good part of that year on auction bridge and assorted high jinks unrelated to the curriculum. One way or another, Jim passed all his examinations, often with good grades—good enough, in fact, to win a Phi Beta Kappa key in his senior year at Columbia. He thought that a great joke, but not nearly so funny as the fact that when he told a doting aunt about this honor award, she asked him, quite seriously, "Did Mortie get one, too?"

In the summer between my junior and senior years, Jim invited me to come to Chocorua, New Hampshire, where the Wises had rented a house for the season. By that time I had read the two volumes of *The Letters of William James,* and the name Chocorua reminded me of the photograph contained in one of the volumes—a picture of William James and Josiah Royce sitting together on a stone fence in Chocorua, with the caption "Damn the Absolute." Jim's invitation beckoned me to that stone fence, but after I arrived, the attractiveness of his sister, Justine, and her Bryn Mawr classmate, Diana Wertheim, diverted my attention from the haunts of Harvard's philosophers. My uncle had introduced me to tennis some years earlier, but my deficiencies made me a liability in mixed doubles and a patsy for either of the girls in singles. Irked by this, Jim spent hours on the court with me to improve my game to the point where I could beat Justine or Diana. I returned to New York and to Columbia that fall, not only with a lively interest in tennis, but with an even livelier one in the two girls. A livelier interest, but no skill in dealing with them. Jim had not realized that there was another sport I needed training in.

My only approach to the girls was to conduct serious philosophical discussions or write equally serious philosophical letters. Having much earlier formed the habit of never typing anything without making a carbon copy, I made carbon copies of the twelve- and fifteen-page letters I wrote Diana and Justine. They were partly instructive and partly argumentative, for I discovered that both girls had very queer notions which required correction. I have recently found some of these carbon copies in the deepest strata of my files, and attached to them, in one or two instances, were brief handwritten replies. I don't know whether I intended my lengthy missives to serve as love letters, but it is perfectly clear that they were not so interpreted by their recipients; nor were they gratefully acknowledged as the useful instruction or intellectual emendation I doubtless thought they contained.

One other vein of carbons, this time with more affectionate replies, comes from the same file. During my senior year, I became acquainted with Helen Berlin. She was a student at Hunter College who earned pin money working in the evenings as an usherette at the theatre where the *Chauve Souris* performed. The theatre was near Columbus Circle close to Columbia's medical school, the College of Physicians and Surgeons, where, two evenings a week, I went for a course in Neuro-anatomy. My class finished about the same time that Helen went off duty at the theatre. We would meet for something to eat and drink, and then I would take her home by subway to the upper Bronx, where she lived with her parents. I managed to be a little less philosophical and pedagogical with Helen than I had been with Justine and Diana, but I still woefully lacked knowledge of, not to mention competence in, the ploys of boy-girl play, even on the superficial level of adolescent puppy-love. My sexual impulses, which it would be more accurate, perhaps, to describe as blandly erotic, would have been satisfied by a good-night kiss when we reached the entryway of Helen's apartment house; but time and time again, I would leave her with lips untouched, kicking myself all the way back to Manhattan for not having had the courage to kiss her. I gave vent to the unfulfilled wish by writing her long letters about it, to which she replied with modestly offered suggestions at first and then delicately worded invitations—none of which helped me to get over the hurdle of my inhibitions, born of the fear of being embarrassed by clumsiness or ineffectuality in the performance of acts that other boys did spontaneously at an earlier age and that they had gone way beyond by the time they were nineteen or twenty.

The summer after graduating—degreeless—from Columbia, I worked as a counselor at a boy's camp, Camp Wigwam in Maine. Since I lacked proficiency in most games and sports, I was assigned to running what were called the camp's "educational activities." These included a Sunday morning session, a substitute for religious exercises, I suppose, at which I would deliver a short speech, something like a sermonette. As the summer wore on, I became infuriated by the petty rules and regulations of camp life, and used one of these Sunday mornings as the occasion for delivering a lecture that contrasted what I called "Greek ethics" and "Jewish ethics." The latter, I said, was a heteronomous ethics, consisting in laws or commandments imposed from without or above, calling for unquestioning obedience to rules and regulations, and allowing for no consideration of the circumstances surrounding particular acts and no calculation of the pleasures and pains, or the goods and evils, that might accrue to the individual from acting one way or another. In terms of the little understanding I had of Aristotle's treatise on the subject, I delineated "Greek ethics" as autonomous rather than heteronomous, with the individual governing his own acts by the use of his reason to determine what was good or bad, right or wrong, in a particular case, rather than simply doing his duty by compliance with rules.

The campers sitting on the grass before me understood only that one of their counselors was recommending that they disobey the camp's rules whenever they could think of a good reason for doing so. That message they gladly received and even more gladly acted on. All hell broke loose the next week. Not only did the boys break every rule; they invented rules to break. The directors of the camp seriously considered giving me my walking papers, which I certainly deserved if for no other reason than the fact, unperceived by them, that I had presented a caricature of Aristotle's *Ethics,* making it sound like that half-baked theory of conduct aired during the early sixties under the title of "Situation Ethics."

Henry Simon, younger brother of Richard Simon of Simon and Schuster, also served as a counselor at Camp Wigwam that summer. Henry was a classmate of mine at Columbia and had sat beside me during the seminar sessions of General Honors conducted by John Erskine. Many an evening, after the campfire died down and lights were turned off, we sat around recalling this or that sally with which John Erskine had spiced our conversations about the great books; and we vied with one another in attempting to show off the understanding we thought we had achieved by reading them—not only a grasp of the pivotal ideas in Western intellectual history, but also an awareness of the main lines and currents in the cultural tradition of the West. We had both passed, creditably enough, the final examination in General Honors, and if anybody had asked us whether we thought that we really understood the books we had read during the last two years, we would not have hesitated for a moment to give an affirmative reply. More than that, we would have given it in a tone of voice that bespoke confidence in our educated judgments about almost any subject we might be called upon to discuss.

I did not realize until some years later that my good fortune consisted in something more than having a paying job when I returned to the city at summer's end, the job of laboratory assistant in Experimental Psychology, to which I had been appointed before the end of my senior year, at a salary of one thousand dollars per annum. My good fortune included something far more important than a position on the faculty and a salary, for I had also been invited to join Mark Van Doren in running one of the General Honors seminars in the coming year. Had the accidents of fortune taken me to some other job or had they not included this appointment to the teaching staff of General Honors, I might not have opened the great books again, assuming blithely that I understood them, having read them all once and mastered them sufficiently to pass a tough examination on them.

Happily, I was saved from such folly. Happily, also, I had sense enough to realize that my undergraduate "mastery" of the great books might not suffice for the purpose of teaching them, not by lecturing, but by asking the kind of questions that could sustain a good two-hour discussion. In that first year of teaching, I was to learn two things that have pervaded my educational thinking ever since. One was that the teacher who takes his job seriously learns more than even the most serious student in his class. What a boon it would be if, in the study of any subject matter, everyone were obliged to teach it to someone else as well as study it under someone else. The other thing I learned—to my surprise and dismay—was that one reading of the great books had scarcely scratched the surface. On the second reading, which I did in order to teach them, I discovered how little I understood them and how much more I had to learn from them; and that discovery has been confirmed again and again in the fifty years that I have been conducting discussions of the great books.

Chapter 3

God and the Psychologists

I N THE EARLY 1920s, becoming a member of the faculty of a leading university, for someone with my name and of my race, was like getting into an exclusive club. The chances were very slim, indeed. How aware I then was of the prejudices standing in my way and how thin-skinned were my feelings about combatting them, I cannot now remember. However, I know that as early as my second year in college, I had fixed my mind on becoming a teacher of philosophy, not just anywhere, but at Columbia. I could think of no other future that interested me at all. I directed all my energies to the one goal that promised the fulfillment of my aspirations.

When I realized in my senior year that I might not make it—a letter from Professor Coss, the head of the Philosophy Department, threw buckets of cold water on my hopes—I somehow managed to readjust my sights. I accepted the invitation to become a member of the Psychology Department, though I still regarded that as a poor alternative. The fact that I had also been invited by John Erskine to teach a section of General Honors in the fall of 1923 made it a little more palatable.

I had spent most of my time in college on philosophy and psychology. Though I took and passed courses in other subjects, some of which I found momentarily fascinating, such as the history of the English language or the study of shades and shadows in the School of Architecture, it was in the fields of philosophy and psychology that I did most of my extracurricular reading and writing. I say extracurricular because the volume of both far exceeded what any student might have been reasonably expected to do. Even though I did nothing but study seven days a week during my three years in college, I find it difficult to understand how, in addition to reading so much, I also turned out so many hundreds of pages of typewritten manuscript.

I must confess at once that, in assessing the sheer quantity of this input and output, I am not relying on unaided memory. The fact is that, from early on, I formed the habits of a pack rat, at least as far as saving, storing, and accumulating paper was concerned. While I was writing for the New York *Sun,* I kept several copies of every editorial paragraph, essay, and poem of mine that had been published in the paper, often both a galley proof copy as well as one from the printed edition, and these my mother pasted up in a series of scrapbooks which I still have.

My file contains, from earlier years, copies of high school journals, the *De Witt Clinton News,* and the *Magpie,* of which I had been editor or in which I had published stories. It even goes as far back as a notebook in which, under my mother's tutelage one summer while I was still in elementary school, I had written a chapter-by-chapter report on a history of English literature that she had taken out of the local library for me to read.

The paper I accumulated in my college years is overwhelming; it is redundant, often containing several variants of the same piece. It includes the registrar's record of the courses I took and the grades I received, official communications from the university authorities, correspondence of all sorts, large manila envelopes of unpublished verse, and copies of the college literary quarterly in which some of my poems were published.

One would have to be egotistical beyond belief to reread some of it without cringing with embarrassment. Nevertheless, the files do contain some materials that I now find helpful to my recollection of the circumstances surrounding my unsuccessful effort to get into the Philosophy Department, the events leading up to my unsolicited appointment to the Psychology Department, and the work I did in both fields while I was still a student and after I had become an instructor.

The students in Professor Poffenberger's course in Experimental Psychology were required to make reports on all lab experiments, not only describing the experiments and their results, but also commenting on technical writings bearing on the subject. Most students wrote cursory comments; their laboratory reports ran to two or three pages on the average. In order to cover all the books or articles I had read on the subject of the experiment, I regularly wrote twenty to twenty-five single-spaced typewritten pages. The collection of these reports fills two very large binders. I would guess that the amount of work this represented, together with a number of lengthy term papers I had submitted in other psychology courses, persuaded Professor Poffenberger and Harold Jones, who succeeded him, that I had sufficient interest and competence in the subject to be appointed a laboratory assistant before I had begun to do a stitch of graduate work in psychology.

The record of the work I did in philosophy is even more voluminous.

As a student enrolled in General Honors, I also had to enroll for Special Honors in a particular field of scholarship, and I did so in philosophy rather than in psychology. The reading I did and the reports I wrote ranged over the outstanding figures in contemporary philosophy—Bertrand Russell, George Santayana, F. C. S. Schiller, Henri Bergson, William James, Arthur O. Lovejoy, John Dewey, R. W. Sellars, C. I. Lewis, R. F. A. Hoernlé, and Morris Cohen—and included the study of Kant's *Prolegomena to Any Future Metaphysic*, together with some reading in the literature of commentaries on Kant, and the further study of Aristotle's *Metaphysics*, to which Professor Woodbridge had introduced me.

I should mention one other book, which had just been published, containing the essays of the six "New Realists" (Professors Montague and Holt of Columbia were among them), to which they had attached a programmatic manifesto for the reform of philosophy. I don't think I ever marked up a book as assiduously as I marked that one, with questions and comments on almost every page. Having at first adopted James's pragmatism as the right remedy for the mistakes of absolute idealism, I now shifted to realism as the proper corrective. It took some time before I discovered how many varieties of realism contended for that honor—naive realism, new realism, critical realism, the naturalistic realism of Woodbridge and Santayana, and the logical realism of Meinong and Husserl—and I would have been shocked had someone told me then that, in quite different senses of the term, Plato, Aristotle, and Aquinas had also been called realists.

My friend John Storck had the habit of exploring the philosophical periodicals as I had explored the books in the College Study. Following his lead, I plunged into the bottomless pit of the periodical literature, more bemused than enlightened by the polemical attacks and counterattacks that I found. However, these explorations did result in my constructing an almost complete bibliography of Professor Woodbridge's essays for the journals—he had published only one book at that time—and I read all of them that I could find. They also led to my discovery of an essay, published in 1917, on some conditions of progress in philosophy. Professor Lovejoy of Johns Hopkins had delivered it as his presidential address before the American Philosophical Association. At the time, I did not appreciate the influence this single paper would exert on the views I was later to form about how philosophical research should be conducted. Nor could I, by the wildest stretch of imagination, have foreseen that when the Institute for Philosophical Research was launched in 1952, I would, in describing the work to be done by the institute, hark back to this paper by Lovejoy because of its insistence that philosophy should become a cooperative enterprise instead of continuing to be, as it had been for centuries, a series of solo performances.

That idea about cooperative work by philosophers, carried on in the same spirit that leads scientists to pool their efforts, must have hit me hard at the time, for I find I mentioned it repeatedly in papers that I read before the Philosophy Club in my junior and senior years.

At regular intervals, the Philosophy Department held a departmental conference at which members of the faculty or graduate students read papers for discussion. My files contain four papers which I read at departmental conferences, three while I was an undergraduate and one toward the end of my first year as a teacher in the Psychology Department. These essays were extracurricular efforts, unlike the five or six long term papers which I wrote for my courses. Looking back over them now, I am astounded to discover how many of the ideas that I would otherwise have thought took hold of me in much later years had already seized my mind and taken shape in it. When I first turned them up, I was inclined to dismiss these early papers as juvenile efforts (and juvenile they are in their rhetorical excesses), but on a closer examination I have found that they contain, not just the seeds, but some elaborations of ideas that have preoccupied me in recent years—in fact, have been developed in books that I have written since my sixtieth birthday.

What I have just said does not apply to all the materials in my file, particularly the detailed notes for the lectures that I gave under the auspices of the People's Institute during the middle 1920s. Glancing over these, what surprises me most is my present inability to follow the thought processes of the young man that I then was. Stranger by far than the repressed unconcious are the layers of thought that lie buried—hidden and unreclaimable—beneath one's present state of mind. I have had this experience with books that I have written. Reading them after they have been published and out for some time often involves genuine puzzlement about why a particular bit of analysis or a particular line of argument took the shape it did. It sometimes requires considerable effort to feel at home with thinking I did at an earlier time. Usually I can succeed in resurrecting and revitalizing the almost-but-not-quite-dead. Not so, in the case of some of my undergraduate essays and the notes for lectures that I gave for the People's Institute. They remain tombstones for me, marking something buried that I cannot revive.

John Dewey's lectures in 1921–1922 on types of philosophical thought began in the first semester of that academic year with a criticism of various theories of meaning and an exposition of his own theory of it. This aroused my interest in the subject and sent me reading the various authors he mentioned and others that I turned up myself. I looked into Bradley's and Bosanquet's treatises on logic and also into J. S. Mill's *System of Logic;* I found secondhand reports of the doctrines of Meinong and Husserl; and I puzzled over Edward Bradford Titchener's discussion of meaning in his *Psychology of the Higher Thought Pro-*

cesses. This led me to accounts of the work of Prof. Oswald Kulpe's Würzburg School and also to an essay on imageless thought, quite revolutionary in its day, by Prof. Robert Woodworth, the senior member of Columbia's Psychology Department. Just a few years earlier, C. K. Ogden and I. A. Richards had published their book *The Meaning of Meaning.* It had occasioned a flurry of articles in *Mind,* all on the meaning of meaning, by Bertrand Russell, F. C. S. Schiller, and C. A. Strong.

Since I could never read material of this kind without making notes that would record or guide my own thinking about the subject, and since that, in turn, almost always impelled me to write about it, I turned out an essay to which I attached an extensive bibliography of the works I had read. Though I was only a junior in the college at the time, I submitted the essay to the member of the Philosophy Department responsible for the departmental conferences. It carried the wordy and pompous title "A Survey and Discussion of the Philosophical and Psychological Aspects of the Problem of Meaning." I am sure that it was not the intrinsic merit of the paper but the novelty of its having been submitted by a college student which persuaded the authorities to give it a hearing. Fifty years later I uncovered it while writing *Some Questions About Language,* in which the problem of meaning occupies the center of the stage. That undergraduate essay of mine had certainly covered the ground, but it had not cleared it of the almost impenetrable thickets which surround the problem of meaning. Worse still, acquaintance with John B. Watson's simplistic behavioristic psychology prompted me to concoct a theory of meaning which tried to explain it without reference to acts of the human mind, the folly of which I did not discover for many years—not until I had become a much better student of Aristotle, Aquinas, and Locke than I was on first acquaintance with their works. In fact, it was not until the late thirties, when I read a little essay on signs and symbols by Jacques Maritain, that I was given the ray of light which dispersed my earlier puzzlement about the subject.

Though I have no clear memory of the occasion, my guess is that the self-importance I felt, as a result of having my words listened to—and even seriously discussed—by the faculty and graduate students of the Philosophy Department, not only puffed me up with pardonable pride but also fueled my engines for an early repeat performance. It occurred just a few months later; in May, I was allowed to present another paper, entitled "Love and Logic in Philosophy, Being a Defense of the Sentiment of Rationality," a recasting of a term paper I had done for Professor Woodbridge's course in the history of philosophy.

I had borrowed the phrase "sentiment of rationality" from William James's essay of that title, but I used it without any reference to the problem which had been James's main concern. Mine was the conflict between those who viewed philosophical systems as works of the imagination, great intellectual poems each presenting its own *weltanschauung,* and those who, on the contrary, regarded philosophy as dealing piecemeal with problems that can be solved in much the same way that scientists solve theirs. In the one case, it seemed to me that logical criteria for assessing the truth or falsity of particular philosophical propositions were as irrelevant as they would be for the sentences in a poem. It was only on the other view of philosophy, conceived as having an affinity with science rather than with poetry, that the truth and falsity of a philosopher's statements, sentence by sentence, would have to be considered. One would then not be satisfied with attributing some kind of "poetic truth" to his world vision as a whole.

In addition, I pointed out that, "if there is no question of validity with regard to philosophical propositions, there is certainly no need to worry ourselves about how philosophy can be made cooperative. The very conception of philosophy as a cooperative enterprise," I went on, borrowing the thought, if not the words, from Professor Lovejoy's presidential address, "implies the conception of philosophy as a system of propositions, the truth of which philosophers are cooperatively attempting to demonstrate. . . . The composition of a piece of music is usually not a collaborative effort; nor the painting of a picture, nor the writing of a poem. . . . It would be just as ludicrous to imagine a poem that William Wordsworth and Algernon Swinburne would attempt to produce together, as to conceive a philosophic system being produced cooperatively by William James and F. H. Bradley."

What bothered me most of all (and I expressed my anguish in anguished language) was the fact that if philosophy were to have no commerce with truth and falsity in the ordinary sense of those terms, then there could be no such thing as philosophical knowledge, for how can there be knowledge divorced from truth? Why bother to become a philosopher or even to be a student of the subject? As I expressed it only a few years ago in the opening chapter of *The Conditions of Philosophy,* the very first condition prerequisite to philosophy's being a socially respectable enterprise in which one may engage with some measure of intellectual self-respect is that it achieve knowledge of the same sort that science achieves and that is recognized as knowledge by the general public.

It is not coming upon points and passages like the above that startles me now, though they do represent insights about philosophy that reappear again and again in much later lectures and books, especially in part 1 of volume 1 of *The Idea of Freedom,* the first published work of the Institute for Philosophical Research in 1958, and even more fully in *The Conditions of Philosophy,* published in 1965. What strikes me most strongly is the passion expressed in this student essay, which begins with the words "I have lived for almost twenty years. For the last three I have been more and more intensely interested in philosophy"; and then, after depicting the position that differing philosophical views are nothing but the manifestation of differing temperamental biases, the essay went on to bewail and bemoan the reduction of philosophy to being a matter of taste rather than a matter of truth. Wearing my heart on my sleeve, I wrote: "If I really thought that truth and falsehood never occurred among philosophical positions, I would cry bitterly awhile for the hours I had wasted and the pains I had suffered, then wipe my eyes, whistle a tune, and dig ditches or study sociology."

Having thus expressed my passion for truth, I at once set it aside as having no relevance to the truth of the view that I was trying to defend—that philosophical propositions must be either true or false, just like scientific propositions. I did not deny that emotions play a role. On the contrary, I admitted that they did and that, therefore, it was necessary to dredge them up from their dark recesses and expose them to the light of day by confessing them, as I was here confessing my passion for truth and for logic. This would help to exorcise them; and that done, one could then get on with the serious business of using logic to get at the truth about the matters under consideration, even the truth about whether truth or falsity is attainable in philosophical thought; for, as I argued in the paragraph immediately following my emotional outburst, to deny that truth and falsity are attainable in philosophical thought involves a theory of truth which is itself a philosophical theory that must be either true or false.

Some years later, in the middle thirties, when I was engaged in delivering a series of lectures at the Institute for Psychoanalysis in Chicago (subsequently published, in 1938, under the title *What Man Has Made of Man*), Dr. Franz Alexander, the head of the institute, gave me, without charge, a portmanteau psychoanalysis of my controlling neurosis. "Mortimer," he said, "the trouble with you is that you are masochistic toward truth and reality." I shall have more to say later about my bouts with psychoanalysis and psychoanalysts; here I wish only to remark that Dr. Alexander was probably right in his diagnosis of my neurosis, springing from an analerotic compulsion toward orderliness that insists upon classifying things and putting everything into its proper place and keeping it there. That is certainly one way of describing my abiding and unabating passion for logic and for using it to get at the truth. Dr. Alexander was quite wrong, however, in thinking that his psychoanalysis of me, no matter how correct it was, had anything whatsoever to do with the truth or falsity of the propositions about psychoanalytic psychology that I had presented at his institute and that all the psychoanalysts in my audience, with the possible exception of Dr. Gregory Zilboorg, rejected out of hand with unconcealed emotional

tantrums. I did not make at the time the appropriate retort discourteous
—that if I were masochistic toward truth and reality, they were sadistic.
If I had pointed that out, I would have immediately added, as I did in
my student paper in 1922, "Having lifted these emotional undercurrents
out into the open, let's push them aside and engage in the serious
business of conducting our discussion rationally and logically, to discover the truth about points on which we differ."

I cannot refrain from picking up one other item from "Love and
Logic in Philosophy," not only because it exposes the passion for truth
that appears on every page, but also because it reveals my feeling about
the conflict between poets and philosophers, using "poets" to include
not just writers of lyrics but writers of imaginative literature—novels
and plays. That feeling may even reflect the conflict in my own life
between the wish to be a poet and the wish to be a philosopher. I had
written a long poem on that subject in which I had failed to resolve the
conflict. The passage I now quote follows a remark about "the great
depression that I suffered in witnessing Bernard Shaw's metabiological
pentateuch" (i.e., *Back to Methuselah*). Describing the play as "a
dramatization of Bergsonism," whose theory of the *élan vital* underlying what Bergson called "creative evolution" I thought sheer poppy-
cock, I reacted violently against the long speeches in which Shaw's
characters discuss Bergson's false doctrines in a manner that put them
out of reach of argument. "I trembled when I heard the puppets describe
the science of their day. I squirmed uncomfortably in my seat as I realized
the supposed transiency of our knowledge and our world"—to be
transcended by the coming of a race of supermen. "As I left the theatre,
I comforted myself by the reflection that the play was only a great poem,
and Shaw a poet in his visions. Then, as never before, did I fully and
clearly appreciate the significance of Plato's banishment of the poets
from the republic!" Only a month or so ago, I found myself expressing
exactly the same view and the same distaste about a piece of science
fiction by Robert Heinlein, in which a storyteller advances a whole series
of political *obiter dicta* and gets away with it because, being only a
storyteller, he does not have to stand up to the tests of logic or truth.

During the summer of 1922, I wrote the head of the Philosophy
Department about the possibility of an appointment after completing
my senior year. Exactly how I pleaded my case with Professor Coss I
do not know, but I do have his reply. My guess is that I mistakenly
thought that my avowed passion for logic and truth—and for philosophy
—would recommend me to him. I overlooked the fact that Professor
Coss was a businesslike administrator, the head of Columbia's burgeon-
ing Summer Session. The only course in the Philosophy Department
that he taught was one entitled "Business Ethics." He had almost no
interest in either logic or truth and very little in philosophy. He prob-

ably found the way I had expressed my emotions about these subjects a little embarrassing, perhaps ungentlemanly, and certainly typically Jewish.

Even if I had not been Jewish, the paper that I had read before the Philosophy Department would have put me in Professor Coss's black book, because it contained slurs on pragmatism and pragmatists. Coss idolized John Dewey and was a pragmatist down to his fingertips, or mainly there. His letter informed me that "our Department is now well-staffed and I do not believe that we would be justified in adding to its number anyone with little or no experience when there might be possible candidates with what seem to be better qualifications. . . . While money remains in this world a real consideration you must think of that along with other things. . . . Think of something other than advanced study in philosophy. It might be worth your while to take psychology, pure or applied."

Either because I was prone to wishful thinking or simply unwilling to admit defeat, I persisted and prepared still another paper to read at a departmental conference in the middle of my senior year. This one, occasioned or provoked by a symposium on the teaching of philosophy which I had attended during the midwinter meetings of the American Philosophical Association, bore the title "The Student: A Dialogical Narrative, Considering Aims and Methods in the Teaching of Philosophy." One passage from the opening pages indicates that in thinking about the problem of teaching and studying philosophy, I was thinking about myself and my own future.

> Last year the problems and solutions of epistemology and metaphysics were ends in themselves, and to teach philosophy meant simply to teach that subject-matter as the data and technique of a science. But this year, fortunately, I have gotten a glimpse of how a person who does not expect to become a professional philosopher must feel toward being taught these subjects. I got this feeling when it first occurred to me that I might not become a professional philosopher. I know that philosophy is supposed to be coextensive with living, that theory and practise are supposed to be inseparable, and therefore, what one learns in the philosophy classroom enhances and improves the quality and worth of any life, and is not only the preparation for a certain professionalism. I accepted this as true until I started to live, and found the problems of life harder to solve than the problems of philosophy. I discovered that economic troubles, and social adjustments, and being in love are difficulties of practise the meeting and solution of which are in no way facilitated by a philosophical education, such as I have had—a very thorough training in specific branches of pure theory.

After this bit of personal confession, the paper dealt mainly with conflicts that I now realize have troubled me during most of my career—

the tension between philosophy as every man's business and philosophy as a technical subject of interest only to professionals, the tension between teaching philosophy as something useful to every student in the class and teaching it as if the only aim were to train another generation of professional philosophers, and the tension between devoting one's time and energies to being a teacher of philosophy and concentrating one's efforts on becoming a philosopher one's self. I did not realize how very recent had been the emergence of university philosophy departments, of professors of philosophy and professional philosophers, though I should have known that most of the great English thinkers— Hobbes, Locke, Berkeley, Hume, and John Stuart Mill—were not teachers of philosophy, certainly not professors in departments of philosophy. If I had thought of it, I would have realized that that was true also of Descartes, Leibniz, and Spinoza, and even perhaps, in a slightly different way, of Plato and Aristotle as well. The glaring exceptions would be found in the German universities of the eighteenth and nineteenth centuries—in such figures as Kant, Fichte, and Hegel— and unfortunately it was the German model that came to prevail almost everywhere else in the twentieth century.

The conflicts to which I have just referred were dramatically presented in my "dialogical narrative" by lengthy quotations from the diametrically opposed views of Professor Lovejoy of Johns Hopkins University and Professor Garman of Amherst College. I have already mentioned the lasting impression that Lovejoy's presidential address made on me. Lovejoy was a prolific writer, but Garman had no books to his name and had never published a single article in a philosophical journal. By accident I discovered a volume on the shelves of the College Study that I read during my first year in college. It was a *festschrift* volume commemorating Professor Garman's long years of service as a teacher of philosophy. It contained essays by some of my own teachers, Woodbridge and Erskine, who had known Garman at Amherst, as well as a letter from Professor Garman to G. Stanley Hall, president of Clark University, in which Garman described his aims and methods as a teacher of philosophy to undergraduates most of whom were not going to become professional philosophers. That letter, like Lovejoy's presidential address, made a profound impression on me, but moved me in exactly the opposite direction. I was torn between the pulls they exerted on my mind.

Here, in my dialogue, is Lovejoy speaking:

Philosophy has long been endeavoring to perform two seemingly identical, but practically incongruous, functions. It has seldom been quite clear whether men chiefly sought from their philosophers the record—often quaintly enough expressed—of interesting and impressive personal reactions upon life or depersonalized science; and as a rule both have been

expected at once and from the same person. Yet there are in human nature hardly any two dispositions more deeply and subtly at variance than
the desire to edify and the desire to verify. There still attaches to the
current conception of the teacher of philosophy, however, much of this
paradoxical duality. . . . This duality in the prevalent conception of the
philosopher affects his work more variously and profoundly than is often
realized. . . . It is more by excellence in the prophetic or poetic character
than by excellence in the scientific character that a philosopher has been,
and often still is, likely to gain academic reputation and influence. . . . If
philosophy is to be treated as a science still in the making; if it is agreed
that it is worth while for society to maintain a small body of men for the
purpose of ascertaining, with as much care and exactitude of procedure as
possible, what can be known about certain of the largest and most difficult
questions that present themselves to the human intellect,—then society
must not confuse this purpose with a wholly different one, that of furnish-
ing impressive, imaginative, edifying, emotionally stirring popular discourses about these same problems.

I then quoted at length from Garman's letter to President Hall, but I
think that the antithesis between Garman and Lovejoy comes out more
clearly in this statement about Garman as a teacher, written by one of
his own students:

The determining note in Professor Garman's teaching of philosophy was
his conception of philosophy. It was for him not primarily a subject to be
studied for its own sake. One might say it was not studied as a subject at
all. He took up the teaching of philosophy not primarily because of his interest in philosophical problems, but because of his belief that it afforded
an excellent educational opportunity. The end always in view was equipment for life, by leading men to see the fixed stars in the heavens and by
enabling them to realize that they were citizens in the universal kingdom
of truth. . . . This then was the first eminent trait of Professor Garman's
teaching: the attempt to teach the student how to weigh evidence, and to
arouse in him the conviction that he could do his own independent weighing, and that truth's ultimate appeal lay in his own mind. In the second
place, the student was quickly led to see that philosophy is a tremendously
serious business—not serious in the sense too often attached to it, of being something remote and well-nigh incomprehensible to be pursued only
in seclusion, but in the sense of being the essential and vitally necessary medium for shaping one's course if one wished for real efficiency as a man and
as a citizen. . . . There was never any splitting of hairs on purely theoretic
issues; the issues were living. The student felt that they must be solved
if he were to go out into the world of action with any confidence or
serenity of mind.

The last ten pages of my paper consisted in mimicry of a Platonic
dialogue, one in which a Socratic questioner tries, by comparing the
teaching of philosophy with the teaching of law and the teaching of

physics, to resolve the conflict between the motives of the edifying teacher concerned to cultivate the minds of students and those of the verifying inquirer concerned to advance knowledge in a highly technical field of scholarship. I am not surprised to find that the paper ended with the issue left unresolved; it has remained so with me for most of my life. Nor am I surprised that the reading of this paper did nothing to change Professor Coss's mind about taking me on as a teacher of philosophy in Columbia College.

Although in the next academic year, 1923–1924, I became a member of the faculty in the Psychology Department, I still continued to take courses in philosophy—a seminar with Professor Woodbridge on Spinoza's *Ethics* and special research under his supervision on Cicero. These undertakings, combined with certain judgments that I had begun to form about scientific, and especially experimental, psychology produced a fourth and final paper, which I read at a philosophy conference in May 1924. Its title, briefer than usual, was "God and the Psychologists." Before writing the paper, I had obviously communicated some of my thoughts—and also feelings—to members of the Philosophy Department, for in March I received the following letter from John Randall, who ran the graduate philosophy conference:

> In view of your desire for a philosophic salvation, I wonder whether you would care to put your ideas on the sins of the psychologists into some kind of shape for the Conference. You might call it "Psychology as it revolts a philosopher, or a metaphysical critique of futility." . . . I think it would do both you and the Conference good. Wouldn't it make your excommunication easier to bear?

As the event itself turned out, my excommunication became more unalterable and no easier to bear. If anything at all were needed to confirm Professor Coss's judgment about me, the delivery of that paper would have done it; it certainly did make me *persona non grata* in his eyes and also widened the breach between me and other members of the Philosophy Department.

Cicero's philosophical writings, undertaken after he had withdrawn from public life, interested Professor Woodbridge as the vehicle by which Greek thought was transmitted to those who read only Latin. He thought that in the process of translation, it had suffered significant distortion; for example, the substitution of *natura* for *physis,* of *virtus* for *aretê,* of *urbs* for *cosmos,* of *ratio* for *logos,* of *res publica* for *polis,* and so on. As I read more of Cicero and reread Aristotle, I became impressed by the profound difference between a philosopher for whom human concerns occupy the center of his thought and a philosopher for whom man is only a part of nature and must be considered in relation to God or to the cosmos as a whole. Bacon and Spinoza, I thought, paralleled Cicero and Aristotle in exemplifying this contrast between the humanist and the naturalist. Bacon, for me, was summed up in his own ringing declaration that "knowledge is power"—power to improve the human condition; while Spinoza, looking upon man as a finite mode of the infinite substance that is identical with God, glorified knowledge as man's salvation only when it resulted in his intellectual love of God. It was easy to find other pairs of opposites to keep them company, but I contented myself with picking John Dewey and George Santayana from the contemporary scene. Why I didn't cite Woodbridge as Dewey's antithesis, I will never know. He was nearer at hand and, for me, much more than Santayana, the paradigm of the speculative philosopher, the metaphysician whose thought both began and ended with wonder about the ultimate shape of things.

The comparisons I drew were, in each case, invidious to the first member of the pair—the humanist, the pragmatist, the man-centered thinker as contrasted with the naturalist, the metaphysician, the God-centered thinker. The paper that I wrote still remains intelligible in its general outlines, though its outrageous errors and its caricatures of all the philosophers discussed now distress me. However, I can still whole-heartedly subscribe to the opening section, which expressed my adverse judgments about experimental psychology and especially about J. B. Watson's brand of behaviorism, a doctrine which has become a little more sophisticated, but not much sounder, in the hands of B. F. Skinner. Watson, it should be said to his credit, did not pretend to be a philosopher as well as a scientist, and certainly did not issue moral and political edicts on the basis of his laboratory findings.

In the closing section of the paper, I directly attacked "the alignment of recent pragmatism with the psychological approach to the problems of human thought and conduct." The prevalence of the genetic fallacy in this approach, I declared, accounted for "the present deplorable state of philosophical speculation."

> The published report of the last meeting of the American Philosophical Association presented a picture of decadence. Philosophers were for the most part neither engaged in understanding the physical universe nor in attacking the problems of man's social welfare.

I then quoted a statement from that published report, to the effect that "philosophy recovers itself when it ceases to be a device for dealing with the problems of philosophers, and becomes a method, cultivated by philosophers, for dealing with the problems of men." Were philosophy to follow that prescription, it would die, I said, at the end of its convalescence; and there were ample signs that that denouement was well on the way. What John Dewey and others meant by "the problems of men" reduced philosophy to an almost exclusive consideration of sociopolitical problems. "The task of future philosophy," Dewey had written, "is to clarify men's ideas as to the social and moral strifes of their own day. Its aim is to become so far as it is humanly possible an organ for dealing with these conflicts." After quoting this passage from *Reconstruction in Philosophy,* I went on as follows:

> There is certainly nothing of the love of God in this utterance, no sense of the infinite weavings of the cosmos, wherein the human is but a pattern; no impulse to detached contemplation of the non-human as well as the human, so that the problems of humanity can be envisaged in proportions and terms befitting man's position in the total scheme of things.

When I read this paper at the department conference, John Dewey sat two chairs away. The other senior members of the department were present—Woodbridge, Montague, Bush, Coss. John Dewey seldom raised his voice or gesticulated for emphasis. I doubt if anyone had ever before seen him explode with rage. But on this occasion, annoyed by my contempt for scientific psychology, angered by the general drift of my remarks, and probably irritated by some infelicitous phrasing of the point I was trying to make, he pounded the arms of his chair, stood up, and walked out of the room muttering that he did not intend to sit around listening to someone tell him how to think about God; he would do that in his own way. John Storck and others present told me later that, even if I had had the slightest chance of getting transferred from the psychology to the philosophy department, that paper put an end to it.

Years later, in February 1952, *Time* reported this incident in a cover story on me. In September of that year, Sidney Hook, who had also been a student of Dewey's, wrote a pastiche—"Some Memories of John Dewey"—in which he questioned the credibility of the story in *Time.* However, my memory of what happened has been recently confirmed by my old friend Richard McKeon, who was there on that occasion, as Sidney Hook was not.

Dewey himself bore me no grudge. I may have become *persona non grata* with others, but not with him. He would certainly have been justified in paying no further attention to the impertinent young whippersnapper who had been so annoying—and so presumptuously smug about it, to boot. On the contrary, three years later, when my first book, *Dialectic,* was published, John Dewey "went out of his way to write a highly complimentary review of [it]." The words just quoted are taken from the piece by Sidney Hook, who went on to say: "I was taken aback because I was getting ready to publish a blockbuster on Adler. Dewey smiled when he read my manuscript . . . agreed that my criticisms were valid, but suggested that I had overlooked some good things in Adler and that he would learn and grow." Unlike John Dewey, Sidney Hook remained unforgiving; he was willing to admit that I had developed, but in all the wrong directions! Try as I might on several occasions much later, I could never get Sidney to acknowledge that I had changed my spots, at least to the extent of my being able to recognize the genuine worth of Dewey's philosophical thought, and my being both willing and able to praise his revolutionary educational insights, while still criticizing the followers who had misunderstood the message of his books on education, especially his epoch-making *Democracy and Education*, published in 1916.

The walking distance between Philosophy Hall, where the philosophers had their offices, and the psychological laboratories in Schermerhorn Hall could not have been more than a hundred yards, but the talking distance between them must have been infinite. Apparently, no word of what I had said to the philosophers about experimental psychology or psychology as a science filtered back to my colleagues in the Psychology Department, for I continued in their good graces. It was fortunate for me that my feelings about psychology remained concealed from them, feelings that were plainly revealed in that paper, which might have been entitled "Mortimer and the Psychologists." Whatever it had to say about theoretical matters on the surface, underneath it certainly was a personal confession of discontent with having to teach psychology, which I found intellectually less and less rewarding. Not only did I think at the time that experimental or scientific psychology had very little to contribute to our understanding of human nature or the human mind, but I also blamed the current state of philosophy on the substitution of psychology for metaphysics as the ruling discipline. I attributed "the dearth and rottenness of philosophy in this day" to the fact that "humanism and psychologism have turned the problems of metaphysics, logic, and ethics over to the anthropologist, the psychologist, and the sociologist. . . . There could be no more appropriate time," I went on, "to raise the cry of 'Back to Spinoza and to the intellectual love of God! Back to Aristotle and to metaphysics!' "

Actually, at the time, I had a much better grasp of what currently passed for a science of psychology and I was much more competent to teach it than I would have been to teach metaphysics. My references to metaphysics were in the nature of reverential gestures rather than signs of intimate contact with its subject matter or principles. My only contact, in fact, had been in a superficial reading of parts of Aristotle's treatise and in Woodbridge's seminar on Spinoza and his lectures on the Eleatic philosopher, Parmenides, and on Aristotle. Those lectures were exciting performances by a man who appeared to be the very embodiment of metaphysics when he told us, slowly and ponderously, in a hushed voice, that the primary object of thought was being itself, being *qua* being, existence *as such,* and then—after a long pause and with a nearly imperceptible smile—*the isness of whatever it is that is.*

Some of us in that class would long remember Woodbridge on *isness,* even some who would never have anything further to do with metaphysics. One of those was "Rondo" Robinson, who sat beside me when, in my senior year, I audited Woodbridge's lectures for the second time around simply because I found them so enjoyable. (I had already taken down, almost verbatim, his whole course of lectures.) Henry Morton Robinson, called Rondo because he wrote reams of light verse, went on to teach English in the college, then turned his talents to editorial work and writing for the *Reader's Digest,* and ended his career as a well-known novelist, author of a best seller, *The Cardinal.* Woodbridge on *isness* stuck in Rondo's mind for a long time after he experienced that performance in 1922. Five years later Rondo wrote a ditty—or perhaps I should call it an ode—"To a Class Room Metaphysician." It was published by F. P. A. (Franklin P. Adams) in his then famous daily column, "The Conning Tower," in the old *New York World.* Someone brought it to Woodbridge's attention, and he found it so fetching that he had it reproduced in the staid pages of the *Journal of Philosophy,* to everyone's astonishment, especially those who perceived the double entendres that Woodbridge had probably missed. I cannot refrain from reproducing it here.

TO A CLASS ROOM METAPHYSICIAN

In the realm of metaphysics I enjoy a daily stroll
Around the rim of Socrates' dominion,
Where philosophers, indulging in catharsis of the soul,
Distinguish cosmic truth from mere opinion.
On the Nature of Reality these gentlemen are hot;
Each local Plato pulls a solemn phiz
While discussing in his lectures the Nothingness of Not
And the fundamental Isness of the Is.

Oh, the Ain'tness of the Wasn't,
And the Isness of the Ain't,
And the Don'tness of the Doesn't
Make your inner spirit faint;
While your tongue gets thickly coated
With a philosophic fuzz
Gained by chewing on the problem
Of the Dizziness of Does.

"Appearances are Many, but Reality is One"
Is the essence of a hundred thousand pages;
When you learn this little formula you think your task is done,
But you get a rude upheaval from the sages,

Who feel duty-bound to ask you in the mid-semester quiz,
(Without apparent vestige of a cause),
"What is the true conception of the Eleatic Is
In relation to their doctrine of the Was."

> Oh, the A-ness of the B
> And the P-ness of the Q
> Open dialectic vistas
> That your eyes cannot see through;
> From whence loose metaphysics
> And Syllogisms roll,
> Deducing from the A-ness
> The nature of the Whole.

Let me recommend philosophy to those who rather doubt
The appearances of Seeming and of Being;
If you really would decipher wotinell it's all about
And appreciate the *Truth* of what you're seeing,
You should decorate your discourse with a dualistic fringe,
Ambiguous and equivocal; and pause
To affirm in every sentence that Reality *must* hinge
On this esoteric business
> Of the Isness
> Of the Was,
On the sempiternal Isness of the Was.

However discontented I was with my lot because I had been exiled into the Psychology Department and was compelled to fuss around with what William James had called "brass instrument psychology" (a discipline, he said, that could have been developed only by the Germans, because they were a people incapable of being bored), I owed a signal improvement in my status and income to the then flourishing interest in psychology. In September of 1924, the beginning of my second year on the faculty, an unexpected number of students enrolled in Elementary Psychology, requiring the department to increase the number of sections for that course. With no time to import additional instructors from outside, the department drafted me to teach two of the added sections, and I was promoted overnight from laboratory assistant to instructor. My salary was raised from one to two thousand dollars a year.

This increase, more overwhelming by its ratio than by its absolute amount, had an unsettling effect upon my spendthrift proclivities. Living at home with my parents, I had been able to get along quite well on $83.33 a month. Now I had twice that amount. Even before the first doubled salary check arrived, I went downtown and charged a new suit of clothes to my father's account. When the bill came and he discovered that I had bought a suit for ninety dollars—more than twice what he had ever paid for a suit—he hit the ceiling and me as well, with words if not with fists. I wish I could say that his harangue on this and other occasions persuaded me to mend my ways, but I never developed the virtue of temperance or thrift in the handling of money, with regard to which I have the self-indulgent propensity to spend as much as happens to be available at a given time, and sometimes a good deal more.

In order to do all the extra reading that I thought necessary for the writing of my laboratory reports, I managed to get permission to use the Psychology Reading Room when it was closed over the weekend. I was given a key to it and also a card authorizing me to get from the Main Library the large brass key that opened the huge, fifteen-foot-high wooden doors to Schermerhorn Hall. At the time that I was preparing to write the essay on the problem of meaning that I was to deliver before the Philosophy Club in January 1922, I spent several weekends in the Psychology Reading Room. On one of these occasions, the door opened and in came a young man who looked and acted as if he were much older than I, though he was barely two years my senior. He was dressed in a very businesslike Oxford grey suit and wore a white shirt with a starched collar and a black rep tie. He glowered at me through dark glasses that gave his powerful, mobile face a rather menacing look.

"What in hell are you doing here?" he wanted to know; "and who in hell are you, anyway?" He hadn't seen me around the department before and demanded that I give an account of myself. Definitely intimidated, I tried my best to reply, but he constantly interrupted me, asking more questions than I was able to make statements. When he finally listened long enough to take in that I was preparing to write a paper about the meaning of meaning, he launched into a series of questions about that subject. This took up the rest of the day. No answer that I could come up with ever stopped him from asking more questions with a pertinacity and in a tone of voice that I am sure Socrates, who was also an inveterate questioner, never used. Glaucon and Adeimantus would never have been able to stand up to Arthur Rubin as they stood up to Socrates. Arthur awakened my compassion for them as I suffered under his relentless onslaught.

Arthur Rubin was a graduate student in the Psychology Department. Less than two years older than I, he was more precocious—working for his Ph.D. while I was still a junior in the college. His family had more than ample means; his father owned American Silk Mills, and Arthur was destined to work there, or at least so his father thought. His tolerance for Arthur's desire to get a Ph.D. in psychology went no further than allowing him just two years to do it. Had he known about it, he would never have countenanced Arthur's equally strong desire to stay on in academic life rather than work for American Silk Mills.

In the next few months, and in the course of more and more frequent sessions, some at Columbia and some in the basement of the Rubins' elegant brownstone house on 93rd Street off Fifth Avenue (where Arthur began my education in food and drink by introducing me to vintage wine accompanied by sliced apples, ripe cheese, and dry crackers), Arthur desisted from asking questions long enough to tell me about the work he was doing for his Ph.D. (It was not until later that I learned more about his habits as a *bon vivant* and a man about town.) He had set up a most remarkable experiment on the conditioned reflex, then one of the most popular themes in behavioristic and brass-instrument psychology. Having studied the works of the two great Russian physiological psychologists, Pavlov and Bechterev, he decided that it would be interesting to see if, by the conditioning process, the action of an innate reflex could be reversed.

Arthur chose the pupillary reflex for this purpose—the contraction of the pupil of the eye to a bright light. By innate reflex, the pupil also expands in response to bodily shock. The apparatus for performing the experiment Arthur had in mind was available at Columbia, a pupillometer which had been devised and used in Wilhelm Wundt's laboratory at the University of Leipzig. Strapping a willing subject to the pupillometer and putting electrodes on his hand, Arthur could simultaneously give the person on whom he was experimenting two contrary stimuli—a bright light and an electric shock. The bright light overcame the electric shock; the result of the two stimuli in conjunction was pupillary contraction. By repeating this hundreds of times, Arthur hoped that he would be able to make the electric shock act by itself as a conditioned stimulus able to produce pupillary contraction, just as Pavlov had made the ringing of a bell, which he associated with the sight of food, a conditioned stimulus for the salivary reflex.

Arthur realized that there were great difficulties in the way of what he was trying to accomplish, but he would never admit that they were insuperable, even when he could no longer get subjects who would submit to the ordeal. Though he failed in this experiment, he might still have obtained his Ph.D. if his father had not insisted to the letter upon Arthur's fulfilling the terms of the contract, which allowed no more than two years to complete his doctoral work. I will save for later the story of what happened to Arthur when his father forced him to go work for the American Silk Mills, and how that affected my own life in significant ways.

Chapter 4

Book Lists without End

THE EXCITEMENT and intellectual profit that made teaching worth doing even if one were not paid to do it came, at the beginning of my career as a teacher, from leading discussions of the great books, not from the instruction I was hired to give in psychology. In fact, that was all my assistant's or instructor's salary covered; my taking part in the General Honors program went beyond the line of duty. What was true at the beginning has been true the rest of my life. Most of the things I have learned from teaching—as well as about teaching itself—I have learned from leading great books discussions not only in colleges and universities but also with adult groups all over the country.

The phrase "great books" was not current at Columbia when Erskine initiated General Honors. The books we read in that course, one a week over a two-year period, were assembled under the title "Classics of Western Civilization." At the end of the twenties, when I tried to convey to Bob Hutchins, after he became president of the University of Chicago, the excitement I felt about Erskine's General Honors course, I think I used "great books course" as an abbreviated reference. The phrase stuck and, in my judgment, it is a much better title for the books than "classics." That word carries an archeological connotation of unearthed monuments from the past rather than living documents in the present.

In Erskine's course, the discussion of the book read that week ran for two hours one evening a week with the students sitting around a large oval table. The fact that students received full credit for attending just one class a week, running for two hours without a break, instead of having to attend three classes, each running the canonical fifty minutes, was itself a revolutionary break with hidebound academic traditions.

But Erskine would not have it any other way, and so he chose evening hours in order not to come into conflict with inflexible schedules.

When General Honors began in 1921, there was only one discussion group, which Erskine conducted by himself. It never occurred to him that his special competence as a scholar in the field of English literature and especially in that of the Elizabethan period stood in the way of his general competence to read and discuss books in every field of learning —in theology, philosophy, and the exact sciences as well as in literature, history, and biography. I am sure he thought such competence belonged to every educated man, certainly to every man with an inquiring mind still trying to educate himself. He approached the great books with the amateur spirit, in the best sense of that term. His colleagues opposed the adoption of Erskine's General Honors program because they insisted upon being strictly professional about the books they taught, and that, of course, restricted them to books in their own specialized spheres of scholarly competence.

The faculty's skepticism about the competence of any teacher to carry on discussions of books in all fields of learning prevailed to a certain extent after the enrollment for General Honors increased. In 1923, when several new sections of General Honors were formed, they were staffed by two instructors on the supposition that each instructor, drawn from a different department, would be able to supplement the incompetence of the other in certain areas of subject matter. It was my great good fortune to be paired with Mark Van Doren.

Six years older than I, Mark was a professor of English, and was to become what even then he displayed remarkable talent for being—an eminent poet, essayist, and literary critic, as well as one of Columbia's most beloved teachers of literature. He inherited from Erskine the course on Shakespeare which generation after generation of Columbia students treasured as their most exciting classroom experience. My good fortune in having Mark as a partner in conducting great books discussions went far beyond the fact that we supplemented each other. It began a lifelong friendship which has been one of the joys of my life, enriched and extended by the close friendships I have had with Mark's two sons, Charles and John, whom I have known since their cradle days and both of whom have been associated with me at the Institute for Philosophical Research in recent years as well as in publishing projects carried out for Encyclopaedia Britannica, Inc.

Initially, Mark and I supplemented each other. In the first few years, we divided responsibility for the books to be discussed according to the fields in which they fell. After that, we both adopted Erskine's policy of proceeding like debonair amateurs, assured that even if the book under consideration was difficult for one of us, we at least should be able to read it better than our students and, in the light of that better reading, ask good questions to sustain a two-hour discussion. The only division of labor we retained consisted in one or the other of us asking the opening question or two. After that, Mark and I carried on as dancing partners do, alternately leading and following, seldom getting out of step. The dance we did was not solely for our own pleasure, though we did get much pleasure out of it. It was designed to draw the students onto the floor and get them into the act, and we counted it a successful session only when a large number of them took part.

Beginning in 1923, I have been conducting great books discussions for over fifty years, most of the time with a co-leader or partner. Not only do I find it more enjoyable that way—one can learn from one's partner as well as from the other members of the group—but I also think that, with two leaders of discussion, the one who at the moment is not actively engaged in asking the question can be more attentive to indications, by facial or other gestures, that someone in the group has something to say. In addition, the second leader can always intervene to try his hand at asking the same question in still another way to make it more intelligible; or, as frequently happens, he can correct his partner's failure to understand someone's response to the last question. Listening with the inner ear to answers is even more difficult than asking good questions; and so, while one of the two leaders is thinking of the next question to ask, the other may prevent him from passing over some nuance or insight in the answer that has just been given.

The only model I had to guide my initial efforts was John Erskine. I tried, not too successfully, to imitate his idiosyncratic, and therefore inimitable, style of questioning. I soon learned much more by observing Mark's style in the opening sessions in which we discussed Homer's *Iliad* and *Odyssey*, the histories of Herodotus and Thucydides, and the tragedies of Aeschylus, Sophocles, and Euripides. By the time we reached Plato's dialogues, I had acquired, by watching Mark, some of the devices that help a great books discussion to take off and soar. The most important is the formulation of an opening question—one that not only opens the discussion but also generates other questions that will reach out in a number of different directions to sustain a coherent discussion for two hours.

I still remember the opening question that Mark posed the first evening our group met. "What is the ruling passion in the *Iliad*?" Mark asked, and then went around the table soliciting proposals from every member of the group. That, by the way, is another advantage to a good opening question; you can call on everyone in rapid succession to try his hand at answering it, and then, with a wide variety of answers on the table, you can play one against another to carry the discussion forward. The question must not be a simple yes-or-no type; it must solicit a diversity of opinions, varying in the degree to which they express some relevant insight.

Relevance is, of course, the *sine qua non*. If a participant reacts to a question as if it were just a stimulus, like a bell, eliciting, as a response from him, whatever happens to be on his mind, the interrogator must point out that the question has not been answered. He must then patiently repeat it, perhaps rephrasing it to be sure it is understood, and he must continue to do so until it gets a general answer. Mark Van Doren had extraordinary ingenuity as well as energy in rephrasing the same question over and over again, so that if, in one version, it did not catch the mind of the student, it might in another. Years of practice in the art of conducting great books discussions have confirmed what I learned from him—that unflagging energy and inventiveness in the asking of questions, as well as unremitting regard for relevance, are indispensable ingredients in cooking up the heady broth of a good discussion.

As the number of sections of General Honors increased and new instructors were added to the program, latecomers who had not sat under Erskine or been inspired by his style reverted to type. They would begin the year by carrying the burden of the discussions themselves, but when books came up which they regarded as "out of their field," they would invite a specialist to come to their seminar to lead the discussion. The result was disastrous—no discussion at all. The expert performed as professionals always do. A lecture about the book, the author, and his importance took the place of a discussion. Most professionals teach by telling; amateurs, among whom Socrates was a paragon, teach by questioning.

Fifteen years later, when the great books program was initiated at St. John's College in Annapolis, Maryland, it took some time to persuade the hastily recruited faculty that each fellow and tutor of the college had an obligation to read all the books that the students were assigned and to be prepared to discuss them. On one of my first visits to the college after my friends Stringfellow Barr and Scott Buchanan had become president and dean, Scott asked me to talk to the faculty about what was then called "the new program." It was to be an indoctrination talk by an old "great bookie." I remember shocking some members of the group by the contrast I drew between the orthodox, professional teacher who is loathe to move beyond the walled enclosure of his speciality and the Socratic amateur who is willing to sacrifice the competence of the specialist in order to achieve the competence of the generalist, even if his doing so causes his orthodox colleagues to charge him with incompetence. "If to be an amateur and a generalist," I said, "is to be incompetent, then be incompetent."

However shocked some of the new faculty were on that occasion, when they began to realize what was expected of them, they were to be even more severely shocked later when Scott Buchanan tried to put into effect his policy, according to the gospel of St. John's, that every fellow and tutor of the college should be able to give instruction in every part of the program—not only lead discussions of all the great books, but also conduct mathematics, language, and laboratory tutorials. St. John's was, and still is, the only college in the United States in which there are no departments of this or that and so no professors of this or that—the only college with no electives and with a completely required four-year curriculum. Scott Buchanan's principle was absolutely sound: in a college thus constituted, with a course of study required of all students, it was certainly fitting and proper that the fellows and tutors who comprised the faculty should also be expected to be students of the whole curriculum and prepare themselves to function as instructors in any part of it. This expectation never became an ironclad requirement; if it had been rigorously enforced, the college might not have survived, or at least some members of the faculty might not have; but for the most part, the rule was adhered to, and still is.

The faculty at Columbia and elsewhere had another objection to Erskine's General Honors course and its lineal offshoots at other places, such as the University of Chicago and St. John's College. How could students be expected to read these difficult books at the rate of one a week? At that pace, their reading would necessarily have to be superficial in the extreme. Bob Hutchins told me of a conversation he had had with Paul Shorey, the eminent Greek professor and Plato scholar, shortly after Bob and I had begun to conduct great books discussions with freshmen at the University of Chicago. Meeting him on the campus, Shorey said to Hutchins: "Mr. President, I understand that you and Mr. Adler are reading and discussing great books with the very young at the rate of one a week." Mr. Hutchins assured him that that was so. "I don't see how you can do that," Professor Shorey went on; "when I was a senior at Harvard, it took us a whole year to study Dante's *Divine Comedy* under Professor Grandgent." Hutchins's reply came quick as lightning and was stunning because of its speed: "The difference, Professor Shorey, is that our students are bright."

Hutchins and I, as well as Barr and Buchanan, had a weightier answer to that objection, to which I will return when I describe how the great books idea in general education developed and became transformed after its inception at Columbia. Erskine's list of authors and books underwent a whole series of changes, changes which began while I was still at Columbia. In almost every case, Erskine's list required the reading of a whole work, not excerpts, though the work, as an artistic unit, might be only part of a large work or collection of works; for example, some of the dialogues of Plato, not all; one or two treatises by Aristotle; some of the tragedies of Sophocles and of Shakespeare; some of Montaigne's essays; but all of Dante's *Divine Comedy*, all of Darwin's *Origin of Species*, and, believe it or not, all of Gibbon's *Decline and Fall of the Roman Empire*. Here is Erskine's list of authors.

Homer	Hobbes
Herodotus	Milton
Thucydides	Molière
Aeschylus	Locke
Sophocles	Montesquieu
Euripides	Voltaire
Aristophanes	Rousseau
Plato	Gibbon
Aristotle	Adam Smith
Lucretius	Kant
Virgil	Goethe
Horace	*The Federalist*
Plutarch	Victor Hugo
Marcus Aurelius	Hegel
St. Augustine	Lyell
The Song of Roland	Balzac
The Nibelungenlied	Malthus
St. Thomas Aquinas	Bentham
Dante	J. S. Mill
Galileo	Darwin
Grotius	Pasteur
Montaigne	Karl Marx
Shakespeare	Tolstoy
Cervantes	Dostoevsky
Francis Bacon	Nietzsche
Descartes	William James

One of the usually unnoticed virtues of Erskine's original list was that it avoided the canonical number "one hundred," which had become connected in the popular mind with the making of such lists, ever since Sir John Lubbock had published in an English newspaper, toward the end of the nineteenth century, his recommendation of "the 100 best books." There were considerably fewer than a hundred in Erskine's list if one counted authors, and more than a hundred if one counted individual works, such as Platonic dialogues, Greek tragedies, biographies by Plutarch, or essays by Montaigne.

By 1925, the staff of instructors in the General Honors program had grown to about a dozen. We met weekly for lunch at the Faculty Club, at first under the chairmanship of Dean Hawkes, and then with Rexford Guy Tugwell in the chair. (Erskine, having just written a best-selling novel, *Helen of Troy*, attended our meetings infrequently.) Conversation at these staff luncheons naturally turned to the books and authors in the course, with dissatisfaction expressed about this or that item included in the list as well as complaints about things that had been omitted. The professors of English and Comparative Literature on the staff called for the addition of works that fell within their field of scholarship; the professors of Latin and Greek, the members of the Philosophy Department, the representatives of the natural and social sciences and of history—each in turn followed suit. Discussion of how to modify Erskine's original list went on week after week and promised to be as fruitless as faculty meetings generally are when curriculum reform is under discussion and the representatives of each department plead for the inclusion of more courses in their area and the reduction of courses in other areas. It looked as if there were little hope for a balanced and well-rounded reading list to result from our staff discussions.

Though I was the youngest member of the group, I persuaded Rex Tugwell to let me try to resolve the conflicting opinions. I proposed to draw up a comprehensive list of all the authors or titles that had been mentioned and then submit this list to the members of the staff in the form of a lengthy ballot on which they were to vote. Tugwell enthusiastically accepted my recommendation and set me to work.

I still have a mimeographed copy of the jumbo list I drew up, containing the names of 176 authors or, in the case of anonymous works, titles. These names were placed in two columns, one arranged in a single, roughly chronological enumeration, the other divided into a number of groups according to the literary genre or scholarly category in which the author or book fell.

How far beyond Erskine's original 52 this jumbo list of 176 went can best be conveyed by citing some of the far-out authors or titles that had been mentioned in our staff discussions. I list a sampling of them at random: *Beowulf, The Kalevala, The Cid,* Camoëns, *The Mahabharata, The Panchatantra, The Zend-Avesta,* Bion, Moschus, Ariosto, Juvenal, Calderón, Lope de Vega, Edgar Allan Poe, Hauptmann, Schnitzler,

Unamuno, Havelock Ellis, *The Arabian Nights,* Cardinal Newman, Jonathan Edwards, Bishop Bossuet, Bunyan, Jeremy Taylor, and so on.

The balloting resulted in unanimous approval for 19: Homer, Aeschylus, Sophocles, Euripides, Plato, Aristotle, Lucretius, Aurelius, Ovid, Horace, and Catullus (the last three grouped together for one assignment), Machiavelli, Spinoza, Montaigne, Shakespeare, Descartes, Molière, Rousseau, and Goethe. The blackballed group consisted of Tasso, Ariosta, Pulci, Camoëns, Musset, Gassendi, Pushkin, Gogol, Unamuno, Schnitzler, Maeterlinck, and Norman Douglas.

The balloting, by itself, did not solve the problem, though it laid the basis for further discussions which, after another year of meetings, achieved a consensus to which everyone was more or less willing to subscribe. The modification and expansion of the Erskine list that emerged at the end of 1927, a list of 76 authors or titles, is below.

Far from putting an end to the making of book lists, that was only the beginning of it. I will just mention here the successive revisions that the original Erskine list went through, reserving for another place an account of the *Sturm und Drang* involved in getting agreement from faculty committees or editorial boards. I will also postpone a statement of the general theoretical principles which should guide their construction. One thing can be said right now. Once the principles for inclusion and exclusion are clearly and explicitly formulated, it becomes possible to get agreement on about 90 percent of the authors or titles proposed.

When Hutchins and I started teaching the great books at Chicago, we adopted the modified Erskine list of 1927 with a few revisions. Scott Buchanan recommended more radical innovations in the list he drew up for the Committee on Liberal Arts at Chicago in 1935–1936, introducing a much larger number of mathematical works and scientific treatises. That enumeration became the basis for the reading list adopted at St. John's College in 1937–1938, enlarged to provide for four, as opposed to two, years of reading, which had been the rule at Columbia and at Chicago. The St. John's list underwent another revision in 1943–1944. In between, I had drawn up the list which appeared as an appendix to *How To Read A Book,* published in 1940. That list contained over 130 authors. A German-Swiss edition of *How To Read A Book* presented a redaction of it, omitting some Anglo-American authors in order to include a larger number of Europeans. There was also a Catholic revision of the *How To Read A Book* list, which dropped a few of the heretics on the Index and replaced them with a number of the faithful. Then, in 1943, when Sen. William Benton asked Bob Hutchins and me to edit a set of great books to be published by Encyclopaedia Britannica, Inc., I drew up the first proposal of authors and titles to be included; but the final list did not emerge until 1946 or 1947, after innumerable meetings at which the members of our Advisory Board debated the composition of the set, which was published in 1952 under the title *Great Books of the Western World*. That Advisory Board included John Erskine, Alexander Meiklejohn, Scott Buchanan, Stringfellow Barr, Mark Van Doren, Hutchins, and me—all "great bookies" of long standing.

Homer	Chaucer	David Hume
Bible (Old Test.)	Leonardo da Vinci	Rousseau
Aeschylus	Machiavelli	Adam Smith
Sophocles	Erasmus	Kant
Euripides	Thomas More	Gibbon
Herodotus	Rabelais	Jeremy Bentham
Thucydides	Montaigne	Goethe
Aristophanes	Cervantes	Thomas Malthus
Plato	Bacon	Hegel
Aristotle	Shakespeare	Schopenhauer
Cicero	Galileo	Balzac
Lucretius	Grotius	John Stuart Mill
Virgil	Hobbes	Darwin
Horace	Descartes	Thackeray
Ovid	Corneille	Dickens
Plutarch	Milton	Karl Marx
Lucian	Molière	Dostoevsky
M. Aurelius Antoninus	Spinoza	Pasteur
Plotinus	Locke	Francis Galton
Bible (New Test.)	Racine	Ibsen
St. Augustine	Isaac Newton	Tolstoy
The Volsunga Saga	Swift	Thomas Hardy
The Song of Roland	Montesquieu	William James
St. Thomas Aquinas	Voltaire	Nietzsche
Dante	Henry Fielding	Freud
Francesco Petrarca		

Since 1952, I have been involved in the making of still other book lists—for Executive Seminars at Aspen, for adult great books groups, and most recently for a revised edition of *How To Read A Book* in

1972, in which Charles Van Doren joined me as co-author. In recent years, some of us have been engaged in thinking about the twentieth-century authors who might be added, at the beginning of the next century, to *Great Books of the Western World,* which ends with Freud; and about the possibility of constructing a list of world books—the relatively small number of works indispensable to a world cultural community, including, along with the ancient and modern greats of Western civilization, the great works of the four or five other cultural traditions in the Near East and the Far East. For me the most interesting game of all is that of trying to list the ten books one would wish to have on a desert island if one had to keep one's mind alive for ten years.

In 1927, I happened upon a recently published book, *To Begin With,* written by Dr. Raymond Pearl, a professor of biology at Johns Hopkins University. In it, he argued that anyone concerned with his own education cannot depend on schools, textbooks, and teachers, but must provide for the enrichment and sustenance of his own mind by independent reading—by recourse to the riches on the shelves of libraries. Having said that, he recommended as "a prophylaxis against pedantry" a list of seventy books. Reviewing Dr. Pearl's essay for the *New York Evening Post Literary Review,* I noted that he had accompanied his book list with an apology for succumbing to the disease of making book lists. He described "the consuming fever of the book-list mania as a very definite clinical picture. . . ." He even dared to recommend a therapy. "If one has the disease, its only effective cure is to construct and publish, *à la* Sir John Lubbock and others, a list of books for other people to read with the purpose, of course, of educating them." I certainly have taken the cure, but up to the present it has not worked. I keep on making book lists without end.

With a superlative model in John Erskine and with an excellent preceptor and co-leader in Mark Van Doren, I nevertheless faltered in my first efforts to conduct great books discussions. For one thing, I made the mistake of overpreparing. I should have been content to jot down four or five questions, with a particularly good one as the leadoff query. Instead, I made pages of notes, largely a record of what I had learned myself on this second reading of a book that I had read once before when I was a student in Erskine's seminar. Impressed by all the things I was discovering for the first time in a book that I had already read and passed an examination on, I could not resist making notes about the points discovered and adding expansive reflections. While it is important for a teacher to carry on with his own learning while teaching, it is also necessary for him to remember that his students are, both in years and experience, a little behind him in the learning process. I was so preoccupied with my own learning that I forgot that the students were reading the book for the first time and could not be expected to find in it the gems I had just discovered. A student's first reading must necessarily be superficial and therefore quick; the great books must be read at least once that way in order to enable him to read them a little better the second time around.

Elaborate notes may be useful for giving a lecture, but they are an obstacle to conducting a discussion. That, however, was not the only reason why I did not do well in my first attempts as a discussion leader; nor was it simply that I had the awkwardness of any novice in an art. The students in my first class were almost my age and some of them were brighter, certainly wittier and more articulate, than I. One in particular, Clifton Fadiman, took the class away from me any time he wanted by asking better questions or interjecting more sophisticated comments. Our ages being so close and our backgrounds so similar, he could not help resenting my sitting at the head of the table when he felt better qualified to conduct the class. He obviously took great pleasure in making his feelings clear not only to me, but to everyone in the room. An instructor, especially one as young and inexperienced as I was, cannot engage in verbal jousting with an overly bright student, returning wisecrack for wisecrack, or witty sally for witty sally. I had no weapons at my disposal to cope with Fadiman.

After four of five disastrous sessions, I began to think that I might never be able to cope. I do not know what would have happened if Fadiman had not solved the problem for me. Encountering him on the campus one day, I told him that he was making my life miserable by the performance he was putting on in class. Obviously pleased, he topped off the sweet taste of victory by a gesture of magnanimity. "Would you like me to help you teach the seminar?" he asked. I played right into his hands by telling him that I certainly needed his help; without it, I might have to give the whole business up. I did not realize then what a lifelong friendship with Kip Fadiman has taught me about him. Nothing motivates him so strongly as a person who needs his help. My cry for help elicited compassionate warmth and unstinting cooperation from him, as it has done again and again for more than fifty years.

That first great books seminar I taught included other students who were to make names for themselves, as Kip was to make a name for himself—as literary critic for the *New Yorker,* as master of ceremonies on the famous "Information Please" radio program, as versatile essayist and author of many books and articles. Among Kip's classmates were Henry Rosenthal, who studied for the rabbinate but subsequently became a professor of philosophy, and Lionel Trilling, who became not only one of the shining lights of the Columbia faculty, but also one of America's most respected literary critics. Recently, when we were at the Aspen Institute together, Lionel told me of his own recollections of that class, and particularly his memory of the question that I asked him on an oral examination in his senior year. "Mr. Trilling," he remembers my saying to him in a bland voice, "tell me what you know about St. Augustine and the pears." He has never forgotten his anguish at not knowing what sin Augustine had committed with pears—one of the high points in the saint's *Confessions*. In his own teaching career, Lionel always devoted a portion of his time to undergraduate seminars of the kind that Erskine had initiated, though from the middle thirties on something called "the Colloquium" supplanted what had been called the General Honors course. In an article recently published in the *American Scholar* entitled "The Uncertain Future of the Humanistic Educational Ideal," Trilling wrote this nostalgic paragraph about the past in the midst of many pessimistic paragraphs about the future:

> Erskine put his mark on Columbia, and, indeed, on educational theory throughout the country. Mortimer Adler as a very young graduate student was one of the first teachers in that enchanting General Honors course that Erskine had devised, and the mention of his name will suggest the response to the Great Books idea at the University of Chicago and at St. John's College and at the innumerable other schools that were led to believe, though of course with varying degrees of intensity, that the study of the preeminent works of the past, chiefly those in the humanities, with what this study implied of the development of the "whole man"—no one then thought of the necessity of saying the "whole person"—was the best possible direction that undergraduate education could take.

Other years, other students; I cannot recall them all by name, but I can remember two in particular. Whittaker Chambers was one of them. He was a brilliant student and a fine poet; his performance in the oral examination on the great books won applause from his examiners; but he did not receive his degree at graduation, because he had just published in the college literary magazine a poem about Christ that the dean thought blasphemous. After leaving Columbia and wandering around the country for a while, he joined the staff of the *Daily Worker* and became a card-carrying member of the Communist party. Our paths crossed a few years later when the People's Institute opened up great books seminars for adults in the metropolitan area; Whittaker Chambers and I became co-leaders in the seminar held at John Haynes Holmes's Community Church. Whittaker's path later crossed that of another person with whom he had been acquainted in his student days —Priscilla Fansler, the sister of Dean Fansler, a young instructor in the English Department. She was later to become Priscilla Hiss, Alger Hiss's wife. I believe I am correct in saying Lionel Trilling's early novel, *The Middle of the Journey*, casts both light and shadows on this episode.

My memory would have placed my first meeting with Jacques Barzun in the great books seminar that Mark Van Doren and I taught, but a recent conversation with Barzun has corrected that impression. Though he was a member of that group, he reminded me that we first met in the laboratory when he was a student in my class on Experimental Psychology. He also reminded me that, after the laboratory sessions were over, we rearranged the laboratory tables and played Ping-Pong together. I don't think we have played Ping-Pong since then, but we have kept in touch, even though his career at Columbia and mine at Chicago took us in different directions. In the last twenty years, we have again become more closely associated, in the work of the Aspen Institute for Humanistic Studies and in the editing of *Encyclopaedia Britannica*. Like Lionel Trilling, Jacques Barzun went on to become one of the luminaries on the faculty of Columbia University, an internationally recognized scholar and author, a member of the History Department, dean of the Graduate Faculties, and provost of the University. While we have had our philosophical differences over the years, some of which still persist, they have always been overcome by the deep bonds of intellectual sympathy that unite us in our judgments about the sorry state of education and of culture in the United States, about the relation of the sciences to the humanities, and about one or another academic fad that gains attention and is in vogue for a short time.

In the spring of 1975, when I had the pleasure of introducing Jacques to a gathering of contributors to the new fifteenth edition of *Encyclopaedia Britannica,* I said that our original roles of teacher and student have been reversed many times since the middle twenties, and always to my profit. I do not mean to give the impression that one does not learn from one's students at the very time that one is teaching them. Learning is a two-way street; the teacher who does not learn from his students while they are learning from him cannot be doing a very good job. Of course, classrooms in which the instructor carries on mainly by lecturing or talking at the students, with very little talking back from them, are seldom places in which much learning goes on—either by the students or by the teacher. Only when discussion replaces lecturing and only when the book being discussed is over the heads of everyone in the room, the teacher as well as the students, is bilateral learning likely to occur. I have been unbelievably fortunate that, in the whole of my teaching career, I have been largely engaged in great books discussions of one kind or another. In fact, apart from my early years as a teacher, I have had little or no experience of the other kind of classroom performance.

I did the other kind of teaching, the unrewarding kind, in discharging my duties as a member of the Psychology Department at Columbia. Teaching a course in elementary psychology consisted in assigning chapter after chapter in the textbook that the students were required to study, and then recapitulating the contents of the chapter in a fifty-minute lecture. Such lectures, it has been remarked, are a process in which the notes of the teacher become the notes of the student without passing through the minds of either. That certainly was so in my case, especially in the second section of Elementary Psychology, which began a mere ten minutes after the termination of the first section. I became so bored with what I was saying in that second hour that I am sure the students in that class went to sleep without even having to suppress a yawn.

My pleasanter memories of teaching psychology have to do with students who became companions or friends. When I was a student, I assumed the posture of a professor, treating my teachers as if they were my colleagues; but on becoming a teacher (when I was still so young in appearance that I was stopped on campus by a sophomore and dressed down for not wearing the regulation freshman cap), I behaved as if my students were my classmates.

One of them, I remember, showed me something of the nightlife on Broadway and took me to my first burlesque show. Another, Fred Atkinson, who became a V.P. at R. H. Macy and Company, took me down to lower Fifth Avenue to an Oriental importing shop where we bought colorful batik ties. I had a short-lived romance with the sister of another; still another student, Jerrold Zacharias (later to become an eminent professor of physics at the Massachusetts Institute of Technology and an innovator in the business of teaching the natural sciences), put his father's automobile and his services as its chauffeur at my disposal on several occasions when Ethel Kremer and I made feints at eloping. Still others, Dick Fitch, Edmund Weil, and Malcolm Stuart McNab McComb, of whom I will have more to say later, became my intimates in a variety of adventures.

I do not think that such carryings-on and intimacies affected my behavior in the classroom. For the most part, I conducted myself as a proper instructor and maintained the normal proprieties. On one memorable occasion, however, I broke through the traces and violated all the rules. It happened in 1927 in an afternoon class in the psychology of art and aesthetics; many of the students whom I have mentioned were in that class. On that particular day, I had had a disagreeable experience at the Faculty Club—some argument with a colleague which left me completely fed up with academics and academic life. Walking back across campus on that balmy May afternoon, I could barely check the impulse to cut the class I was about to teach, though class cutting is a privilege not allowed instructors. As the class began, one of the students inquired about the questions that might be asked on the final examination to take place a few weeks later. That did it: the very thought of the academic ritual of final examinations, blue books, and grades triggered the revulsion that had been building up in me. I responded to the student's query with a proposal that startled the entire class.

I proposed that we should dispense with the final examination. The students immediately called my attention to the fact that that could not be done; they would be expected to turn up at the gymnasium on a certain day for the exam in my course; it would be officially scheduled and there was no way out of it that would not bring the college authorities down on our heads, especially mine. Oh, yes, there was a way out, I replied; I would compose an examination in which all the questions were phoney, full of double entendres and clues to concealed jokes; they were to go to the gymnasium at the appointed hour and write blue books in which they exercised their wits and their imaginations to write funny answers to funny questions. That would reward me for what I next proposed; namely, to hand out grades in advance of the examination. How would I do that, they wanted to know. Reminding them that the authorities would expect the grades to follow something like the pattern of the normal distribution curve, I pointed out that there would have to be a few A's and A minuses; a larger number of B's and B plusses and B minuses, the greatest number centering at the B minuses and C plusses, and then tapering off down to the C minuses, the D's, and the F's. The only problem we had to solve was in assigning these grades, and I proposed to solve that by balloting on their part, after members of the class had indicated the grades they wanted or the grades they were willing to take. No one, of course, was willing to take an F, so I suggested the substitution of an incomplete for a small number of students who would just not show up for the examination. I would turn a passing grade in for them at some later date.

The next three sessions of the class were devoted to hilarious discussions of the merits of the pleas the students made for certain grades. Wonderfully witty speeches were delivered; specious arguments were cooked up; all kinds of horse-trading went on among them in which various quid pro quos were offered in exchange for taking a lower grade so that the other fellow might have a higher one. Just before the end of the semester, we managed to get all the grades handed out more or less to everyone's satisfaction. The high spirits and sparkling wit with which all this had been carried on encouraged me to write as funny a set of examination questions as I could possibly contrive. It also led me to expect from them a set of blue books that would amuse me as much as their antics in class did. To my astonishment, about half the students in that class turned in examination books which contained serious answers to silly questions. If I could have rescinded my agreement, I would have gladly flunked them for breach of promise, if for nothing else. The other students, who had kept to their agreement and had given vent to their imaginations and their sense of humor, wrote answers which, for all the tomfoolery that they contained, nevertheless revealed their knowledge of the subject matter of the course; you cannot write a spoof about something you do not understand. They should all have been awarded A's.

A year or so later, I had the experience of teaching a quite different group of students. Professor Harry Allen Overstreet, head of the Philosophy and Psychology Department at the City College of New York, had invited me to teach a course in Abnormal Psychology. The additional salary being welcome, I took it on. I soon discovered that I could not handle the students at C.C.N.Y. the way I handled my classes at Columbia. They were a rougher lot; if there were any sparklers among them, they were diamonds with very little polish. I later picked up a remark made by Prof. Morris Cohen, who had been in the C.C.N.Y. Philosophy Department for many years. I wish I had known it at the time. At the end of an hour in which Professor Cohen was teaching formal logic, the class bell rang, and without waiting for him to finish his sentence, the students rustled their papers, closed their books, and started to get up. Cohen held up his hand in an angry gesture and shouted: "Wait, wait, I have a few more pearls to cast!"

That class in Abnormal Psychology introduced me to my first painful experience of asylums for the insane and for the feebleminded and also to my first experience of hypnotism. The students informed me that it had always been traditional in the course in Abnormal Psychology to have a demonstration of hypnotism. I told them that I had no competence to put on such a performance. One of them then said that he knew a hypnotist whom he could persuade to do it for me, if I were willing. Since they were very insistent, I gave my permission.

I did not foresee that the hypnotist would bring his own subject with him, or that the subject would be a flashily dressed, gaudily made-up young woman, at the sight of whom the boys in the class uttered wolf cries. The classroom was filled to the brim, for those who belonged there had, without my permission, invited their friends to attend the session on hypnotism. C.C.N.Y. was not a coeducational institution; the girl had to be sneaked in.

The hypnotist, wearing a pin-striped suit with overly large lapels, put his subject through the usual paces—sticking pins in her arm or burning matches under it, which she appeared not to feel while she was in a hypnotic trance. Toward the end of the class hour, the hypnotist announced that he would conclude by giving a demonstration of posthypnotic suggestion. He asked me to cooperate by sitting at the instructor's desk and appearing to be going on with a lecture when he woke the subject out of her trance. I agreed, not knowing what the posthypnotic suggestion would be. I soon learned. Having put the young lady, for whom I had now developed an extreme distaste, into a trance, he said to her: "When I wake you up, you will be standing at the back of a classroom in which the teacher is giving a lecture. You are to walk up the center aisle, go to his desk, and give him a big kiss." The boys in the class howled with glee. It was too late for me to stop him. My face burned; my eyes blurred; my mind almost went blank, but with great effort I managed to continue talking as, with a clap of his hands, the hypnotist woke the wench up. She looked around, seemed to see me with a glance of recognition, and started slowly down the aisle. The next few seconds seemed interminable, but they did come to end with a resounding smack on my lips and with cheers and catcalls from the spectators. Fifty years later I can see how funny it was.

Apart from the great books discussions that I conducted with Mark Van Doren, I cannot say that I took my duties too seriously. For one thing, I found teaching undergraduates in psychology boring; for another, there was too much else, of much greater interest to me, going on in my life during those years, romantic as well as intellectual adventures that had the lure of novelty as well as the lure of learning. In addition I could never take seriously the grading of students on the basis of the ordinary examination questions that called on students to write short essays in which they seldom did little more than hand back to the instructor the words, phrases, opinions, and sentiments which they had put down in their notes on his lectures or on the textbook, then memorized in the few weeks before examination time, and spewed forth on the pages of their blue books. No instructor could ever tell how much genuine knowledge and understanding lay behind the merely verbal memories being displayed. The only way to find out what a student really knows and understands is to put him through the ordeal of an oral examination running a half hour at least, and given by members of the faculty other than his own instructor. Then, when he gives a pat answer, his interrogator can say, "The statement you have just made is quite correct. Now tell me what it means."

As I indicated earlier, oral examinations were given in 1925 to the seniors in the General Honors course, when Fadiman, Trilling, and Chambers were among the students. It took a whole week, from nine to five each day, to schedule a half-hour oral for each student. Either because they had other things to do or because it interested them less than it did me, the other members of the staff took part in only some of the examinations. I alone started on Monday morning and kept at it until late Friday afternoon. It was, in one way, a gruelling and tiring experience, but in another way I found it very exciting. It soon became obvious that the questions would trickle down the corridors to other students waiting their turn. The surprise effect of the questions would be lost unless they were altered in substance or at least in phrasing at each session. I felt great pride in my ability to vary the questions every half hour even though they were being asked about the same set of books and authors.

This performance impressed my colleagues on the staff of General Honors. It moved some of them to act in my behalf. A self-appointed committee, including Mark Van Doren, Rex Tugwell, and Raymond Weaver (whose biography of Herman Melville had just rescued that great American novelist from undeserved oblivion), drafted a letter to Dean Hawkes pleading for my promotion. "Those of us who have this year been working in General Honors," the letter began, "have been increasingly impressed by the unusually splendid work of Mortimer Adler. We are convinced that from the point of view of the best ideals of the College and of Honors, there is no one with finer equipment— with more enthusiasm, reliability, unselfishness, sympathy, and keenness and soundness of mind. He has won our completest admiration and regard."

What the letter writers expected Dean Hawkes to do was indicated by references to the low level of my salary and to my location in the Psychology Department, where, the writers declared, I was not being given sufficient opportunity to exercise my talents. Arguing that "it would be criminal short-sightedness for the College to fail to do all in its power to give him recognition and encouragement," the letter concluded by saying: "Out of our conviction of the great usefulness of Adler to the College, we are instigated to ask if something cannot be done from your Office to allow Adler some of the recognition he so thoroughly deserves."

Nothing happened. Had not a freak accident brought me to the attention of Robert M. Hutchins, I might have gone on being an underpaid instructor in psychology until, perhaps, tiring of academic chores and the routine of academic life, I might have tried to earn a living doing something else. Hutchins saved me from that. Kip Fadiman was not so fortunate. As an undergraduate, he too had set his mind on becoming a member of the Columbia faculty. He wanted to teach English as much as I wanted to teach philosophy; and his undergraduate performance, both in class and out, warranted the most serious consideration of his candidacy for a teaching job. Toward the end of his senior year, the members of the English Department in the College wrote a letter on Kip's behalf to Brander Matthews of the graduate English Department, in whose hands lay the power of appointment. That letter, signed by John Erskine, Mark Van Doren, Raymond Weaver, and others, was more of a panegyric than the letter written to Dean Hawkes about me. Even if the recipients of these letters were to discount the obvious hyperboles they contained, they should not have been able to disregard them so easily. The recommendation about Kip was turned down peremptorily. The administration of the English Department felt that no one of Semitic blood was qualified to teach English literature. I think it is fair to say that Kip suffered deeply from this stumbling block put in the way of what he most wanted to do with his life.

In the summer of his graduation, he married Polly Rush, a student at Barnard College, who had been his high school classmate. He had to do something about earning a living for himself and his wife. I helped him to get a job teaching English to the senior class at the Ethical Culture High School, the principal of which I knew. Subsequently, when he needed to make more money than he could earn as a high school teacher in those days, I recommended him to my friend Dick Simon for an editorial job with his publishing house, Simon and Schuster. All these little favors Kip reciprocated by doing me one good turn that helped me to grow up, which I needed to do just about as much as Kip needed to earn money.

Up to that point—the time is now the summer of 1925—I had continued to live at home with my parents. Even though I was now twenty-two and a half years old, it never occurred to me that I ought to move out and find living quarters of my own. It was Kip who precipitated that move, partly out of self-interest but also out of concern for my well-being. He could not afford a dwelling-place for Polly and himself; in addition, he did not need one that could accommodate Polly all of the time, for she had just won a graduate fellowship at Bryn Mawr and would be living there during the first year of their marriage, returning from Philadelphia to Kip's bed and board only every other weekend. Kip therefore proposed that he and I should share a furnished room together, on condition, of course, that every other weekend I go home to live with my parents.

We found a furnished room on West 76th Street in Manhattan, a few doors from Riverside Drive. Pooling our resources, we could hardly afford the monthly rental of ninety dollars, but we took the room anyway, and it was there I lived, both with Kip and Polly and without them, until I got married in 1927. Explaining to my parents why I felt it necessary to spend money to rent a room away from their home was much more difficult than scrounging up the money to pay the rent. I do not think they ever did fully understand the necessity for the move which Kip had urged upon me. Nor did I at the time. Looking back on it now, I can see how right he was. What happened in that room and during the years that I lived there certainly confirmed his sense that I desperately needed to get away from home.

Chapter 5

A *Summa Dialectica*

THREE-TWENTY-FIVE West 76th Street was just three and one half blocks from where Ethel lived, on the corner of 79th Street. By the fall of 1925, when I moved from my parents' apartment on upper Broadway to share a room with Kip Fadiman on 76th Street, my relationship with Ethel Kremer had already gone through a series of ups and downs. I use that colorless word *relationship* because I do not know how to describe the affair. I regarded myself as in love with Ethel, I was inordinately romantic in my idealization of her, I certainly wanted to marry her, but *love affair, romance, courtship*—none of these words is the right label. The nearest I can come to an apt characterization of it is to say that it was an affair of the heart spoiled by too much intrusion of mind, both on Ethel's part and on mine.

I met Ethel the year I graduated from college. She was a friend of Justine, the sister of my classmate James Waterman Wise. Jim introduced me as a budding philosopher and Ethel as a talented sculptress, thereby setting our relationship on the plane of reciprocal pedagogy. My ignorance of the arts complemented her ignorance of science and philosophy; I gave her books to read and lectured her on them; she took me to concerts and on tours of the museums. Under my tutelage, she came to revere the splendor of Aristotle's *Metaphysics* or Spinoza's *Ethics,* and led by her, I came to see with awe the beauty of Michelangelo's *David* and of Leonardo's drawings. During that first year of teaching at Columbia, I spent more time with Ethel than on my classes and on my graduate work. I had done enough academic work to welcome a vacation from it. The learning that Ethel fostered filled a void in my education.

At times I fell off the lofty intellectual and aesthetic plane on which our endless conversations moved. Ethel was not only my tutor in the perception of beauty; she was herself a thing of beauty—a vivacious, graceful, lovely girl, not only lovely but loveable. While I was still inept and awkward in any effort to display affection or to make love, I must have communicated the stirrings inside me, because toward the end of that first autumn Ethel wrote me a letter telling me how much she valued our friendship and our conversations, but at the same time informing me that she was in love with someone else. If for that reason I chose not to see her anymore, she would understand. The fierce jealousy of the unknown rival which that letter aroused convinced me that I was in love with Ethel; more than that, it made me realize that I should do something about it other than talk, talk, talk. But between the realization and the doing there was still a large gap.

Poor Ethel—beset and besieged by a young man who desperately wanted to make love to her but who did not know how to do so in the masterly manner that she, at twenty, naturally craved. Whatever I did must have been enough to remove the rival mentioned in her letter; but it was certainly not enough to save either of us from being worn to a frazzle by the frustrations suffered in the wake of unrelieved excitement. To make matters worse, both of us, being inveterately discursive, felt duty-bound to talk about what was going wrong and how to set it right; we not only talked about our troubles, we also wrote long letters to each other, even though we were seeing each other almost every other day. Though all the talk and writing did not produce any improvements on the plane of action, it did have the effect of increasing our intimacy on the plane of thought, for we discussed loving and making love in the same speculative manner in which we conversed about philosophy or art. My letters on the subject were analytical and argumentative, not seductive; hers were poetical and imaginative, not emotional; their main thrust was toward the sharing of thoughts and feelings, not embraces.

An additional complication came from the fact that Ethel's mother (her father had died when she was quite young) was having a love affair with an impecunious young man whom she was financing and who, more often than not, sent her into rages by not doing what she expected of him in return for her largesse. Ethel found it difficult to disengage herself from her mother's emotional turmoil. It may have been the loss of her father or the character of her mother or it may have been something else not quite so obvious which caused Ethel the persistent distress that prompted her to try psychoanalysis. That, as far as I was concerned, introduced a further complication into our relationship.

Ethel suffered from psychoanalysis almost as much as she suffered from me. One or the other of us, her psychoanalyst or I, interfered with her work. She would go to her studio only to find herself unable to do a stroke of work, and after days of agonizing inanition, she would have to struggle against a consuming fit of depression. Then suddenly the clouds would lift and she would experience the elation of getting her fingers back into the plasticene with satisfying results. Our ups and downs paralleled the rise and fall in her moods. Toward the beginning of our second year, when things had reached what seemed an unendurable state, she persuaded me to visit her psychoanalyst, possibly with the thought that his helping me out of my torment would be good for both of us. The hour I spent with him, not on the couch but sitting face to face engaged in theoretical discussion, proved to be instructive, but not therapeutic. That one experience gave me the insight that, whether or not psychoanalysis would be beneficial, I had habits of mind which would make it extremely difficult, if not impossible, for me to submit to it.

In the next two years, Ethel occupied more of my time, attention, and energy than my teaching at Columbia. What studying I continued to do, I did mainly with her or for her. There were many interludes of fun and frolic and of romantic exuberance which relieved the spells of misery and soul-searching. We went off on excursions to the country under the chaperonage of her mother, sometimes managing to escape and go off on our own. Twice we contrived elopements by auto—once to Darien, Connecticut, and once to Albany, New York—but we returned from these escapades with nothing but the anger of our families to show for it.

During those years, Ethel infiltrated my life at every point, once producing an effect not a little embarrassing. The previous evening we had gone to a performance of Wagner's *Tristan and Isolde* and wallowed in the music of the famous love-death scene. My psychology class, the morning after, was held in a room under that in which Prof. Daniel Gregory Mason lectured on the history of music. It was a balmy spring day, windows were open, and the strains of the "Liebestod" floated down from Professor Mason's piano overhead. The music reactivated my emotions of the evening before. Suffused with sentimental recall, I found myself unable to see the students in front of me or to think of what I had been talking about. I stood there for some moments as if in a trance, finally regaining enough presence of mind to manufacture a pretext to dismiss the class early.

The aura of Ethel enveloped not only me, but also my friends. That, however, was a product of my behavior, not of hers. I turned my coterie of friends into a band of John Aldens, each in the end pleading his own case with Ethel as well as mine. My motive differed in one respect from that of Miles Standish when he sent John Alden to talk to Priscilla. I wanted to learn more about Ethel and about her relation to me by seeing her and us through the eyes of my friends, either to confirm or correct what I could or could not see for myself. Far from clarifying things, this only tended to confuse them further. Hours of fruitless conversation with Jim Wise, Kip Fadiman, Arthur Rubin, or Herbert Solow were devoted to the intricacies of Ethel, which they found as fascinating and as elusive as I. Other friends—Mark Van Doren and Scott Buchanan —were drawn into such conversations with only secondhand information about her to guide them in giving me advice. One piece of advice, proffered by Scott, I can remember. I did not take it then, but I have thought of it often since then, always finally rejecting it. The life of a philosopher, Scott said, should be monastic. If I really meant to be a philosopher, I should give up Ethel and all thoughts of marriage.

By the spring of 1926, things reached a crisis. Ethel had changed psychoanalysts some months before, and the new man claimed that her involvement with me interfered with her transference to him. He requested her, as a condition of continuing his treatment of her, to discontinue seeing me for at least three months, beginning the middle of February, a time which both Ethel and I thought inopportune. Scott Buchanan, whom I had met at Columbia where he was a teaching assistant, also served as assistant director of the People's Institute under Everett Dean Martin. In addition to the lectures given by Mr. Martin and others at the Cooper Union auditorium, the People's Institute conducted series of lectures at the Manhattan Trade School on the lower East Side of New York. Scott had invited me to try my hand at public lecturing and to give eight lectures on the methods of psychology in March and April. Ethel and I had looked forward to her attendance at these lectures, but now her analyst would prevent her being there. To circumvent him I arranged for Arthur Rubin to take Ethel to dinner on the evening of the opening lecture, bring her to the lecture, take her home, and end up at my place on 76th Street to report on Ethel's reactions.

The lecture and the question period that followed were over by ten o'clock. It seemed to me reasonable to expect Arthur to conclude his escort mission by eleven or eleven-thirty. Midnight came, and then one and two in the morning, but no Arthur. At two-thirty I could stand it no longer. I walked up West End Avenue to Ethel's apartment house and, from across the street, saw a dim light in her living room. A moment later I observed a taxicab standing in front of the building. Noting that his meter was running, I asked the driver how long he had been waiting. Pointing at the meter, which by now registered over twelve dollars, he told me that he had deposited a young man and a young lady at around ten-thirty and that the young man had asked him to wait.

There was nothing for me to do but return to my room and wait for Arthur to arrive, which he did at about four-thirty in the morning—a sight I shall never forget. His collar was open and crumpled, his tie awry, his hair dishevelled, his suit mussed up, and there were splotches of unsuccessfully rubbed off lipstick on his face. He pleaded innocence of intent accompanied by a polite reluctance to rebuff a young lady's advances. I gave him the benefit of every doubt and blamed Ethel, not Arthur, for disloyalty to me. The one thing that Arthur failed to tell me was that he had sent Ethel a spray of orchids before taking her to dinner and had brought a bottle of champagne back to the apartment with him after the lecture, supposedly to toast me but with an effect contrary to that.

Ethel continued to come to the lectures at the Manhattan Trade School, sometimes with Arthur and sometimes with other friends. She also continued to write me frequently; but in the months that followed, it became all too clear that she was infatuated with Arthur, whether with or without Arthur's connivance. By the middle of the summer, the tempest of Ethel's passion for Arthur stirred me to intercede on her behalf. She plainly wanted to marry him as, up to that point, she just as plainly had not wanted to marry me. I pleaded with Arthur only to find that marrying Ethel was furthest from his thoughts and that, apart from having some fun in the process, his dominant motive had been to break up my affair with Ethel. Like Scott, Arthur also thought that emotional attachments and marriage were stumbling blocks to philosophical pursuits. Where Scott merely argued that point, Arthur decided to take direct action to bring about the result which both of them desired—my falling out of love with Ethel, not completely, but sufficiently, so that the ardor of my affection for her could never again be fully restored. The breakup he was trying to bring about eventually occurred.

Kip's wife, Polly, completed her graduate work for a master's degree at Bryn Mawr in June 1926. Kip either had to throw me out of the room that we shared on 76th Street or find other lodgings for himself and Polly. The Fadimans found an apartment for themselves on Morningside Heights near Columbia, and I stayed on. I could not afford to pay the rent by myself, so Arthur volunteered to pay half of it even though he had no intention of using the room except as a place at which to drop in from time to time.

By this time, Arthur was working for his father at American Silk Mills and hating every minute of it. After leaving Columbia at his father's peremptory request, he refused an office job in New York and chose instead to go to Paterson, New Jersey, where he worked as an apprentice in one of the company's factories. During the six months of his apprenticeship, he lived mainly on rotgut bootleg whisky and suffered an ulceration of the stomach from which he never completely recovered. His illness sent him to the hospital and, after that, on a long sojourn in Mexico City to recuperate. On his return to New York, he finally consented to take on an executive role in his father's business. As palliatives for his discontent with the disagreeable job he had taken on, he resorted to speakeasies for one kind of surcease, and to our room at 76th Street for another. Arthur could become as easily intoxicated by a philosophical conversation as by a bottle of whisky, and the former had the distinct advantage of being heady without being injurious to the lining of his stomach.

At Columbia, while still an undergraduate, he had made a nuisance of himself by buttonholing anyone he could to ask, with dogged persistence, a question which he was firmly convinced no one could answer. "Can you explain the existence of apparent qualitative differences in a completely monistic, materialistic universe?" He was well acquainted with the answers that had been given to this question and fully prepared to show why none of them would do. I can remember one occasion when the object of his interrogation was I. I. Rabi, a classmate of ours who later became a world-renowned physicist and Nobel Prize winner. Rabi's failure to understand the question, not his failure to answer it, drove Arthur into a frenzy. When he became philosophically exasperated, his voice rose many decibels, his language became vituperative, and his manner anything but Socratic. In utterances punctuated by shouts and snorts, Arthur outlined the picture of a universe the ultimate and exclusive constituents of which were atoms differing from one another only in quantitative respects—Rabi's world, he thought, the world of the physicist and chemist. Being part of that world, the human body and brain were similarly constituted; so, too, the medium through which waves of light or sound passed between the supposedly sensible object and the sense organs. Nowhere in the whole picture thus drawn did red and green, or loud and soft, appear. Yet in human experience, the physical things with which we had physical contact did unquestionably appear to differ in color or in sound.

Where did these apparent qualitative differences come from? How could they possibly emerge in experience from a world in which they did not exist? To attribute them in any way to the acts of a mind that was not itself materially constituted would violate Arthur's original premise. The supposition of a monistic, materialistic universe ruled out minds and mental acts not completely reducible to atoms and atomic motions. Arthur might have been stopped by someone willing to reject his initial premise, but Rabi could not bring himself to do that; and on the few occasions when someone tried that ploy, Arthur took off on another tack and asked uncomfortable questions about how matter acted on mind to produce the perceptual experiences in which qualitative differences emerged. Whether or not the problem can be satisfactorily solved, no solution that anyone might advance would have satisfied Arthur. His aim was not to get at the truth, but to get at people who claimed to have it.

Like Socrates, but without Socratic irony, Arthur went after anyone who dared to claim that he had a firm hold on the truth or that he knew anything with certitude. Socrates exposed the pretenders to knowledge without precluding the possibility of knowing the truth; but Arthur, with characteristically Hebraic emphasis on the chasm between God and man, reserved for God alone the possession of knowledge or truth. He could not abide the impiety or the sinful pride of a human claim to what was above man's reach. Looking back on our conversations, I realize that I must have lacked both the wit and the courage to ask Arthur how he could be so certain about the existence of God and about God's possession of knowledge. Even if he had answered that he knew these things by religious faith, I might still have called his attention to his inconsistency in asserting, on the one hand, that men had no grasp of the truth, and asserting, on the other, that with the gift of faith they could claim to have a number of unchallengeable certitudes.

If I had made that point, my guess is that Arthur would have told me that what he called his "philosophy of may-be" applied only to philosophy itself and neither to science nor to religion. Scientific findings or conclusions may have a kind of tentative empirical truth, always subject to correction; religious dogmas may have a certitude that is derived from unquestioning, if not unquestionable, faith; but philosophical theories or doctrines—products of the intellectual imagination —must always be entertained as statements of what is possible, of what may or may not be the case, never asserted either as necessarily true or even as actually true of what really exists. Entertaining a philosophical theory as possible, as something that may or may not be true, opens the door to entertaining its opposite as possible, for if the first of this pair may not be true, the second may be, and conversely. A philosophical theory may have—in fact, to be good, it must have—a certain kind of interior truth, wholly a matter of its internal coherence, that is, the logical consistency of its propositions with one another and of its conclusions with its premises. Since its ultimate premises can never be more than postulates, or propositions that can be taken for granted but can never be advanced as self-evidently or undeniably true, the theory as a whole, however admirable its logical structure and its inner coherence, must always remain a mere possibility, and can never become a demonstrably veridical account of the actual world in which we live. On this view of the status of philosophical theories, philosophical work consists in exploring the realm of the possible by comparing diverse theories, delineating their opposition to one another, and then expanding the realm of possibility by developing more comprehensive theories to resolve the conflicts between theories that exclude each other by virtue of being inadequate in complementary respects.

I cannot now give a wholly satisfactory explanation of why this incorrect view of philosophy should have taken so strong a hold on my mind and dominated it for a number of years. I can attribute it in part to the sheer, almost brute, force exerted by Arthur in the conversations we had during those years. In part, it may also have been due to the fact that a somewhat similar view had come to my attention in the conversations I had with Scott Buchanan, for whose mind—the very opposite of Arthur's in style and temper—I quickly developed the greatest admiration. After graduating from Amherst College when Alexander Meiklejohn was its president as well as a teacher of philosophy, Scott had gone on to Balliol College, Oxford, as a Rhodes scholar, and had met there two other Rhodes scholars with whom I was to become acquainted—Stringfellow Barr and Jerry McGill. He subsequently returned to Harvard University, where he received his doctorate for a dissertation entitled *Possibility*. There were enough points in common between Scott's carefully and cogently expounded philosophy of possibility and Arthur's catch-as-catch-can unwritten philosophy of may-be to persuade me that Arthur had his finger on something that could not be easily dismissed. However, that cannot have been the whole story.

Another contributing factor may have been my acute anxiety about the conflicts among philosophical doctrines, or at least among philosophers bent on polemical attack and rejoinder. Regarding each of the contending theories as a possibility—as a theory that may or may not be true—provided a way out of this polemical morass, a much easier way than having to decide which was true to the exclusion of all the rest. Yet the price one had to pay for this way of escaping from the difficulty of deciding or definitely making up one's mind should have been so repugnant to me that I would reject it out of hand. The philosophy of possibility meant abandoning the pursuit of truth in philosophy—not the truth of a theory that is internally coherent, but the truth of a theory that corresponds with facts, with what actually is the case in the real world. It was in that sense of truth that I had been, all through my college years, so passionate about the pursuit of truth in philosophy. Now, a few years later, I seemed to be doing an about-face. But not quite; for, as will presently become evident, none of us—I, perhaps, less than Arthur or Scott—had minds sufficiently mature to be set in one direction and one only.

At about this time, the General Honors staff was discussing the revision of Erskine's original list of readings. Though Thomas Aquinas had been included, the selection chosen seemed odd to me. It was Father Rickaby's translation of chapters from the *Summa Contra Gentiles*—the opening chapters of part 3 dealing with man's last end. I had heard someone refer to a work by Aquinas entitled *Summa Theologica*, though it was not mentioned in Professor Woodbridge's excellent course on the history of philosophy. He jumped over more than a thousand years from the Hellenistic philosophers of imperial Rome to Descartes and the dawn of modern philosophy with the briefest passing reference to the thought of the Middle Ages. (I have subsequently learned that others, taught the history of philosophy by other professors in other English and American universities, had experienced similar lacunae in their first acquaintance with the history of Western thought.) On querying Arthur and Scott, I discovered that their ignorance paralleled mine. Arthur confirmed my impression that no books by Aquinas sat on the shelves of the college library, and Scott reported that he had never seen a copy of any work by Aquinas in his years at Amherst, Oxford, and Harvard.

Richard McKeon, a classmate of Arthur's, had recently returned to Columbia after studying mediaeval philosophy with Etienne Gilson at the Sorbonne. The Columbia Philosophy Department invited him to teach a course in the philosophy of the Middle Ages; in addition, he took on a section of General Honors. He obviously was the man to go to for information about Aquinas. Being able to read St. Thomas in mediaeval Latin, he did not have any English translations of Aquinas's works, but he told me how to get them. In downtown Manhattan on Vesey Street, Benziger Brothers ran a Catholic bookshop. They were also the publishers of the *Summa Theologica* in an English translation by the Dominican Fathers.

I told Scott and Arthur that I would go down to Benziger Brothers early Saturday morning; if they would meet me at our room on 76th Street, we would examine a volume of the *Summa* together. I can remember my amazement on beholding twenty-one uniformly bound red buckram volumes of the *Summa Theologica* on the shelf. I don't know what I expected, but certainly not that. Without knowing about the structure of the work or the significance of its division into three major parts, I decided to buy volume 1, the title page of which bore the subtitle "Treatise on God." It cost two dollars and a half, a price which now seems as amazing to me as the size of the *Summa* did then.

I can remember the excitement with which we three examined the table of contents and turned the opening pages of the Treatise on God. We were too excited to read them carefully; we were satisfied with savoring them quickly. The climax of that process of dipping in here and there came when we reached the first article of Question 4 about the nature of God. This followed two questions about our knowledge of God's existence, one about whether it can be demonstrated by reason as well as known by faith, the other presenting the famous five ways of proving God's existence.

Each article of a question was itself a question, a more specific one than the general question under which it fell. The first specific question under Question 4 was "Whether God has a body?" That question, like all the hundreds of questions that run through the whole of the

Summa Theologica, began with a series of objections that stated the wrong answers to which Aquinas found himself in total or partial disagreement. After presenting these, he would cite a text from Scripture or from some other authority, such as Aristotle or Augustine, before giving his own answer to the question, arguing for its soundness, and concluding with replies to the objections offered at the beginning, sometimes rejecting them entirely and sometimes making distinctions which separated the partial truth in them from some surrounding error.

We were overwhelmed by the cool, evenhanded, quiet rationality of this procedure. None of us had ever read any philosophical work even remotely like this in structure, method, or style. Aquinas managed to combine maximum brevity with maximum coverage of the points to be handled. In spite of our breathlessness in the face of such elegance, we might have gone on reading had Arthur not exploded at the sight of the opening sentence of Objection 1 of Article 1 in Question 4. "It seems that God has a body," he read, and repeated it again and again in a crescendo of exclamations. I cannot remember the innumerable ways in which he expatiated on the wondrousness of that simple phrasing, but I do remember that there was no way of getting him to quiet down so that we could resume our exploration of the text.

I will not here go into the full sequel of that Saturday morning's first acquaintance with Thomas Aquinas, nor can I accurately assess how much it affected Scott and Arthur in the long run, though I do know that its influence on them, however consequential, could not have been as cataclysmic as it was on me. The more I read Aquinas (week after week I went down to Benziger Brothers and bought another volume), the more my mind was turned in a direction away from Arthur's "may-be" view of philosophy and Scott's "possibility" approach. I do not mean to say that reading Aquinas led me to abandon that way of looking at the philosopher's task, but rather that it caused me to be of two minds about it—two minds that did not fit together at all. From time to time, both Arthur and Scott manifested a similar ambivalence, although I think they were as little aware of their intellectual schizophrenia as I was of mine.

My two-mindedness also revealed itself in the book reviews that I was writing for the *Nation* and for the *Literary Review* of the *New York Evening Post.* Serving as literary editor of the *Nation,* my friend Mark Van Doren gave me philosophical or quasi-philosophical books to review; I had also been invited to become a contributing editor to the *Post*'s Saturday book review pages, and though my department bore the title "Social Sciences," most of the books I chose to review myself were of a theoretical cast. Far from entertaining as possibilities the theories proposed in the books under my scrutiny, I criticized them mainly for their failures or deficiencies with regard to the actual truth about the subjects under consideration. While still playing the game of "may-be" with Arthur, I had no reluctance in using words like *erroneous* or *false* when I thought that an author's theory did not accord with the facts, and I was often much surer than I should have been that I knew the facts.

The room on 76th Street was the scene of frivolities, alarms, and excursions that had no connection with the philosophical talk that took place there. When Kip moved out and Arthur took over Kip's share of the rent, the room contained an empty bed that Arthur never used. We invited a classmate of mine, Charles Prager, to use it until he could find work and pay for it or for lodgings somewhere else. For several years after our graduation in 1923, Chick had floundered in the maelstrom of New York business, unable to find a job that he thought worthy of himself. He was one of the most extraordinary persons I have ever known—handsome, always well groomed even when his clothes were a trifle shabby, talented in music and poetry, precise and eloquent in speech, extremely witty, but melancholy to the point of being dedicated to ultimate failure in life, even to self-destruction. On the surface, he had two problems which he persistently tried to solve while firmly believing that they were insolvable, and he read Cervantes's *Don Quixote* over and over again to take his mind off both problems.

One problem consisted in his quest for the ideal girl, whom he searched for in a quixotic fashion by carrying around a three-by-five card on which the characteristics of this ultimate desideratum were precisely specified and enumerated in the order of their importance. The other problem was finding a job that would both pay him enough money and involve him in tasks intrinsically worth doing, both indispensable to maintaining his self-esteem. This he went about in the following manner. Having been out late the night before, either at a concert or in pursuit of his belle ideale, he would sleep late the next day, arise and slowly complete a meticulous grooming, and saunter forth to Broadway with enough borrowed money to buy a good Havana cigar and a copy of the *New York Times* to read while having breakfast at about 2:30 P.M. After carefully perusing the news, he would finally turn to the want ad pages and put a red check against help-wanted ads that held out any hope of satisfying his requirements. There were never many of these. When he had finished doing this, he would look at his watch to discover that it was almost four in the afternoon. Realizing that it was now too late to go downtown to apply for a job, he would go back to our room, read some *Don Quixote,* and prepare himself for the evening's excursion. This he did with stolid regularity, or at least as long as the money he managed to borrow from Arthur or me held out.

On one occasion when Chick was penniless and borrowing more became embarrassing, he earned ten dollars for another week by a gymnastic feat that was breathtaking to behold. On that particular evening, Chick, in a playful mood, had mounted the arms of a rocking chair, one foot on each arm, teetering back and forth. He had on his pajama bottoms and slippers. The sight of him in the precarious position inspired Arthur to offer him ten dollars if he could remain standing on the arms of the chair while removing his pajama bottoms and taking off his slippers. Ten dollars meant another week or more of subsistence; he could hardly refuse the challenge, though the feat looked impossible to perform. He did it in a little less than an hour of painful contortions accompanied by running comments that vilified us as Arthur, Malcolm Stuart McNab McComb, and I doubled up with laughter and with empathized pain watching him.

The end of the story was as sad as it was predictable. Unable to find a job that suited him and unwilling to continue being a parasite, Chick returned home to Baltimore. Bed and board provided, he still had to find a job. Out of sheer desperation he finally became a floorwalker in a local department store, but that only deepened his desperation, and shortly thereafter he committed suicide.

I, too, had my spells of gloom and fits of depression, but never to the point of desperation. Some individuals, like my friend Charles Prager, are obdurately nay-sayers to life; some are yea-sayers. I have always been one of the latter, prepared to mope or muddle through a prolonged depression until some fortuitous turn of events opens the door to new expectations. When that happens, dormant hope quickly revives, and my mood just as rapidly shifts, as if by the turn of a switch, from off to on.

That is precisely what happened in the summer of 1926, after my ups and downs with Ethel. The last episode involving Arthur's intervention had left me down indeed. After a short vacation in Narragansett Beach with Jim Wise and his new bride, I returned to the city and to a listless routine of emotionally and intellectually empty days. Self-pity is a disease that feeds upon itself; it builds up a resistance to anything that threatens to alleviate the misery being secretly enjoyed. Nothing my friends might say or do could break through the defensive barrier I erected to prolong the black mood in which I was indulging.

Some time toward the beginning of the summer, Mark Van Doren asked me to review the recently published *The Story of Philosophy* by Will Durant, one of the then current "popularizations of knowledge," which kept company with H. G. Wells's *Outline of History,* Hendrik Van Loon's *Story of Mankind,* and Lewis Browne's *This Believing World.* Chapters of Durant's book had been previously published by Haldeman-Julius in little paperback blue books that sold for ten cents a copy. Collected in one hardback volume, they were now being offered to the public by Simon and Schuster for five dollars. Through the haze of my indifference to externals, I was aware that Durant's *Story of Philosophy* was being lavishly praised by reviewers. An advertisement in the *New York Times* of August 22, 1926, announced that this "runaway best-seller" had gone through nine printings in less than three months. It quoted extravagant encomiums from Heywood Broun, Henry Hazlitt, and Stuart Sherman, and included John Dewey's statement that in this "thoroughly scholarly, thoroughly useful, human and readable" book, "Dr. Durant has humanized rather than merely popularized the story of philosophy." I was irked by all of this but not enough to move off dead center.

What did it was a telephone call from Mark Van Doren at the beginning of September which reached me in Kip Fadiman's apartment, where I spent many days aimlessly frittering away time. Mark said that he wanted my review of Durant as quickly as possible, and set a deadline which allowed me only ten days to read the book and write the review. It was as if Mark had pressed a button that released energies I had been storing up for the purpose. I read *The Story of Philosophy* with mounting distaste and gave vent to it in my review. Mine was one of only two adverse criticisms that the book received at the time; the other was written by Paul Weiss and published in the *New Republic*. The affinity of our reviews established a bond between Paul and me that has grown into a lifelong friendship.

My chief complaint was that Durant had "humanized" philosophy— exactly the thing for which Dewey praised him. His book, like that of his precursor in antiquity, Diogenes Laertius, author of *The Lives and Opinions of the Philosophers*, dealt mainly with men, not with ideas, or with ideas only as opinions formed by men under certain psychological or cultural influences. An interest in human beings is one thing; an interest in thought another; and one should not be allowed to get in the way of the other. Nor should a man's thought be explained solely by reference to his personality or temperament, or the social and cultural setting of his life. To use that type of explanation as a basis for evaluating his thought, to insinuate that its origins make its validity suspect, is to commit the genetic fallacy—the substitution of psychology for logic—which was my main point of protest against John Dewey and other pragmatists and humanists.

The central blindness of Durant's book, I wrote, lies in the fact that

philosophy is conceived in a manner which would be rudely uncongenial . . . to the minds of the philosophers Mr. Durant has chosen to sketch sympathetically. Where he has achieved sympathetic insight into a philosophic system it has been largely on the side of its vital motivations rather than in terms of its dialectical intent. His implicit acceptance of the pragmatic attitude toward the history of philosophy . . . makes his lack of appreciation for antithetical viewpoints the more distressing, since the prag-matic conception of philosophy is the unacknowledged, pervasive doctrine of the book, underlying its exposition of thinkers to whom pragmatism would have been unintelligible. This doctrine commits the fallacy of genetic interpretation. It assumes that ideas are to be exhaustively under-stood and their validity estimated in terms of their origins; that phi-losophies are most significantly revealed as biographical items in a socio-politico-economic context.

Admitting that "the thinker may be described biologically" and that "thinking may be a psychological process, susceptible to various psy-choanalyses," I went on to insist that "thought itself . . . has a logical structure disengaged from life and a life of its own in discourse which is purely dialectical." And I concluded the review by saying that just as the poets were banished by Plato for writing stories about the gods, so "Diogenes and Mr. Durant would have been exiled with them for telling stories about the philosophers. Not that gossips and collectors of opinions could have harmed the real philosophers who ruled the perfect state; simply that lack of insight into the relation between dis-course and truth would have offended them."

As I now look back upon that review, I can see evidence of my un-resolved state of mind about philosophy, torn between a concern with its being true in the same way that science claims a modicum of truth for itself, and an inclination to disengage philosophy from relation to anything outside the universe of discourse in which it flourishes as a dialectical or logical enterprise. The extreme purism, or intellectual austerity, to which the latter tendency drove me is now as repugnant to me as it must have been to my elders then, some of whom may have had the charity to excuse it as a youthful excess. On one thing, how-ever, I have not changed my mind. The genetic fallacy is an error always to be scrupulously avoided. Nor have I ever found the idiosyncrasies of human beings, including myself, more interesting than their ideas.

In the immediate train of writing the Durant review came another event which completed my recovery from depression. Scott Buchanan asked me to go with him to Harvard to attend the Sixth International Congress of Philosophy. I might not have decided to go had he not also suggested that we stop off at Nantucket Island on our way, to spend the weekend with Everett Dean Martin, the director of the People's Institute, for which Scott worked as assistant director and for which I had given a series of lectures. The purpose of our visit was to get Mr. Martin interested in turning the reading list used in the Colum-bia General Honors course into a program of adult education.

Scott had grown more and more interested in Erskine's reading list and in the method of the seminar discussions which I had described. He regarded the "great books course" as a characteristically American extension of the "ancient greats" and "modern greats" that, in his day at Oxford, were the main undergraduate programs. He also thought that he saw in the discussion method of the seminars something both akin to and askew from the Oxford tutorial. Despite these reservations, he still felt that we should propose to Mr. Martin the project of setting up great books discussion groups for adults under the auspices of the People's Institute. Would I go along with him, not only for the ride but also to see if the two of us together could persuade Mr. Martin?

I did, and we did. Mr. Martin was persuaded. He made an application to the Carnegie Corporation for financial assistance, and when a grant-in-aid of $15,000 came through, Scott was able to set up fifteen adult seminar groups in the five boroughs of New York City. More difficult than raising the money was recruiting the staff. Two discussion leaders for each group meant finding thirty individuals who were both willing and able to do the job, or to learn how to do it. I cannot remember the full complement of the crew we assembled, but I do know it included Kip Fadiman, Dick McKeon, Jacques Barzun, Whittaker Chambers, John Storck, Houston Peterson, Mark Van Doren, and Philip Youtz, as well as Scott and me.

The program ran for two years (1926–1928), one great book a week, in the same chronological order as in the General Honors course. Though it proved to be very well suited to the interests and needs of adults who wished to engage in continued learning, the Carnegie Corporation refused to renew their grant for the usual foundation reason that the initial grant had been for experimental purposes and the experiment had now been performed. The fact that it was successful did not appear, in their minds, to warrant further support for it as an educational venture.

Ten years or more would elapse before Hutchins and I at the University of Chicago, and Barr and Buchanan at St. John's College in Annapolis, revived this form of adult education for the extension departments of our institutions to carry on. Still another five years would pass before we would be able to establish the Great Books Foundation in Chicago to promote great books discussion groups all over the country. From the initial venture in New York, through all the transformations of the idea in Chicago, Annapolis, San Francisco, and Aspen, and right down to my present engagement in an adult seminar that has been going on continuously for more than thirty years, I have never found any reason to amend my conviction that this program represents the soundest idea in genuinely adult education—the continued learning by adults who have been adequately schooled, not the remedial schooling of adults who seek to make up for deficiencies in their formal education.

During that weekend visit to the Martins' summer house on Nantucket Island, one other thing happened that had a long train of consequences. I met the girl whom I would marry before the following summer.

The Martins lived at Wauwinet, a narrow sandspit at the northernmost tip of the island. All summer residents of this little community took their meals in the dining room of the Wauwinet House. The table in the dining room that Scott and I shared with the Martins ran perpendicular to another at which a family with four or five sons and daughters sat. On the first occasion of our being in the dining room, I noticed one of the daughters—pale blue eyes, sun-tanned skin, and wavy auburn hair.

Beyond glancing furtively at the other table from time to time, I thought nothing more about her until Sunday evening came. Scott and I were departing for Boston by early boat on Monday morning. Mr. Martin told us that the Boyntons, living in a nearby house, had invited us all to a beach picnic on Sunday evening, adding that Mrs. Boynton wanted to ask my advice about her daughter's transferring from Smith College to Barnard, the women's undergraduate division of Columbia University. At the beach party, I soon discovered that Mrs. Boynton's daughter, Helen, was the blue-eyed girl at the next table. Toward the end of the evening, her mother asked what I thought about the advisability of Helen's shifting from Smith College to Barnard.

I did not know then that Helen wanted to get away from Northampton because a love affair she had been having with a young man at Amherst College had just blown up. With the prospect of seeing more of Helen if she came to live in New York, I recommended Barnard College to Mrs. Boynton with an enthusiasm that had little to do with the merits of that institution. The next morning on our trip across Nantucket Sound, Scott teased me about what he thought were the ill-concealed motives of my eulogy of Barnard; but that, for the time being, was the end of it. The International Congress of Philosophy at Harvard soon took Helen Boynton off my mind, though I cannot say that the formal addresses delivered at the congress gave me more edifying thoughts, in spite of the eminence of the speakers, among whom were Etienne Gilson, Alfred North Whitehead, John Dewey, Hans Driesch, Sarvepalli Radhakrishnan, and Hermann Weyl. I remember being shocked by the applause that greeted Will Durant when he was introduced by his publishers to this august assemblage. I sat there wishing that I could rise and read aloud my review of his book, due to appear the following week.

Nineteen twenty-six was for me a year of coincidences that had far-reaching effects on my life. If I had not accidentally met C. K. Ogden, I might never have met Robert M. Hutchins, and it is difficult for me to imagine the course my career might then have taken. Ogden happened to be in the United States that autumn, mainly in his role as editor of the International Library of Philosophy, Psychology, and Scientific Method. Always one to multiply his enterprises, Ogden had other irons in the fire; he was trying to get financial support for his Orthological Institute in London and he was starting a magazine called *Psyche* which he hoped would soon be able to publish spin-offs called "Psyche Monographs."

Gardner Murphy, a colleague of mine in the Psychology Department at Columbia, invited me to a tea party that he was giving for Ogden. Ogden had Murphy in mind for a book on the history of modern psychology. In the course of the conversation, our English visitor mentioned a book he was planning to add to his International Library, speaking with some impatience about his difficulty of getting a manuscript from the author. The title was to be *The Technique of Controversy*, and the author a Polish philosopher, Boris B. Bogoslowsky. The mention of that title triggered me into action. I launched into a rapid-fire speech about the ideas which Scott, Arthur, and I had developed concerning philosophical controversy and the dialectical method for dealing with fundamentally opposed theories, to be viewed impartially as equally worthy intellectual objects in the realm of possibility. Ogden's response was as rapid-fire as mine. He asked me whether I would write the book I had just outlined and when he could have the manuscript. Without a moment's thought, I said yes to the first question, and March 1 to the second. I then capped the arrangement by proposing that he simultaneously publish Scott Buchanan's book on possibility, the manuscript of which already existed and probably needed only slight revision, which Scott could easily do between November and March.

I, of course, had no manuscript in existence, or anything more than a few scattered notes, but I quickly calculated that I would have two weeks off at Christmas and another two weeks of academic recess at midterm, toward the end of January. If, before then, I were to make notes on relevant notions culled from our many conversations and construct a working outline of the book, writing the book itself in four weeks seemed feasible. Scott, seven years older than I and a great deal soberer, as well as wiser, expressed some concern about the brashness of my undertaking, though he was delighted that my proposal to Ogden had found a publisher for his doctoral dissertation. In view of the degree to which we sympathized with and shared each other's views, he was particularly pleased that our first books would be published as companion volumes.

Our resolution to go ahead with the project, and especially my determination to meet that difficult deadline for writing and revising a book, became firm when we examined the list of authors whose works had already been published in Ogden's International Library. It included G. E. Moore, Ludwig Wittgenstein, Carl Jung, Charles S. Peirce, Hans Vaihinger, I. A. Richards, C. D. Broad, Jean Piaget, Bronislaw Malinowski, and Bertrand Russell; it also included a book co-authored by Ogden with I. A. Richards—*The Meaning of Meaning*—which I had read five years earlier when I was writing my undergraduate paper on the philosophy and psychology of meaning. Two other books in the International Library I had become acquainted with more recently; both would pop back into my mind when I started to write the book I had outlined for Ogden: one was Vaihinger's *Philosophy of "As If,"* which argued that abstract philosophical ideas are fictions which have little to do with reality, but which we treat "as if" they did; the other Wittgenstein's *Tractatus Logico-Philosophicus,* written by its author before he was twenty years old, on scraps of paper in the trenches while he was serving with the Austrian Army during the First World War.

Christmas came and so did the January recess. With a one-page outline of the contents to be covered, I wrote ten to fifteen pages a day, completing the first draft by the end of January on schedule, with enough time to allow Scott, Arthur, and Kip to read the typescript and make suggestions for its revision before I had to send it off to Ogden in England a month later. At the same time, Scott revised his dissertation, making changes that reflected points we had gone over together and introducing cross-references to my book as I, in turn, made cross-references to his. Both books went off together, were published in the autumn of 1927 together, were advertised and reviewed together, almost as if they were Siamese twins, his under the title *Possibility,* mine called *Dialectic,* a title I had chosen at Scott's suggestion.

The word *dialectic* has a number of distinct connotations, derived from its use by Plato in one sense, by Aristotle in another, by the mediaeval teachers of the liberal arts in still another, and by Hegel in his own special way. The thin thread of common meaning running through them all refers to oppositions in the realm of thought and to logical devices designed to deal with disputation, especially philosophical controversy. I added a purist detachment of thought from reality, a concern with theories in opposition without regard to their truth so far as that is to be judged by their relation to the actual world.

It was in this special sense of the term that, in a concluding chapter of the book, I projected a *Summa Dialectica*—a modern counterpart of a mediaeval *Summa Theologica* in its aim to be a comprehensive summation of thought, but as different in plan and method from its mediaeval paradigm as night from day. Where the great theological summations of the Middle Ages surveyed all human knowledge in an attempt to answer the widest range of questions about God and his creatures, as well as about man's destiny under divine Providence, and where they judged the truth of all possible answers in the light of both reason and faith, a *Summa Dialectica* would rigorously abstain from making comparable judgments, contenting itself with constructing a vast but inherently uncompletable map of the universe of discourse in which theories (which may or may not be true) are placed in revealing logical relationships to one another.

If I may borrow the phrase once applied by William James to a graduate student's dissertation written about himself, I have reread *Dialectic,* after almost fifty years of averting my gaze from it, "with mingled admiration and abhorrence." I cannot dismiss the book entirely as a juvenile effort, for, though fundamentally wrong, it was neither callow nor crass; nor was it wrong in all respects. There are in it ideas that I have held on to or returned to, though in this book they are buried in ground that is now quite alien to my mind. Twenty-five years later, I revived the project of constructing a *Summa Dialectica,* when I proposed to the Ford Foundation the idea of making a dialectical survey of the basic ideas and issues in Western thought. This led much later to the establishment of the Institute for Philosophical Research— in 1952, to be exact.

I should have called the enterprise of my later years an institute for dialectical research. The fundamental error I made when I wrote the book for Ogden was to identify philosophy with dialectic, thereby turning it into a consideration of theories in the realm of the possible rather than an attempt to state truths about the actual world. The proposal that led to the establishment of the Institute for Philosophical Research made quite clear that the dialectical work to be done, far from being identical with philosophical thought, was only a preparation for it. Clarifying the disagreements among philosophers, or the issues on which they stand opposed, and delineating the controversies in which they are engaged can help to clear away the underbrush that impedes progress in philosophical thought, but it does not contribute a single new idea or insight to enlarge our grasp of the truth about the actual world. On this fundamental point, the later formulation of a *Summa Dialectica* repudiated my earlier conception; but the statement of the dialectical method that I prepared at the time of the institute's founding borrowed insights about psychological and linguistic factors in human controversy that I did not then realize were buried in a book that I wrote in 1926–1927.

Looking back on this now, I perceive the origin of the intellectual rift between Scott Buchanan and me. In the years immediately preceding and following the publication of *Possibility* and *Dialectic,* while we were at the People's Institute together, Scott and I seemed to be of one mind. But after he went to the University of Virginia and later to St. John's College, and before I went to the University of Chicago, a subtle barrier, no thicker at times than a haze, made communication between us as difficult as groping for contact in a fog. We continued to exchange ideas, both in conversation and in correspondence, for many years. There was no one with whom I had a more active, wide-ranging, and sustained philosophical conviviality, no one whose mind fascinated me half as much, no one I thought wiser in vision or profounder in insight. But we never regained the oneness of mind which had been so exciting to both of us, and so fruitful, back in the twenties. As the years went on, the rift deepened and we drifted further apart. I think the reason lay in the fact that I repudiated the central thesis of *Dialectic* and did an about-face in my conception of philosophizing, while Scott never forswore the controlling insights of *Possibility*.

We seldom found ourselves in frontal disagreement. It might have been better for us if that had been so. More often than not, we failed to understand one another and failed in ways that we found difficult to identify. We would persist in the illusion that we were talking to one another on the same plane, but in fact the thoughts of one passed over or under the thoughts of the other—his always on the higher plane of imaginative vision, mine always on the lower plane of pedestrian logical precision. I can remember one conversation that exemplifies the pitfalls that beset us. At the time of *Dialectic* and *Possibility*, Scott and I were in complete agreement that all statements, certainly all theoretical propositions, were metaphorical in character—all were suppressed similes. To attempt a literal interpretation was, for us, then, an egregious error. When, later, I moved further away from *Dialectic*, I took exactly the opposite view, eschewing metaphor and attempting to be as literal as possible. The conversation that should have put an end to our efforts to communicate went on for hours; during the whole of it, Scott thought that every time I made a statement involving "is," I meant "is like," and I took his use of "is" to mean just "is," not "is like." Nothing could have been more exasperating, or funny—or, in retrospect, sobering and sad, at least to me.

While I still remained in the toils of *Dialectic,* I gave two series of lectures for the People's Institute, in both of which Scott closely cooperated. One was an attempt to construct "geometries of the soul," an exposition of psychological theories in the style of Spinoza's *Ethics— in ordine geometrico.* This procedure was intended to expose their underlying postulates or assumptions and to reveal them as so many equally entertainable theoretical possibilities. The opening lecture in this series was entitled "The Method and Madness of Geometry."

The other series of lectures bore the title "Philosophy and Silence" and took its theme from the seventh and ultimate proposition in Ludwig Wittgenstein's *Tractatus Logico-Philosophicus:* "that whereof one cannot speak, thereof one must be silent." I had quoted this dictum with approval in an appendix to *Dialectic* and had adapted its meaning to my purpose by saying that "dialectic must confine itself to possibility or be silent." The series of lectures went much further in developing the implications of the Wittgensteinian proposition which I found myself in sympathy with on many counts. In the last of a number of appendices to *Dialectic*, I quoted the following statement from Wittgenstein's *Tractatus*, on the distinction between philosophy and science:

> Philosophy is not one of the natural sciences. (The word "philosophy" must mean something which stands above or below, but not beside the natural sciences.) The object of philosophy is the logical clarification of thoughts. Philosophy is not a theory but an activity. A philosophical work consists essentially of elucidations. The result of philosophy is not a number of "philosophical propositions," but to make propositions clear. Philosophy should make clear and delimit sharply the thoughts which otherwise are, as it were, opaque and blurred.

I wholly agreed with that conception of philosophy at the time. I would still be inclined to agree with it if the word *dialectic* were substituted for *philosophy;* but now I think that philosophy, far from being an "elucidating activity," resembles science in being an effort to achieve knowledge of things as they actually are and to state this knowledge in propositions that can be validated as true in fact. The later Wittgenstein (the Wittgenstein of *Philosophical Investigations*, published in 1953) recanted the "logical atomism" of the 1921 *Tractatus*, a doctrine he had imbibed from Bertrand Russell; but he went on to an even more extreme espousal of the view that philosophy has value only as a therapeutic effort to clarify the thought expressed in ordinary speech and to remedy or remove the puzzlements, or pseudoproblems, that philosophers persist in taking seriously.

Teaching at Columbia, giving lectures at the People's Institute, writing and revising a book for publication, writing book reviews for a number of periodicals, and, with Whittaker Chambers, conducting an adult great books seminar at the Community Church left little time for lighter divertissements. When by accident I met Helen Boynton on the Columbia campus (her mother had taken my advice and allowed her to transfer from Smith to Barnard College), I promised to phone her and invite her out to dinner. Busy months went by; our paths crossed again; again I promised to arrange to spend an evening with her, and again I put it off. After *Dialectic* was out of the typewriter, I had more free time. At last I took Helen out to dinner, several times, sometimes taking her afterwards to hear my lecture at the People's Institute or to the great books seminar that Whittaker Chambers and I were conducting. Occasionally, we went dancing.

I suppose it was natural for Helen to tell me about her affair with the boy at Amherst College (my memory is that he married her roommate) and for me to tell Helen about my long-drawn-out embroilment with

Ethel. In the course of these narrations, I told Helen of one astounding event which had happened a few months earlier.

It was on January 17—I can remember the date well because it was my parents' wedding anniversary and I was at home celebrating it with them. At that time, I had not seen Ethel or heard from her for many months. She telephoned me at my parents' home. Her voice sounded eerily low-pitched. All she said, repeating it several times, was something to this effect: "The stars are changing, the stars are changing." When I pressed her to explain, she told me she would if I came to see her at once. Excusing myself for leaving the family party so abruptly, I made my way through a raging blizzard to Ethel's apartment. She was manifestly distraught and hesitant to tell me what was on her mind. She had been going to Evangeline Adams, the astrologist who had become famous through newspaper reports on her being retained by Wall Street brokers for advice about the stock market. Miss Adams had just that day told Ethel that the constellations which presided over January 1927 made that the month for her to get married. Ethel pointed the finger at me. I said yes. Since she knew I had wanted to marry her, I was embarrassed to say no. The fact that I was no longer in love with Ethel did not then seem to me sufficient reason for not marrying her. However, in the immediate sequel to that evening, that fact became manifest, and I persuaded Ethel that we would be making a mistake to get married.

My telling Helen the story of "the stars are changing" led to a conversation about love and marriage in which we both concurred in the ill-considered opinion that marriage should be contracted for reasons of convenience, not because being in love necessitated it (necessitated it, I should add, under the taboos then prevalent in the society in which we moved). The fact that each of us had been burned by a love affair provided the only possible excuse for so imprudent a judgment on our part. Shortly after this conversation, Helen and I went back for a nightcap to my room on 76th Street after an evening of dining and dancing. While I was getting the drinks ready, she suddenly said, "What would you do if I were to say to you, 'The stars are changing!'" I put the glasses down and replied, "I would ask you to marry me." My reply might have sprung from the same kind of embarrassment that prompted me to say yes to Ethel some months earlier, though in this case it probably also reflected our wishful thinking about the practical advantages of disconnecting love and marriage.

Helen was four years younger than I, but I, at twenty-four, should have had more sense. We arranged to meet the following afternoon for tea to discuss the details of getting married. Helen's "reason of convenience" was that she wanted to get married before she turned twenty-one—earlier than the age at which her elder sister was wed. I cannot remember what my "reason" was or whether I had any. We set a date in May, before Helen would leave Barnard to go to Nantucket for the summer. Since we had also decided, once again for reasons that are not entirely clear and certainly cannot have been prudent, that we should keep our marriage a secret, we planned a brief honeymoon, in Stockbridge, Massachusetts, where, signing the register at the Red Lion Inn, I put down "Mr. and Mrs. M. J. Adler and wife." Our plans for the summer (which included my visiting Nantucket Island as a lecturer at the Fred Howe's School of Opinion at Siasconset) completed our picture of secret married life. How long we then planned to keep the secret, I cannot remember; but I do know that by mid-December we decided to tell our families what we had done. I was not a welcome Christmas present to her parents, or she to mine.

As I now look back on it, my temporary adoption of the philosophy of may-be and my writing of *Dialectic,* while at the same time being disposed toward quite opposite views, indicate a mind still undeveloped. So, too, my secret marriage to Helen, under the circumstances I have described, indicates a character similarly inchoate, or unformed. If to be immature is to be unformed, or inchoate, in both mind and character, I was, in my twenty-fourth year, still immature—irresponsible, thoughtless about the future, and given to convictions insufficiently examined or weighed.

In spite of the careless way in which Helen and I entered into marriage, our marriage lasted for thirty-three years. In the beginning we lived a carefree and adventuresome life in which Helen engaged with as much zest as I, yet at the same time making sure that our frolics did not interfere with my serious pursuits. These she encouraged and fostered without participating in them, her perceptive intelligence and her moral integrity often safeguarding them against miscarriage. The gradual decline and ultimate dissolution of our relationship were the result of personal faults that neither of us had the wisdom or the will to correct.

Chapter 6

The Law of Evidence

MARRIED LIFE REQUIRED larger living quarters and larger income. The one room without bath on West 76th Street that had served well enough as bachelor digs would not do; nor would an income of twenty-four hundred dollars a year. The first problem was partly solved while my marriage remained secret. Shortly after the wedding, I persuaded Arthur Rubin to join me in renting a flat around the corner on 77th Street, somewhat more commodious—two rooms with bath and a kitchenette—but unfurnished. We then proceeded to furnish it as if it were going to serve as a work place for both of us. We bought two huge desks, some tables, bookcases, a variety of office chairs, a couch, and a pair of beds. The bedroom had nothing but a bed in it; the other room, with its two oversized desks and heavy office chairs, looked—so a friend of ours told us—like the office of the president of the Great Atlantic and Pacific Tea Company. Six months later, when the secret came unglued, Arthur retired from the scene gracefully, Helen moved in, and we gradually added a few pieces of furniture that gave the place a less forbidding look.

The problem of finances took a little more doing to solve. The salary scale at Columbia for young instructors without tenure held out no promise of a solution. The only other route open to me was a combination of stipends and fees from multiple sources. In the three years that I remained at Columbia after marriage, I managed to carry a work load involving a wide variety of paying jobs. In addition to my teaching duties at Columbia, which included General Honors seminars as well as instruction in psychology, I held a part-time teaching post at the City College of New York; I took on a research job for the Columbia Law School; I took over the assistant directorship of the People's Institute

97

when my friend Scott Buchanan left to go to the University of Virginia as a professor of philosophy; I gave lectures during the summertime at the Siasconset School of Opinion on Nantucket Island and hired myself out to a lecture bureau; I did a great deal of book reviewing, remuneration for which was slight, though I did receive a small weekly retaining fee as a contributing editor for the *New York Post Literary Review*. To cap all this, I took advances from C. K. Ogden for a number of books that I spent a lot of time thinking about but never wrote, advances which I subsequently had to repay. In one of those years my income from all sources exceeded eleven thousand dollars—a considerable sum in those days; but my recollection is that at the end of that year, I was more deeply in arrears than I had been when I was earning less.

Ogden was an inveterate and untiring editorial entrepreneur. He was always thinking up books or series of them for other people to write, though I must add that he combined this activity with writing a few of them himself, including an interesting one on Jeremy Bentham's theory of fictions. Prodded by his interest in sequels to Scott Buchanan's *Possibility* and my *Dialectic,* I proposed that Buchanan write a book on poetry and mathematics and I do one on philosophy and silence. Scott did eventually write *Poetry and Mathematics,* but not for Ogden to publish; I never came through with the book I had outlined from the lectures about silence which I gave at the People's Institute. However, I did accept small advances from Ogden for two little books that he conceived as units in a series of "Hour" books. My contributions were to be *An Hour with Psychology* and *An Hour with Philosophy.* I cannot now imagine what those books would have been like if I had written them, but I am sure that it was fortunate that, after a certain amount of backing and filling, I gave the projects up and the money back after a number of dunning letters from Ogden.

One Ogden project stands out in my memory not only because of the distress it caused me but also because of what I learned from my failure to deliver. Ogden had come to some understanding with the management at Brentano's, who wanted to go into the publishing business as well as run very successful bookstores. For their first venture in trade publishing, Ogden had suggested a series of biographies about twentieth-century figures in the world of science and philosophy. Knowing my interest in William James's philosophy and my affection for James as a person, he invited me to write his biography. If I had had any premonition at all of what is involved in writing a biography, I might have had the good sense to turn the invitation down, even though I sorely needed the three-hundred-dollar advance. Lured by the money and banking on the fact that I had by this time read almost everything that William James had written, including the extraordinary collection of his letters which had been edited by his son Henry James, I took the job on. I must have realized to a certain extent that understanding a philosopher's thought does not suffice for writing an account of his life, because on the very day that I received the three hundred dollars from the cashier at Brentano's, I spent a little less than a hundred of it buying books that I thought I might need for background—the letters and notebooks of William's brother Henry, the literary remains of William's father, the Swedenborgian theologian, books about Harvard at the turn of the century, and so on.

The remainder of the three hundred did not stay in my pocket long, though my original plan had been to use it to repay debts I had incurred with my father for things I had bought and charged to his account with the stores. The squandering of what remained can partly be explained, and perhaps excused, by the growing distress I suffered as I tried to put my mind, during that June of 1927, on the task of writing the life of William James. Distress turned into depression, which came to a climax the day that Colonel Lindbergh arrived in New York after his solo flight across the Atlantic. Of all the welcomes that New York has ever given to returning heroes, that must have been the most exuberant. Starting at the Battery, proceeding up lower Broadway, going on to upper Fifth Avenue, and ending in Central Park, it drew enormous, boisterous, almost maniacal crowds, drowned in ticker tape and torn-up telephone books. That day I had chosen to go down to lower Manhattan to deliver to the editor a number of reviews I had written for the *New York Post*, and also to pick up some new books to review. I battled with the milling crowds and the snarled traffic at every stage of my journey downtown and back. I suddenly and irrationally developed an active dislike for Charles Lindbergh. The sound of his name repeated over and over again by the hoarsely cheering crowds grated on my ears. I couldn't stand the sight of the banners that waved welcome to him. I focussed my frustrations on him, as if he were the cause of my distress, not William James. By mid-afternoon, I felt that I had to get away from it all—out of the city somewhere, someplace where the sound and sight of Lindbergh would be nil.

Why not take the night train to Lake Placid in the Adirondack Mountains? That would get me out of the city by early evening and in a mountain retreat by early morning. I telephoned Malcolm McComb, who had been a student in one of my psychology classes, and asked him to go with me, and he, always ready for a lark, readily consented. The purchase of the round-trip rail tickets and the sleeping accommodations on the train used up most of what I had left of my advance for the James biography, but getting away from Lindbergh—and, subconsciously, from James—had become an imperious necessity. I breathed easier and felt almost lighthearted as the train pulled out of Grand Central Station. We arrived in Lake Placid at seven the next morning, and as we walked from the station down the main street of the village, braced by the cold, clear mountain air, the first thing that met my gaze was a big bold sign hung across the street saying "Welcome Charles Lindbergh!" That did it. There was no getting away from Lindbergh—or from James. After a day of disconsolate muttering that had no therapeutic effect, I returned to New York to my desk, and to the task which I had come to regard as an unbearable yoke around my neck.

Off and on for some months thereafter, I continued the background reading and went on making notes in preparation for writing, but eventually I felt compelled to abandon the project, give the advance back, and find some other way to repay the debt I owed my father. The facts that one could discover about a man's life from all the recorded details of his actions and from what is known about the external circumstances that conditioned them, even when supplemented by his writings (not merely his published books and essays, but also his collected letters) did not seem to me to provide sufficient evidence for statements about what he thought, felt, or intended on particular occasions. Yet the biographical narrative cannot consist exclusively of statements about externals. It will not come to life without the introduction of passages in which the biographer is willing to surmise what was going on inside the person he is writing about and willing to express those conjectures as if they were known matters of fact. He must put words into the mind of his subject—words that convey his thoughts, feelings, or intentions—but words that the biographer himself has put together for the purpose. In addition, to give some depth to the interior life of his subject, the biographer must add insights of his own about underlying traits of mind or character and hidden motivations or springs of action. No amount of factual research will do. The biographer must be a poet—a teller of likely stories and the creator of a fictional hero; and if in addition to poetic talent, he has some gift for feeling his way inside another person's heart and mind, with or without the aid of psychoanalytical hypotheses, so much the better.

What I discovered about myself was that I totally lacked the requisite talent and gift for the biographer's task. I could not bring myself to write even one sentence which had the form "When he was confronted with this opportunity, William James thought . . . (or felt, or wished)." How could anyone know what James thought, felt, or wished unless he himself expressed it in his own words at the time? And even were that evidence available, how could anyone know why that was his thought, feeling, or wish? Even if he himself had given the reasons why, he might have been self-deceived or deficient in self-understanding. The person who undertakes to write a biography is fully aware of all this and is willing to cope with it, surmounting the difficulties in his way by an overriding interest in the individual human being whose life he is conjuring up. My greatest deficiency, I discovered, was my lack of such interest. It was the published philosophy of William James, not the living man, in which I had so keen an interest.

As I look back at this failure on my part, and the deficiency in me that it reveals, I cannot help thinking that the same defect must impair the writing of an autobiography. I fear that my efforts at self-characterization and self-understanding are woefully inadequate. What I am able to say about myself as a human being as well as about the other human beings mentioned in this narrative is skimpy, imperceptive, and superficial. I can report recorded or recollectable events in their external aspects, but I do not have an eye for perceiving the motivation of the actors who took part in them, or the kind of interest in their human interiors that is needed to delineate their characters in the round. If I had as much interest in human beings as I do in human thought, this would be a different story. On the other hand, such a story, if I could write it, might detract from the interest this one has, which lies in the fact that throughout my life it has been human thought to which I have reacted with the kind of concern that others have for human beings. I have given hurt sometimes because of this, and sometimes I have suffered it.

Ogden did not make a great fuss about my failure to write the biography of William James or about my withdrawal from other projects he had hoped I might complete. As an editor and a publisher's agent, he had become inured to such contingencies. Prof. Wolfgang Köhler had promised him a book on gestalt psychology, a sequel to his book *The Mentality of Apes,* which Ogden had published in his International Library; but somehow the manuscript of that book ended up in the hands of Horace Liveright who, at Mark Van Doren's recommendation, sent it to me to perform the most onerous task I have ever taken on. Instead of writing the book in German and having it translated, Professor Köhler, who had been lecturing in English at American universities, thought he could make himself understood in writing as well as he could in speech. The result was unpublishable broken English. Removing the fractures of syntax, sentence after sentence, while trying to preserve the meaning of the author, barely detectable in the contorted word-order, was many times more difficult than translating from a foreign language. As I recall, I was paid three hundred dollars for a job that took more than three full weeks to accomplish—the same amount that Brentano's advanced on the biography of James, which had to be repaid.

Writing book reviews was more rewarding than remunerative. So was giving public lectures, not the kind that were arranged by a lecture bureau, but the kind that I gave for the People's Institute in New York and for the School of Opinion at Siasconset on Nantucket Island. When

Fred Howe opened the Tavern-on-the-Moors and announced that, in addition to board and lodging, the tavern planned to offer highbrow intellectual fare during the summer months, the natives, many of whom had never been off-island, looked askance at the proceedings. Word passed around among them that a conspiracy was under way—"to form an opinion and foist it on the world." The first series of lectures that I gave at the School of Opinion bore the strange title "The Psychologist Enters the Garden of Eden"; I cannot reconstruct the underlying intent from the notes available to me. The second summer I lectured there, in 1928, I shifted from psychology to philosophy and talked about World Pictures—the big ideas in Western history.

Of these eight lectures, the only one worth recalling is the one that concluded the series—"The World as a Funny Picture: a Tale Told by an Idiot." It argued that the human mind is caught in the coils of relevance, and that, as a result, it always tries to relate and to see things in relation, with the further result that it is always striving to make a cosmos out of the chaos that may exist. As I developed it then, the thesis now seems to me highly dubious; however, toward the end of the lecture, I did one thing that was to prove useful later. To show how difficult, almost impossible, it was to get away from being relevant in thought and speech, I wrote a paragraph to exemplify the point of Shakespeare's statement about life's being a tale told by an idiot, full of sound and fury, signifying nothing. To speak coherently and yet to signify nothing; to construct sentences in which each word could be understood and in which the words fitted together in grammatically correct syntactical order, but the sentences themselves made little if any sense—that was what I tried to do in order to show how difficult it is to speak nonsense grammatically and with recognizable rhetorical form while still using words instead of mere nonsense syllables, such as "glub," "figery," and "trinisted." Here is the paragraph—the first of a dozen or more such pieces of prose that I was later to write and publish as companion pieces to a series of steel point line drawings done by Maude Hutchins.

We have triangulated with impunity in order that sophistication would neither digest nor slice our conventional drainage. Examples of serious solicitude, cleared away with dishes after dinner, leave some of us unfaithful to the beach and others of us unprepared to skate. You, perhaps, individually have bounced in isolation, careless of benefit derived from saracens, but not wholly too late for the Sunday papers. I offer two reasons for suspending my argument. The antlers that the fish wear on Fifth Avenue confuse the ready ear, not through belief but, after all, in admirable restraint. Since the cause of this is the future of our local facts, we must admit that the foregoing does not entirely summarize the absence of philosophy.

Lecturing at the Manhattan Trade School, the Mühlenberg Branch Library, or in the Great Hall of Cooper Union was only part of my duties as assistant director of the People's Institute. Everett Dean Martin, the director, lectured in the Great Hall every Friday night during the academic year, but the institute also sponsored lectures on Sunday and Tuesday evenings, and it was the task of the assistant director to serve as chairman, introducing the speaker and repeating the questions asked from the floor during the forum that followed the lecture. The purpose of that was not only to make sure that everyone had heard the question, but also, by rephrasing it, to increase its intelligibility and to eliminate what was not germane. The Cooper Union audience in those days was remarkably heterogeneous. It included jobless vagrants and idlers, many of whom, during the winter months, came in to get out of the cold, as well as students, teachers, businessmen, lawyers, and physicians, and a scattering of persons who had been attracted by the title of the lecture or the name of the lecturer.

Those who came in to warm up usually sat in the front rows, would often go to sleep during the lecture and, if awakened by the lecturer's rising voice, would listen for a while, then stand up in the aisle, shake their heads in disapproval, and stomp noisily out. Some who remained, having listened attentively, would ask quite searching questions, but usually with a vocabulary and imagery that contrasted with the phrasing of the questions asked by the academic or professional people present. The question-and-answer period often grew quite heated but almost never got out of control. Only once did I have to call the police to clear the hall, when a near-riot broke out, and that was occasioned not by such sensitive subjects as communism, pacificism, or atheism, but by a biologist who defended the scientific utility of vivisection. The vivisectionists and the antivivisectionists in the audience went at each other's throats. On one other occasion, when I was giving the lecture, the chairman had to call for help to remove from the platform a member of the audience who had climbed onto the stage to deliver a competing lecture at the same time.

The lectures and discussions at Cooper Union and a similar program at the Ford Hall Forum in Boston carried on the great Chautauqua tradition which had initiated public lectures as a means of general adult education. I don't think that anything like them now exists. For one thing, the lectures were open to the public without any paid admissions or passing of the hat; they were supported by a large number of small contributions to make up a very lean budget of operating expenses. Fifty dollars was the honorarium for lectures, yet the lecturers included an extraordinary range of talent. To name only some of them, who may or may not be known to later generations: Rexford Guy Tugwell, Raymond Weaver, John Cowper Powys, Babette Deutsch, Irwin

Edman, John Mason Brown, Harry Elmer Barnes, Horace Kallen, Karl Llewellyn, Jacques Barzun, Kirsopp Lake, Gardner Murphy, Harry Overstreet, and, in my own immediate circle of friends, Mark Van Doren, Stringfellow Barr, V. J. McGill, and Clifton Fadiman, who also served as secretary of the Lecture Staff.

The audiences included many regulars who came to lecture after lecture and acquired a wide variety of intellectual interests, which were nourished by the suggested readings that were provided. In addition, the regulars gradually learned how to ask good questions, how to respond to the answers, and even how to conduct miniature debates with the lecturer, often aided by interventions on the part of the chairman. Speaking not only for myself but also for Scott Buchanan, Richard Mc-Keon, and Clifton Fadiman, who served as chairmen at Cooper Union, I must say that chairing these meetings taught us a great deal about the discussion method of teaching—how to listen to questions and make as much sense out of them as possible, how to get the lecturer to answer the question instead of passing it off with a witty sally or a polite re-mark, how to maintain relevance, and how to build up, whenever possible, the framework of a debate by highlighting the opposition of contrary opinions and the thrust and counterthrust of opposing arguments.

Debating—intellectually well mannered disputation, not just exhibition of contentiousness, however eloquent or witty—has always seemed to me one of the most educationally rewarding processes, for the participants as well as for their audience. The great theological and philosophical disputations at the universities of Paris, Oxford, and Cambridge in the thirteenth century performed an educational function as important as the lectures, in the strict sense of that term which means the reading of an important text with an elucidating commentary on it. The tradition of debating persists to this day at the two ancient universities of England, where the meetings held at the Oxford and the Cambridge unions constitute what is probably the most important extracurricular activity in which students and faculty engage. It is difficult to assess the educational impact of these schools without referring to the influence of attendance at or participation in the debates conducted regularly during termtime.

Nothing comparable exists in American colleges or universities. Though many of them have debating societies which become involved in intercollegiate competitions, debating is not regarded by most undergraduates as even a minor indoor sport. I find this most regrettable. If every undergraduate could be persuaded to engage in formal debate and acquired the requisite discipline for the task, as well as the measured judgment needed to perform the function of the jury which has to decide whether the affirmative or the negative prevailed, many of the deficiencies of our colleges might be overcome. The benefits would be maximized by having every participant try to uphold the affirmative side on one occasion and the negative on another, particularly if doing so ran counter to some firm prejudice or belief on the participant's part.

I wish I had done more debating in my youth. The little that I did I remember as having been both pleasurable and profitable—a debate with John Storck before the Philosophy Club at Columbia on likeness and difference; a debate about pragmatism with Horace Kallen, who had been a student of William James's; a debate with James Waterman Wise, the rabbi's son, on whether or not Jews should seek to be assimilated into the Gentile society in which they lived; a debate on the popularization of knowledge at the Community Church with John Haynes Holmes, the leading Unitarian minister in New York at the time. In every one of these instances, I regret to say, the position I undertook to defend represented a firmly held conviction on my part. I would have profited much more from having to defend pragmatism instead of attacking it, from having to argue against the assimilation of the Jews instead of arguing for it; from trying to praise instead of depreciating the educational value of popularizations of knowledge, such as the books by Will Durant (about philosophy), Lewis Browne (about religion), and Hendrik Van Loon (about history), concerning each of which I had written vehemently adverse criticisms. Everyone should be able to argue against himself to achieve a more sympathetic understanding of the contrary views, and even, perhaps, to produce a change in one's convictions. I wish I had been required to do this when I was young. I might have changed my mind more quickly about certain matters.

What I have just said is particularly true of the debate in 1927 with John Haynes Holmes in which I took the unpopular—and, in my present judgment, the wrong—side of the issue about the popularization of knowledge. A somewhat shortened transcript of the debate was published in the *Nation*. Reading it, I can understand why the position I took so incensed the audience at the Community Church that Holmes thought it advisable, after an explosive discussion period, to get me out of the church by the back door. The published version of my remarks outraged many readers of the *Nation,* who wrote letters to the editor condemning the stand I took. As I look back at it now, the view I expressed outrages me; it also puzzles me, for it is inconsistent with other things that I stood for at the time.

With everything that John Haynes Holmes said on that occasion I find myself now in wholehearted agreement. "If we believe in the aristocratic theory of society—the subjection of the many to the few—then we will be opposed, as Dr. Adler is opposed, to the popularization of knowledge. We will argue that knowledge is for those who are fit to use it for their own enlightenment and for the guidance of the people." But, Holmes went on, "there are some of us who still believe in democracy," and to them "the popularization of knowledge is as necessary and beneficent as education itself"; first, because "a democratic society can survive—indeed, it can come into being at all—only by giving the people knowledge"; and second, because "the popularization of knowledge is necessary in a democracy because knowledge itself can survive only by diffusing its light among the people. . . . The case for the popularization of knowledge," Holmes concluded, "is one with the case for democracy."

To all of which I now emphatically say Amen! I wish I had had sense enough then, when I was twenty-five, to have understood the soundness of Holmes's position, but then I was an elitist snob who could loftily say—in a tone of voice which must have smacked of insolence—that "popular education seems to be the unfortunate burden of democracy. . . . But the democratic philosophy itself, so insidiously prevalent in current American thought, is far from being above question." I completely confirmed Holmes's association of me with the Platonic contempt for the many, by going on as follows:

> If, instead of assuming that social democracy is the most desirable state of affairs, one made the equally possible postulate of an aristocratic convention, there would be no ground whatsoever upon which popularizations could be praised. Even if they served in some slight manner to improve the great masses of the population, that would be a totally irrelevant and insignificant item. For the great masses would not matter; the intellectual tradition would be properly the possession and the care of the few who, by economic or eugenic good fortune, were capable of the task imposed upon them. Popularizations would be denounced not as socially evil, but merely on aesthetic grounds as ugly, crude, vulgar objects. The aristocrat would not attack them with Comstockian zeal; he would merely consider them with contempt, along with the tabloids and the public prints in general as the shadows which those who are chained within the cave perforce must view.

The passage quoted suggests that I was simply being dialectical, in the sense in which I then conceived being dialectical—entertaining the aristocratic and the democratic points of view as equally possible theories, each resting on its own unprovable assumptions. However, the indications are plentiful that I much preferred looking down my nose at the *polloi*.

It took me some years to get over this addiction to elitism—that is a much more accurate name for it than "aristocracy"—and to convince myself that the preference for democracy had a solid rational foundation. Fifteen years later, I was able to marshal arguments which, in my judgment, demonstrated that constitutional democracy is the most just, indeed the only completely just, form of government, based not on the assumption, but on the self-evident truth, of human equality. From the same premise, and from the meaning of citizenship in a political democracy, it follows that the liberal schooling of all the people, completed by continuous adult learning after school, is the educational obligation that a democratic society must gladly and inventively fulfill.

On both counts, I have not changed my mind since my conversion to democracy—both intellectual and emotional—in the 1940s. On the contrary, all the thinking I have done in political philosophy and in the philosophy of education during the last thirty-five years has both enlarged and fortified my understanding of the political and educational consequences of the essential equality of human beings (all, without any exceptions), regardless of their individual differences in talent and temperament—an equality in kind which overrides the inequality in the degree to which they all possess the common properties of the human species. For many reasons, I wish I had come to this view earlier, for holding it would have been more consistent with the educational projects I helped to promote in the late 1920s—the formation of adult great books seminars and the organization of popular lecture courses and public forums under the auspices of the People's Institute, the very conception of which was essentially democratic.

What puzzles me, as I look back at it now, is why I was so vehemently opposed to the popularization of knowledge at a time when I was so vigorously engaged in popularizing the great books and the great ideas. The only explanation I can give is that I must have felt, somewhat smugly, that *our* kind of popularization (the kind that Everett Dean Martin, Scott Buchanan, Richard McKeon, and I were promoting at the People's Institute) was sound and beneficial, while *their* kind (the kind represented by the current best sellers, such as Durant's *Story of Philosophy*), was misguided and injurious. I say "felt," because at the time I probably did not think clearly enough about the problems of education to realize the inconsistency between my condemnation of the popularization of knowledge and my willingness to try to popularize what I thought I myself knew or understood.

In 1927 Robert M. Hutchins was acting dean of the Yale Law School and professor of the law of evidence. After graduation from Yale College in the same class with Henry Luce and William Benton, he had put himself through the Law School by holding down the job of secretary of the University. In Dean Winternitz of the Medical School, he found a congenial ally for the idea of creating an interdisciplinary project involving the collaboration of the law and medical faculties with professors in the social sciences. His success in raising money for his projected Institute of Human Relations—he obtained a sizeable grant from the Laura Spelman Rockefeller Foundation, of which Beardsley Ruml was then head—must have attracted the attention of C. K. Ogden, who had a nose for money raisers and especially for those who might be interested in unorthodox academic undertakings, such as his own Orthological Institute in London. While in the United States in the early summer of 1927, Ogden paid Hutchins a visit at Yale to discuss what I am sure he described as matters of mutual interest. In the course of their conversation, Hutchins told Ogden of his desire to examine the rules of the law of evidence in the light of relevant considerations from the fields of psychology and logic. This prompted Ogden to mention my name and to give Hutchins page proofs of the opening chapters of *Dialectic*.

That he should have had page proofs of my forthcoming book in his pocket at the time was one coincidence; another was the fact that these pages happened to contain a footnote about legal casuistry as an example of the dialectical process of thought; still another was the use that Ogden made of this footnote, way beyond anything its content justified, to suggest that I might be the very person Hutchins was looking for to work with him on the law of evidence, about which, at the time, I knew absolutely nothing.

The foregoing conjecture of what happened in the meeting between Hutchins and Ogden, I culled from a letter, dated July 15, which I received from the acting dean of the Yale Law School. It read as follows:

> I have learned with much interest from Mr. C. K. Ogden of your work on Dialectic, parts of which he has been kind enough to show me. Mr. Ogden tells me that you are thinking of doing something in Evidence. Since that is my field I am of course much excited that a psychologist, or a philosopher, or a logician should care at all about it. An ordinary lawyer very quickly exhausts the possibilities of his own background in this field and longs for the assistance (which he does not get) of scholars who really know something about the subject. Is there any chance at all that you might be coming up this way during the summer? I am teaching almost every day in the week, so that it is practically impossible for me to get down to New York. I should appreciate it very much if you could manage to run up here sometime—so much so that I should be very glad to contribute to your expenses!

Before being able to arrange a convenient date for a visit to New Haven, I went to the Law School Library at Columbia and took out the five big volumes by J. H. Wigmore on the law of evidence. In the letter which arranged my visit for Friday, August 5, I told Mr. Hutchins that I had been looking into Wigmore on evidence with growing puzzlement and consternation. It seemed to me, I said, that "either there is a job of profound logical clarification to be done, or the law, in its great respect for the practical, is above or below the ministrations of a merely logical busy-body." Hutchins, in reply, expressed his delight that I had been reading Wigmore. "Mr. Wigmore," he wrote, "is the most eminent living or dead authority on Evidence, and the reflections of the logician, psychologist, and philosopher upon him are of the greatest interest to me." Thus assured that I was on the right track, I managed, in the time that remained before my visit, to go through the five volumes of Wigmore, reading carefully his exposition of the principles of the law of evidence and his interpretation of its controlling rules, but ignoring the many pages of smaller type in which he treated in detail the variations on each rule in the forty-eight state jurisdictions and in the federal judicial system. By the time I boarded the train for New Haven, I had a folder full of notes on the logical problems raised by the law of evidence, especially by its requirements concerning relevance.

My experience with deans and other administrative officers at Columbia led me to expect a man of advanced years, portly in appearance, and somberly dressed. Therefore, I dressed in what I thought to be a style suitable to the occasion. I don't know what Hutchins expected me to look like. He at least had the advantage of knowing from Ogden that I was three years younger than he, but I had no reason to suspect that the dean of the Law School would be only twenty-eight years old. When I knocked at the door of the dean's office, expecting it to be opened by a secretary who would usher me into the deanly presence, I was greeted by a handsome young man in white sneakers, white ducks, and a white T-shirt. When I finally stuttered, "I am here to see Mr. Hutchins," I must have done a double take at the response: "That's me. Come in."

His surprise, I learned later, was as great as mine. As he tells the story, he beheld at his door a young man in a double-breasted black suit, with a black hat, carrying a black cane and a black briefcase, and wearing yellow spats. The yellow spats, I believe, were a pardonable invention on his part; to the best of my knowledge I have never worn spats. Nevertheless, the invention had poetic justification, for by contrast to his informal, sparkling whites, I was ridiculously overdressed— an all-black apparition, straight from a funeral parlor.

The initial shock of confrontation was overcome as soon as we started to talk. Bob Hutchins's charm, his wit, his elegance of manner, and his superabundant intelligence made communication easy. His genuine modesty, accompanied by the absence of any academic pretensions, encouraged me to spew forth what I had just recently learned about the law of evidence, of which he was the professor. He made it quite clear that teaching the subject by the case method made it unnecessary for the teacher—or his students—to understand the underlying principles. Though his initial interest had been in the bearing of psychology on the rules of evidence, he did not insist that I deal with that aspect of the subject, nor did he regard my total ignorance of the cases an impediment to my lecturing him on the underlying logic of the rules.

The basic principle that, in the judicial trial of an issue of fact, no evidence is admissible unless it is relevant was simply the legal way of saying that, in assessing the possible answers to a question of fact, consideration should be given only to matters which rendered one or another of the possible answers more or less probable. Irrelevant evidence has no probative force at all; lacking probative force, it cannot affect the probability of the answers in question.

The second fundamental principle of the law of evidence—that relevant evidence is admissible only if it is also both material and competent—introduces considerations that are more legal than logical. The evidence may have probative force, but it may still be inadmissible because what it tends to prove is not legally adjudged to be at issue in the case (and is, therefore, immaterial); or because, though both relevant and material, it is thought to be untrustworthy for some special reason (and it is, therefore, incompetent). As Bob Hutchins pointed out to me, the American trial lawyer, unlike his British counterpart, blunts the cutting edge of these nice distinctions when he tries to prevent opposing counsel from introducing evidence by raising objection after objection, crying out in one breath "Irrelevant, immaterial, and incompetent."

In the course of a conversation that ran on for three hours without pause, Bob Hutchins instructed me in the vagaries of one of the principal exclusionary rules—the one which declares relevant evidence inadmissible on the grounds that it is hearsay, and, therefore, untrustworthy or incompetent. This rule, which excludes hearsay evidence because the credibility of the person making the hearsay utterance cannot be tested by cross-examination in court, as can the statements of witnesses on the stand, has in the course of common law practice, gradually accumulated thirteen or fourteen exceptions. One exception, for example, favors the admissibility of dying declarations on the ground that a person facing death will be inclined to tell the truth; another favors the admissibility of spontaneous exclamations on the ground that the spontaneity of the utterance precludes the time needed to fabricate a falsehood; and so on. Hutchins wondered, quite properly, whether modern psychology might not throw light on these accretions of the law, either by supporting or by challenging the assumptions of the judges who created these exceptions to the rule excluding hearsay. Just as what I had to say about the underlying logic of the law of evidence opened up a new angle of the subject for Hutchins, so his queries about the factual foundation of exceptions to the hearsay rule started me thinking about the psychological aspects of the law.

The interchange between us was so rapid and so effortless that we were startled to find that we had come to five o'clock and that Mrs. Hutchins had come to fetch us home for drinks and dinner. Maude Hutchins was as tall, as lithesome, as impressively handsome as her husband—and, once started, more loquacious. She had been a student at the Yale School of Fine Arts when Bob had been a student in the Law

School. Their marriage was of recent date. As we walked home, she wheeled the pram that carried their infant daughter, Frania. Martinis, both strong and numerous, loosened my tongue, and before dinner was over, conversation took a much more personal turn. Maude was a sculptress; she had been at work in her studio that afternoon; she exuded the pungent scent of the plasticene that she had been modelling. The whiff of this odor produced a state of embarrassed excitement in me, even to the point of my blushing, which, after some stammering and hedging, I finally explained to my host and hostess by telling them the story of Ethel—also a sculptress, also exuding a similar scent. By the time that Bob put me on the train for New York, I felt as if I had known the Hutchinses all my life, and they certainly knew more about me than was called for by a consultation on the law of evidence.

The immediate consequences of that Friday in New Haven were many and various; the ultimate consequences changed the whole course of my life. Before the summer was over, Bob Hutchins offered me a Sterling Fellowship in the Law School, but though I found myself greatly attracted by the offer which meant our working together on the law of evidence, I was still an unregenerate New Yorker. I could not bring myself to leave the big city to live in a sleepy little village like New Haven. Unable to persuade me, Bob proceeded to promote his project of nonlegal studies of the law of evidence in another way. He engaged Donald Slesinger to work with him in New Haven and he came down to the Columbia Law School and persuaded its dean, Young B. Smith, to engage me to work with Jerome Michael, who was teaching the law of evidence there. The plan envisioned two teams—one at Yale, one at Columbia—working in collaboration. Hutchins and Slesinger chose the exceptions to the hearsay rule as their province and in the course of the next few years produced and published three articles that Michael and I were consulted about while they were in their draft stages.

The initial project that Michael and I undertook to work on concerned the law's willingness to admit testimony about a person's habitual behavior to indicate the probability on a given occasion of specific acts in conformity with his habits, but its unwillingness to regard a person's character as being at all relevant to the question of how he probably acted on a particular occasion. (For example, a witness acquainted with the plaintiff in an accident case is allowed to testify that the plaintiff always stopped, looked, and listened at a railway crossing, and the jury is allowed to infer his having the habit of doing so and then from the habit to infer that, on the particular occasion when the accident occurred, he probably acted as he was in the habit of doing when he came to the railroad crossing and so was not contributorily negligent. But the law will not permit a witness acquainted with the plaintiff to testify that he has the reputation in the community of being a man of prudent and cautious character, on the grounds that a man's character does not provide the jury with the basis for an inference to how he acted on a particular occasion, as evidence concerning his habits does.)

We produced an extensive draft of an article on the habit and character rule, which we submitted to the Yale team; but for reasons that I cannot remember, we never brought our essay on the subject to the point of publication. It may have been because my discussion of the law of evidence with Jerome Michael so frequently turned away from psychological considerations to the logical problems that we both found so fascinating.

Jerome Michael, educated at the University of Georgia, had been as untouched by philosophical thought and by logical analysis as Hutchins had been in his years as a Yale undergraduate. Three years at law school had not alleviated their innocence. Like Bob Hutchins, Jerome was an apt and docile inquirer, much slower than Hutchins as a learner but, at the same time, a much more patient and persistent student, coming back to the same question again and again until he felt reasonably sure that he really understood the point under discussion. His avidity for knowledge beyond the law, his desire to get at the fundamentals no matter how far from the law the inquiry had to be pushed, brought all my instincts as a teacher and all my pedagogical ploys into play, though I must also confess that the pedestrian pace that he imposed on the process by his insistence on taking no steps forward that were not sure-footed, sorely tried my patience, of which, temperamentally, I have very little.

Out of these discussions with Jerome Michael emerged three long essays, only one of which was published, and a large book that the Law School made available for students in the course on the law of evidence. Both of the published works on which Michael and I collaborated —the essay "The Trial of an Issue of Fact" and the book *The Nature of Judicial Proof*—were completed after I left Columbia and went to the University of Chicago. During those early years in Chicago, I returned to New York frequently to carry on my collaboration with Jerome, and spent almost every summer there, working at the Columbia Law School. The book became known in legal circles as the hieroglyphics of Michael and Adler on evidence, because the logical analysis that it made of the steps of proof in a judicial inquiry concerning matters of fact was set forth in an idiosyncratic symbolism that I had needlessly invented and employed. The analysis itself was quite precise and rigorous; it did not need the look of mathematical logic to gild the lily. Generations of Columbia law students, under Professor Michael's relentless tutelage, acquired the knack of reading the symbols and even of using them, but I doubt if anyone outside of Jerome's classes ever made the unaided effort to read the book. The essay we wrote, "The Trial of an Issue of Fact," made that unnecessary. Published in two issues of the *Columbia Law Review*, it expounded the analysis we had developed, without the use of symbols or even much logical jargon. It remains for me a piece of writing—and thinking—to which I would be willing to sign my name today without a stroke of revision. That is more than I can say of most of the things I wrote in those early years.

Of the two essays that did not get a reading outside the confines of Professor Michael's office, one attempted to draw a detailed comparison between the method used by a judicial tribunal to determine the most tenable answer to a question of fact and the method of an experimental scientist in selecting the most tenable among a number of competing hypotheses. I am sure that many of my analogies between what goes on in a courtroom trial by jury and what goes on in the laboratory of an experimental physicist or chemist were farfetched, but writing that essay and submitting it to Jerome's critical scrutiny corrected inaccurate impressions I had formed about judicial procedure and improved my understanding of the experimental method. In the course of reading my manuscript, Jerome would often spend a day on little more than a page or two, asking question after question that pushed our discussion into philosophical nooks and crannies to which I had not given the slightest thought when I wrote the sentence or paragraph from which he took off. As a result, the series of lectures on reason and experience in the law which I subsequently gave at the People's Institute presented a much clearer and more accurate picture than the original essay which Jerome had torn apart, leaving me to put the pieces together again.

The other unpublished essay did not receive the same treatment. Jerome may have read it, but we did not spend hours in his office on a line-by-line examination of it. I had collected a number of theoretical or quasi-philosophical works on the law of evidence, the most recent of which was Wigmore's *Principles of Judicial Proof, As Given by Logic, Psychology, and General Experience*. It had been preceded by J. R. Gulson's *Philosophy of Proof*, James Bradley Thayer's *Preliminary Treatise on the Law of Evidence*, Sir James Fitzjames Stephen's *Digest of the Law of Evidence*, and Jeremy Bentham's *Rationale of Judicial Evidence*, which, as I recalled from John Stuart Mill's autobiography, the teenage Mill had helped to prepare for publication. There was even an earlier eighteenth-century treatise, the title of which I do not remember. Reading these works strung out over three centuries gave me the idea of writing a history of the theory of proof underlying the law of evidence, calling attention to the influence exerted by the then current notions in logic and the theory of knowledge.

Scott and Miriam Buchanan had invited Helen and me to spend the summer of 1929 with them in a house they had rented in Connecticut at Cornwall Hollow, on a hillside just opposite the hill on which Mark and Dorothy Van Doren had staked out a sizeable domain, not only for a summer residence but also for a more permanent future retreat from the city. Just across the road from the Buchanan house was a large barn. That was to be the Adler abode, combining a bedroom and a study for me. I transported books, typewriter, and files from New York, but decided to buy a large unpainted wooden table in nearby Torrington to serve as my desk. In my anxiety to get a table large enough, I overdid it. The table I bought, four feet by eight, was much too large to work at comfortably. I could not decide at which end to sit, where to place my books, how to lay out my work. I spent hours fidgeting at that oversized table, readjusting the things on it in patterns that repeated themselves, none of them satisfactorily. That, combined with the fact that I found quite unnerving the stillness of the country, broken only by the drone of crickets and the buzz of horseflies, induced a mental paralysis that made writing impossible. For many days, going over to the barn after breakfast with the Buchanans, I sat at the typewriter, hour after hour, staring glassy-eyed at a piece of white paper which remained as blank when I pulled it out of the machine as when I put it in.

I finally gave up, and took to the hammock instead of the typewriter, lying for hours in a state of brooding self-pity, fiercely defying the efforts of all concerned to shake me out of it. I must have been a pain in the neck to the Buchanans and the Van Dorens, not to mention my wife. At last a bright idea occurred to me. Why not pack up all my gear and go back to our hot, dusty, and noisy flat in New York and to my own desk, where I would surely be able to do the writing that rural quiet and a gargantuan table had inhibited me from doing? I did precisely that to good effect. Less than ten days after my return to the city (without Helen), I had completed a forty-thousand-word essay on the development of the theory of judicial proof. Still enough of the summer remained for me to return to Cornwall for a vacation and for conversations with Scott about a book that we were collaborating on. The gargantuan table, I should add, I bequeathed to the Van Dorens, who turned it into a Ping-Pong table on which the two Van Doren boys, Charles and John, learned to play the game.

The book that Scott Buchanan and I contemplated co-authoring bore the working title "The Religion of Science: Scientific Apologetics." What started us off were the Gifford Lectures, in which eminent scientists such as Arthur Eddington, James Jeans, and J. S. Haldane, exceeded their competence as scientists to pontificate about matters metaphysical and theological. The book was to consist of essays, some written by Scott and some by me, on the aforementioned Gifford Lectures, as well as on Percy Bridgman, Ernst Cassirer, Alfred North Whitehead, and John Dewey. Each of us wrote one or two essays, but we never finished the book. Instead, we used the work we had done together to give jointly a series of lectures on scientific apologetics at the People's Institute.

That summer in Cornwall was, for both Scott and me, a first experience in communal living. Our wives managed to stand the strain of it better than we did. Though Scott and I had much in common philosophically, especially our admiration for Plato, Aristotle, and Kant and our dissatisfaction with contemporary scientism and pragmatism, we were temperamentally poles apart. His mind was constantly reaching for all-embracing analogies that would reveal the underlying unifying similarities among apparently dissimilar and conflicting things. Mine always tried to spell out in painstaking detail the differences that distinguished even closely similar things from one another. Our friend Dick McKeon coined the words *holoscopic* and *merescopic* to name the opposite Platonic and Aristotelian turns of mind that Scott and I exhibited. Scott's mind soared, jumping from insight to insight without touching the ground between the peaks on which it alighted. Mine moved at a pedestrian pace, stumbling over little obstacles in the terrain and trying to smooth them out so that the whole surface would be covered snugly by a closely-knit network of analysis. In addition, my conversational technique with Scott involved asking question after question, much as Jerome Michael had done with me—to my annoyance, I must admit. Scott responded to my persistent questioning by flashes of wit, by making arcane remarks that had the appearance of jokes, and even by forms of teasing that I found hard to take. If my questions drove him to desperation, he increased the frenzy of my interrogations by his evasiveness, and left me uncomfortably baffled when, on the rare occasions when he did answer a question, he said something that sounded profoundly true but which I could not translate into any terms in my own philosophical vocabulary—the only way I know of being sure that you really do understand what the other fellow is trying to say.

That September Scott took up his post as professor of philosophy at the University of Virginia. In a letter that he wrote me from Charlottesville in October, he did a postmortem on our summer in Cornwall together. I quote a passage from it at length, not only because it throws light on what had happened during the many hours that we wrangled across the table with each other from breakfast through lunch and until dinner (our wives removing one set of dishes and replacing them with another without disturbing us), but also because it reveals the remarkable phenomenon of Scott Buchanan so much better than I can describe it.

> Communal living is such a serious matter that it requires the most delicate and refined instrumentation; it requires omniscience and omnipotence, both of which are beyond human limitations. Therefore, nothing in it can be taken seriously without serious damage. It needs a religion to draw off

the passions, or a sense of humor to humor the passions. You, for one reason or another, began the summer seriously and I found myself the victim
of an inquisition. I tried to escape by systematic pursuit of the obviously
trivial. It was all good fun—for me—until I realized that it was not the
kind of game that you wanted to play. Among other things, it made you
trivial, too. The rest of the summer I wavered between trying to find something that both of us could take seriously, and finding some private modus
vivendi that would be neutral as far as you and I were concerned. I think
this explains the distance that you felt between my values and yours—mine
were assumed for the communal comedy, and couldn't be shaken off when
I wanted to get rid of them later. I was so clumsy that I was just nasty in
the end. This, of course, is reasoning after the fact; I didn't know what
was happening this summer. The worst of it is that I don't know yet what
I could have done to make myself clear. I've done this same thing before,
and I don't seem to learn from the experience. I realize the futility of taking the value of humor seriously, but I haven't yet found out how to take it
humorously. The problem is the problem of types, the humor of humor. Of
course, the conclusion is that I have no sense of humor, and the fact that
I find it a problem is the proof of the conclusion. There is something
wrong with this tragicomic metaphysics. Tell me, O Mr. Dialectician, what
the trouble is.

Despite its pains and misunderstandings, on both sides, that summer
in Cornwall left no lasting scars. Dick McKeon and I drove down to
Charlottesville during Scott's first year at the University of Virginia to
give lectures before the local Philosophy Club, as well as to carry on
the three-sided conversations that we had enjoyed so much in New York,
conversations in which Dick persisted in trying to explain Scott's position to me, and mine to Scott, to nobody's satisfaction but his own.
Over the next five or six years, as long as Scott remained in Charlottesville, I visited him frequently, sometimes with Dick McKeon, sometimes
alone, usually to give a formal lecture at the university, but always re-
lentlessly in pursuit of a goal that I sought with passionate persistence—
a meeting of minds that could be registered in a series of precise propositions to which both Scott and I would subscribe without reservation or
qualification. That consummation, however devoutly wished by me,
was never to happen, either in the Virginia years, or in the year Scott
spent at the University of Chicago as a member of the Committee on
Liberal Arts, or in the many years thereafter when he became dean of
St. John's College in Annapolis, Maryland, and our interminable conversations continued when I went there as a visiting lecturer.

One other involvement with the Law School at Columbia was to
have consequences later at the University of Chicago. My conversations
with Jerome Michael ranged beyond the law of evidence to general
questions in jurisprudence and to the techniques of legal scholarship and
the art of teaching law. It occurred to me that both legal research and

legal pedagogy might be improved if the members of the law faculty
had not come to their jobs solely from training in a law school—training aimed principally, if not exclusively, at proficiency in the practice
of the law. Might not fresh winds blow through the law school corridors, I asked Jerome and other members of the Columbia law faculty,
if the law school were to give fellowships to advanced graduate students
in mathematics and the exact sciences, with a view to persuading them
to bring their special skills to the study of law? Some of these, who had
developed a serious interest in law and acquired knowledge of it, might
then be invited to join the faculty. This would leaven the faculty and
might result in significant advances in legal research. The response to
this suggestion was, to my surprise, affirmative, but with reservations.
Dean Smith suggested that the proposed procedure be reversed—that
top-ranking law students be given, upon graduation, fellowships to pursue studies in other academic disciplines, and when they had become
competent in other techniques of research, they might be invited to return to the Law School and become members of the faculty.

To the best of my knowledge, neither my proposal nor Dean Smith's
modification of it was ever adopted so far as cross-fertilization between
law and the exact sciences was concerned; but the idea did take effect,
with remarkable results, in the wedding of law with the social or behavioral sciences at the law schools of Yale, Columbia, and Chicago. The
original seed had been sown by Hutchins at Yale with the establishment
of the Institute of Human Relations, which brought the Law School
into contact with the social sciences. "Cross-fertilization" became the
slogan of the advanced law schools that added economists, sociologists,
statisticians, and accountants to their faculties.

With regard to the teaching of law, as opposed to legal research, another proposal emerged from our discussions at the Columbia Law
School. I cannot recall whether the proposal was mine or someone
else's, but it was generally agreed that it might be enlightening to the
faculty if an outsider—someone trained in another discipline and with
no interest in becoming a practicing member of the bar—were to attend all the first-year courses in the Law School as an observer of teaching methods, and then, at the end of the year, submit a critical appraisal
of the pedagogy to the faculty as a whole. The Law School obtained
a grant-in-aid from the Social Science Research Council for this purpose, and since I was near at hand and available, I became the guinea
pig for the experiment. When I accepted the job (in addition to all the
other things I was doing in 1929–1930), I did not foresee the difficulties
that would confront me when it came to writing the report at the end
of the year—a report in which I would have to exercise more tact than
I normally possess.

The three courses I attended that year were the basic bread-and-butter courses for future practitioners: Torts, taught by Dean Smith; Contracts, taught by Karl Llewellyn; and Real Property, taught by Richard B. Powell. I must confess that I so enjoyed the experience of learning what I could about these subjects that, half the time, I forgot the purpose for which I was there. This being my first acquaintance with the style of teaching that pervades professional schools, the antics of the law professors amused me. The somewhat sadistic trick of saying to the students at the opening session of the course "Turn your head to the left; now turn your head to the right; at least one of the two men you have just looked at will not be here at graduation time" is merely one example of the many devices employed to keep the professional student on his toes. The one that I recall most vividly, because it seemed to me both wittier and more effective than the others, was used by Dean Smith. Instruction by the case method normally proceeds by calling on the students to answer very specific questions about the case under consideration. The professor never lectures, never expounds the principles of the law or explains the rules. One morning Dean Smith departed from his usual procedure the moment he assumed the rostrum. He lectured for twenty minutes without pause. Every student in the class frantically took notes, heads down, pencils scurrying. Suddenly the dean stopped and silence reigned. With that, pencils stopped and heads came up to attention. The dean waited for every head to come up, and then he said: "Gentlemen, tear out from your notebooks all the pages on which you have written what I said. Everything I said was wrong."

At the end of the year, I submitted to the dean, for transmittal to the faculty, a report entitled "Some Aspects of First Year Work in the Columbia Law School." In addition to specific comments on the teaching techniques of the three professors I had observed, my chief constructive recommendation consisted in a criticism of the case method of teaching law. However effective it may be in the training of future practitioners, it is certainly not designed to give the student an understanding of the underlying principles and the nonlegal context of the legal subjects he is studying. If the law is to be a genuinely learned profession, then lawyers should be more learned about the law than instruction by the case method can equip them to be. I did not realize how much law students are dominated by the bar examination, which accredits them as practitioners of the law, not as members of a learned profession in my sense of that term. This is so much the case that Bob Hutchins was later to propose the creation of a university law school designed primarily for the study of the law as an intellectual subject matter and as one of the basic human institutions, a law school only incidentally concerned with the bread-and-butter courses that prepared students for the bar examinations.

In the closing pages of my report, I reverted to the idea of cross-fertilization between law and other disciplines, by means of which hybrid scholars might be produced, now, however, restricting my plan of hybridization to the social sciences, with the possible addition of philosophy and logic. Prof. Karl Llewellyn, in writing a response to my report, endorsed this recommendation and suggested that Columbia join with Yale and Chicago in carrying it out. (One paragraph of his commentary, concerned with ways of improving legal writing and argumentation, referred to "one recent graduate student who had a lively interest in training men for argument and expression. Wayne Morse was, I believe, his name." The reference was to the future senator from Oregon.) I also received a gracious letter from Dean Smith, written from Paris, in which he accepted my description of his own teaching as accurate and my criticism of it as sound. Most of the letter was devoted to my concluding suggestion about cross-fertilization and hybridization, and developed at length the modifications of it that I have already mentioned.

All these early thoughts about the study of law and legal education were to exert an influence on discussions I had with my colleagues after I became, under extraordinary circumstances, a member of the law faculty at the University of Chicago. Bob Hutchins, from whom I absorbed many of these ideas by a process of osmosis, pushed them much further than I did after he left Yale and became president of the university. Under a succession of progressive-minded deans, among whom the most effective as a reformer of the Law School was Edward Levi, later president of the university and attorney general of the United States, the Chicago Law School became a model of education in the law as a truly learned profession. My work with Jerome Michael on evidence was to bear fruit in a somewhat different fashion. I taught a seminar on the law of evidence with Judge Hinton. The judge, who was from Missouri, would sit by silently, smiling blandly and nodding his head, while I went to the blackboard and covered it with the Michael-Adler hieroglyphics to explain a step in judicial proof or procedure. When I had finished, the judge would always sum it all up by telling an apt story drawn from his experience on the bench. I do not to this day know how he always managed to make the story so apt, for I was under the impression that he did not understand my logical high jinks at the blackboard.

During those last years at Columbia, many letters passed between Bob Hutchins and me, those he wrote me always addressed "Dear Doctor." I do not know whether that was simply a humorous acknowledgment of my claim to being a scholar of sorts or an oblique reminder that I had not yet earned the title. The reminder I did not need. It came in no uncertain terms from Professor Poffenberger, head of the Psychology Department in which I had been teaching since 1923. Poff

said, gently but firmly: "Mortimer, you've been around now for almost
five years. It's about time you got your Ph.D." That meant finishing a
piece of "experimental" research, writing a dissertation, and defending
it in the final oral examination that all doctoral candidates had to go
through. Some years earlier, I had passed the preliminary written examinations, which consisted mainly in a day-long ordeal of answering
questions about every aspect of the science of psychology—its history
and its present state.

In earlier pages, I may have given the impression that psychology as
a subject was of little interest to me. Far from it! The study of the human mind and of human nature was from the beginning and always has
remained one of my main interests and a field in which I have done a
great deal of thinking, lecturing, and writing. What bored me or irked
me, because I thought it so often trivial and insignificant, was the so-
called "experimental science" of psychology, whether the experimental
work was done in line with the structuralist, or introspective, approach
represented by Wundt at Leipzig and Titchener at Cornell, the be-
haviorist approach of Watson at Johns Hopkins, the functionalist approach of Angell at Chicago and Yale, or the dynamic school of psychology that had been developed at Columbia under Woodworth. The
theoretical framework and the conceptual apparatus of these various
schools did not seem to me adequate to the task of understanding the
nature of man and the acts of the human mind, nor did their experiments do anything but confirm this inadequacy.

The very fact that the science of psychology was divided into conflicting schools of thought showed, as Professor Boring pointed out, that
psychology had not resolved its ambiguous relation to philosophy. That,
after all, was the focus of my deep interest in the subject: the philosophy
of man and of the human mind—philosophical, not experimental or
scientific, anthropology and psychology. Nevertheless, I was sufficiently
diligent as a student to have passed with flying colors the written examination covering the various contemporary schools of psychological
thought. Only one of the books I studied for that examination stands
out as a work worth reading again and again—William James's two-
volume *Principles of Psychology*—and it is included in *Great Books of
the Western World* precisely for that reason. The writings of Freud
are also included; I had begun reading his books and papers early in
my career, but in the 1920s, academic psychologists ostracized Freud.
There was no mention of him or his work in the preliminary Ph.D.
examination.

The work I had done as an undergraduate in neurophysiology, and
the wider reading I had subsequently done in physiological psychology,
together with the questions raised by the James-Lange theory of the
emotions, determined the direction of my first efforts to do the laboratory

research required for a Ph.D. To collaborate in this research, I was fortunate in having a classmate, George Schoonhoven, who was well trained in physiology. We proposed to test the hypothesis that the emotions fell into two main groups according to their affective tone—the unpleasant emotions of fear and anger on the one hand, and the pleasant emotions of hunger and sex on the other. Since, according to the James-Lange theory, the emotions consist in widespread bodily changes, we proposed to measure the physiological reactions that occurred simultaneously when, under laboratory conditions, we induced fear and anger, or hunger and sex. The pupillometer that Arthur Rubin had used for his Ph.D. research was still available. Schoonhoven rigged up the pupillometer so that we could take a continuous reading of pupillary dilations and contractions and register them on the smoked surface of a moving kymograph. The subject was hitched up to the pupillometer in a small room that had to be absolutely dark for the purpose. A sphygmomanometer was attached to his chest to register changes in respiration on the kymograph; electrodes were attached to his wrists to register psychogalvanic changes; the apparatus needed to measure blood pressure was attached to his arm, and a blood sugar test to measure adrenaline discharge was made at the end of the experiment.

On the physiological side, the hypothesis being tested involved a division of the emotions into two groups of visceral reactions—the unpleasant and relatively intense emotions consisting of reactions innervated by the thoracico-lumbar segments of the sympathetic nervous system, the pleasant and milder emotions consisting of reactions innervated by the cranio-sacral segments: the first group of bodily changes would include pupillary dilation, accelerated respiration, heightened blood pressure and blood sugar, positive psychogalvanic response, and so on. Supposedly, the milder, pleasant emotions would involve an opposite set of bodily changes. To test this, we first had our subjects—all students in my experimental psychology class—suffer anger, shock, and fear. Anger was produced by my kicking the subject's shin under the table on which the pupillometer stood; shock by Schoonhoven's firing off a revolver behind his head; and fear by wrapping around his neck a young boa constrictor which George had borrowed from the zoology lab, the extremities of which he held firmly in his hands.

Up to this point the experiment was a great success. The kick on the shin, the revolver shot, and the cold coils of the boa constrictor all elicited the same set of violent physiological reactions, as we expected. The visceral content of fear and anger appeared to be exactly the same state of excitement and stress. If there is any difference in the psychological content of these two intense emotions, it must lie in the cognitive and conative contexts—what is being perceived and what impulses the perceptions set in motion, recoiling and running away from what is perceived as dangerous, as contrasted with aggressive behavior toward what is perceived as aggressive. If hunger and sex are emotions of a different sort from fear and anger, not only should their impulses to action be different, but their visceral content should also be different. In putting that part of the hypothesis to the test, we faced the difficulty of inducing the appropriate emotions under controlled laboratory conditions. For sex, I persuaded the students who volunteered as subjects to bring to the darkroom some girl with whom they had established at least a minimal degree of intimacy. When George had strapped the subject to all the pieces of apparatus that we used, I instructed the young lady to enter the darkroom and engage in mild forms of fondling accompanied by affectionate speech. The only result we obtained was embarrassment on the part of the subject, hardly mild, and the recorded visceral reactions were the same as those of fear and anger. A similar thing happened when we tried hunger by asking the subjects to starve themselves in the twenty-four hours before they came to the darkroom. Then, after they were strapped up, we passed a hot cup of coffee and a redolent bacon and tomato sandwich under their nostrils, only to elicit pain and anger on their part, the frustration, not the satisfaction, of hunger.

We should have known, of course, that it was impossible at that time to measure the visceral pattern of satisfied sex or hunger under laboratory conditions. In the case of sex, that is no longer the case. My guess at the time was that the visceral content is exactly the same in all violent emotional excitement, whether the emotion is called fear, anger, or sexual passion by the person experiencing it. It is experienced differently because of the differing perceptions and the differing impulses to which they give rise. I wish we could have tested that conjecture; but in addition to difficulties that we did not know how to surmount, George Schoonhoven fell ill, and we could not go on with our work together. We made a preliminary report on our findings, and that won us membership in Sigma Psi, the equivalent of Phi Beta Kappa for graduate students in the laboratory sciences.

When, to the great sorrow of all his friends, George died of cancer, I decided not to go on alone to complete the work we had begun. That left a hole to be filled. A few years later, I hit upon an easier piece of research to do for the Ph.D. It would be empirical, if not experimental in the laboratory sense of that term; it would involve tests and measurements, and it would call for statistical computations and graphs—all the paraphernalia needed for a dissertation in the Psychology Department at that time. Professors Abbott and Trabue, at Teachers College, had constructed a "poetry appreciation" test by taking verses written by Shelley, Keats, Wordsworth, or Tennyson, and spoiling each in three different ways, one version spoiling the meter, one spoiling the rhyming scheme, one spoiling the sense. The original and the three spoiled versions were then submitted to students to number in the order of their preference—from most liked to least liked. By testing groups of students, different in age, in intelligence, or in scholastic background, correlations might be obtained between these factors and the appreciation of excellence in poetry. That, at least, was the theory behind the work of Abbott and Trabue, and since it was then regarded as a competent piece of psychometric research, I saw no reason why I could not submit a similar piece of research for my Ph.D., substituting music for poetry in the construction of the tests.

Douglas Moore was then a young instructor in the Music Department in Columbia, and when I told him my idea at a Faculty Club luncheon one day, he volunteered to produce the musical equivalent of the Abbott and Trabue poetry test. Gifted composer that he was, he easily turned out amusingly spoiled versions of passages from musical classics —one version spoiled by being made musically dull, a second by being made musically sentimental, and a third by being made musically chaotic. Douglas Moore constructed two series of tests, in the first of which the originals to be spoiled were drawn from Chopin, Bach, Beethoven, and Wagner; and in the second of which he used Mozart, Rameau, Brahms, Weber, and Chopin. In addition, he persuaded friends of his at the Aeolian Company to record his playing of these pieces of music on duo-art piano rolls that I could use on the aeolian player piano. The Aeolian Company obligingly sent one of their player pianos around to the various schools and colleges in the metropolitan area, at which I had permission to conduct the tests.

Over a period of two years, I accumulated a vast pile of raw data in the form of test results. All that remained was to score the papers on which students had registered their preferences, work out statistical correlations of the results with other supposedly relevant factors, construct tables and charts, and write the dissertation itself. I found myself either too busy or too bored to do much of this busy work, so I hired two of my students to do the scoring and my sister, Carolyn, who had graduated from Barnard and was working for her own Ph.D. under Professor Boas in the Department of Anthropology, to do the necessary statistical computations. A girl who had been a classmate of my wife at Barnard and was now working with her at R. H. Macy's department store volunteered to construct the graphs or charts that an orthodox Ph.D. dissertation had to include in order to look right. As for the dissertation itself, I had examined so many of them that I knew exactly how one had to be written: an introductory chapter stating the problem, followed by a description of the method and the materials devised to solve it; then a series of chapters summarizing the findings, accompanied by tables, charts, and graphs; finally, a chapter or two stating the writer's interpretations of his findings and the conclusions he could draw from them. Once all the data was in hand and the statistical work had been done, there would be no difficulty in writing the dissertation. In fact, I did it in twenty hours at the typewriter, turning out seventy-seven pages between 9:00 A.M. one day and 5:00 A.M. the next.

Before I tell the rest of the story, I must confess that I had little or no interest in this Ph.D. project; in fact, little or no interest in getting a Ph.D. I had not yet read William James's telling attack on the Ph.D. octopus in American institutions of higher learning, but if I had been acquainted with it at the time, I would have given it to Professor Poffenberger as expressing my reasons for not thinking it necessary to get a Ph.D. I had been teaching the subject for five years and had demonstrated in the preliminary written examination my knowledge of it. Why did I need to do some trivial piece of research, have it published, and get awarded a Ph.D. for it in order either to go on teaching or to win advancement in rank and increase in salary? I realize, of course, that Poff would have listened to me patiently, been tolerant of my complaints against the system, but he would also have told me that I had to do it whether I liked it or not. He was so insistent on my conforming to the requirements that he even conspired to help me conform by maneuvering enough credits on my graduate school record to fulfill the course requirements (I had cut some of the graduate courses that I had registered for, and so received only attendance credit for them, which was not sufficient for the purpose).

In addition, I had never taken the examinations in French and German which were among the requirements for a Ph.D. in psychology at Columbia. On this score, I must confess a profound disinclination on my part to become competent in foreign languages. I had passed my French courses in college, but I did nothing to maintain or improve my ability to read that language. I began the study of German, but found its irregular verbs and its peculiar word order so annoying that I gave it up. The secretary of the Psychology Department, a few months before my oral examination, called my attention to the fact that my records showed that I had not passed my qualifying examinations in French and German. She, too, was willing to conspire, and said she would not mention this to Professor Poffenberger if he did not specifically ask her a question about it.

The morning of the oral examination finally came. It was held in the Trustees Room in Low Library and attended by four professors from my own department, together with three or four from other departments. The dissertation I had submitted bore the title "The Experimental Measurement of the Appreciation of Music." Professor Woodworth sat at the head of the long conference table, chairman of the meeting. He opened it by a startled exclamation as he looked at the matriculation parchment in front of him, which contained the candidate's record. "The candidate," he said with a smile, as if it could not possibly be true, "does not seem to have passed his French and German examinations." Then, with another, even gentler, smile he added: "Let's do something about that here and now. You, Professor Garrett, ask him a question in German, and you, Professor Lecky, ask him a question in French." Garrett asked me what time it was, and I replied, *"Zehn Uhr"*; Lecky asked me how I felt, and I replied, *"Très bien"*; and Woodworth, with a final smile of benign content, said, "Examination passed!"

Since I felt that the dissertation itself was not worth two full hours of questioning, I diverted the attention of the examiners from it by proposing a theory of pleasure and displeasure in the aesthetic experience. The theory contended that pain had no sensory opposite, and that displeasure was not the opposite of pain, but the opposite of pleasure as an affective response that had no specific sensory basis. I argued for this contention on the physiological grounds that we have specific nerve endings for pain, but none for pleasure. The theory was novel enough not only to get everyone's attention, but also to set my examiners to quarreling among themselves about it. This used up most of the two hours, and after returning to the Board Room, which I had been asked to leave while my examiners discussed the merits of my dissertation and its defense, I was told that I had passed but that my examiners recommended that the title of the dissertation be changed to "Music Appreciation: An Experimental Approach to Its Measurement." It was published under that title as Number 110 in the *Archives of Psychology*, edited by Professor Woodworth, and its preface expressed, not fully enough, my debt to all the persons who did the real work on it—Douglas Moore who wrote the music, the technician at the Aeolian Company who made the recordings, two students of mine, Richard Fitch and Sigmund Timberg, who scored the papers and tabulated the results, and, last but not least, my sister Carolyn, who did or supervised the statistical computations, graphs, and charts.

That morning in April 1929, when I finished writing the dissertation a little before 5:00 A.M., I did not go to bed, but lay down for a brief nap until the morning milk and paper arrived. While breakfasting, I looked at the *New York Times* and, on the first page of the second section, found the announcement that Robert Maynard Hutchins had just been elected president of the University of Chicago at the age of thirty. I can recall vividly the thought that jumped into my head the moment after I felt a surge of exuberant gaiety at this announcement. Why, I asked myself, had I drudged through this tiresome Ph.D. business when it might no longer be necessary for me to have that union card for academic advancement? Then, almost as quickly, I remembered the repeated salutation "Dear Doctor" in the letters Bob Hutchins had written me. I might just as well go ahead and justify the epithet, even if I regarded it as having little significance.

Chapter 7

The Young Rush In

THAT MORNING in late April 1929, when I learned of the appointment of Robert Maynard Hutchins as president of the University of Chicago at the age of thirty, I sent him a wire. It consisted solely of the punch line of a joke that I mistakenly thought I had told him—"Some son of a bitch, I'll take pie!" Bob replied by return mail: "The Western Union balled up your telegram so badly that I shall have to see you to find out what it said. Meanwhile, I shall take it to mean congratulations. If it signifies anything else, let me know. We ought to have a talk sometime. Tell me when we can get together."

During the following weeks, the public prints indulged in a wide variety of comments on "the boy President of the University of Chicago," most of them a mixture of amazement and applause. I quote from one that appeared in the *Nation* on May 8.

> To be in succession a graduate of Yale College, secretary of Yale University, professor of law, dean of the Yale Law School, and now president of one of the country's largest universities—all in less than a decade in the life of one person—must be as dizzying a progress viewed from the inside as it seems kaleidoscopic from without. Mr. Hutchins has paused long enough as dean of the Law School, however, to give us some idea of what turns his energies take when they radiate from a relatively fixed point. He has been one of the most audible spokesmen for the renovation of the university law school in the direction of making it a graduate and research institution rather than a mere preparation for bar examinations. Toward this end he not only forcibly changed the curriculum at Yale, reduced the number of students, and brought economists, sociologists, and psychologists into the law faculty, but he has even had time genuinely to participate in some of these researches, in the field of evidence. There is good reason to doubt, however, that Mr. Hutchins's future services will be directed to-

ward scholarship. His capacity for high-powered organization, such as the recently founded Institute of Human Relations, his zest for all the academic intrigue and machination required to put such "big ideas" across, is so great that it seems to outrun his interest in the schemes themselves—whatever be their merit. His ability to raise money and to wangle his way through the most intricate academic politics certainly recommends him for his new office.

That is the way it must have looked at the time; I had no reason to think otherwise. Only from the vantage point of retrospection, many years removed, can I now see how far from the truth the *Nation* was in attributing to Bob Hutchins a "zest for all the academic intrigue and machination" and an "ability to wangle his way through the most intricate academic politics." He had more than enough intelligence and energy to play the game of academic politics, but he was too young and, therefore, too inexperienced in that arena to play it well. In addition, his youthful impetuosity and impatience found all delays irksome; his superabundant intelligence, habituated to being as reasonable as possible, sought to bring things about by rational persuasion rather than by intrigue or machination. He wanted to build Rome in a day and he felt that if he openly laid a well-designed blueprint on the table for his colleagues to examine, they would, with equal frankness, either tell him how to improve the plan or else enthusiastically cooperate in carrying it out. He had not learned from his brief experience as dean of the Yale Law School that professors do not operate that way, least of all when their vested interests are threatened.

My initial efforts to collaborate with the new president of the University of Chicago did not help him. On the contrary, my very first suggestion to him led him to make one of the most disastrous mistakes of the early years of his administration, and one from which he—and I—never fully recovered. I was younger than he, twenty-seven, even less experienced in academic politics (I had shown very little taste or tact for it in my dealings with the Philosophy Department at Columbia), and equally, if not more, impetuous and impatient. Even more than Bob, I felt that if good reasons could be advanced for a proposal, the only ground for not pushing it forward would have to be better reasons against it.

I cannot now recall when I made the fatal suggestion to Bob Hutchins. In a letter of May 29, Bob referred to our "conversation of a week ago," in which I had proposed to him the creation at the University of Chicago of a philosophy department that might eventually rival the great department at Harvard at the beginning of the century when it included William James, Josiah Royce, George Santayana, and George Herbert Palmer. My frustrations at Columbia had left me with an obsessive desire to get out of a psychology department and into a philosophy department—not any philosophy department but one made congenial by colleagues with whom I could communicate and collaborate. Hence, without any thought of the rank immodesty of my proposal or the obstacles in the way of its execution, I suggested to Hutchins that he appoint not only me but also my philosophical buddies to the University of Chicago—Scott Buchanan, Richard McKeon, and V. J. McGill. It never occurred to me that academic appointments are not made by presidential fiat.

If it occurred to Bob, it did not give him a moment's pause. In his letter of May 29, he requested complete academic biographies of the four of us and asked, "What ideas will the three or four of you, as the case may be, have developed in another year as to rank and salary?" He went on to say that he was "most optimistic about the possibilities. What I want to do next is to make a concrete suggestion at Chicago. When it comes to answering the question [about rank and salary], be your age." Congratulating me on my having just received a Ph.D., Bob added: "Standards are slipping every day."

During the next month, occupied with his departure from Yale and by frequent trips between New Haven and Chicago, Bob nevertheless tried to arrange a meeting at which I would introduce him to Buchanan, postponing until later meetings with McKeon and McGill. The plans fell through. He sailed for Europe on July 6, writing me from the ship that he had already "found the budgetary situation in Philosophy not impossible. What the reaction of the members of the staff would be to the appointment of the three or four of you, I do not know." Before I received that letter, I received one from Miss Hadley, Bob Hutchins's secretary at the Yale Law School. She said that my letter to him of July 2 had not reached him before he sailed, and that he had not had time on his way through New York to see Buchanan and me. He would go directly to Chicago upon his return, she wrote, adding: "Until then, I think Mr. Buchanan will have to dream of Mr. Hutchins, and nothing he will dream will compare with the actuality."

In October, after he had returned from Europe and assumed his duties at the University of Chicago, Bob Hutchins wrote me that "the chairman of the Philosophy Department has been informed of my interest in you three gentlemen, and the most important member of the department, who is not the chairman, has enthusiastically endorsed my proposals. I have told your wealthy father-in-law twice that the only obstacle to your coming to Chicago is lack of funds. From his response I gather that he doesn't care whether you come to Chicago or not. If he has any preference I judge that it is that you should stay in New York. I can understand that. He lives in Chicago."

That same month, Bob and I spent an evening together at the Yale Club in New York. On that occasion, Bob confessed to me that, in his career so far, he had never given much thought to the subject of educa-

tion. He found this somewhat embarrassing now that he was president
of a major university. I had never ever given much thought to the subject either. However, I could tell him what had been the most important factor in my own education—the Erskine General Honors course
at Columbia. Reading the great books, both as a student and as a
teacher, I said, had done more for my mind than all the rest of the
academic pursuits in which I had been so far engaged.

After I described how the General Honors course was conducted at
Columbia, Bob asked me to name the books we read. I rattled off a
long list of authors and titles in roughly chronological order, to which
Bob's response was that his own education at Oberlin and Yale had not
included most of them. In a speech that he gave some years later, entitled "The Autobiography of an Uneducated Man," he recalled that
he had arrived at the age of thirty "with some knowledge of the Bible,
of Shakespeare, of *Faust,* of one dialogue of Plato, and of the opinions
of many semi-literate and a few literate judges, and that was about all."
Bob then went on to say that Mr. Adler had told him that unless he
"did something drastic he would close his educational career a wholly
uneducated man." It was Bob himself, not I, who proposed the drastic
remedy.

Though his proposal, which he communicated to me early in 1930,
was originally designed to initiate the education of Hutchins and continue the education of Adler, it had much more far-reaching effects. It
developed into one of the main parts of the program of educational
reforms associated in the thirties with his name and with the University
of Chicago. Though John Erskine and Columbia had done the pioneering work ten years earlier, Hutchins and Chicago were to become, in
the public mind, the promulgators and promoters of the "Great Books
Movement" in liberal education.

After our meeting at the Yale Club, I wrote Bob a long letter, not
about General Honors and great books or educational reforms in general, but about the importance of doing something about philosophy at
the University of Chicago and what Buchanan, McKeon, and I might
contribute toward doing it. I told Bob, for the first time, that while I
would much prefer to have him succeed in bringing all three of us to
Chicago, I was willing to come alone if only that could be arranged.
Bob replied that he was delighted with my decision, adding: "The
dean of the Law School has manifested great interest in you. As soon
as the inauguration is over I am going to follow up the matter with the
department of Psychology and the boys in Philosophy." That was November 11. The inauguration took place on November 19, and on
December 4 Bob wrote me:

Our present plan is to retire two men and appoint you in their place. It
should give you a feeling of satisfaction to learn that you are regarded

as the moral equivalent of two individuals of the combined age of 135. By the time I talk to you on the phone I hope this will be absolutely definite. The financial situation is such that we probably can't swing Buchanan and McKeon this year. I have great hopes however that we can bring them in the year following.

Two weeks later I received a formal notification from the secretary of the Board of Trustees that I had been appointed associate professor of philosophy for three years at a salary of $6,000 a year. At that time, having been an instructor in psychology at Columbia for a number of years, I had reached a salary grade of $2,400 a year. When I told Professor Poffenberger, the head of the Psychology Department, about the Chicago appointment, he rejoiced in my good fortune, at the same time confessing his concern about my future at Columbia. Even if all the powers affecting my future were benign, which Poff gently intimated might not be the case, it would take many years for me to attain that rank and salary at Columbia.

Though my official designation was associate professor of philosophy, it had been my understanding with Hutchins that I would teach courses in the Law School and in the Psychology Department as well. But Professor Tufts, who was then head of the Philosophy Department, did not share our understanding. I reacted with ill-concealed discomfort to his proposal that I teach certain courses that were already included in the Philosophy Department's offering. My somewhat irritable correspondence with Professor Tufts and later with Professor Mead, his successor as head of the department (both of whom had been eminent associates of John Dewey in the establishment of what William James referred to as "the Chicago School"), did not get me off to a good start with my future colleagues.

At Christmastime, visiting my wife's family in a Chicago suburb, I had the opportunity to meet some of the members of the Philosophy Department and also Dean Bigelow of the Law School and Judge Hinton, who taught the law of evidence. Shortly thereafter Professor Burtt, whom I had known at Columbia before he went to Chicago, wrote me that the Philosophy Department had accepted my proposal to teach two courses during the fall quarter—a course in the history of logical theory and an introduction to formal logic. At the same time, the Law School agreed that, in the winter quarter, I would teach a course in legal analysis and conduct a seminar on the law of evidence with Judge Hinton. Similar arrangements were concluded for two courses to be offered by the Psychology Department during the third quarter. For the moment, it looked as if I had jumped the first hurdle and my interdepartmental status had been confirmed. It was not until June that a letter from Professor Mead informed me that, by a regrettable accident, reference to my courses had been omitted from the bulletin of the Philosophy Department. However, he wrote, attention would be called to them during registration that fall.

In his inaugural address, delivered in November 1929, President Hutchins recommended, among other things, a "scheme of pass and honors work," which would divide courses into large lectures and small discussion groups. The general and special honors program at Columbia, about which I talked to Hutchins again when I visited Chicago during the Christmas season, had obvious relevance to what Bob had in mind, and consequently he asked me to send him detailed information about the Columbia program. I did this in a letter in which I warned him that "organized departments and departmentally-minded individuals don't understand it, resent it, distrust it" and that "specialized scholars think that it is pretentious, and that the work must be sloppy because it isn't their type of scholarship." Nevertheless, I urged him to adopt something like the Columbia honors program, especially the great books seminars, because, I said,

> it is one of the strongest attacks upon specialism and departmentalism; it is the best education for the faculty as well as for the students; the use of original texts is an antidote for survey courses and fifth-rate textbooks; and it constitutes by itself, if properly conducted, the backbone of a liberal education.

I would not have been surprised to learn of Bob Hutchins's willingness to advocate the adoption of this program, but I was certainly surprised by a telephone call in which he asked whether I would be willing to teach the General Honors course with him the following September. We would, he said, take a select group of freshmen from the entering class and read the great books with them for two years—in the Columbia fashion, by discussing one book a week for two hours. He hoped he would prove as good a co-leader of the discussion as Mark Van Doren had been; he hoped that the introduction of this course in the college would be an opening wedge in an effort to reform the college curriculum; but, most of all, he hoped that reading and discussing the great books would remedy some of the defects in his own education.

Up to that point my acquaintance with university presidents had been limited to a remote awareness of the personality and posture of Nicholas Murray Butler at Columbia. The picture of a university president reading great books with freshmen, for his own sake as well as for theirs, was as shocking as it was refreshing. When it was announced, without any reference to great books, that Hutchins planned to teach freshmen the following autumn, a shock wave spread from the campus through the whole community. By that time, the newspapers had been filled with multifarious stories and with pictures of the handsome, young new president and his almost as tall and even more strikingly handsome wife, Maude. The faculty and the general public had come to expect the unexpected, but this piece of news exceeded even that expectation.

Bob asked me to write a description of the course for insertion in the college catalogue. I sent him a statement twelve to fifteen lines long which he cut down to three lines, writing me that he had translated my statement into English and had forwarded it to the dean of the college. Under the heading "General Survey," it was listed as follows: "110. General Honors Course. —Readings in the classics of Western European literature. Limited to 20 by invitation. This is a two-year course, one two-hour class session each week. Credit is deferred until completion of the course." Chauncey Boucher, who was then dean of the college, found everything about this venture disturbing. It was not only that the president had volunteered to become a member of his faculty; in addition, the course departed from the prevalent academic orthodoxy of full course credit being given each quarter for passing an examination in a course that met three times a week in fifty-minute periods and was taught by a single instructor. He was also troubled by the problem of selecting the twenty students to be invited to participate, eventually solved by my interviewing about eighty members of the entering class, chosen on the basis of their high school records. What probably upset Dean Boucher most of all, as being most irregular, resulted from my pressing Bob Hutchins to have a special room set aside in which the General Honors class would meet and which the students could use as their reading room at other times. That took some doing, but finally in June Bob wrote:

> Just a word to say that we are going to get a room for our class to study in. We are going to move the library of the Art Department to bring this about.
>
> If there are any other little changes that you would like to have made in the structure of this University in order to accommodate your whims, just let me know.

I had not waited for that invitation to do so. Three or four months earlier, I had proposed to Hutchins the creation of a new department in the university—a Department of Philosophical Studies. The aim was not to replace the existing Philosophy Department, which would continue to conduct undergraduate teaching and graduate research in the usual fashion, but to initiate and promote the penetration of philosophical thought into other areas of the university—the Law School, the Medical School, the School of Education, the social sciences, the Psychology Department, and so on. My proposal was, of course, accompanied by the suggestion that the new department would be the ideal location for the likes of Buchanan, McKeon, McGill, and me. I pointed out that it would not only begin to break down departmental barriers and introduce cross-fertilization, both of which were announced Hutchins objectives, but it would also have the effect of giving philosophical inquiry and analysis the pivotal function it should have in a modern university, analogous to the role played by theology in its mediaeval progenitor.

It was in this context that I reminded Bob of the possibility of producing a modern analogue of the mediaeval synthesis that had been provided by a "Summa Theologica"—what Scott Buchanan and I had described as a "Summa Dialectica." That idea, and the idea of a Department of Philosophical Studies—or of a separate Philosophical Institute—was never far from the surface in the conversations that Bob Hutchins and I had about the future of the university, and in the letters that passed between Scott Buchanan and me during those years of hope for an early realization of the dream we shared. Our hopes were nourished by miscalculated optimism on Hutchins's part.

In reply to my long letter about the Department of Philosophical Studies, he wrote: "Your idea is excellent and can be worked out here with the greatest ease provided you follow my instructions as to naive inquiry and intelligent humility." His estimate of the ease with which the proposal might be accomplished could not have been more inaccurate; its misjudgment was exceeded only by his miscalculation of my ability to follow his advice about approaching my colleagues in the spirit of "naive inquiry and intelligent humility."

No advice ever given to anyone could have been more ill suited to the temperament and style of the person advised. In the months that followed Bob's giving me this advice, my youthful exuberance and wild imprudence led me astray on at least three occasions.

In April, Bob and I spent an evening at the Yale Club in New York, an evening of plotting made hilarious by our consumption of a fifth of bootleg Bacardi rum mixed with ginger ale, a vile potion made potable by the exigencies of prohibition. I still have a vivid memory of driving home late that evening—under the elevated tracks on Sixth Avenue. I drove with abandon, swerving in and out around the pillar supports as if they were the poles on a slalom course. A few days later I wrote Bob that I had enjoyed our evening at the Yale Club, "including the difficulties I had in not committing torts while driving home." I should have said "manslaughter and suicide." I also reported reading a volume of essays in honor of John Dewey, a volume which contained contributions by leading members of the Chicago Philosophy Department—Dewey's old associates, James Tufts and George Mead, and newer members of the "Chicago School"—T. V. Smith and Edwin Burtt. I expressed in no uncertain terms my distaste for the brand of philosophizing that these essays so plainly exhibited.

That letter, intended only for the eyes of its recipient, could do no harm. Bob had not instructed me to exercise rhetorical reserve in talking to him. But a little later that spring, at a cocktail party in New York, I thoughtlessly and impulsively failed to exercise restraint when asked for my opinion of my colleagues-to-be. In a voice somewhat above a whisper and in a tone that was unmistakably derisive, I repeated the judgments I had conveyed in my letter. My remarks were overheard by someone who reported them to friends in the Chicago Philosophy Department. He did not need to embroider or exaggerate this juicy bit of gossip to produce the hostility I deservedly experienced when I arrived in September.

That was my first inexcusable transgression of the Hutchins precept. My second occurred in the autumn after I had been at the university a very short time. During the spring and summer of 1930, my friend Arthur Rubin harangued me endlessly about the scientific pretensions of the social studies which had just begun to assume a certain prominence on the academic scene. He prodded me into writing a number of critical memoranda on the logic and method of the so-called "social sciences," all of which pointed out how far they fell short of the precision which entitled the disciplines involved in the study of nature to be called "exact sciences." I showed some of these memoranda to Robert Lynd, of *Middletown* fame, who was at that time secretary of the Social Science Research Council. He suggested that I might turn them into a paper on logic and method to deliver to an assembly of social scientists at Dartmouth in August. When I reported this to Hutchins, he encouraged me to accept, saying that he thought I had "the right dope on the social sciences" and that the paper "might do the Social Science Research Council a great deal of good," but, he added, "remember our slogan!"

The notes, or memoranda, I had prepared for Arthur Rubin and had shown to Bob Lynd were entitled "Theses on the Distinction between the Exact and the Inexact Sciences." At Lynd's urging, I turned these into a paper, written in outline form for ease of presentation to an audience; it was entitled "The Social Scientist's Misconception of Science." For some reason I cannot now recall I did not go to Dartmouth in August, but Bob Lynd mimeographed my lecture outline and circulated it amoung his colleagues.

It was thus that a copy fell into the hands of Donald Slesinger, who had worked with Bob Hutchins at Yale on psychology as applied to the law of evidence while I was working with Jerome Michael at Columbia on the logic of judicial proof. Hutchins had brought Slesinger to Chicago with him in the fall of 1929, and by the time I reached there a year later, Slesinger was secretary of the local branch of the Social Science Research Council, a meeting of which had been scheduled for mid-October or early November. Its membership included all the leading professors at the university in the departments of sociology, economics, political science, and anthropology. Donald, who had read the paper and who had no reason to doubt that, if invited to do so, I would deliver it in my usual brusque and blunt style, should have known better than to invite me to address the local branch of the council. But he did, and I did, with disastrous results as far as making friends and influencing people was concerned.

My address opened with the flat statement of its controlling thesis: "Current research programmes in the social sciences are misdirected and methodologically ill-advised because of erroneous conceptions of the nature of science which comprise the 'raw empiricism' characteristic of contemporary social science." A moment later, I was saying: "The distinction between exact science (the physical sciences) and inexact science (the social sciences) is a distinction between good and bad science, not between two different kinds of science." After a brief but very compact statement of the methodology of the exact sciences, I went on to captivate my audience of social scientists by saying: "In the light of the foregoing statement of the nature of the exact sciences, we can now enumerate the leading misconceptions which prevail among social scientists"— nine of them in all, followed by a quick summary of the fallacies underlying these misconceptions. The address ended with some praise for theoretical and mathematical economics as an approximation to exact science, and with a condemnation of sociology as the worst offender— the furthest removal from what a science should be.

I need not dwell on the reaction my address elicited from an audience of social scientists who were dedicated to empiricism, raw or otherwise. I had now succeeded in alienating a larger and more diverse group of colleagues than those in the Philosophy Department. Donald Slesinger, who must have been as imprudent as I, took great glee in the commotion I had caused, but Charles Merriam, professor of political science, an elder in the council, and very well disposed toward Bob Hutchins and me, gently reprimanded me for having trodden so heavily and clumsily on the toes of persons with whom I would have to work if I were to serve Hutchins's interest in bringing about educational and intellectual reforms at the university. He admonished me to ask questions every now and then instead of laying down theses in the flat declarative mood of my recent address.

That was my second egregious transgression of the precept to practice "naive inquiry and intelligent humility." The third occurred repeatedly over a more extended period of time—during the meetings throughout the academic year 1930–1931 of the Curriculum Committee that the new president had set up to reform the program of undergraduate studies. At session after session, I failed to adopt Professor Merriam's kindly suggestion that I employ the interrogative, rather than the declarative, approach. Other friendly colleagues, among them Professors Harold Lasswell, Ralph Gerard, and L. L. Thurstone, who had observed my performance at faculty meetings with a mixture of amusement and dismay, tried to soften or deflect my style, but to no avail.

The piece of advice that I remember most clearly, even though I could never manage to follow it, came from Ralph Gerard, who phoned me one day and asked if he could visit me in my office. After a few pleasantries, he got down directly to the business at hand—improving my performance with my colleagues. "The trouble with you, Mortimer," he said, "is that your mind moves much too fast. You don't wait until one of your colleagues finishes a sentence before telling him what is wrong with what he was going to say. You anticipate the statement he is going to make, and without letting him complete it, you start disagreeing with it. What you should do instead is to hear him out, look puzzled without frowning while you are counting to ten, and then slowly, hesitantly, and even stumbling in speech, if you can manage that, express some vague concern about the direction of his thought, intimating, again with some diffidence, that your own thought tends in the opposite direction."

Gerard's diagnosis was accurate and his prescription correct, but my temperamental disabilities made it impossible to follow. I continued to challenge my colleagues instead of trying to persuade them, but I do have to add that, even if my conduct had been exemplary in every respect, the deliberations of the Curriculum Committee would not have produced a revision of the college program in line with the objectives that Hutchins and I had in mind. The changes we wanted to see effected were simply too much against the grain of vested interests to be accomplished as quickly and easily as both of us thought they might be— simply because, in our judgment, they were fundamentally sound. What we hoped might be accomplished in that first year of effort was finally achieved more than ten years later, after Clarence Faust became dean of the college and after the new program at St. John's College in Annapolis, Maryland, had been set in operation by Scott Buchanan and Stringfellow Barr, partly as a result of the year they spent at Chicago (1936–1937) as members of the Committee on the Liberal Arts.

Before I say more about the vicissitudes of that first year's effort to reform the college curriculum, I should describe certain discomforts that I suffered on moving to Chicago, after having spent the whole of my life in the precincts of Manhattan Island. The contrast between the personalities of Robert Maynard Hutchins and Nicholas Murray Butler, together with the remarkable difference in the degree of my cantact with each of them, was not the only striking change I registered emotionally. At Columbia, members of the faculty resided all over town and in the suburbs, whereas in Chicago almost the whole faculty lived within a five-block radius of the campus, in a tight little enclave the social life of which resembled that enjoyed by the officers and their wives in an army camp. At Columbia, in contrast, most of the colleagues with whom I had become friends not only lived at remote distances from the campus but also moved in social circles that were predominantly nonacademic.

The university residential neighborhood in Chicago consisted of tree-lined streets, a sharp contrast to the treeless streets of my whole life hitherto. I found this disturbing, because it suggested country life that I did not like as compared with city life that I was used to and liked. I wanted to establish my residence on the Near North Side of Chicago, ten miles or so away from the university, but I was strongly advised against it, and so, as the best alternative we could muster, Helen and I rented an apartment on the fourteenth floor of a new building some ten blocks away from the campus. It had a superb view of the lake and the city's skyscrapers, reminiscent of Manhattan, and it overlooked the Michigan Central tracks. This afforded me the pleasure of watching trains on their way to and from New York. I not only regretted leaving the city of my birth; I also returned to it as frequently as I could in order to carry on my work with Professor Michael on the law of evidence and in the development of another project (in the field of criminology and criminal law) in which he persuaded me to join him.

One other difference between living in Chicago and in New York was that my wife's family were prominent residents of Chicago. My father-in-law, a retired, wealthy industrialist, was a member of the Chicago Club. I had no such connections in the city of my birth. I mention this because still another mistake I made during that first year was to allow Freddy Boynton, my father-in-law, to give a luncheon in my honor in a private room at the Chicago Club, to which he invited not only the president and several vice-presidents of the university (Butler at Columbia had no vice-presidents!), but also various deans, heads of departments, and other colleagues with whom I might have close association. Putting together that kind of rank and swank hardly ingratiated me with my professorial colleagues, those present at the luncheon or those who heard of it through all the avenues of local gossip.

During the summer of 1930, Bob and I corresponded about the great books that he was reading in preparation for the honors seminar in September. Toward the end of August, I must have written him—I hope jocularly—about raising my salary. Since it was much larger than was normal for a person of my age and rank, my request was probably prompted by the fact that Hutchins, in his first trustees dinner address the preceding January, had proposed as an ideal "a faculty of one hundred men and women, all getting and deserving $50,000 a year"—an unthinkable sum at the time. In any case, in a letter in which he reported that he was just finishing Virgil, he wrote:

> I have received without surprise your request for an increase of your salary
> of $500, and have repelled it without effort. A recent editorial in the
> *Nation* attacking me for wishing to raise professors' salaries has convinced

me that in your case at least no change should be made now or at any future time in your stipend.

Teaching the great books with Bob Hutchins was the one fine experience that first year at the university. It was neither complicated nor spoiled by the mistakes that he and I made in dealing with the faculty about other matters, such as curricular reforms and appointments to the Philosophy Department, mistakes that sowed the seeds of the Chicago fight that almost blew the university up in our faces. Distinctly different in his style from Mark Van Doren, my partner at Columbia, Bob, like Mark, was a witty interrogator of the students, catching them on vague or airy statements about the readings. Just as Mark and I had learned to do, Bob and I would argue moot points with one another, as much for the amusement as for the elucidation of the students. I was no match for Hutchins in repartee. No one was. His lightning flash rejoinders left me speechless, astonishing those who were already his friends, but confounding others not so well disposed.

When he was a dean of the Yale Law School, Hutchins had been invited to attend a reception for the justices of the Supreme Court. On that occasion, one of the stuffier old men on the court, either Mr. Justice Reynolds or Mr. Justice Butler, said to him: "I understand, Mr. Dean, that you are teaching your young men at New Haven what is wrong with our decisions." To which Hutchins instantaneously replied: "Oh no, we let them find that out for themselves."

Partly because of Hutchins's wit and gift for repartee, which punctuated our discussion with the kind of laughter that, in my judgment, promotes learning, and partly because newspaper stories about the great books seminar that the president of the university was teaching freshmen had given the performance nationwide notoriety, we had a constant stream of visitors to the class. I cannot recall all the transcontinental travellers who included a visit to the Hutchins-Adler seminar as part of their stopover in Chicago while travelling between the East Coast and California or the other way around; but I do remember the actresses Katharine Cornell, Lillian Gish, and Ethel Barrymore; the actor Orson Welles; the columnists Westbrook Pegler and J. P. McEvoy (whose son Dennis was one of our students); and also the publisher of the *Washington Post,* Eugene Meyer, and his wife, Agnes, whose daughter Katherine (to become Kay Graham) was also a member of the class. Agnes Meyer, being an active promoter of progressive education, did not hesitate to express her qualms about the kind of intellectual discipline that we were imposing on her daughter.

Of all the celebrities who, for one reason or another, found some fascination in these great books seminars, the only one who challenged the whole enterprise was Gertrude Stein. She had been invited to give lectures at the university. Bob and Maude Hutchins gave a dinner party for her during her visit, and as chance would have it, the dinner had to be set for an evening when our great books class met between seven-thirty and nine-thirty. Consequently, Bob and I could not be at the dinner, but after class was over, we turned up in time to join the guests for coffee and cognac. The party included Thornton Wilder, whom Bob had persuaded to do a stint of teaching at the university, and a trustee of the university, Charles Goodspeed, and his wife, Bobsy, at whose home Gertrude Stein and her companion, Alice B. Toklas, were staying.

As we took our places at the table—and certainly before we had been fortified by coffee and cognac—Gertrude turned on Bob and said, "Where have you been, Hutchins, and what have you been doing?" A little weary at the end of the day, Bob was taken aback by the abruptness and forcefulness of the attack (the energy Gertrude exuded in a small room hit one like Niagara Falls). Bob replied, as briefly and effortlessly as possible, "Miss Stein, Mr. Adler and I have been teaching the great books." Gertrude pounced on him again with even more vigor. "Don't call me Miss Stein," she said; "call me Gertrude Stein. What are the great books?" Bob tried to explain the basic educational idea involved in reading and discussing great books with college students, but he kept forgetting how she insisted upon being addressed, and so he was forever being interrupted by Gertrude's peremptory injunction "Don't call me Miss Stein; call me Gertrude Stein."

At one point I decided to come to Bob's rescue by going downstairs to my briefcase and getting out the list of the great books. I showed it to her. She scanned the list quickly and just as quickly asked, "Do you read these books in their original languages or in English translations?" Hutchins explained that our freshman students did not have competence in Greek and Latin or Italian and French, and were finding it difficult enough to read the books in English. This infuriated Miss Stein, I mean Gertrude Stein. She laid it down as an unchallengeable axiom that great literature was essentially untranslatable. Hutchins and I then tried to argue with her, pointing out that we were concerned mainly with the ideas that were to be found in the great books. She might be right, we admitted; fine writing suffers in translation, but ideas somehow transcend the particular language in which they are first expressed.

"Not so," our grand inquisitor replied, "not so at all! Greek ideas must be studied in Greek, Latin ideas in Latin, French ideas in French, and so on." Hutchins tried to explain that the idea of justice, for example, is the same idea whether it is discussed by Plato in Greek, by Cicero in Latin, by Kant in German, or by John Stuart Mill in English; but he got nowhere, largely because he was so courteous, calm, and long-suffering. I decided that Gertrude needed a dose of her own medicine; so I began to ask her questions, one after another, with gathering force and rising pitch. The argument grew heated. Gertrude rose from her chair, came around the table to where I was sitting, and tapping me on the head with a resounding thwack, said, "I am not going to argue any further with you, young man. I can see that you are the kind of young man who is accustomed to winning arguments."

At that very moment, the butler came into the room and announced, "The police are here." Gertrude turned on him and with an imperious gesture waved him out of the room with "Have them wait!" We all looked puzzled. Thornton Wilder learned over and whispered in my ear, "Gertrude wants to tour Chicago at night in a squad car. Mr. Good-speed has arranged this for her. Two police captains are waiting down-stairs to take her for a ride." The way I felt about her at that moment, I wished they had done it earlier and taken her for a ride Chicago-style.

Shortly thereafter, the party broke up. As we were all standing in the doorway expressing the usual amenities, Alice B. Toklas turned to me and said, "This has been a wonderful evening. Gertrude has said things tonight that it will take her ten years to understand." She was always saying things she did not understand, as well as things that she did not know had been said by others before her. At Hutchins's invitation, she visited our great books class the following week to lead a discussion of Homer's *Odyssey*. We tried to persuade her to ask the students ques-tions, but most of the time she harangued them with extempore re-marks about epic poetry which she thought up on the spot, but which none of us, including Gertrude, could understand, then or in the years to come.

The students in that first great books class had one other unforget-table experience. Partly because I wanted Mark Van Doren, Dick McKeon, Scott Buchanan, and Stringfellow Barr to visit Bob Hutchins and me in Chicago, and partly because of my own experience with oral examinations in the General Honors course at Columbia, I persuaded Bob to invite my friends to come to Chicago as external oral examiners. Buchanan and Barr came from the University of Virginia in June of 1931, Van Doren and McKeon from Columbia University in June of 1932, to conduct a half-hour oral examination of each student in our class. They put the students on the spot in a way that was good for them, exposing the shallowness of their verbal chatter, full of clichés that had stuck in their memories, often in a fragmentary fashion. No written examination by instructors in a course, or even an oral ex-amination by them, could possibly cut under the surface of students' answers to find out whether or not they really understood what they were saying. Only an oral inquisition by outsiders can do that effec-tively in a way that is instructive as well as corrective to the examinees, not to mention its similar effect on their teachers. Without anticipation of what the examinations might reveal, Hutchins had invited a half-dozen or more members of the faculty to attend the first round of oral examinations in 1931, and afterwards solicited comments from them. The responses were, to our surprise, most complimentary, though almost everyone pointed out that this method of examination must be very expensive and, therefore, not generally applicable to courses in the college.

By May of 1932, we had completed the assigned readings from Homer to Freud. After their second oral examination, and perhaps because of it, a committee of the students approached Hutchins with a refreshing request. Realizing how poorly they had read the books assigned, and how little they had understood them, would it be possible, they asked, to repeat the course for another two years, in order to read and discuss the same books a second time? Bob and I were simply delighted with this unusual request. He submitted it to the dean of the college, who, in turn, submitted it to a ruling group of the faculty. Their immediate response was that it could not be done. Whoever had heard of students taking the same course a second time and getting credit for it?

Bob conceded that ordinarily that might be a questionable procedure, but he tried to explain that in the case of reading and discussing great books, it did not seem at all questionable that students might advance in their learning by reading and discussing the same books a second time—or even a third and a fourth time—and so might deserve credit for each repetition of the course. The faculty, unpersuaded, grudgingly complied with the president's wish to grant the students' request. The second round of General Honors showed that the students deserved academic credit for the same course taken a second time. The third and fourth set of oral examinations completely confirmed that. In addition to academic credit, the students should have been given medals to honor the soundness of their unorthodox suggestion.

It was not until the winter quarter of the academic year 1930–1931 that the Hutchins-Adler troubles began in earnest. Until then, what in national politics has come to be called "the honeymoon period" of the new president prevailed in the academic politics at Chicago. Hutchins had succeeded, with almost no opposition, in reorganizing the structure of the university by setting up a fourfold division of the faculty—physical sciences, biological sciences, social sciences, and humanities. The Department of History straddled the fence that divided the social sciences from the humanities, and there were some unresolved problems about the relation of the Medical School to the division of the biological sciences, and of the Law School to the division of the social sciences. Hutchins had not yet achieved one objective that, in fact, it took him many years to accomplish—the establishment of an autonomous faculty for the undergraduate college. In those first years, teachers in the college held positions on one of the divisional faculties and, in consequence, were deeply influenced by the specialized educational objectives of the graduate school rather than by the concerns of general education at the college level. The conflict between these quite distinct aims led to the dissensions in the Curriculum Committee that was formed to construct a program of general education for the first two years of the college.

Though suspect by virtue of being a personal friend of the new president, I was still in sufficiently good standing for Hutchins to be able to propose me for membership on the Curriculum Committee, which Dean Boucher set up in January 1931. I lunched regularly with my colleagues at the Quadrangle Club, sitting one day with my associates in the Law School, another with members of the Psychology Department, and still another with the philosophers. Until the quarrels over the college curriculum reached the stage at which I was made uncomfortable by the conspiratorial air of whispering groups at nearby tables in the club, I continued to "fraternize" with my colleagues. I remember only two occasions when I inadvertently stepped on tender toes. Once during a lunch with members of the Philosophy Department, I angered Professor Mead by my blithe espousal of what he regarded as the undemocratic elitism of President Hutchins's proposal of small-class instruction only for honor students, and large lecture classes for the rest.

My second blooper took place during a luncheon with eminent members of the Physics Department, including several Nobel laureates. They were discussing the then regnant Bohr theory of the atom, which involved the instantaneous passage of electrons from one orbit to another without traversing the intervening space. It never occurred to me that they would think I was being facetious or making light of a serious scientific theory when I remarked that electrons, according to the Bohr theory, behaved exactly the way that angels did. An angel, according to the theory of Thomas Aquinas, could move from one place to another without taking any time to do so and without passing through the intervening space. When one of the physicists chided me by insinuating that I would probably also claim to know how many angels can stand on the point of a needle, I could not restrain myself from lecturing him on the main tenets of the mediaeval science of angelology, a science which had, I declared, as much intellectual rigor as modern mathematical physics. Only those ignorant of it continued to pose the problem of the number of angels on the point of a needle as a way of ridiculing the folly of mediaeval thought. That question was never raised in the Middle Ages; nor, had it been raised, would it have caused any agitation, because all competent angelologists knew that there could be only one answer. The intensive occupation of space by angels, I tried to explain, is as exclusive as the extensive occupation of space by bodies; as only one body can fill a certain space at a certain time, so only one angel can exert spiritual power at a certain place at a certain time.

Far from persuading the physicists that angelology might be a respectable science, my remarks on the subject, delivered with some heat and without any apology, generated doubts about my sanity as well as fears about a recrudescence of mediaevalism—the hobgoblin of a modern university dominated by experimental or empirical science. In the subsequent ten years in which the Chicago fight reached one boiling point after another, "mediaevalism" became the most explosive expletive in the rallying cry of the opposition to Hutchins and Adler, though "Aristotelianism," "Thomism," and even "metaphysics" and "philosophy" took on a related resonance, connoting attitudes and aspirations that sprang from what were regarded as the twin sins of being antimodern and antiscientific.

The first two boiling points, one of which altered my status at the university, resulted from Hutchins's intense desire to create a program of general education in the college, one that would disregard the narrowly specialized requirements of the upper divisions; and his equally intense interest in changing the face of the Philosophy Department. My appointment as a member of the College Curriculum Committee landed me right in the center of the first cauldron; my recommendation that Buchanan and McKeon be appointed to the Philosophy Department lit the fires under a second.

In my early conversations with Bob Hutchins about instituting a program of general education in the college at Chicago, I suggested the possibility of four honors courses, each corresponding to the subject matter of one of the four divisions in Bob's restructuring of the university, each a two-year course of readings and discussions built around great works in the appropriate field. He liked the idea and asked me to try to construct the four reading lists. That was easier said than done, but I finally came up with four lists, ranging from 85 recommended works in the physical sciences to almost 120 in the biological sciences. In each case, the reading lists comprised three types of books —classic, original contributions to the subject matter, commentaries on or criticisms of these contributions, and historical treatises. The lists were ample and varied enough to be cut in half during a process of selection, still leaving enough for a two-year program.

When the College Curriculum Committee came into existence in January 1931, Bob suggested that I propose the consideration of the four divisional reading courses as an honors program for the college.

No move could have been more naively brash. With Dean Boucher as chairman, the membership of the committee included a chemist from the Physical Sciences Division, a botanist from the Biological Sciences Division, an economist and a psychologist from the Social Sciences Division, and a professor of English literature from the Humanities Division. One additional member was the man whom Bob had appointed as chairman of the Board of Examiners, charged with constructing the examinations that would certify satisfactory completion of a program of general education in the college. With the possible exception of him, and one or two others, the committee had little interest in general education and even less appetite for reading and discussing with students great works in their own field of specialization. My reading lists were quickly disposed of as an utterly fantastic suggestion.

Not willing to give up so easily, I tried to lobby for them with members of the faculty not on the Curriculum Committee. I met with the same dismal results. I can remember a luncheon I had with Professors Compton, Millikan, and Dempster of the Physics Department. I asked them whether reading Galileo, Newton, Huygens, Pascal, Clerk Maxwell, and Faraday might not go a long way toward producing educated physicists. They admitted that that might be a good way to educate men who wanted to become physicists, but doubted that it was the best way to train them to be good physicists. Professor Compton went so far as to say that he felt that being a good physicist might be more important than being an educated man. Shortly after that conversation, and a number of others even more distressing, I wrote Scott Buchanan that Bob and I had decided to drop the proposal of the four reading courses for honor students not only because it had been greeted by the faculty as wildly bizarre, but also because it had become plain that, even if the plan were adopted to please the president of the university, it would be impossible to staff it.

The work of the Curriculum Committee concluded with a set of recommendations that Bob and I regarded as a poor compromise. It included only one point that completely satisfied Hutchins—comprehensive examinations at the end of two years, constructed by a group of external examiners, to replace the usual examinations given at the end of each course and prepared by the instructor of the course. Otherwise it was a far cry from the hoped-for program of general education that would have eliminated all electives from the first two years of the college, would have introduced honors seminars for selected students, and for all students would have had the effect of opening their minds to the whole world of learning, instead of narrowing their vision to the tunnel which led to proficiency in one or another field of academic specialization.

That is primarily what the divisions and departments fought for—the retention in the curriculum of courses that would prepare students in the first two years to specialize in the last two years of the college and, in effect, would initiate them into graduate work before they had been graduated. From the faculty's point of view, they had compromised far enough by accepting a plan that required *all* students in the first year of the college to take four divisional lecture courses, which came to be known as "survey courses," in which the main reading would consist of a syllabus prepared by the divisional faculty.

The disappointment that Hutchins and I felt over what we regarded as an unmitigated defeat was not assuaged by the fact that the so-called "New Plan" was hailed, both locally and nationally, as a victory in the battle for general education and against too early specialization. How very slight and almost negligible that victory was can be measured by its distance from the achievement, first at St. John's College in Annapolis in 1937 and then at the University of Chicago in 1943, of a required program for all students, with electives completely eliminated and with small groups engaged in the reading and discussion of great or important books in all fields of learning.

In the interim, Hutchins and I continued to criticize the New Plan that we had been instrumental in getting adopted. Several years later, when our dissatisfaction with the New Plan reached the faculty through critiques written for the campus daily, the *Chicago Maroon,* by students in our General Honors course, that only had the effect of hardening the opposition and postponing for almost ten years the reforms which Dean Faust was finally able to institute. But before I tell the story of the fight that developed in the middle thirties, I must report the second blowup during that first year, which enlisted concerted action by the faculty to redress the grievances suffered by the Philosophy Department.

Anyone who recalls the national furore over FDR's attempt to pack the Supreme Court of the United States with justices friendly to the New Deal will be able to understand the intensity of the reaction to the attempt by the president of the university to pack the Philosophy Department with a coterie of his and Adler's friends. It started in the fall of 1930, when he appointed Professor Mead to succeed Professor Tufts as head of the department, though Mead's term of office would run for only a short time as he was almost of the same age as Tufts. Mead's retirement being imminent, Bob decided that he would not appoint any of the other full professors in the department his successor. He discussed with Mead the possibility of inviting Buchanan and McKeon to join the department, but found him extremely cool to the suggestion.

To overcome Mead's reluctance, Bob devised a ploy that was ill conceived for the purpose he had in mind. It soon generated an academic atmosphere increasingly hostile to any further maneuverings on the president's part. Bob drafted a letter asking leading philosophers in the United States and abroad to give him an appraisal of a number of candidates for appointment to the Philosophy Department. The list included my friends Buchanan, McKeon, and McGill, along with the names of men proposed by the department—Charles Morris, a man named Blake, and one or two others. This letter and the list were sent to Morris Cohen at the City College of New York, C. I. Lewis at Harvard, F. C. S. Northrop at Yale, and W. P. Montague at Columbia; to Bertrand Russell, Alfred North Whitehead, and G. E. Moore in England; and to Etienne Gilson at the Collège de France in Paris.

This polling of professional opinion did not give Bob results he could use to overwhelm the opposition to his wishes in the matter; on the contrary, when, by grapevine and scuttlebutt, the rumor spread that the members of the Philosophy Department were having trouble with an administrative officer who was trying to encroach on their prerogatives, the opposition of the department to the president became fortified by expressions of sympathy and encouragement from their colleagues in other universities. Morris Cohen passed the gossip on to Scott Buchanan when they ran into one another at the annual meeting of the American Philosophical Association in December. Shortly thereafter Scott wrote me what Cohen had told him.

> He says that Hutchins is doing a very dangerous thing in picking on the Chicago department of philosophy. That department contains men who have more respect from the profession at large than any other department in the country. He admits that the respect is partly irrelevant to their intrinsic merits as philosophers, but as philosophers and graduate schools go, they are very strongly entrenched in the esteem of the profession. . . . They have trained about 25 substantial teachers of philosophy and have served the Middle West in many ways. Their social evangelism is an integral part of the most strongly established American tradition.

Either unaware of these facts or undeterred by them, Bob Hutchins continued, in the spring of 1931, to make trouble for the philosophers at Chicago, even though at that time he was no longer pushing to bring Buchanan and McKeon to Chicago the following academic year.

Buchanan had accepted what amounted to a fellowship, with a substantial stipend, from a wealthy Chicagoan, Mrs. Frances Dummer. She had read Scott's recently published *Poetry and Mathematics* and decided that Buchanan was just the person to do a year's research in England on the mathematical logic of George Boole and the mathematical pedagogy of Mary Boole, his wife. Obtaining leave from the University of Virginia, Scott, his wife, Miriam, and their son, Douglas, planned to spend the academic year 1931–1932 at Cambridge University on the Boole project, a move which precipitated my first visit to England and to Europe in the summer of 1932. Scott and I maintained a steady correspondence during his year abroad, not only about developments at the University of Chicago, but also about our current philosophical concerns. To facilitate communication, we even registered cable addresses with Western Union: his was "Philoboole, Cambridge," mine "Analerotic, Chicago," which I managed to get registered because the operator who took the order could not spell the word as I pronounced it and certainly did not know what it meant.

Dick McKeon, when he learned that Bob had included his name in the list of potential candidates for rating by leading philosophers in this country and abroad, became furiously indignant and, in effect, removed himself from the picture. "In the future when you send out lists of 'candidates,' for ratings," he wrote, "leave my name out of them. I resent having my friends asked to pass on them. . . . The picture of Lewis and Cohen coming on my name in the list makes me sore as hell; the picture of Gilson and Moore embarrasses me. If you get a favorable report from the lot, I'll turn your offer down."

With Buchanan and McKeon temporarily out of the picture, Bob still remained intransigent in his dealings with the Philosophy Department. When Professor Mead proposed the appointment of a man from Texas named Brogan, it was accompanied by an ultimatum that either Brogan be appointed a full professor or the president would receive his resignation and, perhaps, the resignation of other members of the Philosophy Department. Hutchins, who was hardly the man to threaten with resignations, replied with a flat refusal. Mead asked if that decision was final, and Bob said that it was.

This occurred during the mounting turmoil over reforming the college curriculum. Matters came to a head a little later that spring with Bob's refusal to appoint another Texan, Charles Morris, to the Philosophy Department. While Bob was absent from the university for a period of weeks—in Arizona with Maude because of illness on her part—the threatened resignation of the Philosophy Department as a whole precipitated an open revolt against the president by senior members of the faculty in other departments. They held a mass meeting in the Rockefeller Chapel and passed resolutions calling not only for a redress of the philosophers' grievances, but also for legislation by the University Senate to prevent further presidential intrusion in appointments. When Bob returned from Tucson, Woodward, vice-president of the university, met him at the train and informed him that the university had blown up in his face and that he had to take immediate and drastic steps to get things under control.

The concessions Bob had to grant included the appointment of Charles Morris, the acceptance of legislation that greatly curtailed his prerogatives with respect to faculty appointments, and last but not least the removal of Mortimer Adler from the Philosophy Department.

Shortly thereafter I received a formal communication from the secretary of the university which read: "The Board of Trustees, at its meeting held July 9, 1931, voted that your title of Associate Professor of Philosophy be changed to Associate Professor of the Philosophy of Law (in the Law School)."

That put an end to my career, not as a philosopher, but as a professor of philosophy. Since my early days at Columbia I had wanted that professional status, because I had mistakenly regarded it as an indispensable condition for doing philosophical work. Yet I did almost no philosophical work during my short-lived term of office as a professor of philosophy, and in the years since then I have never found the deprivation of that office even the slightest obstacle to engagement in philosophical thought or the writing of philosophical books.

The only other appointment that Hutchins made which turned out to be as short-lived as mine was his appointment in the Medical School of Dr. Franz Alexander, an eminent psychoanalyst and an associate of Sigmund Freud. Bob was not trying to pack the Medical School with Freudians, but one Freudian psychoanalyst on the faculty was one too many for the Medical School in the 1930s.

Chapter 8

The Chicago Fight

AFTER BEING REMOVED from the Philosophy Department, I removed myself from academic politics and turned my attention to writing in the field of law; to teaching the liberal arts, especially grammar and logic, in the college and in the laboratory school attached to the university, in the Law School, and in the Social Science Division; and to giving university lectures on a wide variety of subjects. In addition, I continued to teach the great books with Bob Hutchins. My relegation to the law faculty did not confine my activities to that area, as some of my less friendly colleagues probably hoped it would. From their point of view, I was still provocatively at large.

In an article that appeared in *Fortune* in 1937, John Chamberlain presented his version of the quarrels at the University of Chicago which reached their first crisis in the spring of 1931. Relating the events that led to the resignations submitted by members of the Philosophy Department and the general blowup that followed, Chamberlain concluded:

> Whether Adler was misconstrued or mistreated is a question that is still endlessly argued, but the fact remains that Hutchins, to preserve the peace, had to find a place for his protégé in the law school, as associate professor of the philosophy of law—or, as one of Hutchins's more vocal opponents puts it, "Professor of the Blue Sky."

Although I had never taught the philosophy of law, my activities at the Columbia Law School gave some justification for my appointment to the law faculty. The work with Jerome Michael on the law of evidence, which had culminated in our collaboration on a book on the nature of judicial proof, prepared me for the seminar on evidence that I taught with Judge Hinton. A defense of realistic jurisprudence had just recently been written by Jerome Frank, entitled *Law and the Modern Mind*. The *Columbia Law Review* invited Prof. Karl Llewellyn, Prof. Walter Wheeler Cook, and me to review it in a symposium. My contribution, the only adverse criticism that Frank's book received at the time, made a distinction between law in action and law in discourse and argued that, while psychoanalysis of the judge on the bench might have some bearing on law in action, logical analysis of the relation between legal principles and judicial decisions threw more light on law in discourse.

One other Columbia engagement provided background for my teaching in the Law School. The Bureau of Social Hygiene had given a research grant to the Columbia Law School to conduct an inquiry which would determine "whether or not it is desirable at this time to establish an institute of criminology and criminal justice in the United States" and, in the event it were found desirable, to establish one. Jerome Michael was assigned the task of heading the inquiry. After he had spent considerable time pondering the reports of the criminologists, sociologists, and psychologists who surveyed the relevant fields of knowledge, he invited me to join him in the enterprise as a critic of the surveys. I accepted, largely because it provided me with numerous trips to New York as well as whole summers there working with Michael at Columbia.

My general appraisal of the state of the social or behavioral sciences, reinforced by the even lower estimate Arthur Rubin gave at my behest to Jerome Michael, persuaded Jerome to sign his name to a report which said that our lack of knowledge of the causes of crime and of the effects of various methods of treating criminals made it undesirable to establish an institute of criminology and criminal justice. Our colleagues at the Columbia Law School were somewhat chagrined by what amounted to our rejection of a gift of five million dollars to establish the proposed institute at Columbia.

When Helen and I went to England in the summer of 1932 to visit the Buchanans at the end of their year abroad, I took along with me a copy of our report. In the course of conversations that Scott and I had with C. K. Ogden, I showed it to him. He offered to publish it in the International Library of Philosophy, Psychology, and Scientific Method —the series in which Buchanan's *Possibility* and my *Dialectic* had earlier been published. He rushed it through the presses and it appeared in the spring of 1933 under the title *Crime, Law and Social Science*. In 1971, the book was republished in a reprint series dealing with criminology, law enforcement, and social problems. On reading the introduction to the reprint edition, I discovered that the original had been very favorably reviewed in the law journals as well as in the *Times Literary Supplement*. Michael and I had persuaded others that the study of human behavior had not yet produced a body of respectable and reliable scientific knowledge.

However, none of this really prepared me for my first attempt to give a lecture course on the philosophy of law. Having constructed an elaborate bibliography of the subject, which concentrated mainly on modern and contemporary writings, I spent months reading and making notes. The more I read and the more notes I made, the less able I felt to outline a course of lectures that had the order and intelligibility I regarded as essential to decent philosophical discourse. I can still remember vividly my suicidal nightmare during the week just before the term began. I dreamed of opening the window of my study in our fourteenth floor apartment and throwing out bundle after bundle of my notes. As the bundles fell apart and the loosened sheets fluttered to the street below, I flung myself out of the window to dive through the scattering notes. A few days later, just in time to save me from despair and the course from floundering, the subject finally took philosophical shape for me when I read the first eight questions in the Treatise on Law in the *Summa Theologica* of Thomas Aquinas.

I repeated that course a number of times, each time making more effective use of the basic insights of Aquinas. I also taught a course in legal analysis and one on logic and argumentation for students of law. My teaching took still other directions in 1933–1934, when Bob Hutchins and I undertook to read the great books with a selected group of juniors and seniors in the university high school. Though younger than the students in our General Honors course in the college, the high school students did just as well; in fact, having had less schooling, they were somewhat less inhibited in discussion. However, one aspect of this educational experiment was, perhaps, ill conceived for youngsters of their age. I prepared a series of formal lectures on the trivium— grammar, logic, and rhetoric—which I delivered at breakneck speed to them in a sequence of fifty-minute sessions. I was too intent on a systematic exposition of the principles of these liberal arts to pay any attention to pedagogy. Both in preparing the lectures and in delivering them, I was so exhilarated by what I was myself learning that I probably could not imagine their listening to the lectures without learning as much as I. As one of them told me many years later, they just sat there in a daze, patiently suffering a torrent of analysis which for them had neither rhyme nor reason.

One other teaching experience in 1933–1934 is memorable, not only because of its unusual nature, but also because of the two persons who were my associates. One was Beardsley "Bee" Ruml, who, after having been head of the Laura Spelman Rockefeller Fund, came to the University of Chicago as dean of the social sciences. The other was my old friend Arthur Rubin, who, no longer able to tolerate working for his father in the American Silk Mills, had negotiated a financial settlement on his potential inheritance that turned him into a remittance man. He moved to Chicago to become involved in the various fracases he had heard about from me, and most particularly to carry on his vendetta against the social sciences.

Bee Ruml was a most unconventional dean. He never sat in his office at the center of the dean's suite. Instead, he appropriated a smaller office down the hall, which he kept relatively dark, with a desk that never had any papers on top of it or anything in its drawers, except a box of cigars—cigars that he smoked incessantly while dreaming up schemes for reforming the Social Science Division. He also maintained a suite of rooms at the nearby Hotel Shoreland, where he entertained department heads and senior faculty members. Bee did his deaning of the Social Science Division at these daily luncheons, elaborately planned both as to food and drink, and lasting two or three hours.

Only after the cumulative effect of cocktails, good food, and fine wine did the dean think it opportune to propose to his associates some academic departure that might have shocked them more if they had not been benumbed. He would often recount his sorties of the day before to Arthur and me in his office the next morning, and Arthur, who was even more intent than Bee on sticking pins into social scientists, would egg him on to further sallies. Both Bee Ruml and Bob Hutchins grew very fond of Arthur and found him useful as an *agent provocateur*— a role that to him was second nature. Bob's only discomfort in this relationship arose from Arthur's unrestrainable desire to underline the obvious, which he feared would be overlooked, and to repeat himself ad nauseam even though the person he was addressing had already acknowledged the soundness of his point. In order to check him, Bob Hutchins had a sign made which he put on the edge of his desk whenever Arthur came in for a conference. It read: "Please don't tell the President things he already knows!"

From these three-sided or four-sided conversations about the state of the social sciences gradually emerged a project that was Bee's brainchild. As he viewed the departments in the Social Science Division, he concluded that they all dealt with closely related or overlapping aspects of the same subject matter. Society, after all, was one thing and should be studied as one thing even though sociologists, economists, political scientists, and cultural anthropologists each approach it differently. Great progress might be made, Bee thought, if these differences in approach and in technical jargon were overcome to produce a unified social science. The more Bee Ruml, Arthur Rubin, and I batted this one around, the more we became fascinated by that vision and the less inclined to recognize how visionary or illusory it was. Our self-hypnotism culminated in the announcement for the following year of a seminar entitled "Systematic Social Science," to be conducted by Ruml and Adler.

The announcement and the rumors that accompanied it resulted in the most unusual assembly of persons. When the seminar met in October 1933, its membership included three graduate students, two of whom later became professors of anthropology and heads of the department. All the rest were senior professors in the departments of economics, sociology, political science, and anthropology, including department heads. Looking back now, I am more embarrassed by the brashness of my performance in that seminar than I am about any of my other early exploits at the university when I acted without constraints that would have been wise and without the modesty appropriate to my youth. The seminar met for two afternoon hours each week. Session after session, through the autumn and winter, I lectured my elders, allowing no time for questions or discussion. Since the dean, their superior officer who supervised their budgets, sat Buddha-like beside me at the head of the seminar table beaming benignly, they felt compelled to audit these lectures in long-suffering and unsmiling silence. For reasons I cannot recall, I had decided that lectures on pure and applied logic, including the theory of probability, would provide the prolegomena necessary for unifying the social sciences; and when, after many months, I finished my exposition of the requisite liberal arts, I followed that with instruction in philosophical psychology.

How this could possibly produce the result that Bee and I had in mind, I cannot imagine. Nor can I figure out why Bee did not stop me from continuing my utterly mad performance. His only criticism was a mild reproof. One day, after a session, as we were walking to his house for a drink, I asked him how he thought the seminar was going. "Fine," he replied, "but could you, when making a point, just once in a while manage to say 'We' instead of 'I'?" Totally oblivious to the effect I was producing, I continued into the spring quarter until, at last, the floodgates burst: the assembled professors allowed their three graduate students to unleash an attack on the very idea of a unified social science and on the total irrelevance of all the logical distinctions and metaphysical principles with which I had been wasting their time.

My only explanation, and it is hardly an adequate excuse, is that I allowed my fascination with formal logic and philosophical grammar to run away with me. I had indulged myself similarly in the work I did with Jerome Michael on the law of evidence and on criminology; I had permitted this penchant of mine to blind me to the pedagogical inappropriateness of my lectures on the trivium to youngsters in the university high school; even the course I gave in the Law School on logic and argumentation was designed less to give them practical guidance than it was to pursue my own theoretical interest in the three arts of the mediaeval trivium.

The Law School further abetted my monomania by permitting me to construct a course of study for pre-law students that, because of its concentration on the three liberal disciplines of grammar, rhetoric, and logic, came to be called "the Trivium course." In its own way, it was as odd an academic offering as Systematic Social Science had been. It began in the academic year 1934–1935 and went on for three years. The idea of the course emerged from discussions within the law faculty about the requirements that should be set for students preparing to enter the law school. I suggested that, instead of prescribing a set of courses already being offered in the college, we should develop our own course, specifically designed to give pre-law students background in the humanities and training in the liberal arts of reading and writing, listening and speaking—the skills to be acquired through the disciplines of grammar, rhetoric, and logic.

The humanistic background would be provided by the close reading of a few great books—not one a week, as in the great books seminar, but two or three at most during the whole year. I would give the course with Malcolm Sharp, who, before he came to Chicago to teach the law of contracts, had been associated with Alexander Meiklejohn in the experimental college at the University of Wisconsin; in addition, there would be two assistants who would meet the students individually in tutorial sessions. It would be the only course that the students would take for a whole year, and they would receive full academic credit after passing the examination in this one course. The academic unorthodoxy of such a procedure must have excited student interest, for in each of the three years that the course was offered, it enrolled an intellectually responsive and lively group of students.

Like the students that were enrolled in the Hutchins-Adler great books seminar, they became devoted disciples—too devoted, in fact. Their enthusiasm led them to spearhead a frontal attack on the compromise college curriculum adopted by the faculty. The other unanticipated result, also born of their excessive enthusiasm for intellectual high jinks, was the decision on the part of many of the students in the pre-law course not to go on into the Law School, but instead to study philosophy, literature, or history. Two who did go from the Trivium to the Law School eventually became professors of law.

Of the two young tutors in the Trivium course, one, James Martin, after studying law, went on to become a member of the faculty teaching the great books at St. John's College in Annapolis. The other, William Gorman, after a year of graduate work at the Institute of Mediaeval Studies at the University of Toronto, also joined the faculty at St. John's College. He subsequently left St. John's to join me in producing the Syntopicon for *Great Books of the Western World,* and over a period of twenty-five years, since 1952, he has been associated with me in the work of the Institute for Philosophical Research. I owe my long and fruitful friendship with Bill Gorman to Bob Hutchins. Bob invited him to come to the University of Chicago as a result of reading an essay that Bill had written for *Hound and Horn,* which carried the title "Nostalgia for the Trivium." Accepting Bob's invitation, Bill came to the university to be plunged at once into the Trivium course.

The students met with Malcolm Sharp and me eight hours a week, in two-hour sessions, morning and afternoon on Mondays and Wednesdays. Individual tutorial conferences with Gorman or Martin were also arranged. The morning sessions were devoted to expositions of the liberal arts; the afternoon sessions, to the examination of a text. The afternoon sessions were the most exciting for me, partly because I had by this time reached a plateau in my own learning curve in matters grammatical and logical, and partly because it was my first experience in reading a text with students line by line, almost word by word. In the first year of the Trivium we read a short dialogue of Plato, the *Meno,* with that kind of intensive care. We spent more than six months on a little less than fifty pages, drawing out of every sentence not only all the meanings we could find there but also noting reflexively the grammatical, rhetorical, and logical rules that governed our process of interpretation, or the tactics we used to apply the rules to words, sentences, and paragraphs in order to come to terms with the author, to discover the propositions that he was affirming or denying, and to construct the arguments implicit in the sequence of his thought. The afternoon sessions thus provided practical applications of the principles and distinctions expounded in the morning sessions.

That experience in the close reading of the *Meno,* accompanied by reflexive observations of the techniques we employed in doing it, laid the groundwork for my formulation of the rules and recommendations that became the substance of *How To Read A Book* five years later. That book grew out of all my teaching of great books seminars at Columbia and Chicago, but particularly it germinated in the exegetical exercises that we performed in the Trivium course. The Trivium experience also gave me pedagogical insight into how training in the liberal arts should be conducted.

Courses in formal logic or lectures on the arts of grammar and rhetoric, even when accompanied by exercises, will not produce the desired result. Students can pass examinations in such courses without acquiring the habit of putting the rules to use in reading and writing, or speaking and listening. Competence in the arts of grammar, rhetoric, and logic must manifest itself in skilled reading and writing, or skilled speaking and listening; mastery of the formal principles and rules without acquiring such skills is as hollow an intellectual achievement as knowing the rules of French syntax without being able to write or speak the language.

Courses in logic and rhetoric were once required elements in the curriculum of a liberal college because it was mistakenly thought that they developed discipline in the liberal arts. They are no longer required courses, it having been discovered that they failed to inculcate the requisite skill; but, unfortunately, they have not been replaced in our colleges by instruction in the liberal arts that takes the form of teaching students how to read and write, or speak and listen, with grammatical, rhetorical, and logical skill. If liberal schooling did nothing else but develop these abilities as firm habits, it would restore the B.A. degree to its original significance. It would signify, as it once did in the Middle Ages, that a bachelor of art is one who is skilled in the liberal arts of reading and writing, speaking and listening.

In the second and third years of the Trivium course, we repeated the same general procedure, substituting other books for the *Meno* as texts to be intensively explored. In the second year we chose the Treatise on God in the *Summa Theologica* of Thomas Aquinas; in the third, Aristotle's *Physics* and Hegel's *Phenomenology of Spirit*. These last two were much more difficult than the *Meno*, partly because they were much more difficult texts and partly because of a profound deficiency that I discovered in myself, one that I have never been able to cure. I simply cannot read Hegel in the way that I can read Plato and Aristotle, Aquinas and Kant. An intransigent intellectual antipathy to his cast of mind prevents me from making the requisite effort. When I discovered this in the spring of 1937, some weeks after Hegel had been assigned, I had to ask Malcolm Sharp and the tutors to take on the task of reading Hegel with the students as I had read other authors earlier in the course. I should have sat by silently, but I could not conceal my intellectual distaste or repress my emotional discomfort at almost every turn in the discussion.

The year before, the reading and discussion of Aquinas's Treatise on God proved to be as rewarding an exercise as the one we had performed with the *Meno*. We spent weeks on the three articles of Question 2: (1) Whether the existence of God is self-evident?; (2) Whether it can be demonstrated that God exists?; and (3) Whether God exists? The students and I agreed that we would not move beyond that third question either until I persuaded all of them that Aquinas had succeeded in demonstrating God's existence, or until they persuaded me that he had failed. Session after session we stuck at this task until, finally, all but one student had assented, probably out of boredom or fatigue, for I must add that at the time I had a deplorably inadequate grasp of the difficulties and intricacies involved in the demonstration of God's existence—an inadequacy that it has taken me many years of work since then to overcome. Charles Adams, the one student who held out, remained obdurate despite everything I was then able to say on the subject, and he was righter than he knew. Malcolm Sharp intervened to break the deadlock. He suggested that, instead of persisting in my effort to persuade young Adams, I spend the rest of that particular session telling the class something about the life and work of Aquinas.

Relieved of the burden of proof I was unable to discharge, I launched into an eloquent account of the saint's career, his travels by donkey across the Alps from France to Rome and back, and the dictation of voluminous works to scribes at various monasteries during daylight hours, frequently interrupted by compulsory attendance at religious services. When I stressed the fact that Aquinas had composed a vast number of treatises of extraordinary complexity and systematic rigor, involving innumerable quotations from Scripture, from the writings of Plato, Aristotle, Cicero, and other ancient philosophers, as well as from the works of Augustine and other early Fathers of the Church, without the aid of libraries, such as we now have, or other scholarly implements, Charles Adams chided me, "Why didn't you tell us all this in the first place?" When I expressed puzzlement, he went on to say, "If you had told us all this, you wouldn't have had to argue for God's existence. It would have been obvious that Aquinas could not have done what he did without God's help."

In addition to the courses I taught and the books I wrote during the early thirties, I also managed to find time for other intellectual diversions. One of these, a performance in which I collaborated with Maude Hutchins, later developed into a book, *Diagrammatics,* that was published by Random House in a limited edition of 750 numbered copies. It opened up my interest in the whole field of the philosophy of art and aesthetic theory, subjects to which I had paid little attention before. Another divertissement consisted in a series of lectures that I delivered in the social science auditorium in 1932–1933. Attended not only by undergraduate and graduate students, but also by a substantial sampling of the university's faculty, the lectures evoked a variety of favorable and unfavorable reactions. On the favorable side, one of the lectures resulted in my being drawn back once more into academic politics and into the second round of the Chicago fight about general liberal education at the college level.

When Maude Hutchins was asked to lecture before the ladies of the Friday Club, she persuaded me to join her in the effort. In addition to her work as a sculptor, Maude had begun to do silver-point drawings in which anatomical figures appeared but in a manner that defied realistic viewing. Her artistic purpose was to present linear forms devoid of

representative content. As she said in the address that she gave at the
Friday Club, "they are non-narrative and non-representative. It is incidental that the human form may be recognized in them. The forms
you see are not necessarily people." When she asked me what I could
produce to parallel her drawings in the medium of language, I remembered a piece of prose I had written some years earlier to illustrate a
point in a lecture on sense and nonsense. The paragraph manifested
grammatical and rhetorical form even though the sequence of words in
it made no sense.

When I read this piece to Maude and told her that I thought removing the sense heightened one's perception of the form, she saw
at once the affinity between her linear and, as she referred to them, my
"lingular" constructions—the same artistic intention executed in line
and language. It was agreed that I would attempt to produce fifteen
such pieces of prose—or "proses," as we called them—to go along with
an equal number of drawings by her; and that, after brief introductory
remarks by each of us, her drawings would be projected on a screen
in a darkened room while I read my proses as the audience looked at
the drawings. Between a particular drawing being shown and a particular prose being read at the same time, there was, of course, no intelligible
or intended connection.

To give some impression of what the performance was like, I will
quote the opening lines of a few of the proses, though the total effect
is not reproducible without the conjunction of each prose with a drawing to which it was as irrelevant as the prose itself was nonsensical.
Each prose bore a title that indicated the rhetorical form being exhibited in abstraction from significant content. Here, for example, are
the opening lines of a prose entitled "Prayer," modelled on the prayer
with which St. Augustine begins his *Confessions:*

> Blue art thou, O Last, and deeply to be raised; blue is thy pagination,
> and of thy fistula there is no wing. And most, being a court of thy crema-
> tion, conspires to raise thee—most who flays a tendency, the illness of his
> fort—yet most, this court of thy cremation, conspires to raise thee.

The prose entitled "Invective" exhibits a distinctly different rhetorical form. It begins as follows:

> He is an example of insuperable skulduggery. It is difficult to believe that
> a more distressed and encrusted man could exist. His incestuous bearing,
> his conical and irreducible connivance, his undisguised infibulation make
> him an object of frenzy. No home in this fair land would castigate his
> presence.

How different in stylistic line is a prose that has the form indicated
by the title "History."

Render Hibernica, the heredity exotic, developed far beyond the nexus
of his contemporaries the theory of epibenthic provinces. Elevated to the
post of syntax, his influence enlarged to more commodious consent in
the prevailing guild-hall. The rapid advance of his placental inquiry fore-
shadowed the scientific method of later protection.

And so on with other proses, bearing such titles as "Definition," "Description," "Dilemma," "Interrogation," "Contention," "Analysis," and
"Peroration."

It should not be too difficult to imagine the effect of this performance
on the ladies of the Friday Club. In 1932, abstract or nonrepresenta-
tive art still raised hackles in many quarters; the shock waves set up
by the Armory Show in New York twenty years before were still rever-
berating. Were the wife of the university's president and Professor
Adler perpetrating an elaborate spoof at which the audience should
feel free to laugh, or were they being serious—and outrageous? In fact,
the feelings of the audience were mixed that Friday morning, but when
the dust settled the predominant reaction was one of outrage over having
their legs pulled. If Maude Hutchins had initially planned the event
in lighthearted fashion, the reaction of the audience transformed her
mood into one of deadly seriousness. When the furore spread from the
social circles of Chicago to the campus of the university, Maude and
I became involved in repeat performances—one before the members of
the Renaissance Society and another in Mandel Hall before a large
audience of students and faculty—in each of which Maude became
more defensive of what had now become for her an aesthetic dogma.

I could hardly abandon ship in the midst of such a storm, and so I
went along with these sequelae, half-serious and half-amused. At
Maude's urging, I persuaded Donald Klopfer and Bennett Cerf at
Random House to undertake the publication of our materials in a
book to be entitled *Diagrammatics*. The limited edition of 750 copies
sold out before publication, former heavyweight champion Gene
Tunney getting copy number one as the first subscriber. After the book's
publication, I too became defensive of its thesis when reviewers and
others who discussed it failed so utterly to understand the simple point
that was being made about the significance of form divorced from
significant matter in a work of art.

During the same month of 1932, I delivered four lectures in the
auditorium of the Social Science Bulding—one on form and subject
matter in the intellectual disciplines, which paralleled the distinction
that Maude Hutchins and I were trying to make in the field of the
arts; one on the position of psychology among the social sciences; one
on the relation of law to the social sciences; and one on the nature of
history. In the course of the last lecture, I quoted Oswald Spengler's
statement that physiognomy is to the history of anything as system is

to the science of anything. When my audience looked puzzled, I invented an etymological derivation for the word *physiognomy*. I ignored the presence of the letter *g* in the word and made it out to come from the Greek words *physis* and *nomos,* thus rendering its relevant meaning as "the law of change." A week or so after the lecture was delivered, I received the following communication from Prof. Paul Shorey of the Greek Department:

My dear Professor Adler—

To be quite frank, I was unfavorably impressed by your lecture on History, and I have the courage to tell you so because I have since been reading your book on Dialectic, and now think much more highly of your methods and point of view than I did when I heard the lecture. I am not such a pedant as to attach great importance to false etymology, though I do think that a university professor ought to verify his etymologies before presenting them to students. If Spengler uses the word in that sense, it would only verify my impressions from a hasty reading of his work that the colossal scholarship which his admirers attribute to him is a good deal of bluff.

Sometime later, I received an opposite reaction from Prof. Ronald Crane of the English Department. At first hostile to the president's educational ideas, Crane changed direction as a result of understanding better what Hutchins was driving at. He invited me to have lunch with him at the Quadrangle Club and asked me to send him some papers of mine that might further amplify his understanding of the program with which he identified both Hutchins and me. Among the papers I sent him was a copy of my lecture on the nature of history, concerning which he wrote me:

I have read it with much interest and, for the most part, with entire agreement. I expect to make good use of some of your points not only in the Committee on History, but also on the course I give each year on the nature and methods of literary and intellectual history.

From Professor Crane's reversal of attitude, many things ensued— the formation of a group of young instructors in the Humanities Division which met regularly at his home in 1933–1934 with whom, at his invitation, I discussed the teaching of the liberal arts and the reading of the classics; the appointment, at Crane's initiative, of my friend Dick McKeon as visiting professor of history in 1934–1935; and the emergence of a small coterie in the faculty who, friendly to Hutchins and me, gave us some support when the second round of the Chicago fight broke out early in 1934. I should, perhaps, mention here that among the young instructors who attended the sessions of the "Crane Group" were men who many years later became pivotal figures in the

educational reforms that Clarence Faust, who was one of them, instituted when he became dean of the college in 1941.

John Barden, who as an entering freshman in 1930 joined the
Hutchins-Adler great books seminar, became in his senior year editor
of the *Daily Maroon,* the university newspaper. Both in its news columns
and in his editorials, he advocated the president's educational program
and criticized the faculty opposition, precipitating an intellectual
tempest that swept over the campus from January to June in 1934.
Hutchins, in his convocation address of December 1933, had made a
number of acerbic comments about the place of facts and ideas not
only in the education of students, but also in the researches carried on
by scientists and scholars. At the beginning of the new term, Barden
reported the effect of this address in a story headlined "Hutchins
Address Divides Faculty into Two Camps"; and if that was not true at
the time, a succession of more inflammatory articles, which Barden
wrote, succeeded in producing a campus confrontation that aligned students and professors on opposite sides of the issue.

Day after day, the "Letters to the Editor" column carried answers to
and defenses of Barden's criticisms, written by members of the faculty
as well as by students. Prof. Harry Gideonse, later president of Brooklyn
College in New York, posted *Maroon* editorials on the college bulletin
board with his own caustic comments; to which Barden responded by
publishing a glossary "to aid those who criticize *Maroon* editorials," in
which he instructed Gideonse and others on the meaning of such terms
as general education, ideas, facts, propositions, principles, and theories.
The running feud between Barden and Gideonse, together with heated
exchanges between adherents of both parties—exchanges which occurred
in classrooms as well as in locker rooms, cafeterias, and taverns—became
the chief, in fact the all-absorbing, extracurricular activity at the university. Excitement about an intellectual conflict took the place of the
usual excitement about athletic contests and made the latter look
pallid by comparison.

My own involvement resulted from a challenge issued to me by
Prof. Anton J. Carlson, an eminent physiologist, who along with
Gideonse, a social scientist, led the opposition. He had been particularly
provoked by what he interpreted as slurs on the scientific method in
the president's convocation address the preceding December, and which
Hutchins repeated in his address to the faculty at the annual trustees
dinner in January. What Hutchins said on both those occasions he had
said many times before, but his earlier statements just did not happen
to light the spark that set the tinder on fire.

As early as 1931, in an address to the graduating class, Hutchins had
declared:

Science is not the collection of facts or the accumulation of data. A discipline does not become scientific merely because its professors have acquired a great deal of information. Facts do not arrange themselves. Facts do not solve problems. I do not wish to be misunderstood. We must get the facts. We must get them all. . . . But at the same time we must raise the question whether facts alone will settle our difficulties for us. And we must raise the question, too, whether an educational system that is based on the accumulation and distribution of facts is likely to lead us through the mazes of a world whose complications have been produced by the facts we have discovered.

And a little later in the same address, which he entitled "The New Atlantis" because it was an attack on the scientific utopia envisioned by Francis Bacon, Hutchins declared that "upon the proper balance of fact and idea depends our eventual escape from the New Atlantis," adding that he hoped the system of general examinations which had just been set up would "emphasize ideas rather than facts."

The subsequent convocation address in December 1933 contained remarks slightly more incendiary, such as:

The gadgeteers and data collectors, masquerading as scientists, have threatened to become the supreme chieftains of the scholarly world.

As the Renaissance could accuse the Middle Ages of being rich in principles and poor in facts, we are now entitled to inquire whether we are not rich in facts and poor in principles.

Rational thought is the only basis of education and research. Whether we know it or not, it has been responsible for our scientific success; its absence has been responsible for our bewilderment. A university is the place of all places to grapple with those fundamental principles which rational thought seeks to establish.

The system has been to pour facts into the student with splendid disregard of the certainty that he will forget them, that they may not be facts by the time he graduates, and that he won't know what to do with them if they are.

The three worst words in education are character, personality, and facts. Facts are the core of an anti-intellectual curriculum. Personality is the qualification we look for in an anti-intellectual teacher. Character is what we expect to produce in the student by the combination of a teacher of personality and a curriculum of facts.

The scholars in a university which is trying to grapple with fundamentals will, I suggest, devote themselves first of all to the rational analysis of the principles of each subject matter. They will seek to establish general propositions under which the facts they gather may be subsumed. I repeat, they would not cease to gather facts, but they would know what facts to look for, what they wanted them for, and what to do with them after they got them.

When he came to deliver his address to the faculty at the trustees dinner a month or so later, Hutchins took note of the reaction that these remarks had aroused. Remarking that he had said such things repeatedly in earlier statements, which had been printed in the *University Record,* he added: "Were the editor of the *University Record* still alive, he would, I am sure, be grieved to learn that any of you were surprised at my remarks at the last Convocation." He then quoted appropriate supporting passages from eminent scientists and philosophers—Alfred North Whitehead, Bertrand Russell, Stanley Jevons, Claude Bernard, and Henri Poincaré. But instead of leaving matters at that, he poured fuel on the fire he had lit by a series of *obiter dicta* about anti-intellectualism, which could not fail to antagonize the leading members of the faculty:

> An anti-intellectual attitude toward education reduces the curriculum to the exposition of detail. There are no principles. The world is a flux of events. We cannot hope to understand it. All we can do is to watch it. This is the conclusion of the leading anti-intellectuals of our time, William James and John Dewey.

> Anti-intellectualism dooms pure science; it dooms any kind of education that is more than training in technical skill. It must be a foreboding of this doom which accounts for the sense of inferiority which we find widespread among academic people.

> . . . the recognition that ideas are the essential elements in the development of a science . . . is a repudiation of the anti-intellectual position. The anti-intellectual position must be repudiated if a university is to achieve its ends.

It should not be difficult to understand why these remarks stung and stunned the faculty at a university which, since its inception and certainly in its heyday, had been dominated by the scientific spirit, by empiricism and pragmatism, and by the instrumentalism of John Dewey. The faculty response issued in a variety of documents—a speech by Prof. Frank Knight, a widely respected economist, entitled "Is Modern Thought Anti-Intellectual?" and a paper by philosophy professor Charles W. Morris entitled "Pragmatism and the Crisis of Democracy," the latter published in a pamphlet series by Professor Gideonse. The controversy over facts and ideas, and intellectualism versus anti-intellectualism, spread from the campus to the city. Leading articles appeared in the *Chicago Daily News* under such headlines as "Hutchins Stirs University by Questioning Science as a Basis for Philosophy" and "Scientific Writers Challenge Dr. Hutchins' Statement Fact-Finding Art Is Empiric." But by far the most dramatic confrontation on the issues occurred in February in a debate between Professor Carlson and me which took place in Mandel Hall, the university's largest auditorium, jam-packed with both students and faculty, and with an over-flow crowd seated on the platform behind the speakers.

Professor Carlson, it must be said, was the kind of "personality" on the campus that Hutchins had in mind when he made his invidious comment about "character, personality, and facts." His disciples fondly referred to him as "Ajax," a sobriquet derived from his initials *A. J.* His addiction to getting at the facts and always arguing in terms of them earned him another epithet, based on his strong Swedish accent: "Vat-iss-de-ef-fidence-Carlson." That phrase became the watchword of his followers. His study of the physiology of thirst and hunger had won him recognition as an experimentalist. It was said of him that he "inspired several generations of students to cling to the facts" by being the kind of classroom showman who climbed on a laboratory table "in order to explore, albeit uncomfortably, how the digestive system worked."

Late in January, I was visited by a graduate student in the Biology Division who reported that the president's recent speeches had caused a great deal of confusion and anxiety which needed to be clarified and removed. To this end, would I be willing to explain as well as defend the Hutchins position in a discussion with Professor Carlson at a meeting of the Graduate Club of the Division of the Biological Sciences. He stressed the fact that it would be staged as a discussion, not a debate, and that the audience would be limited to graduate students in the division. Given these limiting conditions, I could hardly refuse the invitation. I accepted without consulting Bob Hutchins, Bee Ruml, or Arthur Rubin. Before I learned about it or could do anything to stop it, the conditions that had been set were abandoned; the polite, private discussion had been turned into a meeting of antagonists in a public debate open to the whole university population.

The *Daily Maroon,* of course, publicized the event. The demand for admission to Mandel Hall led to the sale of tickets to an event that should have been free. Departments bought boxes for faculty members to view the event, as if it were going to be a bullfight that should be seen from a vantage point. Now, when it was too late to do anything about it, I sought the advice of my friends. They took a very dim view of the whole affair and tried to persuade me to withdraw, which was, of course, impossible. Bee Ruml summed up my chances most succinctly: "You can't possibly succeed," he said; "you will lose either way, either because Carlson gets the better of you in the argument or because you anger the crowd by getting the better of him."

In spite of this warning, expressed even more emphatically and grimly by Bob Hutchins and Arthur Rubin, I proceeded quite blithely to prepare a careful statement about the relation of theory and observation, and their correlatives—ideas and facts, in the laboratory sciences or, for that matter, in any kind of empirical research or scholarship. Not until the very day on which the debate was to take place did I become scared, as I should have been from the very beginning if I had had any sense. During that day, I could not escape a growing awareness of the carnival atmosphere that surrounded the forthcoming event, and so I began for the first time to be apprehensive. When I walked from my home to Mandel Hall that evening, struck by the excited and noisy crowds that were converging on the entrances from all directions, I could not help feeling that I was going to be the bull who would end up on the floor of the arena rather than the bullfighter who would end up bowing to the cheering multitude.

I took my place on the platform at the appointed hour, white-faced, I am sure, but I hope not visibly trembling. Professor Carlson had not yet come in. Long minutes passed before he did, and when he did, he strode down the aisle in his white laboratory coat, greeted by thunderous applause from the crowd. He later explained his lateness by saying that he had just come from his laboratory where he was working late— again eliciting a burst of applause. I delivered my precisely worded speech, constructed in my customary analytical style, which I had taken great care to keep cool and reasonable, devoid of even the least trace of caustic criticism or disparaging innuendoes. It also made no mention of Hutchins or of his recent addresses. When I finished reading it in an even voice, I received a smattering of polite applause, with a spotty "hurrahing" added by students of mine scattered in the hall.

Professor Carlson then got up and began by saying that he had been much too busy of late in the laboratory to prepare a speech (applause), but that he would get down at once to the nuts and bolts of the occasion by challenging Professor Adler to defend the outrageous statements recently made by the president of the university (loud applause). Whereupon he took from his pocket a sheaf of cards, on each of which he had written a statement that I was challenged to defend. After he read each of these statements to the audience, he turned in my direction and threw a card at me as if it were a gauntlet, saying, "What about that?" (applause).

Luckily, I had brought with me copies of Bob's speeches, which I knew almost by heart, having read them and gone over them with him a number of times before he delivered them. I found myself able to connect each of the cards that Carlson threw at me with the very passage in the speech from which Carlson had wrenched it out of context. When Carlson had finished and sat down with all-too-obvious satisfaction in his performance, reinforced by the wild applause of the audience, I took the rostrum and proceeded to the rebuttal by putting each of Carlson's quotations into the larger context that explained the president's statements and made them appear much more reasonable and defensible than Carlson would have the audience believe.

To my surprise, this procedure won a noticeably intensified and more widespread applause—from the faculty boxes as well as from the students on the main floor. This turn of events angered Carlson. Since he really had not prepared himself for a serious debate and had nothing more of substance to say, he flailed about rhetorically in the closing moments of the evening, exhibiting an obvious irascibility and even an unbecoming loss of temper. The applause that greeted him at the end was much less hearty and affectionate than it had been at the beginning, the very reverse of what had happened to me. My friends admitted the next morning that, though I had not won the debate, neither had I lost it. I had gained enough friends and supporters for the president's position to turn it into a draw.

The debate took place on February 9. Its repercussions were scarcely over when less than a month later, John Barden published an "education issue" of the *Maroon,* which he introduced with this front-page statement:

> Critically campaigning for the intellectual as opposed to the memoriza-
> tional approach to education, The Daily Maroon brings its three-month
> battle to a stormy close with today's issue. . . . New Plan Syllabi for the
> four general courses are reviewed in other columns of this issue.

All four of the reviews were written by seniors who, like Barden himself, had been students for almost four years in the Hutchins-Adler great books seminar. The faculty had every reason, therefore, to infer that the criticisms levelled by these students at the syllabi which they had prepared for the four New Plan survey courses had either been inspired by Hutchins and Adler or, to say the least, reflected indoctrination by them. Some impression of the tone and direction of these criticisms may be gathered from the headlines that Barden attached to the reviews:

> —Humanities Syllabus Lacks Needed Accuracy
> —Social Science I Presents Facts, Overlooks Ideas
> —Logic Missing in Physical Science Course Outline
> —General Biology Course Is Termed Biased, Partial.

To top it off, Barden wrote an editorial that presented the vision of a college in "the Utopian future" which would be the answer to "American mediocrity in education"—a college in which all the students would be engaged in the reading and discussion of great books, accompanied by tutorials in grammar, rhetoric, and logic. At the end of four years of such a program, the students, Barden concluded, would rejoice "that education for them had been philosophical, not scientific."

Leading members of the college faculty as well as a substantial portion of the students in the New Plan courses were now drawn into the fight. In the ensuing weeks, what might be characterized as civil war broke out on the campus. The Hutchins-Adler student contingent engaged in public debate with equally vocal and vociferous representatives of the other side. Commenting on this debate, the *Maroon* declared: "To anyone who has had the privilege of reading Mr. Hutchins' address, it will be evident that both philosophically and rhetorically he has said the last word on education as well as the first." It also opened its columns to the opposition by publishing rejoinders to the earlier critical reviews, which charged the critics with being dogmatic, making unsupported statements, deifying the infallible Aristotle, and aiming to constitute themselves a new Inquisition. In addition, in mid-April the *Maroon* published an editorial written by Prof. James Weber Linn of the English Department, who dismissed the whole controversy by saying that "the belief that such discussion is particularly important is characteristic of the inexperienced and immature. . . . In education, 'principles' are of little importance in comparison with people." Barden could not let that pass without a comment that verged on insult. "Those who have taken courses in the personality of Professor James Weber Linn," he wrote, "will realize the inevitability of his editorial."

The winds of doctrine that swept across the campus were by now approaching hurricane velocity. On April 21, the College Curriculum Committee drafted a resolution on the educational objectives of the college, which they submitted to the faculty for adoption. I quote from it only the passages that must be read in order to appreciate the way in which the battle lines were drawn.

> The University of Chicago has been characterized by its devotion to research and its sense of responsibility to the community. . . . Its attitude has been at once scientific and humanistic.
>
> Certain of the criticisms which have been made concerning the present College program are related and coherent expressions of a common metaphysical background and basis. They grow out of the acceptance of a thoroughgoing rationalism, a commitment to the Aristotelian-Thomist realist view of *universalia in re*. . . . They postulate as orthodox a belief in a rational soul engaged in abstracting eternal and unchangeable ideas from experience. . . .
>
> We believe that any form of rationalist absolutism which brings with it an atmosphere of intolerance of liberal, scientific, and democratic attitudes is incompatible with the ideal of a community of scholars and students, recognizable as the University of Chicago. For over forty years the University has led a distinguished existence without being officially committed to any single system of metaphysics, psychology, logic, religion, politics, economics, art of scientific method. To follow the reactionary course of accepting one particular system of ancient or mediaeval metaphysics and dialectics, and to force our whole educational program to conform thereto, would spell disaster. We cannot commit ourselves to such a course.

The college faculty adopted the resolution as drafted by the Curriculum Committee. This action impelled John Barden to write a letter to the dean of the college in which he said:

> If you were surprised by the Maroon's mild comment on the resolution passed by the college faculty, you deserve to know the reasons for such mildness.
>
> The resolution could only have been directed at the following: President Hutchins, the Crane-Adler group within the faculty, and The Daily Maroon. . . . I shall assume that it was unmistakably directed at The Daily Maroon. But I hope that you never admit that such was the intention of the resolution.
>
> I don't care how good or bad a college newspaper may be, it is *never* worth official notice by any division of the faculty. I feel that the college faculty have immeasurably degraded themselves by officially recognizing that The Daily Maroon even exists.

Before the term ended in May, the overheated controversy took a lighter turn. A hundred or more students spent a weekend at a Wisconsin lake in a conference on education. Thornton Wilder and Harold Swift, chairman of the Board of Trustees, addressed them in tones that aimed at reconciling differences of opinion. But when Prof. Louis Wirth, a member of the Sociology Department and a spokesman for facts rather than ideas, talked about "group relations in the university," any chance of reconciling the opposing groups faded away. The *Daily Maroon*'s subsequent report of what then occurred ran as follows:

> After those in attendance had been divided into two camps, someone with the right idea as to how intellectual disputes should be settled, suggested that a ball game be played. Sides were chosen and the Aristotelians took the field against the Social Scientists. After seven hectic innings, the Aristotelians claimed a 5 to 4 triumph. But there were several Social Scientists to be found who thought that the Aristotelians had forsaken their immutability of ideas and for once made two and two equal five.

That evening after the ball game, around a campfire, light verse ditties were chanted by the opposing forces. The Aristotelians had not lost their sense of humor, for they sang, to the tune of "Nobody Knows the Trouble I've Seen,"

> Nobody knows what Aristotle means,
>   Nobody knows but Adler.
> Nobody knows what Adler means,
>   Let's ask The Daily Maroon.
>
> *Chorus:*
>   The whole is greater than its parts, L . . o . . g . . o . . s
>   Logos is the essence of the arts, L . . o . . g . . o . . s

Everybody knows that Aquinas is dead,
  Everybody knows but Adler.
Nobody knows what Adler knows,
  Let's ask The Daily Maroon.

In the final issues of the *Maroon* that academic year, Barden wrote an editorial on intolerance, in which he characterized as a specious form of tolerance the view that everything is a matter of opinion, one opinion being as good as another, even when they are contrary or contradictory. By way of rejoinder, Professor Gideonse, after ridiculing the flight into the past of the neo-Aristotelians, reminded everyone that "not the least of the university's many distinguished contributions was that of the so-called 'Chicago School' of philosophy, identified with the names of Dewey, Mead, Tufts, Moore, and Ames." That, he said, represented the main tradition of this university.

Gideonse was correct. By the same token, the resolution adopted by the college was wide of the mark in asserting that the university had never in its history been committed to a relatively homogeneous doctrine or point of view. The "Chicago School" of philosophy did represent the main tradition of the university from the beginning of the century until Hutchins became president. The empiricism, pragmatism, and relativism of Dewey, his associates, and followers, were not confined to the teachings of the Philosophy Department; they gave inspiration and direction to the leading professors in other fields, resulting in a relatively homogeneous doctrine and spirit diffused throughout the university as a whole. In a retrospective article that I wrote for *Harper's Magazine* in 1941, entitled "The Chicago School," I pointed out that Chicago's school of thought gradually came to dominate the work of other institutions—in philosophy and education, in biology, social science, and religion. "Chicago had, in its first long period," I wrote, "both homogeneity in itself and affinity with the general trend in American culture. It was the larger community in microcosm."

This led me to ask why anyone should have wished to reform the University of Chicago. Was it not everything that a university should be, doing everything a university should do? "The answer," I said, "is simply that its unity had been achieved too quickly and at too great a cost. The price must be measured in terms of the things which Chicago, and American culture generally, had been willing to give up, had, in fact, renounced as outmoded. At its *very* center, exercising centrifugal force, was a hard core of negations and exclusions," such as the denial of metaphysics and theology as independent of empirical science, the denial of moral values transcending adaptation to environment and escaping relativity of time and place, the denial of intellectual discipline in education, and so on.

If the positive points in the Chicago movement had been temperately affirmed, truth might have been increased, even transformed, by their addition; but there would probably be no record today of any Chicago School of Thought. Given a sharp, negative twist, they not only created a school of thought but also unified its members in a crusading movement against the old and supposedly outworn. Once remove the negations and make the contrary supposition—that the old is not outworn, but must be integrated with the new—and you will see how hollow at its center was Chicago's unity before Hutchins came along.

I then went on to explain that "what Hutchins attempted to establish at Chicago was not a new school of thought, just as exclusive in its own way as its predecessor." The faculty misinterpreted him in terms of their own extremism. They charged him with wanting "nothing but Thomism," "nothing but principles," or "nothing but the past" where before there had been "nothing but Dewey's brand of pragmatism," "nothing but facts," or "nothing but the present." On the contrary, Hutchins sought to relate science, philosophy, and theology harmoniously without sacrificing the autonomy of each. He wished to be contemporary and American in education without promoting militant modernism or cultural isolationism.

In the past ten years there have been numerous references to "the neo-scholastic movement at Chicago," "Chicago Thomism," "Aristotelianism on the Midway," "the revival of classicism," "the return to the Middle Ages" —all suggestive of the fact that Chicago had become the center of another orthodoxy, the seat of an opposite school of thought. That, however, is simply not the fact . . . I do not believe that Hutchins ever wished it to be. It was not merely that he and his associates in reform were vastly outnumbered by the dissident voices on the faculty. . . . The truth is rather that Hutchins fought the old school not to replace it by another, but to place its positive contributions, shorn of their "nothing-but" exaggerations, in the perspective of the whole European tradition. Justice could be done to modernity without throwing ancient wisdom out of court.

Looking back over those ten trouble-filled yet intellectually exciting years, I summed them up by saying that "the Chicago Fight now plays the role . . . once played by the Chicago School." The extraordinary intellectual vigor of those ten years resulted from the fact that the parties to important issues concerning education, the organization of knowledge, and the structure of the university were "willing to see the fight through, wherever the chips fell." They did not "run away from trouble by insisting upon academic dignity, by hiding behind the false face of academic politeness. Dispensing with kid gloves and Queensberry rules, the discussion turned into something of a public brawl, with all sorts of kibitzers on the sidelines mixing in. But, however lamentable some aspects of the controversy now seem, the Chicago

Fight, like the Chicago School, performed the type of service which a university owes to the community."

Comparing those ten years at Chicago with my previous ten years at Columbia, and also in terms of what I knew about academic life at other universities, I could applaud, without qualification, "the exceptional character of Chicago's intellectual vitality."

> . . . there has been more real tangling over basic issues at Chicago than has occurred at a dozen other places during the same time, or at some places during their whole existence. . . . Their faculties may harbor differences of opinion about fundamentals, but you would never know it by listening to the talk at the faculty club, reading the student paper, or detecting signs of strife in administrative decisions. From this usual state of affairs, Chicago differs almost in kind, not degree. The campus has been a seething ferment these past ten years, and everybody has been involved from the President down to the janitors—the students as well as the faculty.

The phase of the Chicago fight that I have just described centered mainly on issues concerning the aims and methods of general education at the college level. But implicit in that controversy were more fundamental issues concerning the hierarchy of disciplines in the organization of knowledge and the structure of a university—questions about the relation of philosophy, and also theology, to the empirical sciences, questions about the architectonic position of metaphysics, questions about the validity of ethical principles and the objectivity of moral standards. These issues were peripheral or in the background of the interchanges between Barden and Gideonse, in the Carlson-Adler debate, and in the jousting of student groups who aligned themselves with the Aristotelians or the Social Scientists. They came to the fore with the publication in 1936 of Hutchins's *Higher Learning in America* —based on the Storrs Lectures he delivered at Yale the previous year— and they occupied the center of the stage in the final rounds of the Chicago fight.

My account of the fight may give a false impression which I wish to correct. What I have reported so far and will report in the chapter to follow is only a small part of the Hutchins years at the university—the part in which he and I collaborated. The activities in which we were engaged together represent only a fraction of the time and energy he expended on educational innovations in which I played no role, on administrative duties as burdensome as they were multifarious, on the never-solved problems of the university's finances, and on the daily round of dealings with deans, members of the faculty, members of the Board of Trustees, prospective donors, and representatives of government or of the public. When the going got tough, the philosopher could retreat to his ivory tower; the president always had to remain on the firing line.

Chapter 9

The Final Rounds

Toward the end of June in 1935, *Time* magazine carried a cover story on "Chicago's Hutchins." It was generally congratulatory, especially with regard to the New Plan for general education adopted by the college faculty. Hutchins and I regarded the plan as a poor substitute for the one we had originally outlined and submitted. Considering as defects the compromises we had been forced to make, we indulged in premature despair. As early as 1933, we talked to one another about leaving the University of Chicago and setting up "Cornwall College."

Our choice of Cornwall, Connecticut, as the site for the college of our dreams sprang from the fact that Mark and Dorothy Van Doren owned a house there. Scott and Miriam Buchanan lived across the valley in a house that the Adlers shared for several summers. At Cornwall College, we envisaged a curriculum that would provide not only general but also genuinely liberal education, revolving around the reading and discussion of great books and discipline in the liberal arts. As we talked about this fancied institution, Bob pointed out that it would have one serious defect: being only a college and not a university, it would not be able to support or accommodate an institute of philosophical studies, which remained part of my dream.

However fanciful may have been our talk about Cornwall College, serious, indeed, was Bob's relatively early willingness to consider other jobs to which he might go from the presidency of the University of Chicago. After visits to the White House at President Roosevelt's invitation, there appeared to be some likelihood of Bob's being offered an important New Deal post. That did not come through, but he was subsequently considered first for the chairmanship of the Securities and Exchange Commission and then for a seat on the Supreme Court—to which, however, Roosevelt eventually appointed Bob's old friend Bill Douglas.

The reasons why these jobs did not materialize for Hutchins are of less importance than the reason why he seriously considered them— his despair, born of impatience, about effecting genuinely innovative changes in the higher learning in America. But he kept on thinking of ways to break through the impasse that had developed at the university. This persistence on his part led to another scheme for bypassing faculty opposition and getting something done on the educational front. It took the form of establishing a special Committee on the Liberal Arts, with Scott Buchanan, Dick McKeon, and Stringfellow Barr as members. Hutchins had never really given up on the idea of bringing to the University of Chicago men he had come to know through me. The university blowup that resulted from his efforts in this direction during 1930– 1931 did not stop him from trying again.

When Scott Buchanan returned from his year in England and his work on George and Mary Boole, he became involved in educational reforms at the University of Virginia. President Alderman of that institution created a committee to consider curriculum changes, to which he appointed Scott and his close friend Stringfellow "Winkie" Barr. Barr, a professor of history, had been a Rhodes scholar at Oxford at the same time as Scott. From 1933 until 1935, Scott and Winkie did a great deal of thinking about the materials and objectives of liberal education, the fruits of which they brought with them to Chicago when they came there in 1936 as members of the Committee on the Liberal Arts.

The path that led Dick McKeon to membership on the committee took a somewhat different course. Through the intervention of Ronald Crane, McKeon received an invitation to come to Chicago as a visiting professor in the History Department in the academic year 1934–1935. For once, an appointment that Hutchins desired had been submitted for his approval by the faculty. During his year as visiting professor, McKeon, aided and abetted by Crane, won the favor of his colleagues in the Humanities Division. Not only did his impressive scholarship and his striking intellectual attainments justly earn their respect, but McKeon employed tactics in dealing with his colleagues which, unlike those employed by Hutchins and me, were designed to be conciliatory and persuasive. An objective desired by Hutchins was achieved without his intervention when the Humanities Division nominated McKeon for the deanship, and he became dean of humanities, as well as professor of philosophy and Greek, to take office at the beginning of 1935–1936.

McKeon did not have to learn what not to do by observing the miscarriages that resulted from the tactics employed by Bob Hutchins and me. He was temperamentally addicted, as well as intellectually inclined, to a different method of gaining his point—in the longer, rather than the shorter, run. On a visit to the University of Virginia in April 1935, after his appointment to the deanship, McKeon outlined his plans to Scott Buchanan, to Scott's dismay, for Scott put little trust in the results to be achieved by the adroit maneuvering on the part of academic administrators. He told Dick this in so many words when Dick tried to persuade him to come to Chicago under his auspices. Scott really lost his temper when Dick got around to talking about the mistakes that I had made in my dealings with the faculty at Chicago. According to Dick, I had been utterly blind to the possibilities of a more subtle approach, and in consequence I had all but eliminated myself from the picture. Nevertheless, Dick assured Scott that if I would "behave myself," he would succeed in getting me reestablished in the course of the next five years.

Shortly afterward, Dick and I had a conversation in which he repeated his promise to get me established, even going so far as to say that he could get me reappointed to the Philosophy Department, but only, of course, if I were willing not to rush things and to tread lightly. I responded, as politely but as plainly as possible, by telling him not to trouble himself about my future. I did not tell him that I no longer had any desire to be in the Philosophy Department, and most certainly not under the conditions that Dick envisioned.

In the spring of 1936, Arthur Rubin came up with a scheme that involved a gift to the university of funds for the president to use at his discretion for educational purposes. Among Arthur's friends in Chicago were Alfred and Marion Stern, with whom he gossiped about university affairs. He persuaded Marion, who had inherited a fortune from her father, Julius Rosenwald, to put $25,000 at the disposal of Bob Hutchins to use as he saw fit. Since in Bob's view the appointment of Barr, Buchanan, and Rubin to a special committee did not require the approval of the faculty, the gift from Marion Stern led to the creation of a Committee on the Liberal Arts, with the three aforementioned on it, and with McKeon and me also included. In addition, the funds allowed Barr and Buchanan to bring with them from the University of Virginia two young men, Catesby Taliaffiero and Charles Glenn Wallis, who during 1936–1937 doubled as junior members of the committee and as tutors in my Trivium course. McKeon also invited three of his graduate students from Columbia to become junior members of the committee, among whom were Paul Goodman and William Barrett. Bill Gorman, who had been a tutor in the Trivium course, also became a junior member. The committee, numbering ten, met for the first time in October 1936.

I think it is fair and accurate to say that the committee's explorations and discussions during 1936–1937 laid the groundwork for the New Program at St. John's College in Annapolis, initiated there in the fall of

1937 with Stringfellow Barr as president of the college and Scott Buchanan as its dean. But Bob Hutchins was greatly disappointed in his hope that the work of the committee might advance the cause of liberal education at the University of Chicago. Far from doing that, it occasioned another academic setback for him. The fact that special funds had been available to finance the work of the committee, together with the fact that the members of the committee, other than McKeon and Adler, had no official status on the faculty, encouraged the "Stop-Hutchins" contingent on the faculty to take further restrictive action against the president's appointive power. At a meeting of the Humanities Division, McKeon could not prevent the passing of a motion which called upon the University Senate to inform the president that he had to consult the division as a whole if he wished to make an appointment in it. The college faculty passed a similar resolution. These actions finally led to the creation by the University Senate of a committee to investigate the administration of the university and to propose reforms, among which would be a severe curtailment of the president's prerogatives.

In addition to his disappointment over the failure of the committee to effect changes at the University of Chicago, Bob Hutchins was sorely perplexed by the tensions that broke into open strife among persons whom he thought able to work together amicably as friends. A rift developed between Arthur Rubin and Barr and Buchanan when these two pursued a line of thought that Arthur felt was fruitless for Chicago. Both Buchanan and I found ourselves at odds with McKeon after his appointment as dean. In my case, the disaffection stemmed from philosophical differences that had arisen since our days together at Columbia.

By 1935, my growing sense of a body of important philosophical truths to be found in the writings of Aristotle and Aquinas had caused me to abandon the dialectical stance I had adopted at Columbia. I was no longer willing to entertain the tenability of positions on opposite sides of any issue. My inclination was now to come down flatly in favor of certain propositions as true, rejecting their contraries or contradictories as false. McKeon, on the other hand, now appeared to me to be taking the approach that I had recommended in *Dialectic*. Even though his method of doing so rested on principles different from mine, it nevertheless enabled him to accommodate, or even to attempt to reconcile, conflicting points of view. Observing Dick straddling issues that Bob Hutchins and I thought required one either to be with us or against us, I wrote Bob a letter in which I criticized Dick:

> He makes the basic issues a matter of difference in method, not a matter of difference in doctrine. He can take any position and justify it by interpreting it as one method of approaching the problem. This, it seems to me, is

simply a way of avoiding the dilemma of having to decide which position is true, and which false. Either Aristotle is right, and Plato wrong, or conversely. I'll be damned if they do not contradict one another and I'll be damned if, contradicting one another, one of them isn't right and the other wrong. Dick is today taking the position which I took in *Dialectic* eight years ago, and which I now think is nothing but clever sophistry. It is simply a way of avoiding the obligation to take sides and take the chance of being wrong. If you straddle all issues by Dick's method, you can never be found off-side.

With all these strains and tensions among its members, the Committee on Liberal Arts was foredoomed to split up. After a few meetings of the group as a whole, in which we could not agree about what books to read or how to read them, the committee blew apart. Buchanan and Barr, with Arthur Rubin as a noncooperative member, set up a rump committee with their students in which they read great books and worked on the plans for an ideal curriculum along the lines they had followed in Virginia. I concentrated on my Trivium course, now in its third successive year. For a short while, Barr and Buchanan attended its sessions to observe, as an example of training in the liberal arts, the exercises we were performing in an effort to read and interpret Aristotle's *Physics*. McKeon was teaching graduate courses in Plato's *Republic* and Aristotle's *De Anima,* which most of the younger associates of the committee attended. These younger men formed a group of students who kept in touch with what the senior members were doing in their separate ways, and they continued in their own discussions to explore the liberal arts. Their experience created a pool of available talent that could later be drawn upon to staff St. John's College and liberal arts programs elsewhere.

The growing despair that Bob Hutchins felt about his failure in the sphere of educational reforms increased with what appeared to be the dismal failure of the Committee on Liberal Arts and the heightened faculty opposition it had aroused. But, in a larger perspective, this phase of the Chicago fight was not without its positive results. The plan to be adopted as the New Program at St. John's College took shape in the work of the Committee on Liberal Arts. Both Bob and I would have good reason to feel a strong identification with the educational experiment at St. John's for its central core involved the reading and discussion of the great books. The educational experiment that was begun at St. John's in the late thirties influenced the formation of a completely required college curriculum at the University of Chicago in the early forties. These two developments might have changed Bob's mind about which side could reasonably claim a victory in the Chicago fight were it not for the fact that the final round, more hard-bitten than anything that preceded it, left us both with a sense that the most critical battle of all could not be won—at least not in this century.

Bob Hutchins delivered the Storrs Lectures at Yale in 1935 to an academic audience that listened without batting an eyelash to views about the indispensability of the great books, about philosophy's superiority to science, about the pivotal place that metaphysics should occupy in the organization of a university. Why, then, did these lectures, published the following year under the title *The Higher Learning in America,* raise the hackles of faculty members at the University of Chicago when they read the book (which sold 8,500 copies—an amazing circulation for a book on education published by a university press)?

The answer is that the intellectual atmosphere at the University of Chicago had become overheated and was filled with inflammable gases. The slightest spark would set off an explosion. Also, the views expressed renewed fears that Hutchins was resolutely antiscientific and antimodern—that he wanted to restore the hierarchy of disciplines that had given structure to the mediaeval university. The very dogmas that his opponents had been attributing to him were now boldly stated and unequivocally affirmed. One other factor, operative at Chicago, may help to explain the reaction there. The views being expressed were not just those of a professor writing about the philosophy of education; they were received as a message from the president of the university and interpreted as an indication of the lines along which he wished to reform the institution he headed.

Three or four years later, Milton Mayer wrote a two-part article about Hutchins for *Harper's Magazine:* "I. The Daring Young Man; II. The Flying Trapeze." After criticizing Hutchins for the rhetorical mistake of referring to metaphysics as the science of first principles without explaining the meaning of this statement, Mayer went on to say:

> Whitehead has been deploring the neglect of "basic ideas" for forty years. For thirty years Nicholas Murray Butler had been saying that "the great thinkers of Greece and Rome and the Middle Ages sounded the depths of almost every problem which human nature has to offer." Coming from Hutchins, these modest notions aroused the wrath of the educational world. "First principles," "Aristotle," and "Middle Ages" suddenly matured into fighting words.
>
> Why? Because Hutchins was a university president who threatened to do something about it all.

In the third chapter of *The Higher Learning in America,* Hutchins called attention to the distinction between permanent and progressive studies, educational content which remains the same generation after generation as contrasted with educational content which changes as new

discoveries are made. The distinction had been made by William
Whewell a hundred years earlier when, as master of Trinity College,
Cambridge, he defended retaining permanent studies as the core of
liberal education. Employing this distinction, Hutchins identified the
reading of great books and training in the liberal arts as the permanent
studies to be given a central place in any college that had liberal education as its objective. Progressive studies are not to be excluded from
the curriculum, but they should be pursued in the light that the permanent studies can shed on them. As Whewell had said, "the progressive
studies which education embraces must rest upon the permanent studies
which it necessarily includes. The former must be its superstructure,
the latter, its foundation."

Praising the great books as "a part, and a large part, of the permanent
studies," Hutchins quoted Nicholas Murray Butler's remark that "only
the scholar can realize how little that is being said and thought in the
modern world is in any sense new." Why, Hutchins then asked,

> should this insight be confined to scholars? Every educated person should
> know the colossal triumph of the Greeks and Romans and the great think-
> ers of the Middle Ages. If every man were educated—and why should he
> not be?—our people would not fall so easily a prey to the latest nostrums
> in economics, in politics, and, I may add, in education.

The great books should be an essential part of everyone's education
"because it is impossible to understand any subject or comprehend the
contemporary world without them. . . . Four years spent partly in
reading, discussing, and digesting books of such importance would,
therefore, contribute equally to preparation for specialized study and
to general education of a terminal variety." In addition, Hutchins
pointed out, it would provide the basis for understanding modern science, and would save us from "the false starts, the backing and filling,
the wildness, the hysteria, the confusion of modern thought and the
modern world [which] result from the loss of what has been thought and
done by earlier ages."

The complementary part of the permanent studies for which Hutchins
appealed consisted of "grammar, or the rules of reading," together with
"rhetoric and logic, or the rules of writing, speaking, and reasoning."
Summarizing his idea of general education as "a course of study consisting of the greatest books of the Western world and the arts of reading, writing, thinking, and speaking, together with mathematics, the
best examplar of the processes of human reason," he concluded by saying that "all the needs of general education in America seem to be
satisfied by this curriculum," and by asking, "What, then, are the objections to it?"

Hutchins dismissed the objection that this course of study is "too diffi-

cult for students, who can read or who can be taught to do so. . . .
No," he continued,

> the students can do the work if the faculties will let them. Will the facul-
> ties let them? I doubt it. The professors of today have been brought up
> differently. Not all of them have read all the books they would have to
> teach. Not all of them are ready to change the habits of their lives. Mean-
> while they are bringing up their successors in the way they were brought
> up, so that the next crop will have the habits they have had themselves.
> And the love of money, a misconception of democracy, a false notion of
> progress, a distorted idea of utility, and the anti-intellectualism to which all
> these lead conspire to confirm their conviction that no disturbing change
> is needed.

William Whewell and Nicholas Murray Butler may have cherished the
same idea of liberal education that Hutchins was trying to promote;
they may have had as little hope as he of persuading those whom they
knew to hold contrary views; but unlike Hutchins, they did not tell
those whom they had little hope of persuading that it was their own
intellectual and moral defects which stood in the way. No wonder that
Hutchins's message was received with as much equanimity as would be
produced by a shower of barbs and nettles.

The final chapter of *The Higher Learning in America* criticized the
modern university for failings that its faculties regarded as virtues rather
than defects. A graduate student at a modern university, Hutchins
wrote, finds "a vast number of departments and professional schools all
anxious to give him the latest information about a tremendous variety
of subjects, some important, some trivial, some indifferent. He would
find . . . that all these subjects and fractions of subjects must be regarded as equally valuable. . . . He would find a complete and thorough-
going disorder." What is worse, Hutchins declared, the university takes
pride in this disorder and has "resisted attempts to correct it by calling
them undemocratic and authoritarian." And the reason why disorder
is the chief characteristic of the higher learning is that there is no ordering principle in it.

> The modern university may be compared with an encyclopedia. The en-
> cyclopedia contains many truths. It may consist of nothing else. But its
> unity can be found only in its alphabetical arrangement. The university
> is in much the same case. It has departments running from art to zoology;
> but neither the students nor the professors know what is the relation of
> one departmental truth to another, or what the relation of departmental
> truths to those in the domain of another department may be.

Hutchins then contrasted this picture with the hierarchical structure of
the mediaeval university in which theology was queen of the sciences
and philosophy was her handmaiden. Theology provided the mediaeval

university with its principle of unity and of order. In ordering the truths
that dealt with the relation of man to God, the relation of man to man,
and the relation of man to nature, it also placed the three faculties of
the university—theology, law, and medicine—in an order that subor-
dinated medicine to law and both to theology. Theology, Hutchins admitted, could no longer be appealed to as the source of unity and order.
He proposed that we go back to the Greeks and employ metaphysics, as
they conceived it, to perform this function. Concerned with first principles, ultimate causes, and the basic categories involved in the understanding of any subject matter, metaphysics can serve as "the ordering
and proportioning discipline. It is in the light of metaphysics that the
social sciences, dealing with man and man, and the physical sciences,
dealing with man and nature, take shape and illuminate one another."

> Metaphysics, then, as the highest science, ordered the thought of the
> Greek world as theology ordered that of the Middle Ages. One or the
> other must be called upon to order the thought of modern times. If we
> cannot appeal to theology, we must turn to metaphysics. Without theology
> or metaphysics a unified university cannot exist.

Hutchins's reiterated disclaimer that he was not "arguing for any specific theological or metaphysical system" did not save him from the justifiable suspicion that he had one secretly in mind. That, however, was
not the main disquietude on the part of those who opposed him. Even
if he had not proposed that metaphysics take the place that theology
once occupied; even if he had admitted that theology failed to unify the
mediaeval university on points of doctrine; even if he had used the word
philosophy instead of that troublesome word *metaphysics* to name a
mode of inquiry and a body of truths distinct from the whole range of
empirical sciences, the reaction would have been essentially the same,
though it might have been less violent. In the eyes of his contemporaries, he would still have been guilty of the twofold heresy of calling
for a hierarchy of disciplines in the higher learning, with one sovereign
over all the rest, and of giving that sovereign place to philosophy as
regulative of the empirical sciences and other fields of scholarship.

In fact, if Hutchins had done no more than insist that empirical science is *not* the only valid knowledge to which we can appeal, that the
scientific method is *not* the only reliable mode of inquiry capable of
achieving approximations to the truth, and that philosophy, having a
method of its own, is an organized body of respectable knowledge, *not*
an assortment of personal opinions, and is capable of discovering and
establishing truths *not* attainable by science, such pronouncements
would have been as passionately rejected by the scientists in our universities and by most of the philosophers as well. Their passions would
have been further aroused if that error were compounded by saying that

philosophy can answer questions that science cannot answer, and by declaring that the questions philosophy can answer are more fundamental and more important—more fundamental because they are concerned, in the speculative perspective, with the ultimate features of reality; and more important because, in the sphere of action, they are concerned with values, with good and bad, or right and wrong.

Before Bob Hutchins delivered the Storrs Lectures at Yale, I had learned these things from my own experience at Chicago. In 1935, I had written, as a guide for the students in the Trivium course, a fairly elaborate analysis of the kinds of knowledge. It ran to eighty-three single-spaced typewritten pages and it was circulated in mimeographed form by the university bookstore. When this bulky pamphlet found its way into the hands of my colleagues, it did not take them long to spot what they regarded as outrageous and untenable assertions about philosophy's distinction from and superiority to science. Looking back at it now, I can see that no amount of caution would have avoided controversy. There was simply no way of saying what both Hutchins and I thought should be said about philosophy in relation to science that could have elicited the kind of cool consideration and rational debate appropriate to what, after all, were theses in a theory of knowledge. Like another set of theses that had been nailed to a church door, this set called for reforms that threatened the existing order and its vested interests.

Harry Gideonse, the professor of economics who several years earlier had tangled with editor John Barden in the columns of the *Daily Maroon,* spearheaded the faculty opposition at the University of Chicago. His critique of *The Higher Learning in America,* which he delivered orally on the campus, appeared in book form in 1937. Its title, *The Higher Learning in a Democracy,* plainly implied that Hutchins's views were antidemocratic. Hutchins himself had anticipated that this would be said about views that called for a hierarchical ordering of the various fields of learning instead of treating them all as of equal importance.

Gideonse's critique began by asking whether the unification of the university is to be voluntary or mandatory? If voluntary, should it not be developed by the community of scholars employing their diverse methods of research? If mandatory, who will impose it? The tendency of these questions was, of course, to imply that the unification would be imposed from above—by Hutchins and by means of philosophy, not by the scientific method. Hence, in the name of science and democracy, Hutchins's proposals must be rejected.

Gideonse did not believe that Hutchins had no particular system of metaphysics or philosophical doctrine in mind. Hutchins kept on reiterating that by philosophy he did not mean the doctrine of any particular

philosopher, any more than he would be referring to *Newton*'s physics
when he spoke of physics or to *Lyell*'s geology when he spoke of geology.
Nevertheless, Gideonse and others charged him with trying to promote
the philosophy of Plato, Aristotle, and Aquinas. Even though they had
considerable justification for the allegation, the point had little importance, since Gideonse's main contention was that, in a modern university and in a democratic society, the only kind of knowledge that can
and should be respected as valid is the kind achieved by the methods of
investigative science. Therefore, philosophy, in Gideonse's view, must be
precisely what Hutchins repeatedly said philosophy was *not*—subjective
opinions, personal insights, even wild conjectures.

Where Hutchins proposed that metaphysics or speculative philosophy
should provide the ordering and unifying principles for the higher
learning, Gideonse countered by asserting that "the true scholar finds
his unifying principles in the . . . methods of science." It is these "that
unite him with his associates into a community of scholars and scientists." The role that philosophy should be playing in a modern university, according to Gideonse, is that of handmaiden to science, confining
itself (as positivistic and analytic philosophers were currently recommending) to therapeutic clarifications or methodological subtleties, and
definitely eschewing any attempt to achieve knowledge of the world
that, as Hutchins conceived philosophy, would be as valid in its own
right as scientific knowledge was in its, yet independent of science and
unaffected by advances or alterations in scientific thought. While refus-
ing to acknowledge that philosophical questions can be answered by
knowledge rather than opinion, Gideonse nevertheless did concede that
philosophy might make a positive contribution through clarifying the
values by which we live.

In a number of addresses to the faculty at Chicago, Bob Hutchins
tried to overcome Gideonse's misunderstanding or misrepresentation of
his views, without yielding an inch on the main tenets of his position.
During the summer of 1937, I wrote Bob a series of long letters analyz-
ing Gideonse's critique, pointing out the weaknesses in his arguments,
and formulating more precisely the principal points that should be
steadfastly maintained against Gideonse and others. Bob made good use
of my letters in his speeches to the faculty the following year.

> Both science and philosophy arise from experience [I had written in a let-
> ter to Hutchins], but there is a difference between the sorts of experience
> from which these two types of knowledge arise. Science arises from special
> experience, the data of research. Philosophy arises from the common ex-
> perience that all men have without investigation. The method of science
> involves both observation and reflection or theorizing; so does that of
> philosophy. But the method of science stresses observation because it is
> from the acquirement of new data by observation that science grows and

advances. The method of philosophy stresses reflection or analysis, because common experience does not change, and philosophy grows or advances through better and better analyses.

In the light of this differentiation between philosophy and science, Hutchins took pains to make two other points clear: first, that the truth of philosophical formulations is independent of the changing content of scientific knowledge, for their truth is not tested by reference to scientific data, but by reference to common experience; and second, that one clear indication of the superiority of philosophy lies in the fact that questions about the nature, validity, and limits of scientific knowledge are themselves philosophical questions—questions that philosophy can answer, but science cannot.

To Gideonse's suggestion that philosophy might be consulted on questions of value or concerning the ends to be sought in human life and society, Hutchins pointed out that philosophy's answers to such questions would be of little practical use if the answers do not have the status of objective knowledge rather than that of subjective opinion. If science cannot answer such questions at all and if the answers that philosophy gives lack objectivity, then mankind in an age of science and technology has more and more power at its disposal and no knowledge to direct its use of that power for constructive, rather than destructive, ends. This should have been a telling point, as should have been Bob's reiteration that he was not advocating the substitution of philosophy for science (he had never questioned the place of science in the university), but rather the restoration of philosophy to the place it should occupy in relation to science.

Nothing he said, however, mollified his adversaries or moved the controversy to a plane where the issues might be resolved by rational debate. The Chicago fight soon spread from the university to the nation. As more and more reviews of *The Higher Learning in America* appeared in popular as well as professional journals, the adverse criticisms being uttered in Chicago were echoed across the land. The biggest gun fired off against Hutchins—a review written by John Dewey, which appeared in two issues of the *Social Frontier* in January 1937—was the only one that elicited a published rejoinder from Bob, except for a summary response to all the adverse reviews, which he wrote for the *Nation* in 1940.

Dewey's criticism contained the same oft-repeated charges—President Hutchins's "authoritarianism," his "contempt for science," his appeal to "fixed and eternal truths." Bob's reply, entitled "Grammar, Rhetoric, and Mr. Dewey," began by saying that "Mr. Dewey has stated my position in such a way as to lead me to think that I cannot write, and has stated his own in such a way as to make me suspect that I cannot read."

Mr. Dewey says (1) that I look to Plato, Aristotle, and Aquinas; (2) that I am anti-scientific; (3) that I am withdrawing from the world; and (4) that I am authoritarian.

Hutchins then went on to answer each of these charges by citing passages in *The Higher Learning in America* which refuted them. He pointed out, for example, that "the words 'fixed' and 'eternal' are Mr. Dewey's; I do not apply them to principles or truths in my book"; and he ended up by saying

Mr. Dewey has suggested that only a defective education can account for some of my views. I am moved to inquire whether the explanation of some of his may not be that he thinks he is still fighting nineteenth-century German philosophy.

Dewey, not Hutchins, had the last word in this interchange. Declaring that he had originally thought Hutchins's book "a work of great significance," he now reported a change of mind. In his judgment, Mr. Hutchins's reply avoided the main issues. "I cannot find in his reply any indication that he either repudiates the position I attributed to him or is willing to defend it. . . . I must ask his forgiveness if I took his book too seriously."

The furore at the University of Chicago and, in the rest of the country, the controversy about what was going on at the university, had reached proportions that, in the judgment of the editors of *Fortune,* merited extensive coverage in their magazine. They commissioned John Chamberlain to write the article. Chamberlain's confessed difficulty with certain aspects of the Hutchins position did not seriously impair his effort to present a fair picture of the two sides in the controversy at Chicago. His *Fortune* article, which appeared late in 1937, reported, for example, the view, on one side, that

science, no matter what its glories, can't advise you on your likes and dislikes; it cannot give you a scale of values. It can tell you *how* to fight a war, but it cannot tell you whether or not you *ought* to have a war.

This he balanced against the view on the other side by saying:

Even those who are willing to admit Hutchins's preoccupation with values, with the *oughts* of life, are unwilling to grant the final authority to the Aristotelian tradition to define values. They insist that no values can be fixed, and [argue] that a valid modern philosophy need not reckon with ideas as they are expressed in the books of ancient and mediaeval times.

The final episode in the Chicago fight, in its intellectual, if not its administrative, aspects, occurred in 1940. Before I come to that, it is necessary to describe the mood that had by this time become chronic with both Bob Hutchins and me. The letters that passed between us in

the summers of 1938 and 1939 contained repeated expressions of unrelieved despair. Bob's hopelessness led him to write me that he ought
to be looking for another job; yet he was reluctant to consider leaving
Chicago. For a while I tried to persuade him to become president of
St. John's College. My despondency led me to flirt briefly with the possibility of going there with or without Bob. When I put that out of
mind, my hopelessness took the form of resolving once more to withdraw from active participation in the affairs of the university and use
my academic tenure and salary to provide myself with the means for
carrying on my own work—writing books and giving lectures.

Acting on that resolution, in 1938, I reworked four lectures I had
given at the Institute for Psychoanalysis in Chicago; they were published
under the title *What Man Has Made of Man*. I delivered the Aquinas
Lecture at Marquette University, entitled "St. Thomas and the Gentiles," also published that year. In 1939, in addition to writing a number of articles on education that were published in *Commonweal*, the
Social Frontier, Better Schools, and the *Educational Record*, I delivered
an address at the annual meeting of the American Catholic Philosophical Association, setting forth my conviction that it was possible rigorously to demonstrate that democracy is the only perfectly just form of
government. In the same year, I wrote two books, *How To Read A
Book* and *Problems for Thomists: The Problem of Species*. Obviously,
I had little or no time left for stirring the stew which continued to sim-
mer at the university.

The stew came to its final boil as a result of the address I delivered
in September 1940 at the first public meeting of the Conference on
Science, Philosophy, and Religion. The idea of the conference had
been conceived by Rabbi Louis Finkelstein, head of the Jewish Theological Seminary in New York City. In order to prevent the complete
destruction of religious values, he felt that it was necessary to achieve a
better understanding of the relation of religion to science and philosophy; and that, in view of the increasingly ominous threat of Hitlerism—
1939 was the year of appeasement at Munich, 1940 the year of the assault on Poland—something should be done to give the American people a greater faith in democratic institutions and in the ability of those
concerned with religion and democracy to lend it support.

Rabbi Finkelstein raised the necessary funds to underwrite the conference and to create a group of seventy "founding members," of whom
a dozen would serve as a steering committee to plan the first meeting,
scheduled for September 1940. He visited me in Chicago in the spring
of that year to invite me to become a founding member and a member
of the steering committee. Two things persuaded me to accept his invitation. One was the extraordinary impressiveness of his gentle de-
meanor, his intense earnestness and dedication, and his striking appear-

ance—finely shaped face, gleaming prophetic eyes, and exquisite Old Testament beard. The other was the affinity of his objectives with my own—a modern synthesis of science, philosophy, and religion, and an understanding of the underlying principles and values of democracy, indispensable to ensuring our adherence to and defense of its institutions.

The founding members included the most eminent names in American academic life, representing the entire range of disciplines relevant to the theme of the conference—"Science, Philosophy, and Religion in Their Relation to the Democratic Way of Life." The much smaller steering committee, whose meetings I attended on several occasions, included Prof. William Albright of Johns Hopkins University, Prof. Lyman Bryson of Teachers College at Columbia, Prof. Harlow Shapley of Harvard University, Prof. I. I. Rabi of Columbia, and Prof. Harold Lasswell, who had been a colleague of mine at Chicago. My friend Jacques Maritain was also a member of the steering committee, but other obligations prevented him from attending its meetings.

I went to these meetings with the hope that something might be done that would sharply distinguish this conference from the annual meetings of learned societies at which professors read papers at one another. No one feels compelled to listen, because the papers can be read in the published proceedings. I have always regarded such sessions as exercises in futility. What I hoped might be planned under Rabbi Finkelstein's auspices was a disciplined colloquy of scholars representing the three great areas of science, philosophy, and religion, in the course of which they might make a patient effort to understand one another's positions and gradually reach agreement on a small number of fundamental propositions about the relation of their disciplines; or, failing that, to acknowledge the roots of their disagreement. If that could be done, then this conference might make a genuine contribution to modern culture, in a manner comparable to the contribution made by the great disputations in mediaeval universities to the culture of their day.

My hope did not survive the month of May. What shattered my illusion was the reaction of my fellow members to my proposal for the conduct of the conference. No delivery of formal addresses; no polite discussions from the floor afterward; no publication of proceedings. Instead, I urged the steering committee to draw up an orderly list of questions about the relation of science to philosophy and about the relation of both to religion—questions of the sort that had been the focus of the disputes at Chicago—and to agree to try to answer them in the order in which they were placed. I proposed that we then carry on discussions aimed at formulating answers to which we could get substantial agreement from all parties to the conference. The least we should settle for was a frank acknowledgment of our inability to agree, and an appraisal of the causes and consequences of our disagreements—consequences not only for our universities but also for democracy.

Accustomed as I was to being rebuffed, the reaction to this proposal surprised and dismayed me. I was told that the very idea of laying down a set of questions to be answered by all conference participants in a certain order was fundamentally authoritarian and undemocratic. When I observed that all we had to agree upon initially was a set of questions and their orderly arrangement, and that I was neither dictating the questions nor the answers, I was told that that made no difference. Any attempt to prescribe the content of the conference that went beyond the statement of a theme which the scholars should have in mind when they prepared their papers departed from the democratic ideal of freedom of thought and discussion.

I should not have been so astounded by this reaction to my proposal, given a recent experience in Chicago. When my "Demonstration of Democracy" was published, I sent an offprint to my associate in the Trivium course, Malcolm Sharp, thinking that he who, I knew, agreed with the conclusion of my essay would be pleased with it. Instead, his only comment was that he hoped he could show me that I had failed in my effort to demonstrate that democracy was the only perfectly just form of government, because if my demonstration turned out to be rigorously valid and, therefore, unanswerable, the ultimate effect would be undemocratic—it would preclude a difference of opinion, so essential to freedom of thought.

When I realized that Rabbi Finkelstein's conference would be exactly like all other scholarly conventions, I decided to withdraw from the whole affair. At the end of May, I wrote Rabbi Finkelstein that though I was deeply devoted to the original project, I now thought that nothing of any distinctive value would or could come of it. "My reason," I wrote to him,

> is very simple: the professors you have gathered together for these discussions are not willing to make the effort to understand one another, and even less are they interested in trying to reach agreement about anything, or even to join issue clearly in disagreement. . . . The best thing for me to do is to withdraw. I'm an impolite sort of fellow and I am likely to insult my colleagues if they talk the way they usually do. If no real good comes from the sessions, you would like them to be at least gentle and friendly, and I am likely to be a gadfly and a nuisance to you.

Many letters passed between Rabbi Finkelstein and me during the rest of June and July, in which he persisted in urging me not to withdraw. Finally, toward the end of July, I sent him a six-page memorandum in which I set forth my reasons for thinking that the conference could not achieve any objectives that I thought worthwhile. I also sent my friend Jacques Maritain a copy and found that his attitude toward the conference resembled mine. Yet he, too, urged me not to withdraw.

When he received my letter, Rabbi Finkelstein suggested that I come to the conference and present a paper that incorporated the substance of my memorandum. I could not believe that he really meant me to deliver an address in which I expressed my dissatisfaction with the procedure of the conference and predicted that it would fail to accomplish any significant results. When he assured me that that was precisely what he wanted and that he was fully cognizant of both the content and the temper of my message, I yielded. That was a mistake on my part, as it was a mistake on his part not to accept my resignation.

The conference sessions took place in the inner courtyard of the Jewish Theological Seminary. I delivered my paper on a bright sunny afternoon in mid-September to an audience of about two hundred academicians. They were protected from the sunshine by canvas awnings stretched across the courtyard. It had rained the night before, and little pools of water had gathered in the corners of the awnings.

"God and the Professors" was the title of my paper, as I had warned Rabbi Finkelstein it would be. It plainly signalled the tenor of my remarks. If my aim had been to make friends and influence people, or to persuade any part of my audience, I could not have been more misguided or inept in the rhetoric I employed. But persuasion was no part of my intention, because I had no hope of succeeding. My sole intention was to tell the professors exactly what I thought of them in relation to the theme of the conference. That purpose my rhetoric served effectively.

The tone and temper of my remarks can be judged from the following excerpts:

> Since professors come to a conference of this sort with the intention of speaking their minds but not of changing them, with a willingness to listen but not to learn, with the kind of tolerance which delights in a variety of opinions and abominates the unanimity of agreement, it is preposterous to suppose that this conference can even begin to realize the ends which justify the enterprise. . . .

> It is a little naive, therefore, to suppose that the professors can be called upon to solve the problem of the relationship of science, philosophy, and religion in our education and in our culture—as naive as it would be to invite the professors to participate in a conference about what is wrong with the professors.

I then declared that it was not necessary to wait until this conference was over in order "to discover its futility and the reasons therefor."

> The glorious, Quixotic failure of President Hutchins to accomplish any of the essential reforms that American education so badly needs, demonstrates that for us. In fact, if he could have succeeded, this Conference would not be necessary now.

I asked the professors in front of me to consider why Mr. Hutchins had failed. The answer, I said, should be obvious to "anyone who has ever attended a faculty meeting. It can be discovered by anyone who will read the reviews of *The Higher Learning in America,* written by the professors or, what is worse, the professional educators."

He failed not because his analysis was patiently *demonstrated* to be in error; not because someone *proved* that philosophy does not exist or is inferior to science; or that religion is superstition, and sacred theology a rationalization of some make-believe. He failed because he was asking the professors to change their minds. He failed as much with the professors of philosophy as with the professors of science; he failed even more with those teachers of religion who regard themselves as liberal. What Hutchins proposed ran counter to every prejudice that constitutes the modern frame of mind and its temper.

At the center of my address, I stated eight propositions about philosophy, the denial of which I said was tantamount to a denial of philosophy. "Let the professors who claim to respect philosophy—and this goes as much for the professors of philosophy as for the others—decide whether they affirm every one of these propositions." Having flung down that gauntlet, I then stated eight propositions about religion which must also be affirmed. To deny them, I said, is to deny the very existence of religion "in any sense which makes it distinct in character from science and philosophy."

I would still affirm many of these sixteen propositions without attenuation or amendment. In fact, I have done so in books and lectures during the last ten years. But some of the theses I advanced that September afternoon in 1940—and these were among the ones that struck the quickest fire—went far beyond views that I now think can be reasonably held or rationally defended.

If propositions about supernatural religion, revealed truth, and the demonstrability of God's existence caused my audience to recoil, what I said about the present crisis of democracy produced an even more violent convulsion. What had been happening in Europe in the thirties, and the calamities that had befallen the Western democracies in the spring and summer of 1940, made it unseasonable for me to say that "democracy has much more to fear from the mentality of its teachers than from the nihilism of Hitler." The fact that I followed that comment by explaining how the anti-intellectualism in our colleges and universities precluded an adherence to democracy on rational, rather than emotional, grounds did not alleviate the painfulness of my remark.

One event occurred that afternoon which caused my audience, otherwise stonily grim, to smile or even laugh out loud. After presenting the propositions which I thought ought to be affirmed if the conference were to become a significant enterprise, I read the passage in my paper which said:

> If a group of men do not come together because they have common problems, and ultimately seek to reach common answers, there is no more community among them than there is in a modern university, or in modern culture itself.

Then, in a tone of voice that I probably hoped would sound like an Old Testament prophet predicting impending doom, I declared: "The tower of Babel we are building invites another flood." At that very moment, the seams of some of the awnings opened up and the rainwater that had gathered there fell on the professors below.

Before September was over, Sidney Hook, professor of philosophy at New York University, published in the *New Republic* a long article denouncing me, under the title "The New Mediaevalism." During October, "God and the Professors" was published in a variety of public prints, including all the newspapers served by the International News Service syndication. The *Daily Maroon* at the University of Chicago, prompted by this publishing flurry, decided to reprint my address. This enraged a large section of the faculty, who insisted that the *Daily Maroon* give equal space to Professor Hook's attack on me, to balance my attack on professors. In November, the *Maroon* issued a special six-page supplement which went through several printings and sold over 5,000 copies, in response to off-campus requests for them.

Hook's piece was on page one and mine on pages three and four. The other two inside pages were filled with a variety of denunciations. Even my most friendly colleagues, Professors Malcolm Sharp and Ronald Crane, came out against me, and they were followed by Prof. Quincy Wright, with a piece entitled "Absolutism and Democracy," and by Prof. Frank H. Knight, with a piece entitled "God and Professor Adler and Logic."

The *pièce de résistance,* however, was written by Milton Mayer, a devoted disciple of Bob Hutchins and a close friend of mine. Earlier in the decade, Milton had been a reporter on the Hearst paper in Chicago. His contacts with Hutchins soon converted him from the promulgation of opinions to the pursuit of knowledge. He became a regular visitor at the Hutchins-Adler great books seminars, and later a full participant in the class.

Milton Mayer's piece filled the back page of the *Maroon's* special supplement. It was a hilariously funny essay taking all of us to task for our failures to be persuasive and reasonable. Its most telling comment on the hubbub in the pages preceding blared forth in large black type across the top of the last page: "I CAN'T HEAR MYSELF THINK."

Chapter 10

Extracurricular Activities

THE EDUCATIONAL SEEDS Chicago sowed led to the establishment of the New Program at St. John's College in Annapolis and to similar programs of liberal education at Notre Dame University and at St. Mary's College in California. Experiments with adult great books seminars led to the establishment of the Great Books Foundation and the spread of the great books movement to all parts of the country. It also led to the publication by Encyclopaedia Britannica, Inc., of *Great Books of the Western World* in fifty-four volumes, including the two-volume Syntopicon of the great ideas; and it gave an initial impetus to the development of the Aspen Institute for Humanistic Studies.

In 1939, the campus newspaper, the *Daily Maroon,* reviewed the advances made at the university in the ten years since Hutchins became its president; in 1945, *Life* magazine published an elaborate and generally laudatory account of the innovations and accomplishments that distinguished Chicago from other leading universities; and in 1949, Hutchins, in a report to the trustees, did his own summing up of what had been achieved under his stewardship. All these retrospective appraisals give a more balanced and a much less gloomy picture of the Chicago scene than our experience of it at the time. If they had taken into account the influence Hutchins's Chicago exerted on other institutions, more than balance would have been restored. The total result would be judged predominantly positive—one that Bob Hutchins might look back at with justifiable pride.

Beginning with the war years, my attention and energy shifted to affairs beyond the university campus. In fact, a number of such shifts occurred in the thirties, at moments when my despondency about our efforts at Chicago prompted me to turn elsewhere for relief or a way out. In this chapter, I want to tell the story of some of these extracurricular adventures, the most successful of which helped to promote the New Program at St. John's College.

The first began one day early in 1934 when I was visited in my university office by a representative of the Motion Picture Producers and Distributors of America, otherwise known as the Hays Office because its president was Will Hays, who had been postmaster general in the Harding administration. My visitor told me that *Crime, Law and Social Science,* the book Jerome Michael and I had written a few years earlier, was regarded as "the Bible" in the Hays Office. It made a very strong case against the claims of criminologists and sociologists to *know* the causes of crime; and so, when the movies were charged with being responsible for increased juvenile delinquency or a rise in the crime rate, the representatives of the movie industry could cite our book as authority for challenging the charges.

When I expressed puzzlement about the purpose of his visit, the reason was disclosed. The attorney general of the United States had called a National Conference on Crime and Juvenile Delinquency. Would I accept an invitation from the attorney general to attend the conference? And would I be willing to express from the floor of the conference what Michael and I had said in our book about the prevailing ignorance of the causes of crime—just in case someone pointed a finger at the movies as the villain?

The one brief speech I made at that conference led to a meeting with Will Hays, who was a fascinating mixture of political astuteness and naivete about the arts, the sciences, and philosophy. That meeting was followed by further conferences with members of his organization and by a growing interest on my part in books about the movies—on the one hand, books about the art of the cinema; on the other hand, books about the baleful influence of motion pictures upon the behavior of the young. A few years earlier, Jacques Maritain's *Art and Scholasticism* had aroused my interest in the philosophy of art and in the problem of the relation between art and morality. Greatly influenced by Maritain, I had written and delivered a number of lectures on art and aesthetics at the University of Chicago. The books about the movies not only invited the kind of critique of the behavioral sciences that *Crime, Law and Social Science* contained, but also suggested the desirability of applying to the cinema the kind of analysis I had been developing in my lectures on art and aesthetics.

I spent the summers of 1935 and 1936 writing and revising a book which did precisely that. It was published in 1937 under the title *Art and Prudence.* The first part, dealing with the history of censorship of the arts, especially storytelling and the theatre, provided background for a critical examination of current efforts to censor the movies and for a general discussion of the restraint that the prudent man must exercise in his concern with the moral content of a work of art or with its effect on the moral character of an audience. The reviews of the book, largely unfavorable and even hostile (the frequency with which I quoted Plato, Aristotle, St. Augustine, and St. Thomas Aquinas had something to do with that), completely ignored the long last section, entitled "Cinematics" in which I adapted the principles of Aristotle's *Poetics* to the art of the motion picture. That section of the book, in my judgment, made a significant contribution and would be worth revising and republishing today in the light of the developments that have taken place in the art of the cinema since the middle thirties.

With the onset of World War II, the movies came under criticism from the Congress on the grounds that certain films released in 1939 and 1940, in the course of telling stories about Nazi spies and Nazi infiltrations in the United States, propagandized for our joining Great Britain and France in their struggle with Hitler's Germany. A congressional committee was set up to hold hearings on these charges, and Will Hays was called upon to testify for the movie industry in the fall of 1941. He phoned me to ask if I would come to New York to work with him on the formulation of his speech for that occasion. Vacationing on Cape Cod that summer and writing a book—*A Dialectic of Morals*—that put together arguments that I had had with students about the basis for sound moral judgments, I was reluctant to go, but Hays prevailed. He set me up in a hotel suite at the St. Regis and provided me with research and secretarial assistance, and I worked around the clock to draft a statement for him to make—a careful analysis of that slippery word *propaganda* and a defense of the films against political regulation, extending to the movies the First Amendment's safeguarding of a free press. I still have in my files a printed copy of *Freedom of the Films,* which Hays would have delivered to his congressional interrogators had the hearings not been postponed and then cancelled as a result of Pearl Harbor and our entrance into the war.

Will Hays was so delighted with my ability to put his ideas and sentiments into words that made him feel comfortable that he invited me to become a consultant of the Motion Picture Producers and Distributors of America, on an annual retainer that was more than half the amount of my salary from the University of Chicago. This involved my being available for occasional conferences in New York, but it mainly meant my working up a first draft of Hays's annual report to the members of his association. I found the invitation tempting not only because of the retainer, but also because I had experienced, from time to time, an impulse to get as far away as I could from the academic world. Adventuring into the movie business would certainly achieve that. I yielded to the lure and served as consultant and ghostwriter for the next four or five years, until Hays retired. Eric Johnston, who succeeded him, asked me to stay on for one year more to draft his first annual report. I did so, and when it was released to the press, it was hailed, to my astonishment, as "the sounding of a new voice in the movie industry."

I must confess that what I enjoyed most about this excursion into the New York end of Hollywood, even more than the pleasure of ghost-writing, which has its own secret satisfactions, derived from the per-quisites attached to the job. Will Hays had an apartment in the Waldorf-Astoria Towers, and when I came to New York in the spring of each year for two or three weeks of work on his annual report, he put me up in a luxurious tower apartment—once in the Prince of Wales suite, once in the Queen Wilhelmina suite, and once in a suite dedicated to Lana Turner. It did not take me long to discover my susceptibility to lavish surroundings and their accompaniments. When I shamelessly re-ported my evident pleasure in such baubles, Bob Hutchins chided me for being a sybarite, to which I responded by calling him an anchorite, thinking that one appellation had no more truth in it than the other. However, on reflection, I must confess that I do have the propensities of a sybarite. In addition, I have flirted with the thought that Socrates was wrong in Plato's dialogue, the *Phaedo,* when he contended that a philosopher should strive to forgo worldly pleasures and aspire to lead an ascetic life. If asceticism is an indispensable prerequisite to philo-sophical thought, I have some doubt whether my love for philosophy and my excitement in it would have prevailed. But my life in the last thirty years or more has tended to confirm the view that high living is not necessarily incompatible with high thinking.

My adventure with the motion picture industry (which led Mark Van Doren to call me "Merton of the Movies") was not my only ex-cursion into the world of business. Another—this one aiming at sever-ance of my connection with the university—occurred in the late thirties. In this case, it was Beardsley Ruml's departure from the university that set the stage for me.

After being dean of the Social Science Division for a number of years, Bee Ruml severed his connections with academic life to become vice-president and treasurer of R. H. Macy and Company in New York. On learning of this, Bob Hutchins's wife, Maude, remarked, "Poor Bee! He has given up ideas for notions." The remark turned out to be more witty than true, for during his early years at R. H. Macy, Bee conceived the idea of the Ruml Plan—the pay-as-you-go income tax—and by his single-handed campaigning for it across the country got it adopted. He also continued to write and publish penetrating articles about the organization and financing of institutions of higher education.

Several years after Bee Ruml went to Macy's, Bob Hutchins tele-phoned to ask me to meet with a young man who was then in his office—Richard "Bobby" Weil, Jr., nephew of Percy Strauss, Macy's chairman, and himself president of the Bamberger department store in Newark, New Jersey, a Macy subsidiary. I found Bobby Weil a most attractive and engaging fellow, about my age, full of ideas rather than notions. He had come to the University of Chicago to talk with Hutchins and me, he explained, in order to find another Bee Ruml to work with him at Bamberger's. I told him that I doubted whether the university harbored another Bee Ruml, but after a moment's thought, I proposed that he interview my friend Will Munnecke, who was an officer of Marshall Field and Company. I phoned Will and arranged a luncheon for the three of us.

The next day, Will, who was fairly taciturn, failed to display the interesting turns of mind that had prompted me to recommend him to Weil. In order to draw him out, I thought up all kinds of questions about the retail business, about the organization of a department store, about marketing and advertising new products, and so on. But it was Bobby Weil, rather than Will Munnecke who responded to my questions and carried the brunt of the conversation. Luncheon over, Bobby asked me to ride back to his hotel and talk while he packed his bag. When he reached his suite at the Blackstone, he bowled me over by a quick, crisp speech in which he said that my performance at lunch had per- suaded him that I was the Bee Ruml he had come to the University of Chicago to find. Would I consider becoming an officer of L. Bamberger? When I expressed some doubt about the seriousness of his offer, he said that he would talk to his uncle, Percy Strauss, the next day and, with his approval, would phone me to confirm the offer.

I continued to doubt, but when before noon the next day Bobby Weil phoned to say that his uncle approved and wished to see me, I agreed to go to New York to sit down with him, Bee Ruml, and Bobby to discuss the kind of work I might do in a department store. When I asked what my title would be, Bobby said "Vice-President of Depart- ment X," and when I asked about Department X, the answer was "Thinking!" I observed at once that if you can think at all, you can think about anything, and suggested a number of things I might do as a thinker about the department store business.

I asked Percy Strauss how many hours a week he and his top execu- tives spent around the conference table. About a third of their time, he said. It's expensive time, isn't it? I asked. Very, he replied. Well, I said, I can save you at least one-half of that time and, perhaps, more, by acting as moderator of your business conferences; by organizing the agenda; by keeping the discussion on the point and moving ahead when a point is settled; by serving as rapporteur of earlier discussions; in short, by running executive conferences in the same way that I conduct great books seminars. This proposal not only persuaded the others that

I was the man for the job, but it even convinced me that I might enjoy doing it.

Offer and acceptance had now reached a stage of seriousness that required me to discuss the whole affair with Bob Hutchins. Far from being shocked at my wish to leave the university and go into business (he had had similar hankerings himself for service in government), Bob encouraged me to proceed with the negotiations and laid down the minimal conditions for taking the job: at least a three-year contract and a salary large enough to enable me to save enough to withdraw from business in three years and, with the income from the money saved, supplemented by writing and lecturing, be able to lead the kind of life I really wanted. The Macy organization would not agree to these conditions. They quickly perceived that I was interested in their offer only as a means to an end, and frankly told me that they were not interested in me as a philosopher in transit through the Macy organization. That became quite clear at one point in our conversations when I suggested that I could perform all the duties of Vice-President in charge of Thinking and more than earn my salary by part-time attendance in the store, reserving the rest of my time for studying, writing, and lecturing.

However, this did not completely terminate my association with Bobby Weil or, for that matter, with L. Bamberger. Bobby and I continued to correspond and spend time together. He asked me to help him write a book on the technique of effective thinking in business or practical affairs, which I did. It was published by Simon and Schuster some years later under the title *The Art of Practical Thinking*. That book, together with many of the daring, even somewhat outrageous, things that Bobby did when he became head of R. H. Macy, made him a natural for a two-part profile in the *New Yorker* magazine entitled "White Sales and Aristotle."

Remembering some of the things I had suggested might be done in the course of thinking about a department store's business, Bobby asked me whether I would be willing to come to Bamberger's, to conduct occasional seminars for his top executives. I gladly accepted, and after a conversation in which he explained to me that the essential function of a large department store is to act as middleman between producers and consumers, we planned a first seminar on the theory of merchandise origination.

L. Bamberger's, I learned, carried an inventory of well over 300,000 different items. Of this number, in the course of any year, about one third dropped out of the picture to be replaced by an equal number of new products. Since the department store, as middleman, is in closer contact with the consumer than the manufacturer is, its merchandising executives should be able to guide manufacturers in the invention of new products or in the improvement of old ones. Precisely how to think about this problem was the theme of my seminar on merchandise origination.

As I outlined points to be considered—which I might submit in advance of the seminar—it occurred to me that the theory of the origin of species through natural selection and through the extinction of maladapted varieties provided a model for a theory of merchandise origination. The more I thought about it, the more I became fascinated with playing the role of Darwin in a department store. But I could not do the whole job with Darwin alone. I dragged in Aristotle also, in a section of my notes dealing with the final, formal, material, and efficient causes operative in the origination of any artifact. I finished this eleven-page memorandum a little after noon on Sunday, December 7, 1941. Putting it into an envelope addressed special delivery to Weil, I rang for the elevator man to post it at once. When he opened the door of the elevator, he greeted me with the news of Pearl Harbor. Although the seminar on merchandise origination did take place in January 1942 with great success, no further seminars were planned or held, and shortly thereafter Bobby Weil went off to the war as a member of Colonel Donovan's O.S.S.

In the years immediately before our entry into World War II, my extracurricular activities included lecturing at other institutions or under other auspices. I turned the substance of the lectures into books. The four books I produced in this period were *St. Thomas and the Gentiles, Problems for Thomists: The Problem of Species, How To Read A Book*, and *What Man Has Made of Man*. The last was based on a series of lectures I gave at the Institute for Psychoanalysis in Chicago, of which Dr. Franz Alexander was director.

Alexander's removal from the Medical School at the University of Chicago followed shortly after my removal from the Philosophy Department. A few years later Dr. Alexander and I found ourselves co-residents of an apartment house on the Near North Side and became close friends. Arthur Rubin, who was living with Helen and me, also came to know Dr. Alexander and took an active interest in his Institute for Psychoanalysis, which had been founded with financial assistance from Alfred and Marion Stern, friends of Arthur's and mine. Conversations between Arthur and Dr. Alexander led to my being invited to lecture at his institute.

My controlling intention in preparing the lectures was to praise psychoanalytical psychology for its contribution to the understanding of human nature and to acknowledge the discoveries and insights of Sigmund Freud as genuine advances in the analysis of the human psyche and its operations. It never occurred to me that I would be damning psychoanalysis with faint praise by suggesting that, in order to carry forward the promising start it had made, it had to correct the philosophical errors of its founder. This was how I regarded Freud's wholesale acceptance of the then current positivistic view that only the empirical sciences can provide us with valid or verifiable knowledge of nature, including human nature, and his uncritical acceptance of the Darwinian dogma that man differs from other animals only in degree, not essentially in kind. Nor did it occur to me that I was belittling Freud's stature as a revolutionary innovator in psychology by suggesting that his innovations must be viewed as additions to, rather than departures from, the tradition of philosophical psychology as initiated by Aristotle and developed by Thomas Aquinas. For the psychoanalysts in the audience, including Dr. Gregory Zilboorg of New York and Dr. Karl Menninger of Topeka, Kansas, my intentions to praise psychoanalysis and to acknowledge Freud's genius could not have miscarried more completely.

In addition, the psychoanalysts present were riled by my argument that the fact that only human beings are psychoanalyzable and not other animals showed that humans differed in kind, not degree, from brutes. They were uncomprehending of and uncomfortable with my spelling out in detail the errors of Platonism and positivism, in order to point out the consequences of these doctrines for philosophical and scientific psychology, and so they were resistant to reiterated recommendations that they should correct the error of their ways. But, most of all, they were incensed, even to the extreme of a livid display of bad temper, by my putting them into a logical box out of which they could not extricate themselves without loss of face.

This occurred in the discussion period that followed the third lecture. Both Dr. Alexander and Dr. Thomas French, the institute's associate director, were gentle and mild-mannered and seldom raised their voices in discussion. That made their loss of temper on this occasion all the more astounding at the time, though on reflection I understand why they were so provoked.

At the end of the third lecture, I called attention to the psychoanalyst's unqualified commitment to the proposition that all thinking is, in one way or another, "wishful thinking"—a rationalization of emotional drives or instinctually based desires. It is always nonobjective thinking in the sense that the conclusions reached are predetermined by the passions, not by the weight of the evidence or the implication of premises adopted and the cogency of inferences made on purely rational grounds. On the other hand, the psychoanalysts resolutely claimed for psychoanalysis the status of an empirical science and for themselves the character of scientists. But empirical science, not to mention philosophy, cannot be distinguished from personal opinion, subjective prejudice, or plain superstition unless its conclusions are established, however tentatively and corrigibly, by objective thinking in the light of all available evidence and on the basis of logical criteria for the validation of premises and inferences. Therefore, I said to the assembled psychoanalysts, you are confronted with the following dilemma: either you have to admit that psychoanalytical doctrine is flatly wrong in one of its fundamental dogmas about the nature of human thinking, or you have to admit that psychoanalysis is not a science and that you are not scientists.

They could not bring themselves to embrace either horn of the dilemma. While outwardly rejecting both alternatives, they remained inwardly aware of the contradiction they had been forced to embrace. Though they should have been above being disturbed by self-contradiction (since, after all, wishing to avoid self-contradiction is only an emotional addiction to rationalism), their frustration exhibited itself in a psychoanalytic diagnosis of me. I pointed out that such diagnostic name-calling had no bearing at all on the truth or falsity of the matters under consideration.

In preparing my lectures for the Institute for Psychoanalysis, I employed a style I had begun to develop in earlier lectures at Chicago—a style that has since become a lifelong habit. Instead of either speaking from relatively brief notes or reading out loud a manuscript written in consecutive prose paragraphs, I wrote my lectures in fully formulated sentences and paragraphs, but in outline form. The sentences and paragraphs were put down with all the spacing, indentations, and subordinations of a well-structured outline to capture the structure of the thought and make it evident to the eye of the lecturer and perhaps also to the ear of the listener. This style enabled me to give a lecture which had the kind of spontaneity that characterizes a speech given from fragmentary notes. I found it easy to take my eyes off the page in front of me and appear to be talking without a written script, even though that is precisely what I had on the lectern. The fact that everything was completely written out enabled me to cover all the points that I wanted to be sure to make and yet keep the whole within an appointed time limit, as too frequently is not the case when one speaks from notes.

Almost all the books I have written since the thirties have been expanded versions of lectures or series of lectures composed in this way. In the case of *What Man Has Made of Man* I was so enamored of the outline style that I felt its virtues would be as evident to the reader as they were to me. I could not have been more mistaken. Against the advice of Scott Buchanan, Arthur Rubin, and others to whom I showed the manuscript, I persisted in publishing the lectures just as they were delivered—in outline form. For reasons that I still do not understand, most readers find an outline either terrifying or repugnant. Instead of helping them, it seems to paralyze them. Maybe it is because the page is too full of punctuation marks for them to move smoothly from point to point, as they can when they are presented with even a poorly organized sequence of prose paragraphs.

The outline form was not the only stumbling block I put in the path of the reader of *What Man Has Made of Man*. I also added numerous bibliographical footnotes. Not satisfied with using the first part of every lecture to answer objections or comments advanced in the discussion that followed the previous lecture, I wrote seventy-five commentaries, some quite long, to expand and elucidate propositions, distinctions, and arguments too briefly stated in the lectures. Far from aiding the reader, these complicated the task for him and impeded his efforts to follow the argument. Writing these commentaries on my lectures satisfied my passion for dotting every *i* and crossing every *t*— a passion that horrified Scott Buchanan as he watched me expanding the commentaries and even adding to them at the last moment while I was handling the proofs during the summer of 1937. I must confess that his sympathy for the reader anticipated the reaction I would get from producing a monster in the form of a book.

Nevertheless, concocting the commentaries did serve one purpose. I invited Dr. Alexander to write an introduction to the book, on the basis of a manuscript of the lectures in his possession. He at first accepted the invitation and then, a month or so later, asked me to reconsider my request. Would not the public think it strange—perhaps even somewhat exhibitionistic—for a book to carry an introduction that adversely criticized its author and his views? That bothered me not in the least, I told him. Since I had given these lectures at an institute of which he was the director, I thought it only fair that the book should contain a record of the disagreements which he and his colleagues expressed. He demurred; I persisted; he reluctantly acquiesced. The book was published with his somewhat denunciatory, and also somewhat unfounded, comments.

That his characterization of my views did not accurately reflect what I said, I took some pains to indicate in the commentaries which I wrote after seeing a draft of his introduction. That restored the balance as far as I was concerned, but when my friends Jacques Maritain and Étienne Gilson received copies of the published book, they expressed their typically Gallic amazement at finding a book introduced to the public by an adversary of the author rather than by a friend. After reading the "fascinating Preface by Dr. Franz Alexander," Gilson wrote:

> I really don't know how to think of the man who prefixed it to his own book. I am sure Dr. Alexander feels convinced that you were prompted to print it by nothing but the most generous motives; but I faintly suspect that one at least of your reasons to do so was to show the whole world

what a dear old fool Dr. Alexander really is—and you certainly did succeed in achieving that result.

The title of the published book, which carried as its subtitle "A Study of the Consequences of Platonism and Positivism in Psychology," came from the last line of a quatrain by Wordsworth. It seems to me, now as then, perfectly apt, though it did take the addition of an epilogue to the book in order to explain its appropriateness.

> If this belief from heaven be sent,
> If such be Nature's holy plan,
> Have I not reason to lament
> What Man has made of Man?

The Buchanans and the Adlers again shared a house in Marlboro, New Hampshire, in the summer of 1938. Mark and Dorothy Van Doren, with their sons, Charles and John, visited us there. Conversations late into the night about marriage and family persuaded Helen and me that we should repair our childless marriage by adopting children. Late in August, we adopted the first of our two sons, Mark, aged two months; and two years later, a second, Michael, also an infant. Adopting Mark created a financial problem which I solved by writing *How To Read A Book*.

Until 1938, Arthur Rubin lived with Helen and me in a spacious duplex apartment the rent of which he helped to defray. His bedroom was now needed as a nursery for Mark. The full burden of the rent would fall on me and become even heavier because of a rent increase due the first of the year. Helen, who controlled the family budget with a tight fist and was loathe to contract obligations beyond our means, told me that we could no longer afford to live at 20 East Cedar Street and had to move. I asked her how much more money in our bank account would persuade her to let me sign the new lease. A thousand dollars at least, she said, and she would not settle for the promise of that sum at some future date; it had to be in the bank on or before March 31, when the new lease went into effect.

With that challenge, intensified by my reluctance to relinquish living quarters so pleasant, I went to Bob Hutchins and asked for a thousand-dollar raise. Bob, while teasing me about being a sybarite, was sympathetic, but said he could not promise to get a raise for me through the Board of Trustees by the appointed time. Feeling that I must try another tack, I thought of getting an advance on a book I might write.

The preceding May, at the end of the academic year, I had been invited by the Alumni Council to address a gathering during alumni week at the university. I chose to deliver a lecture on the art of reading, based on what I had learned from years of conducting great books

seminars. In this instance, I departed from my habitual style of a fully
written outline and spoke from the briefest of notes covering two sides
of a three-by-five card.

The lecture proved to be an effective bit of instruction for the audience. Transcribed, it was published in the *Chicago Alumni News;* and
during the fall of 1938, I delivered it on several other occasions, to both
adult and student audiences. The interest aroused by the rules of
reading I had developed prompted me to propose to Kip Fadiman, who
was then editor in chief at Simon and Schuster, that I write a book on
the subject. He asked me for an outline of the book to submit to Dick
Simon and Max Schuster, whom I knew from my Columbia days. When
I sent the outline, I wrote Kip that I would do the book on one
condition—a thousand-dollar advance paid to me on or before March 31.
No advance, no book. Kip said he would do what he could, but that S
and S were not in the habit of paying advances that large. He could not
promise to deliver what I wanted—on time.

Correspondence and telephone calls between Kip and me during
March brought me to a state of frantic despair as I neared the end of
the month with the problem still unsolved. With less than a week to
go, I returned to my office after lunch one day and found two messages
on my desk, one from Kip Fadiman in New York, the other from Bob
Hutchins. I put the New York call through first, to have my spirits lifted
by Kip's message that a check for $1,000 was on its way to me. I then
called Bob to learn that he had just obtained approval for the raise I
had asked for. I had solved the problem in spades.

All that remained was to write the book. I did that in July 1939—a
chapter a day for seventeen consecutive days, with a movie every night to
turn my mind off. Milton Mayer and Bob Hutchins went over the first
draft and improved it by their criticisms and suggestions; Kip gave it
an even more thorough going over, with additional emendations from
his wife, Polly. When it was finally whipped into shape, Kip crowned
these efforts by inventing a title for the book; the working title had been
something as dull as *The Art of Reading.* His title, *How To Read A
Book,* not only precisely described its contents but also was provocative
in exactly the right way. Kip helped me write a preface that began by
saying, this is "a light book about heavy reading." It also indicated that
the book was concerned not just with reading as one of the liberal arts,
but with liberal education itself, indispensable not only to citizens in a
democracy, but also to human beings in the pursuit of happiness. The
art of reading, the subtitle declared, is "the art of getting a liberal education."

The first chapter, addressed "To the Average Reader," announced in
its opening sentence: "This is a book for readers who cannot read." The
appearance of contradiction in that statement, I explained, "arises only

from the variety of senses in which the word 'reading' can be used. The reader who has read thus far surely can read, in some sense of the word." But there are other senses of the word in which, perhaps, he cannot read as well as he would like to; hence "it is not contradictory to say that this book is for readers who want to read better or want to read in some other way than they now can."

I then described the one circumstance in which most persons might be expected to engage in "making an effort to read better than they usually do"—and that is "when they are in love and are reading a love letter." Then

> they read for all they are worth. They read every word three ways; they read between the lines and in the margins; they read the whole in terms of the parts and each part in terms of the whole; they grow sensitive to context and ambiguity, to insinuation and implication; they perceive the color of words, the odor of phrases, and the weight of sentences. They may even take the punctuation into account. Then, if never before or after, they read.

As publication day drew near, I began to hope that the book might sell well, but Kip took a dim view of this. Simon and Schuster took an even dimmer view: the first printing numbered only 3,500 copies. Their more than modest expectations might have proved right were it not for a number of happy accidents.

The New Program at St. John's College, now in its third academic year, had attracted nationwide attention for its innovations—a completely required four-year curriculum eliminating the vagaries of the elective system; four years of reading and discussing great books, accompanied by tutorials in ancient and modern languages and in mathematics, and laboratory exercises in both the physical and the biological sciences; and only one required formal lecture a week, attended by the whole student body and followed by an extended discussion period. While the examples I used in *How To Read A Book,* to illustrate this or that defect in reading, came from my experience in great books seminars at Chicago rather than at St. John's, it was the college curriculum at St. John's rather than at Chicago which I held up as the model of what liberal education at the college level should be. It was the only college in the country, I said in no uncertain terms, at which a genuinely liberal education was being offered.

How To Read A Book was scheduled for publication in February 1940. Late in January, *Life* magazine published a picture story about St. John's College. Two-thirds of a double-page spread consisted of a photograph of the great books being read at St. John's, arranged in five shelves of a bookcase. One column on the remaining third of the two-page spread described the New Program, concluding with a short paragraph which announced the forthcoming publication of *How To Read A Book*—a guide, it said, to the reading of the great books on the St. John's list. On publication day, Scribner's bookstore on Fifth Avenue in New York filled its window with a display of rare editions of many of the great books, with a blown-up replica of the two-page spread in *Life,* and with copies of *How To Read A Book* scattered all about it. Within the week, Marshall Field and Company and Kroch's Bookstore in Chicago had similar window displays.

These unplanned promotions of the book, combined with a large number of early and favorable reviews, turned it into a best seller overnight. During the first month, it sold over a thousand copies a day, went through many reprintings, reached the top of the best-seller list, and after dropping from first place, stayed on the list for the rest of the year. During that first month, Simon and Schuster sent me a special delivery postcard every day reporting the previous day's sales—my only experience of something akin to watching ticker tape as one's stocks go skyrocketing in a bull market. *How To Read A Book* not only solved the financial problem which had occasioned the writing of it (its dedication to my son Mark and to Arthur whom he displaced in our household could hardly have been more appropriate); it also made my fiscal relations with Helen easier. On the negative side, my success as a best-selling author did little to endear me with some of my colleagues at the University of Chicago.

Of all the books I have written to change the minds of others and to move them a little nearer to the truth as I perceived it, none has achieved any great measure of success. Judging by the hundreds of letters I have received from its readers over the years, the one book I wrote to make money succeeded better than all the others in changing their minds or at least in directing their efforts to do something about changing their minds. It is also the only book of mine that gained worldwide attention. After going through almost a dozen printings in the first year, it was published in Great Britain and Australia and translated into French, Spanish, Italian, Swedish, Japanese, and German (the slip cover of the German translation carried a picture that made me look like the Nazi minister of propaganda, Joseph Goebbels).

The popularity of *How To Read A Book* in 1940 occasioned a cartoon in the *New Yorker* by Helen Hokinson, in which two of her typical clubwomen are standing at the desk in the club's private library and one of them is saying, *"How To Read A Book* is out. Secretly, I'm relieved!" It also elicited a spoof entitled *How To Read Two Books* by Eramus G. Addlepate, and a serious rejoinder by I. A. Richards, of Basic English fame, entitled *How To Read A Page,* the title page of which announced that it offered a course in serious reading together "with an introduction to 100 great words." I have always been grateful to Professor Richards and to the jokester "Addlepate" for the aptness of their titles. It afforded me the opportunity to point out in lectures and articles that the technique of reading analytically must be applied microscopically to the interpretation of a page or even a sentence—with close attention to its important words, as well as applied macroscopically to the comparative understanding of two or more books about a common theme.

For some years *How To Read A Book* kept me spinning around the country on the lecture circuit and pounding out articles for popular journals. One for *Reader's Digest,* entitled "How To Mark A Book," has been reprinted more frequently than any other piece of mine, especially in anthologies for high school and college English and humanities courses. That, together with another on "How To Read A Dictionary," and still another on why the first reading of a difficult book should be quick and superficial, elaborated the rules of reading set forth in *How To Read A Book,* as did lectures I gave on the special techniques involved in reading different kinds of books—reference books, history books, and books on other subject matters. The gradual accumulation of additional insights called for a thorough revision and updating of the 1940 version, which remained in print and continued to sell in substantial quantities year after year, largely because it was required reading in many schools and colleges. Charles Van Doren collaborated with me in overhauling the original version in 1972. He brought to the rewriting of the book an expertness in the reading of novels, plays, and poems, and a skill in the reading of mathematics, which complemented my own proficiency as a reader of history, science, and philosophy.

The revision provided guidance in reading other things than great books as well as specific rules for dealing with different kinds of reading materials; it put the fad of "speed reading" in proper perspective by showing the importance of reading some things as slowly as possible while, at the same time, being able to inspect—inspect, not really read—everything as quickly as possible. In addition, by distinguishing four levels of reading—elementary, or fourth-grade, reading; inspectional, or speed reading; analytical, or interpretative, reading; and, finally, the syntopical reading of many books in relation to one another—the revised version of *How To Read A Book* provided more thorough and more useful instruction than the original.

The grave deficiency in modern education (in England as well as in the United States and also, perhaps, elsewhere), which *How To Read A Book* expressly sought to correct, had become, by 1972, an even more serious cause of complaint against the school system. The deplorable fact is that, with the establishment of almost universal schooling, functional illiteracy on the part of a sizeable fraction of the population has increased relative to the school population. Even more shocking is the fact that an overwhelming number of those who are functionally literate because they can read signs, business forms, newspapers, and popular magazines leave secondary schools and even colleges with the same reading ability that they had developed by the time they reached the fourth grade. The reason is simply that the liberal arts, which occupied a central place in the curriculum of the eighteenth and nineteenth centuries, have been progressively displaced by "progressive education" in the twentieth. The relatively small number of children who were schooled in prior centuries, probably less than ten percent, acquired discipline in the arts of reading, writing, speaking, and listening in courses of instruction called "grammar," "rhetoric," and "logic." Now, with most children in school for at least twelve years and many for sixteen, few receive specific instruction in reading after the fourth grade. Instead, courses in English composition are given over largely to "creative writing" (where the word *creative* connotes a negation of discipline) and fail to instill respect for the demands of grammar, rhetoric, and logic, which are indispensable to the direction of the mind in its efforts to analyze, interpret, and judge a paragraph, a page, a book, or a collection of books.

Over the years, I have discovered a way of explaining the failure of our schools in the matter of reading and writing to people who clearly do not understand what I mean when I say that a very large proportion of our college graduates are seriously deficient in the skills of communication. It draws on an analogy between instruction in the art of reading and in the art of playing the piano. In the latter case, the beginner acquires elementary techniques by practicing finger exercises and playing scales or musical compositions about as simple as grade-school readers. Imagine what would happen if a child who had become proficient at this elementary level and who had received no further instruction on the piano found himself some years later on a concert stage expected to play a Mozart piano sonata. If you recognize the impossibility of that occurring, you should be able to see that it is equally preposterous to expect a person to do very much with his mind in handling a great book, if he or she has received no formal instruction in reading beyond the fourth grade.

Two side effects of the original publication led me back to educational enterprises that occupied a great deal of my time and effort in the early forties. One was the development of great books seminars for adults; the other, the New Program of liberal education at St. John's College. The wide circulation of *How To Read A Book* served to promote both undertakings. Together with Mark Van Doren's *Liberal Education*, it persuaded a certain number of prospective college students to choose the little college in Annapolis, Maryland, as the place to get the kind of discipline and the kind of mind-lifting that the reading and discussion of great books affords. Speeches that I gave to adult groups often elicited questions from the audience concerning what they could do on their own to remedy the defects of their schooling. My answer always included the recommendation that they and their friends form a great books discussion group. Not only did being involved in such discussion groups put the pressure on you to do the reading which you might otherwise indefinitely put off; having to exchange views with others also helps you to read a book better after the discussion is over. In comparison, solitary reading was as little to be preferred as solitary drinking. This quip found its way into a book of verse by Phyllis McGinley (*A Pocketful of Wry*), in which the following poem appeared:

THE OUTCAST

"Solitary reading wrong, says Adler. . . . Likens it to drinking alone."
—Headlines in the *Times*.

> Consider the poor sinner,
> The desperate wretch by decency forsook,
> Who, after dinner,
> Stealthily from his shelves takes down a book
> And like as not,
> A drunken fool, a literary sot,
> Creeps to his lonely cot,
> There to swig down and out of public view
> Immoderate tankards of the Pierian brew.
>
> How sunk in vice is he! Look how he gloats,
> Taking no notes,
> Letting his febrile fancy roam at large in
> Frivolous tomes and gay,
> Despised by Mr. A.,
> And annotating not a single margin.
>
> Pity the fate
> Of this inebriate.
> Shunned by his fellows, none in his ear will shout
> How the plot ended, how it all came out.
> None —in a Poetry Morning will enroll him,
> No one will buttonhole him
> To be an audience for some deathless prose
> Recited through the nose.
>
> But, all the precepts dead to,
> Unsung at and unread to,
> He'll end in squalor,
> A miserable bookworm or a scholar.

I have already told the story of the internal disharmonies and the external hostilities that beset the Committee on the Liberal Arts at Chicago in 1936–1937, the first year of its existence. The committee, with altered membership, continued under the direction of Arthur Rubin for two more years; it produced studies bearing on the place of different subject matters in a liberal curriculum, but as far as having any effect on the collegiate program at Chicago, it might just as well never have existed. It did, however, provide a stepping-stone to the development of the New Program at St. John's College in Annapolis. The shift to Annapolis came about through a set of accidental circumstances, but what came into being there sprang from the educational ideas that Hutchins had been trying to put into effect at Chicago, from Barr and Buchanan's deliberations at the University of Virginia, and, perhaps, most of all, from our common feeling that the reforms we would like to see instituted could not be effected at Chicago.

In the spring of 1937, Winkie Barr learned that a little college in Annapolis, having survived for more than two centuries, faced bankruptcy and would have to close its doors unless some group took it over, refinanced it, and renovated it. Winkie at once suggested that we move our base of operations to the shores of Chesapeake Bay. We all agreed that the opportunity to take over a derelict institution and revivify it offered us an irresistible challenge to try out our ideas in actual practice. Negotiations moved very rapidly from that point on, but it now seems to me almost a miracle that by the summer of 1937 the first bulletin of the New Program was issued, that financial arrangements were completed to keep the college going on a borrowed shoestring, that senior professors of the old college were willing to become fellows and tutors of the new college, that additional instructors were recruited, and that the New Program was ready to go into operation by September, when the term began.

The famous St. John's Reading List—never a "hundred great books," as it was always inaccurately described—included almost all the works that Hutchins and I had been using at Chicago; it added the great contributions to ancient and modern mathematics and works of ancient and modern natural science. The rationale of this composite reading list, together with an explanation of the supporting elements in the New Program, Scott Buchanan set forth with his customary imaginative daring in a widely circulated manifesto: "In Search of a Liberal College: A Program for the Recovery of the Classics and the Liberal Arts."

These events precipitated a barrage of publicity including, of course, the same charges that had been levelled against us at Chicago—revival of scholasticism, return to mediaevalism, seedbed of fascism. A long article in the Baltimore *Sun* carried the headline "St. John's 'New Program' No Mere Reading Bee: Revolt against confusions and contradictions of modern intellectualism seen in Hutchins-Barr-Buchanan-Adler retreat to Thomistic formula." Catholic educators and professed Thomists were not entirely comfortable either with the St. John's reading list (it included more heretical authors and more forbidden books than it did representatives of orthodoxy) or with certain other elements in the curriculum and their underlying objectives. A dispute between Father Bull, a Jesuit priest who was president of Fordham University, and Father Slavin, a Dominican who was president of Providence College, about the acceptability of the St. John's program in Catholic institutions appeared in the pages of the Jesuit weekly *America*. As a matter of fact, in all the years since the inception of the New Program, only two Catholic institutions adopted it, and then with certain modifications and in the form of a "special program," to live alongside the conventional college curriculum, not to replace it. One was St. Mary's College in California; the other, the University of Notre Dame in Indiana, in both of which adoptions I had a hand.

On the favorable—and, of course, minority—side, the most eloquent praise for the St. John's experiment appeared in a newspaper column by Walter Lippmann. He reported his amazement at discovering how the men who created the United States had been schooled. Reading a book entitled *The Education of the Founding Fathers of the Republic* by Dr. James J. Walsh, Lippmann learned that they "had been drilled in the Liberal Arts, arts which are called liberal because they were what the *liber homo,* that is to say the free man, must know if he is to be in fact free." At first, Lippmann confessed, "it seemed to me odd, for I was a child of my generation, that the men who had made the modern world should have been educated in this old-fashioned way."

> And then I began to think that perhaps it was very significant that men so educated had founded our liberties, and that we who are not so educated should be mismanaging our liberties and be in danger of losing them. Gradually I have come to believe that this fact is the main clew to the riddle of our epoch, and that men are ceasing to be free because they are no longer educated in the arts of free men.
>
> . . . We have emptied education of rigorous training in the arts of thought, and having done that, we are no longer able to read in any language the classical masterpieces of the human mind. Between ourselves and the sources from which our civilization comes, we have dropped an iron curtain of false progress that leaves us to the darkness of our whims, our vagrant opinions, and our unregulated passions.

Mentioning the efforts to do something about this which had been begun at Columbia, Virginia, and Chicago, Lippmann then called attention to the full-fledged revival of liberal education at St. John's

College—"the third oldest center of higher learning in the United States."

> This is the second academic year in which the so-called new program has been taught at St. John's, and there are now thirteen sophomores and forty-five freshmen. They have some fine buildings which survive from Colonial days, no football stadium, a fair library, no modern laboratory but an old building where . . . they repeat the classical and crucial experiments of science, an uncomfortably large debt left over from their progressive predecessors, and a profound conviction that they are on the right track at last and headed in the right direction.

Not all the attention showered on St. John's College by educators and the general public expressed itself in the form of serious comment or debate about the pros and cons of the enterprise—an undertaking that Barr and Buchanan thought should not be referred to as an "experiment," since in their view nothing new was being tried out. After the wide circulation of *How To Read A Book* and of *Liberal Education* by Mark Van Doren (both of which celebrated the uniqueness and soundness of the St. John's undertaking), the following piece of light verse appeared in the pages of the *New Yorker:*

ON THE GOSPEL ACCORDING TO ST. JOHN'S

(AFTER READING THE CATALOGUE OF ST. JOHN'S COLLEGE
AND ITS PRESCRIBED LIST OF "GREAT BOOKS")

by William W. Watt

> My knowledge of Lucian
> Is quite Lilliputian,
>   I'm feeble on Gibbon and Hume,
> I couldn't finagle
> A study of Hegel
>   From now to the trumpet of Doom—
>
> Do *I* have a true education today?
> Nay!
>
> The course at St. John's is the liberal par,
>   All other curricula foreign,
> Say Hutchins and Adler, Buchanan and Barr,
>   And Van Doren.
>
>   My stock of Plotinus
>   Is shamefully minus,
>   I've never consulted Justinian,
>   My notion of Grotius
>   Is worse than atrocious—
>   So how can I have an opinion

Mortimer J. Adler in front of the John Stuart Mill residence in Kensington Square, London, September 1974.

Clarissa and Ignatz Adler;
their son Mortimer at the age
of three.

Adler with his sons Mark and
Michael.

Adler in academic gown but
without degree. He did not get a
diploma from Columbia because
he could not swim and would not
take physical education.

Adler, years later, no longer averse
to a swimming pool, but still
unable to do more than splash
about.

"How To Read A Book is out. I'm secretly relieved." (*The New Yorker*)

ABOVE Scribner's window on Fifth Avenue, New York, March 11, 1940, during the week of publication of *How To Read A Book*.
BELOW Marshall Field's window on State Street, Chicago, a few months later; in it is *How To Read A Book* and some of the great books. (*Hedrich-Blessing Studio*)

The Great Books course generally met around an enormous table. Adler and co-instructor Milton Mayer led discussion from one end of the table while students listened, wrote, argued, or twiddled their thumbs. (*Time-Life Picture Agency*)

Adler addressing the Syntopicon staff in "Index House," on the campus of the University of Chicago, 1947. (*Time-Life Picture Agency*)

"He doesn't know anything except facts."

The indexers of the great ideas posed for a *Life* photographer with the 102 file drawers containing references to the ideas and with the works of the 74 authors from which the ideas were culled. (*Time-Life Picture Agency*)

The original Board of Directors of the Institute for Philosophical Research at their first meeting in May 1952. Bottom row, from left to right: Thomas Parran, surgeon general of the United States; Harold McKinnon, lawyer and author; Adler. Top row, from left to right: Harold Linder, president of Import-Export Bank; Meyer Kestnbaum, president of Hart Schaffner & Marx; Hermon Dunlap Smith, president of Marsh & McLennan and trustee of the University of Chicago.

Lawrence Kimpton, chancellor of the University of Chicago, addressing the banquet at the Waldorf-Astoria, New York, in April 1952, at which the first edition of the *Great Books of the Western World* was presented to its patrons.

"And don't come back until you believe in God!"

(Esquire)

Adler at the Dominican House of Studies in Washington, D.C., sometime in the mid-1930s. From left to right: Father Egan, Father Farrell (with whom Adler collaborated in writing a series of essays on the theory of democracy); Father Slavin. The identity of the Dominican at the far right is not known.

Adler and his wife Caroline at a private audience with
Pope Paul VI, 1964.

That's worthy to enter the brain of an ant?
I can't!

So say with the confident tones of a czar,
    And not with the peep of a straddler,
Van Doren and Hutchins, Buchanan and Barr,
    And Adler.

    My store of Lucretius?
    Now don't be facetious.
        I'm rusty on Darwin and Dante.
    Racine? Apollonius?
    Vague and erroneous.
        Bentham? Thucydides? Scanty.

I'm brilliant on Whither-democracy's-fate books,
Whether-to-pity-the-Germans-or-hate books,
Fighting-will-end-at-a-definite-date books,
I-was-aloft-in-a-battlescarred-crate books,
Private-initiative-vs.-the-State books,
Can-we-control-them-or-must-we-inflate books,
How-to-get-on-with-a-difficult-mate books—
All of them second- or third- or fourth-rate books—
Not Great Books!

Such trash couldn't possibly sully or scar
    The bright intellectual scutcheons
Of Adler, Van Doren, Buchanan and Barr,
    And Hutchins.

At the same time that Barr and Buchanan became, respectively, president and dean of the college, Bob Hutchins assumed the chairmanship of the Board of Visitors and Governors and I became a visiting lecturer. Barr and Buchanan repeatedly tried to prevail on Hutchins and me to give up Chicago entirely and join them at St. John's—even to the point of Barr's turning the presidency of his institution over to Hutchins. I can remember our deliberations about this; there were many moments when we were sorely tempted to make the move. Hutchins finally decided that St. John's was Barr and Buchanan's educational arena, not his; and, while remaining for some years a member of the board, gave up the chairmanship of it to Richard Cleveland, a son of President Cleveland. I resisted the invitation to become a fellow and tutor of the college, because I felt a full-time engagement in college education would leave no time or energy for the philosophical thinking and writing which had become my major occupation at Chicago in the late thirties and early forties and which afforded me more intellectual excitement than teaching. In the middle forties, when Barr and Buchanan left Annapolis to establish another version of St. John's at Stockbridge,

Massachusetts, they again invited me to join them—to be a member of the founding triumvirate—but by that time I had become completely preoccupied with the work of editing, with Bob Hutchins, *Great Books of the Western World,* and with the even more time-consuming work of producing a Syntopicon of the Great Ideas to accompany the set that was to be published by Encylopaedia Britannica, Inc. Probably, under all the surface reasons I gave for not making the move to either Annapolis or Stockbridge, lay the feeling that the temperamental as well as intellectual differences between Scott and me made it a lot easier for me to cooperate with him at a distance, rather than in close daily contact.

I certainly did cooperate—not always at a distance. During the first year of the New Program, I commuted from Chicago to Annapolis on a monthly basis, delivering ten lectures on the philosophy of Aristotle: two on his theory of the liberal arts of grammar, rhetoric, and logic; two on his philosophy of nature; two on his contributions to biology and psychology; two on his metaphysics and theology; and two on his moral philosophy. In the following year, 1938–1939, I gave another ten lectures at the college, on the theory of signs, on interpreting texts, on the liberal arts as the arts of learning and teaching, and ending with three lectures on the philosophy of Thomas Aquinas. In the early forties, my lectures at Annapolis became less frequent, but, with relatively few exceptions, I have managed to visit the college at least once a year since then.

From the beginning, my relation to the changing student body at St. John's has retained an unchanging element of good-humored personal tension. It started with the exorbitant length of the lectures on Aristotle which I gave during that first year. Consisting of single-spaced typewritten notes running to 35 and 40 pages, they took me at least two hours to deliver. That first year, the students, not yet realizing that this was much more than they should reasonably be expected to suffer, sat through them with admirable patience, and even returned, after a short break, to engage in open discussion. Before I made my first visit to the college the next year, word passed around that something must be done to prevent Adler from going beyond the limits of an hour. My first lecture, though not quite as long as those of the preceding year, could not be delivered in an hour. When the hour was up, every alarm clock in the college, hidden in the balcony of the lecture room in McDowell Hall, went off simultaneously. I stood my ground, waited for the din to subside, and then, with a smile and bow to acknowledge their ingenuity, completed the lecture. The students plotted another way to defeat me. On the occasion of my next lecture, someone pulled the main electrical switch when the canonical time was up. Utter darkness—and silence—reigned for a moment. I knew they expected me to rise to the challenge, so I took matches out of my pocket, and continued the lecture by matchlight for the brief interval it took for a member of the faculty to restore the electricity.

I subsequently shortened my lectures to an hour and a half or an hour and a quarter, warning the audience that I would go beyond an hour, and also telling them that I would find a resting place within the hour, at which I would pause and ask them to stand up to take three deep breaths before I resumed. In the years since then, there has seldom been a lecture of mine at St. John's when the students, inheriting the tradition of playing some prank on Adler, have not graced the occasion with some form of good-humored frivolity. Once, quite recently, just before I reached the rostrum to give a lecture on the defense of man against Darwin, the figure of an ape walked across the stage. Another time, the whole front row was occupied by students wearing the whitened faces and reddened lips of clowns (I asked them to stand up, face the audience, and take a bow); still another time, my lecture was interrupted by a repeating sound that no one in the room could identify and that was so mysterious that it distracted everyone's attention from the lecture, including mine. Someone in the rear of the auditorium, which was sloped and graded, had dropped on the stone floor marbles that pinged as they rolled down from level to level.

It is not because I could always expect some prank of this sort that I have always looked forward to giving a lecture at St. John's. With hardly a single exception, my lectures there have been prepared especially for that occasion and have represented an intellectual venture or a phase of thought in which I was intensely engaged at the time. I would not have dared to give anywhere else lectures as heavy in substance and as complex as the ones I prepared for the St. John's audience. Not only were St. Johnnies an alert and attentive audience, but they took part in an open forum for an hour or more after the lecture, often asking questions that advanced my own thinking about the subject of the evening. This, it seems to me, is an extraordinarily significant measure of the intellectual vitality of a college devoted to reading the great books and to acquiring some discipline in the liberal arts by discussing as well as by reading them.

I never taught a great books seminar at St. John's—never was invited to do so, never volunteered. The deepest disagreement between Scott Buchanan and me, or, perhaps, I should say, the most intractable difference in style, manifested itself in the way we conducted seminars. He, as moderator of the discussion, regarded himself as first among equals, presiding over a conversation among peers who, without being questioned, would express their differing views of the book under consideration. I regarded myself as a teacher leading students to a better understanding of the book by persistent interrogation and argument. While we both took Socrates for our model, his dialectical pursuit of the truth was more Platonic, mine more Aristotelian. From my point of view, his imitation of Socrates gave him the look of a benign Buddha smiling at the folly of those around him; from his point of view, my Socratizing barely concealed the pertinacity of a Torquemada rooting out error.

Nevertheless, we saw eye to eye on the great books and the liberal arts as the indispensable core of a schooling designed to prepare the young for continued learning in adult life and for the duties of citizenship in a democracy. My admiration for Scott's ingenuity, imagination, and wisdom in putting together the elements of the New Program at St. John's was unqualified. I took every opportunity to praise and promote it—by publishing articles in its defense when in the middle forties it was attacked by Sidney Hook and by John Dewey (his critique of St. John's, which appeared in *Fortune* magazine, also elicited a spirited rejoinder from Alexander Meiklejohn); and by holding it up as a model whenever I was invited to talk about education or to educators.

During the late forties and early fifties, I was frequently asked by one institution or another to meet with a curriculum committee which had been set up to reform the collegiate course of study. On such occasions, I laid out a set of negative conditions which I regarded as prerequisite to any reform aimed in the right direction. If these conditions were observed, I said, then any positive proposals for the content of the curriculum, and for its administration, would be satisfactory. The conditions were as follows: (1) there should be no vocational training of any sort; (2) there should be no electives, no majors or minors, no specialization in subject matter; (3) there should be no division of the faculty into professors competent in one department of learning rather than another; (4) no member of the faculty should be unprepared to teach the course of study as a whole; (5) no textbooks or manuals should be assigned as reading material for the students; (6) not more than one lecture a week should be given to the student body; (7) there should be no written examinations.

These seven negatives described the revolutionary changes that Scott had instituted at St. John's. If any other college were to adopt them, it would be compelled to adopt also, I felt, some of the positive aspects of his program—the replacement of departmentally divided professors by a community of fellows and tutors obligated to teach everything the students were asked to study; the replacement of written by oral examinations; the replacement of textbooks and manuals by other books, some of which would have to be better and might even be great; and so on.

This way of preaching the gospel according to St. John's produced a variety of animated responses, but gained no converts. Only a small college about to go out of business offered a fertile field for proposals as revolutionary as Scott's. No flourishing institution with a tenured and indentured faculty could be expected to turn the somersaults that the St. John's program demanded. There were other obstacles, too. I remember a session with the curriculum committee at Stanford University in California, at which I proceeded to outline my set of negative conditions. When I had finished, the members of the committee faced me in stony silence, finally broken by a question from the dean of the college. "Dr. Adler," he asked, "if we were to comply with these conditions, what would you then recommend we do in a college that enrolls seven thousand students?" It was now my turn to sit in stunned silence until I could summon the wit to apologize for not having inquired in the first place about the size of the student body.

I said that I gained no converts, but I have already mentioned two exceptions, both to be attributed to the enthusiasm I had aroused for St. John's in friends of mine. One was James Haggerty, a professor of philosophy at St. Mary's College in California, who helped me persuade some of his colleagues to adopt elements of the St. John's program. The other was Father John Cavanaugh who, as president of Notre Dame University, presided over a series of faculty conferences that went on for almost two years, at which I outlined the kind of adaptation of the St. John's curriculum that might be made by a leading Catholic university. In this case, Father Cavanaugh's persistence, rather than my persuasiveness, finally won out, and resulted in the creation of a General Program of Liberal Studies which enrolled a small fraction of Notre Dame's undergraduates. Otto Bird, who had been at the University of Chicago during the days of the Committee on Liberal Arts and who later worked with me on the production of the Syntopicon, became the first director of the General Program, got it off to a good start, and nursed it to maturity. It still flourishes today.

In all the controversies about the St. John's program, I found it useful to borrow from Winkie Barr two answers to objections frequently advanced by critics who pointed out that the great books were too difficult to be mastered by college students. Barr responded by saying that the students were not expected to master the great books; few if any adults could be expected to do that. At St. John's, he said, the great books serve the purpose of a very large bone thrown to a young puppy. The puppy will wrestle with it, will probably not get much meat off it while agitating it, but will certainly sharpen its teeth in the process. To the criticism that a completely required curriculum imposes too much discipline and reduces freedom, Barr replied by reminding the critics that the undirected often suffer a worse fate than loss of freedom. The ship that will not answer to the rudder, he remarked, must answer to the rock.

Chapter 11

The War Years and After

I N MY LONG association with Bob Hutchins, spanning a half century, there was only one matter about which we did not with little effort agree—America's posture in relation to the war in Europe and to the threat grown large with the success of Hitler's military machine. With the onset of the European war, a revival of American isolationism, under the banner of "America First," enrolled a large following. Among the leaders of that movement were Colonel Lindbergh, Gen. Robert E. Wood (chairman of the board of Sears Roebuck), Bob Hutchins, and Bill Benton, then vice-president of the University of Chicago. For Bob, the central proposition was peace, and in defense of that proposition, he made two of the most eloquent speeches of his life, in nationwide radio broadcasts over NBC, the first in January 1941; the second in April. At the end of March, in the university chapel, he delivered a third plea for America's total abstention from the European conflict.

Most of faculty were in the opposite camp, and on this occasion I found myself siding with them. We all displayed "Aid to Britain" buttons in our lapels. The college newspaper, the *Daily Maroon,* published a "special war supplement" in the week of Hutchins's radio talk. It carried, in large boldface type, the headline "Adler Opposes Hutchins on War." At the time of Hutchins's second broadcast, it issued another special which carried the full text of Bob's chapel address together with replies by six eminent members of the faculty, including my friend and Bob's, Dick McKeon. These replies were also aired over the radio.

After Pearl Harbor, Hutchins, still convinced that it would have been ultimately better for the future of the United States if it could have remained unembroiled, committed the university's facilities to the war effort. Later, when the War Department shopped around to find a location for the ultrasecret Manhattan Project, in the race to produce nuclear fission before the Nazis, Bob Hutchins accepted for the University of Chicago the perilous challenge involved in taking on this billion-dollar contract from the government. On the one hand, the project might fail disgracefully; on the other hand, it might succeed in creating an atomic bomb, abhorrent to Bob in ways that he then only dimly foresaw. But, told by the War Department that if we did not produce the bomb first, the Germans would, Hutchins agreed to house the Manhattan Project at the University of Chicago. It is paradoxical that he, a zealot for peace and a proponent of total disarmament, should have been the university president who so crucially committed his institution to the war effort, whereas the heads of three or four leading eastern universities, all of whom had spoken out in favor of our fighting Hitler, refused to accept responsibility for the Manhattan Project.

In the controversy about the war, I found myself disagreeing with Hutchins's negative conclusion while wholeheartedly agreeing with all his affirmative principles. It seemed to me that the conclusion he reached did not inexorably follow from his premises. In the case of his faculty opponents, whose disagreement with Hutchins's conclusion I shared, I found their lack of principles disheartening. Abhorrence of Hitler had caused even Bertrand Russell, not only an avowed pacifist but also a relativist in morals, to advocate taking sides in the struggle because what Hitler stood for was, in his judgment, morally wrong. But my university colleagues would not forsake their skepticism about the objectivity of moral values in order to come out flatly against Nazism as politically and morally outrageous. They were willing and anxious to have us go to war against Nazi Germany, but could not bring themselves to declare that the issue involved rights and wrongs that were not a matter of subjective opinion or entirely relative to the declarant's prejudices, feelings, or point of view.

My intellectual discomfort and dismay boiled over in an article that I wrote in October 1940 for *Harper's Magazine*, "This Pre-War Generation."

For some years now at the University of Chicago President Hutchins and I have been teaching courses in which the students are asked to read great works in ethics, economics, and politics. They have already had enough education to be suspicious of Plato and Aristotle, St. Thomas Aquinas and John Locke. They react at once against these, or any other authors, who write as if truth could be reached in moral matters, as if the mind could be convinced by reasoning from principles, as if there were self-evident precepts about good and bad. They tell us, emphatically and almost unanimously, that "there is no right and wrong," [and] that "moral values are private opinions," [and] that "everything is relative."

This happened when we read Rousseau and the *Federalist Papers,* just as much as when we read Aristotle and Aquinas. "For those who suppose that American colleges are hotbeds of radicalism," I pointed out that

> the same thing happened when we asked them to read Karl Marx's *Capital.* We tried to show them how Marx had proved the injustices inherent in the historic processes of capitalism. They resisted, not because they could answer Marx's arguments, but because they initially rejected the very notion that a moral judgment about capitalism, or anything else, can be proved.

All such judgments, our students had learned from their teachers, "can be reduced to statements of what I like or what I dislike. There is no 'should' or 'ought.' "

The *Harper's* article reported a number of recent brushes that I had had with my colleagues.

> On one occasion last spring an eminent professor of history at the University took the position in after-dinner conversation that, while he didn't *like* Hitler, no one could *prove* that he was wrong.

This historian had no place in his scheme of things for truth in moral matters, self-evident or demonstrated. "There were just primitive urges which could be rationalized in different ways." He himself "was a democrat 'by faith'—by the way he felt at the time. It is easy enough," I wrote, "to imagine how a change of heart might be forced on him; his mind would present no obstacle to such a change."

> On another occasion I was dining with the local authority on international law and a professor of medicine. It was shortly after the Nazi invasion of the Low Countries. Both my colleagues were hot under the collar about American isolationism. They wanted immediate action in support of the Allied cause. What was that cause? I asked. It was the cause of democracy, our cause, and we must act at once. . . . After dinner I reported the conversation I had had with the professor of history, and again I said that I thought the political truth of democracy could be demonstrated. *No such thing!* Democracy could be saved by force of arms, but it could not be proved by weight of reason. The professor of international law told me that his "preference" for democracy was simply a cultural bias, arising from "postulates" which could not themselves be examined for truth or falsity.

During the summer of 1941, when Hitler's panzer divisions opened the Nazi invasion of Soviet Russia, I completed work on *A Dialectic of Morals,* a book that reported the dialogues Hutchins and I had had with our students in an effort to combat the influence of skepticism and relativism about moral judgments. And that autumn, in an article in

Harper's on "The Chicago School," I asked once more the question that was my repeated refrain for many years—"whether a culture can be healthy, whether democracy can be defended, if theology and metaphysics, ethics and politics are either despised or, what is the same, degraded to topics about which laboratory scientists pontificate after they have won the Nobel Prize or are called to the Gifford Lectureship." Is science by itself—without philosophy—enough, either theoretically or practically, to guide us in leading good human lives or to lay the foundations of a good society?

That question framed the issue of the second public debate that I had with Bertrand Russell. My first debate with him took place in January 1941. In that dispute, Lord Russell challenged my thesis that the objectives of education were always and everywhere the same because education must be defined as "the process whereby the powers of human nature become developed by good habits." He doubted that we could know enough about human nature and its powers to know which habits were universally and objectively good for human beings to form. In his rebuttal of my affirmative position he regaled the audience with quips and sallies—a display of great wit rather than wisdom. My distaste for Russell's performance still lingered when, a year later, the People's Church in Chicago asked whether I would debate him again. My first inclination was to say no, but after some reflection, I said I would be willing on one condition—that this time he would take the affirmative position and allow me the pleasures of rebuttal. It took at least six months or more for Russell to come up with a proposition he was willing to affirm, and when he did, it put him on the affirmative side of the resolution that science is enough for the good life and the good society.

Preparing for the debate, I put into my file a letter from Bertrand Russell to the *New York Times*. It filled three columns on the editorial page. The headlines conveyed the gist of the message: "Long-Time Advocate of Peace Approves Present War: Professor Bertrand Russell States Reasons for Changing Positions, Disputes Stand of Dr. Hutchins, and Hopes Ultimately for Federation of the World." Though the letter fell short of being explicit on the point at issue, I thought I could cite Russell's approval of the present war, in spite of his resolute commitment to pacificism, as some indication that he regarded the Allies as being on the right side of this conflict—right in some rationally arguable sense, not just a reflection of personal feelings about what was at stake. I could, therefore, use this letter to rebut Russell's position out of his own mouth.

I was mistaken in my impression that Russell had changed his views about the nonobjectivity of value judgments. As it turned out, I did not need to quote Russell against himself. In the first ten minutes of his defense of the affirmative position, he contradicted the proposition he had undertaken to affirm. In rapid order, he made the following assertions: first, that empirical science constitutes the only objectively valid knowledge available to us; second, that our knowledge of the world and of man is by itself incapable of answering any questions of value, for we have knowledge only of matters of fact, and what is good or bad, right or wrong is not a matter of fact; third, that our decisions on questions of value as opposed to questions of fact are determined by our feelings. From these three propositions, only one conclusion logically follows—that knowledge by itself does not enable us to decide how to lead a good life or establish a good society. That conclusion directly contradicted the proposition Russell was supposed to be defending— that science (for him, equivalent to knowledge) is enough for the good life and the good society.

In my rebuttal, I pointed out this contradiction, but that hardly settled the matter. I proceeded to put Russell into the logical box of a *reductio ad absurdum*. Feelings, he had said, decided our judgments about good and bad, or right and wrong. Was there a difference, I asked, between good and bad feelings, right and wrong feelings? The Nazis and the Allies harbored opposite feelings about which party in the present war had right on its side. Could Lord Russell, I asked, tell us on what grounds he thought his feelings were right and Hitler's were wrong?

If he could not provide us with objective grounds for asserting that rightness or goodness attached to one set of feelings, and wrongness or badness attached to the opposite (if, in short, our feelings are purely personal and subjective), then only might or force in the awful arbitrament of war can decide which of conflicting feelings about what is right and wrong shall finally prevail. I then argued that Russell, in order to avoid this horn of the dilemma, was logically compelled to impale himself on the other: if might should not be allowed to decide who is right, then reason must, and reason can do so only by having recourse to objectively valid knowledge of right and wrong.

Were he to adopt this view, Russell would be able to assert that his feelings about the issues in the European war were objectively sounder than Hitler's, not just an expression of his personal prejudices. However, in doing so, he would also once more contradict the proposition he was supposed to be affirming—that science is enough for the good life and the good society. He had himself maintained, and I fully agreed, that science gave us knowledge only of matters of fact, not about values. For there to be objectively valid answers to questions of value, there had to be valid knowledge other than empirical science. Such "knowledge other than empirical science" was clearly not mathematics or history. There was nothing left for it to be but philosophy.

Russell was correct in thinking that we needed something more than science to settle questions of value; that something more, however, was not feelings, but moral philosophy—the objectively valid principles and conclusions of ethics and politics. If he were to agree to this, in order to avoid embracing the view that might makes right, then he would also have to change his mind not only about the character of philosophical knowledge in differentiation from empirical science, but, even more radically, about the validity of moral philosophy. He would have to abandon his endorsement of the then current view of ethics as completely noncognitive (as emotive, an expression of feelings rather than of knowledge) which he, with characteristic wit, had epitomized by saying that "ethics consists in the art of recommending to others what they must do in order to get along with one's self."

I wish I could report that my arguments had some effect on Russell. They did win the audience over to my side, but Russell quipped his way out of the box I had put him in without even trying to resolve the contradictions. When I was a philosophy student at Columbia, I had great respect for Russell's views, his philosophical writings before World War I, especially his contributions to the philosophy of mathematics and to mathematical logic. But the more I studied the books he wrote from the twenties on, especially his writings on the philosophy of language, the more my respect for him as a philosopher diminished.

However, on one point I found myself in complete agreement with him at the time of our second debate. In the concluding paragraph of his letter to the *New York Times,* Russell wrote:

> There is one hope that is important and, I think, not utopian; that at the end of the war some step, less ineffective than the League of Nations, may be taken toward the Federation of the World.

It may be questioned whether the United Nations has turned out to be that more effective step, but the goal toward which effective steps should be taken is certainly, as Russell indicated, world federation to create world government and to institute and preserve world peace.

That goal, as Russell observed, should be regarded as a practicable objective, not a utopian one. There may be many causes of war, but there is only one cause of peace, and that is government. Civil government produces civil peace. Anarchy, or the absence of government, is identical with a state of war: either the cold war of the diplomats and of espionage or the actual warfare of the generals with guns and bombs. To identify the state of war with the violence of actual warfare is to misconceive the state of peace in purely negative terms as the absence of fighting. Civil peace, positively conceived, consists not in the absence of fighting but rather in conditions that make it possible to settle all differences without recourse to violence or bloodshed. Civil government, by providing that set of conditions, establishes and preserves civil peace.

Up to this point in history, there has never been a single moment of world peace, though there may have been periods when no actual warfare was being waged. There has been a multiplicity of local peaces, each the civil peace of a political society under civil government. The argument for world government as the indispensable condition of world peace can be boiled down to a single proposition: if local civil government is necessary for local civil peace, then world civil government is necessary for world civil peace.

I had learned this lesson from a few extraordinary paragraphs in the great books—one in Dante's tract on monarchy, one or two in Hobbes's *Leviathan,* several in Kant's *Science of Right* and his essay on perpetual peace; and in particular one brief statement by Cicero that is paraphrased by Machiavelli and then by Locke, to the effect that brutes have only one way of settling their differences, by fighting, whereas men have two ways of doing so, by fighting or by conversation and recourse to law. The first way is the way of war; the second, of peace.

Government, with a monopoly of authorized force, provides the apparatus for settling differences by debate and litigation, and so it is the *sine qua non* of peace. When, in the course of diplomatic negotiations between sovereign states, the conversations break down, actual warfare breaks out to settle serious differences that cannot be settled any other way. The diplomats having failed, the generals take over. Actual warfare, said Clausewitz, is nothing but the continuation of international politics by other means.

The foregoing summarizes the gist of a book that I wrote in 1943, during the long, dark summer of the siege of Stalingrad. I wanted to entitle it "The Cause of Peace," but Simon and Schuster wanted another how-to book and so it came out in 1944 under the title *How To Think About War and Peace.* In addition to presenting the argument that world government is the indispensable cause of world peace, the book attempted to show that world government is not only necessary, but also possible and desirable—just as possible as the federation of the thirteen independent colonies "to form a more perfect union" under the Constitution of the United States; and desirable for the same reason that their federal union under a national government was preferable to the loose association of the thirteen states under the Articles of Confederation, analogous to the loose association of states in the League of Nations.

Necessary, possible, and desirable though world government might be, how probable was it? In 1943, before the explosion of the first atomic bomb, it seemed to me that for millennia history had been moving slowly but inexorably toward the expansion of local peaces and that the establishment of world peace might be expected within the next five hundred years. Not until the twentieth century did technological advances make global warfare an actuality. These same technological advances, together with the economic interdependence of all human societies, might increase the probability of global peace.

During 1944 and 1945, I took every opportunity to talk about world government. Through Mark Van Doren, who had been giving lectures for the Army Air Force, I was invited by the Air Transport Command to tour various bases. My repertoire consisted of three lectures—one on liberal education, one on the future of democracy, and one on world government and world peace. Repeated hearing of these lectures did persuade at least one of my listeners—Peter Krehel, a young lieutenant, my military escort on the tour. At a base in Wilmington, Delaware, I talked about democracy and world peace to a large audience of both officers and enlisted men—white officers from the South and black enlisted men from the North. I argued for universal suffrage and civil rights without any discrimination. I also made the point that democratic institutions could not prosper in a world at war; the future of democracy depended on the establishment of world peace through world government. In the question period, a young major expressed the sentiments of most of his fellow officers by saying, with a pronounced Southern drawl, "Professor Adler, you say you are talking about democracy, but I think it is plain that it is communism, not democracy, you are speaking for."

With the dropping of atomic bombs on Hiroshima and Nagasaki in August 1945, the nascent World Federalist movement burgeoned overnight. Wendell Willkie, after a whirlwind global tour, published his best-selling tract, *One World,* that gave wide currency to the slogan "one world or none"; in an essay on the unification of the world, Arnold Toynbee predicted that world government would come into existence, in the not too distant future, either by world conquest or by a world constitutional convention. During the next two years, not satisfied with the charter of the United Nations, the legislatures of 36 out of the 48 states passed resolutions calling for a worldwide people's convention to take steps toward the formation of a world federal government. What seemed then like the imminent threat of a global holocaust not only reduced the time scale of my thinking about the probability of world government (I was now prepared to think in terms much less than 500 years), but also heated up my rhetoric in the effort to persuade others that world government was now more necessary than ever.

In the year of the atomic bomb and afterwards, I redoubled my efforts at persuasion. My overcharged rhetoric on one occasion generated a chain of consequences it would have been difficult to foresee.

Lecturing at Notre Dame College in Cleveland, Ohio, less than three months after the bombs had been dropped, I told my audience that we must be prepared to relinquish the sovereignty of the United States, and other peoples must do likewise, in order to form a world government, just as Massachusetts and Virginia and the other states gave up their external sovereignty to form the federal union of the United States. The *Cleveland Plain Dealer,* reporting the lecture, opened its story with the following statement attributed to me: "We must do everything we can to abolish the United States." An irate citizen of Ohio sent a clipping of this story to his congressman, who read it into the Congressional Record. Some weeks later, my father-in-law, who had received several copies of the Congressional Record, called me into his study to give an account of myself. I had some difficulty in explaining the difference between the actual statement made in my Cleveland speech and the misreport of it in the *Cleveland Plain Dealer.*

The consequences did not stop there. More than six years later, asked to make a speech on world government at Texas Christian University in Fort Worth, I arrived at the auditorium to find, outside of it, a parade of the "Mothers of America" carrying banners denouncing my views. Ten years after that, in 1963, the John Birch Society of Spokane, Washington, tried to prevent my speaking at a state educational conference. Failing to get my invitation cancelled, they distributed a pamphlet, the front cover of which blazed forth in large red letters "We must do everything we can to destroy the United States — Mortimer J. Adler." Underneath this was the following statement:

> Mortimer J. Adler, high priest of the liberal-left, leaves little doubt to the imagination regarding his loyalty to the United States. The above quotation is from the October 29, 1945, *Cleveland Plain Dealer.* The Vigilante finds it very difficult to understand why this character was selected to be the keynote speaker at Spokane's 61st annual session of the Inland Empire Educational Association.

An inside sheet of the four-page pamphlet carried the *Plain Dealer* story in full; and on the back was a letter to a local John Bircher from J. Edgar Hoover, charging me with "urging the complete abolishment of the United States" and adding that he had "no information that this statement was ever repudiated."

In view of these events, I half expected to be grilled for disloyalty to the United States during the years when Senator McCarthy's Un-American Activities Committee ran rampant. The reason why that did not occur probably lay in the fact that I am an inveterate nonjoiner and nonsigner. I never even went so far as to become a member of the World Federalist organization; I have never signed my name to any public manifesto or published appeal. Nevertheless, with a black mark against my name in J. Edgar Hoover's files, and aware of the plight of friends who had suffered interrogation during the McCarthy era, I thought up the answer I might have given the senator if he had ever asked me whether I was a member of the Communist party, "Senator," I would say, "if I were a member of the Communist party, I would not hesitate to lie to you and tell you that I am not a member; but since I am not a member of the Communist party, I refuse to answer your question."

The destruction of Hiroshima and Nagasaki produced tremors on the campus of the University of Chicago, especially among the scientists who, through their participation in the Manhattan Project, had helped to create the bomb. They held meeting after meeting in which they cross-examined each other on questions of moral responsibility. With smarting consciences, they asked themselves whether an atomic bomb differed in kind, rather than degree, from other destructive weapons of warfare. Scientists of the stature of Enrico Fermi, Edward Teller, and Leo Szilard discussed the issue without the same assurance, and certainly without the same precision of speech or thought, that they displayed in their laboratories. They now sought answers to questions in moral and political philosophy which, several years before, they would have dismissed as unanswerable, that is, by objective knowledge rather than subjective opinion. For many years after the earth-shaking event of atomic explosions, the *Bulletin of the Atomic Scientists,* published at the University of Chicago, continued to record the agitation of scientists about matters philosophical that required them to wade in unfamiliar waters. The issue of April 1957 contained an article of mine entitled "The Questions Science Cannot Answer."

Nuclear fission produced another reverberation at the university. Those of us who had been thinking during the war years about the conditions prerequisite for world peace now felt the need for action that might accelerate the movement toward world unification. Bob Hutchins and I, Dick McKeon, and Guiseppe Antonio Borgese, an anti-Fascist émigré from Mussolini's Italy, a poet, and a profound as well as a passionate teacher of Dante, formed the "Committee to Frame a World Constitution," which Bob could not resist referring to as "the committee to frame Hutchins." It enlisted Prof. Robert Redfield, a distinguished anthropologist who became dean of the Social Science Division, and Wilbur Katz, a professor of law who became dean of the Law School. Its membership, outside the university, included Stringfellow Barr, Rexford Tugwell, Erich Kahler, who was then at Princeton, Charles McIlwain of Harvard, and Albert Guérard of Stanford. James Landis, dean of the Harvard Law School, and Reinhold Niebuhr, of the Union Theological Seminary, took part in some of our meetings, but did not sign the *Preliminary Draft of a World*

Constitution, which was completed in July 1947 and published in 1948. Dick McKeon, who had been one of the founding members and who participated in most of our sessions, resigned from the committee before its work was concluded, largely because of differences of opinion between himself and Borgese.

Between November 1945 and July 1947, the committee held thirteen meetings, each running two or three days. It produced 150 position papers, totalling about 4,500 pages. In July 1947, it also started a monthly magazine, *Common Cause,* to publish some of the papers prepared in the course of our work. After the publication of the *Preliminary Draft of a World Constitution,* the magazine continued in existence to publish commentaries on the World Constitution analogous to those written by Hamilton, Madison, and Jay on the Constitution of the United States. Indefatigable in his efforts to promote world government, Borgese planned a series of three books in support of the constitution. He lived to complete only one—*Foundations of the World Republic,* published in 1953.

The meetings of the committee were vivid—I would almost say, livid—affairs, because of Borgese's style of speech and manner of thought. He had the immense and unusual vocabulary of a poet who taught himself English by almost total immersion in its best literature. His study of *The Divine Comedy* had drawn him into the byways of both philosophy and theology, and that, combined with a massive knowledge of history, gave him unusual intellectual resources which he exhibited with passionate pleasure, but not without discomfort to one or another member of the committee. One day, Jim Landis, impatient with what he regarded as an unnecessary burst of elocutionary fire on Borgese's part, stopped him in the middle of a sentence by saying with some disdain, "Oh, that's just rhetoric." Antonio glared at him for a moment of breathless silence. Then, pointing a finger as if it were a gun about to go off, he uttered the warning made famous by Owen Wister's Virginian: "When you say that again, smile!"

His style included unforgettable dicta, some original with him, some borrowed from Shakespeare or Dante. Instead of saying "in my opinion" or "in my judgment," he would preface a weighty declaration by saying "according to me." At large dinner parties, he would begin some injunction to his wife at the other end of the table by saying "Elizabetta, *cara mia,* be ruled by me!" That expression, I discovered years later, Antonio had lifted from Shakespeare: Hamlet's mother, the queen, is thus addressed by her husband. Most extraordinary of all was Borgese's invention of a new mood and tense in English grammar. After a series of disputes between Borgese and McKeon had raised barriers to their direct communication, I undertook to serve as intermediary, trying to interpret the views of each to the other in tones more placating than either of them would have used. One day, when I was reporting to Antonio something I had said to McKeon on his behalf, he raised his eyes and hands in horror and sought the retraction of my statement. "Oh, Mortimer," he commanded, "do not have said that!" We subsequently called this novel grammatical construction "Borgese's past imperative."

During those postwar years, my collaboration with Antonio and his wife, Elizabeth, deepened my thought about world peace and world government, and my friendship with them enlivened my life. Elizabeth was the youngest daughter of Thomas Mann. When the great German novelist and his wife visited Chicago, Helen and I were invited to dinner at the Borgese household. Those dinner parties were highly charged with electric sparks set off by the verbal swordplay of two eminent literary figures, one German, the other Italian, but one also the father-in-law and the other a son-in-law of almost the same age; for Antonio was thirty or more years older than Elizabeth. That April-October marriage had much to recommend it over other conjugal unions with which I was intimately acquainted, including my own. Years later, after Helen and I were divorced, Elizabeth Borgese helped me to persuade Caroline Pring that the difference in our ages (I was then sixty, she twenty-six), far from being an impediment to a good marriage, could contribute to one. My experience during the last fourteen years has confirmed that promise.

What turned out to be the last or next to the last gasp of the world government movement occurred in Stockholm in the late summer of 1950 when representatives of world federalist organizations from all over the world assembled for a conference. The Borgeses and I attended it as representatives of the Committee to Frame a World Constitution. Winkie Barr and Scott Buchanan represented the World Government Foundation, of which they had become the directors after they left St. John's College. Lord Boyd-Orr, for some years president of the Congress of World Federalists, now wanted to resign, and so the election of a new president became the concluding business of the conference. Antonio persuaded me to phone Hutchins in Chicago and ask permission to nominate him. Permission granted, I made the nominating speech, only to discover that Barr and Buchanan, who disagreed with Hutchins, Borgese, and me about the means for reaching our common goal, had persuaded Lord Boyd-Orr to withdraw his resignation. When that was announced, seconds after I concluded my nominating speech, he was reelected by acclamation.

Since the middle fifties, the world government movement has become almost moribund. No one, in my judgment, has shown the basic idea to be unsound or has come forward with any practicable alternative for establishing and preserving world civil peace. A seminar on war and peace, which I conducted for the Ford Foundation in the early fifties, reinforced all of my earlier convictions on that score. There are certain subjects on which I have not changed my mind in the course of the last thirty years, and this is one of them. Why has the movement for world government lost its vigor and its adherents? Not because events since 1945 have introduced new difficulties and obstacles. If anything, recent technological advances, the growing economic interdependence of all parts of the globe, and ecological problems of global proportions have made political unification of all peoples not only more feasible, but also more necessary and desirable. I think the reason is that it is only during the devastation of war, and in the years of rehabilitation following a war, that the minds of men turn with vigor to thoughts of peace. As the horrors of the last war recede from memory, and the ability to imagine the next becomes feebler, people yield to the preoccupations of their daily round and devote their energies to more immediate goals. Horrible as the thought is, it may take a third world war that will bring all mankind to its knees in rubble before the survivors will do, under dire need, what they should and could have done before.

Another, if less significant, waxing and waning, I find more difficult to account for. Like the world government movement, the great books movement gained impetus during the war and reached its high-water mark in the postwar years, but it continued to flourish throughout the fifties and into the sixties before it began to wane. Why it initially won and subsequently sustained widespread interest across the nation must have been due to factors other than the zeal of its promoters. It is, perhaps, more difficult to say what caught the public fancy at the beginning than it is to explain why, in the generally iconoclastic and antiretrospective atmosphere of the middle and late sixties, the great books movement slid into a decline.

The rapid growth of the great books movement in the early forties throughout the United States, and even in Canada, required a national organization to carry on the work that University College had begun. Bob Hutchins and Bill Benton sponsored the formation of the Great Books Foundation, which came into existence in 1947, with some help from the University of Chicago and with contributions from several charitable sources, including the Old Dominion Foundation, founded and chaired by Paul Mellon. Later, the Ford Foundation's Fund for Adult Education gave its support to the Great Books Foundation.

With some income derived from the sale of paperback reprints of selections from the great books, the Great Books Foundation has managed, on relatively meager means, to train generation after generation of great books leaders, to organize discussion groups, to publish and circulate training manuals and other aids, and to extend the program in a variety of ways, most recently in the form of junior great books discussion groups organized in elementary and high schools and with parents as well as teachers serving as discussion leaders. Lynn Williams became the first president of the foundation. When he became a vice-president of the University of Chicago, he was succeeded by Wilbur Munnecke; and he, in turn, was succeeded by C. Scott Fletcher, who subsequently became president of the Fund for Adult Education.

Within a year, over 7,000 adults in the Chicago area enrolled in seminars organized by the Great Books Foundation, and less than a year later, over 43,000 persons had become members of great books groups in 300 cities all over the country. The mayor of Chicago proclaimed the week of September 25, 1948, "Great Books Week." Tributes were sent to the Great Books Foundation from the governor of Illinois and from President Truman. During Great Books Week, I delivered a number of addresses, one entitled "The Great Books in Today's World" to a large audience in the auditorium of the Fair Department Store on State Street; and Bob Hutchins and I conducted a discussion of Plato's dialogue on the trial of Socrates before a capacity audience of 3,000 in Orchestra Hall; an additional 1,500 were turned away. The participants in the discussion, seated on the stage around a table with microphones, included a number of eminent Chicagoans—Marshall Field, Jr., publisher of the Chicago *Sun*, Meyer Kestnbaum, president of Hart, Schaffner and Marx, and Ralph Helstein, head of the meat-packers union. A similar event in Milwaukee (Machiavelli's *Prince* was the book under discussion) reached an even larger audience through radio and TV coverage. Milwaukee's City Hall displayed a large electric sign, "Register for Great Books." In 1950, the University of Chicago's Round Table, nationally broadcast by NBC, devoted a half hour to a conversation between Clare Boothe Luce and me about the great books and the great ideas. The next year, Clare Luce and I took the stage of a large packed auditorium in Los Angeles to demonstrate a great books seminar by discussing the Declaration of Independence with a select group of local citizens. Encyclopaedia Britannica, Inc., published *Great Books of the Western World* in fifty-four volumes in 1952, and less than a decade later sales reached the record high of over 49,000 sets in a single year.

It may be difficult to explain why the great books movement spread so fast and so far during the twenty years between 1945 and 1965, but not how it began and got off to a good start. The idea of using the great books in adult education through the organization of informal discussion groups antedated the Second World War by many years. As the reader already knows, Scott Buchanan and I had set up an experimental effort in this direction in 1927–1929 under the auspices of the People's Institute in New York City. After Hutchins and I began teaching the great books to freshmen at the university, the publicity about that enterprise prompted a group of university alumni to propose that

I moderate discussions of the same books at regular meetings in the homes of different participants. What came to be known as the Highland Park Great Books group started small, grew as it enrolled newcomers, and flourished for over fifteen years. In 1939, University College, the extension division of the university, began including a great books seminar as one of its course offerings, and continued it without notable success for three or four years. The turning point came in 1942–1943 with the formation at the University Club in Chicago of a great books seminar for adults, which Bob Hutchins and I conducted for businessmen, industrialists, bankers, and lawyers of the city, together with their wives. Because of the affluence of its participants, the University Club group was soon referred to in newspaper stories and even by the members themselves as "the Fat Man's Class."

The idea of setting up this class came from Wilbur Munnecke, who had left Marshall Field to become a vice-president of the university. Munnecke, aware that many of the university trustees still did not understand the purpose of the educational program that Hutchins was fighting for, thought that having a select group of trustees, together with other leading Chicagoans, read and discuss the great books with Hutchins might not only enlighten them about what was going on at the university, but also win their sympathy for Hutchins's position.

The series of reading assignments that Hutchins and I constructed for the University Club Class took ten years to get through; from that point on, we began rereading some of the same works, other works by the same authors, and books not included in the original list. The discussion of certain works produced some amusing interchanges that I can still remember. On the occasion when we were discussing Sophocles's *Oedipus the King*, Ellen Smith, the wife of Hermon Dunlap Smith, a university trustee, expressed some puzzlement over the horror which the Greeks apparently felt about incest. Milton Mayer, sitting at my side, responded by saying, in an audible stage whisper, "There's nothing wrong with incest just as long as you keep it in the family." During a discussion of the Treatise on God in the *Summa Theologica* of Thomas Aquinas, Hughston McBain, a feisty Scotsman who was then president of Marshall Field and Company, held up the discussion for half an hour, hammering away at an incidental remark of mine that even God could not reverse the order of past events. How could anything be impossible for an omnipotent God? When I tried to explain that being unable to do the impossible in no way detracts from the divine omnipotence, which consists in the power to do anything that is possible, Mr. McBain castigated my impiety for claiming to know what was possible or impossible for God. Another year, when we were reading Dante's *Divine Comedy* and finally came, in the third session, to the discussion of the *Paradiso*, Clay Judson, a Chicago lawyer, asked

Hutchins what the saints did day after day in Heaven. Told by Hutchins that those who enjoy the blessing of the Beatific Vision spend a changeless eternity contemplating God, Clay Judson asked whether that was all they did, and to Bob's affirmative reply, he responded by declaring his distaste for life in Heaven, saying he thought it was distinctly un-American.

The University Club class developed side effects more far-reaching than those Will Munnecke had in mind. It did what he hoped for. It helped to create a better understanding of Bob Hutchins's educational ideas on the part of the university's trustees. The chairman of the board, Harold Swift, and his brother Charles were members; and so were Marshall Field, Jr., Paul Harper (son of the first president of the university), Laird Bell, Walter Paepcke, and Hermon Dunlap Smith. William Benton was also in the class, as were Meyer Kestnbaum, president of Hart, Schaffner and Marx, and Lynn Williams, vice-president of the Stewart-Warner Company. The idea of a group of well-known citizens reading the great books and discussing them with the president of the university caught the popular fancy. It generated a shower of colorful reports in the press, news photographs, and favorable comments. These, in turn, put into the minds of less well known citizens of Chicago the thought that they, too, should go and do likewise. Applications for membership in the great books course offered by University College exceeded that institution's capacity to satisfy. It was this that led to a novel plan for expanding the great books program and later to the establishment of the Great Books Foundation to develop that program on a nationwide basis.

In 1944, the year after the University Club class started, Cyril Houle took over the administration of University College and served as chairman of a governing committee, of which I was a member. At one of our meetings, the question was asked whether it would be possible to train persons who had no prior teaching experience to serve as leaders or moderators of great books discussion groups. My immediate response was that such persons might become better discussion leaders than professional teachers, because the latter were so used to teaching by telling instead of teaching by asking that it was almost impossible to get them to change their ways. If we took persons from other walks of life and taught them the Socratic method, they might turn out to be much less pedantic and pedagogical than the professionals. The fact that they would know less about the great books and their cultural contexts might even prove to be an advantage, for in their ignorance, they would be forced to inquire and thus inspire inquiry in others, instead of being tempted to convey their accumulated knowledge by lecturing.

The head of the Public Library in Chicago offered to help us launch this experiment by enlisting librarians, among others, in a training course for those who wished to try their hand at becoming leaders. I prepared a series of talks about the great books, the art of reading them, and the method of asking questions about them to start and sustain discussion. We also staged a series of ten sample great books discussions to demonstrate the method. When the training course had been completed, University College and the Chicago Public Library organized great books discussion groups all over the metropolitan area, most of them meeting in local public libraries. The recently graduated trainees served as leaders.

The remarkable success of this experiment in adult education led to more training courses and more discussion groups. It also quickly aroused the interest of library administrators in other cities, who sought help from Chicago in setting up similar programs. My lectures to the original training group, revised and expanded, were published as a *Manual for Great Books Discussion Leaders;* and, between 1945 and 1947, I travelled extensively across the United States as a missionary to the library systems of Detroit, Cleveland, Minneapolis, St. Paul, Milwaukee, Rochester, Syracuse, Louisville, Seattle, San Francisco, Los Angeles, Buffalo, Boston, and finally New York City. One of many variations on the experiment occurred in Indianapolis. When Lynn Williams, an original member of the University Club seminar, became manager of the Stewart-Warner plant in Indianapolis, he suggested organizing a great books discussion group for the plant personnel. Milton Mayer and I flew to Indianapolis to conduct it. This led to the formation of a great books group in Indianapolis under the auspices of Butler University, and to the subsequent formation of a leader training course there.

During the early years of the Great Books Foundation's existence, I continued to act as a travelling missionary of the great books movement —conducting demonstration seminars for civic groups and educational institutions and giving lectures on the role of the great books in adult education. As early as 1940, after *How To Read A Book* had become a best seller, I spoke out against the prevailing misconception of adult education. For most of the professionals involved in adult education, it was either regarded as remedial schooling for those adults who had been deprived of sufficient schooling in their youth or regarded as an avocational or even recreational pursuit, such as basket weaving, folk dancing, or the learning of a foreign language.

The underlying mistake in this conception of adult education consisted in the identification of education itself with schooling. While schools of all sorts, from the kindergarten to the graduate school, are educational institutions, education should not be identified with schooling. Rightly conceived, education is the process of a lifetime, and schooling, however extensive, is only the beginning of anyone's education, to be completed, not by more attendance at educational institutions in adult years, but rather by the continuation of learning through a wide variety of means during the whole of adult life. Schooling can and should be terminated at a certain time, but education itself cannot be terminated short of the grave. I said all this in 1946 to a joint national conference of five adult education associations. I also argued that, of all the materials available for continuing education, only the great books have the power to sustain the growth of the mind—the gradual development of some measure of insight, understanding, and wisdom, possession of which at the end of life signifies an educated human being.

The fact that youth or immaturity (or worse, the pathological adolescence that is perpetuated by prolonged schooling) presents an obstacle to becoming educated is not the only reason why everyone should engage in learning throughout adult life. Another equally important reason is that mind, like muscle, atrophies with disuse. Just as one cannot keep one's body alive and growing on last week's feeding, much less on last year's feeding, so one cannot keep one's mind alive and growing on last week's or last year's reading. The mind, unlike the body, can continue to grow throughout one's life. Therefore, we have an obligation to take good care of our minds by continued learning—an essential part of our obligation to pursue happiness by making the most of our potentialities.

Conducting great books discussion groups, and rereading the great books over and over again to do so, has served me well in this regard. The University Club seminar, begun in 1943, is still in existence today, and some of its original members—Elizabeth Paepcke and Gertrude Kestnbaum still attend, as did Daggett Harvey until his death in 1976. Hutchins retired from it in 1950, when he became vice-president of the Ford Foundation in Pasadena. I found substitutes to take my place during my first few years in San Francisco, where in 1952 I established the Institute for Philosophical Research. But I resumed my role as moderator in 1957, flying back to Chicago for monthly sessions until I again became a resident of Chicago in 1963. During my ten years in San Francisco, I organized a similar group which met in the library of the institute. Its members were reluctant to disband when I returned to Chicago, and so I flew back to San Francisco once a month to meet with them.

The longevity of both of these groups testifies to the liveliness of the discussions as well as to the vitality of the great books and to their contemporary relevance. What is true of the members of these groups is equally true of me. I have enjoyed my participation in our sessions together year after year, and I have continued to improve my understanding of the books with each successive year. Some of them I have now read and discussed at least a score of times or more. My files contain notes for leading a discussion of the same book on successive occasions. By putting them in order according to the date of each occasion, I can observe changes of mind that show a growth of insight and understanding. Over the span of more than fifty years, the great books have proved inexhaustibly rereadable—always over my head and, therefore, always stretching my mind and, I hope, lifting it up a little.

I must express one other debt of gratitude to the University Club class. Among its original members, as I have said, were Walter and Elizabeth Paepcke, and William and Helen Benton. The development of the Aspen Institute for Humanistic Studies under the leadership of Walter and Elizabeth Paepcke, and the publication of *Great Books of the Western World* by Encyclopaedia Britannica, Inc., under the proprietorship of William Benton changed the course of my life in ways I shall relate in chapters to follow.

Chapter 12

The Great Ideas

O N DECEMBER 9, 1941, Gen. Robert E. Wood and William Benton lunched together at the Chicago Club. Benton was then a vice-president of the University of Chicago; Wood was chairman of the board of Sears, Roebuck and Company, which, since 1920, except for a short interval, had owned the *Encyclopaedia Britannica,* an enterprise that Bill Benton thought would be more appropriately affiliated with the University of Chicago. Toward the end of lunch, Benton asked Wood whether it was wise for a mail-order house to own the *Encyclopaedia Britannica.* Wood expressed his long-felt discomfort over their ownership of so venerable and world-honored an institution, remarking that Sears should never have acquired it in the first place. No more was said at the table, but as they left the club, Wood offered to give the *Britannica* to the university.

Early in 1943, after protracted deliberation by the university's Board of Trustees, the transfer was arranged in a way that enabled the university to profit without having the burden of managing a business involved in sales and advertising as well as editorial production. Only the latter fell within the university's competence to supervise. The university became the owner of the preferred stock and received an annual royalty on sales. Bill Benton, who had put up $100,000 to provide the needed working capital, acquired in return two-thirds of the common stock, headed the management of the publishing company, and became publisher of the *Encyclopaedia Britannica.* Shortly after Benton assumed the chairmanship of the company's Board of Directors, he created a Board of Editors and made Bob Hutchins chairman, a post he held continuously until I succeeded him in 1974.

Bob Hutchins and Bill Benton had been classmates at Yale. Both came from families involved in missionary work and in education, but Bill went into business after graduating in 1921 while Bob stayed on in academic life. In 1935, after Bill retired from Benton and Bowles (an advertising firm that he had founded with another Yaleman, Chester Bowles), he accepted Bob Hutchins's invitation to come to the University of Chicago to advise him on public relations. In 1935 and 1936, the university was under fire from the local newspapers as a result of charges made by Charles Walgreen, head of a national chain of retail drug stores, that his niece was being subjected to "Communist influence" in her social science courses, where, among other things, she had been asked to read the *Communist Manifesto*. This led to a public hearing on the charges by an investigating committee of the Illinois state senate. The university was not only cleared by the senate committee of all the allegations made by Walgreen, but, with Bill Benton's help, Bob Hutchins also persuaded Walgreen to make a gift to the university to set up the Charles R. Walgreen Foundation for the Study of American Institutions.

Benton stayed on at the university in a part-time capacity as vice-president for another eight years, until President Truman appointed him assistant secretary of state. In addition to other academic duties, Bill took a great interest in the weekly radio broadcasts of a discussion program called "The University of Chicago Round Table." Benton and Bowles had been one of the first advertising agencies to appreciate the potentialities of radio, and their innovative use of it had earned Benton his first fortune. Never content with existing projects, always impelled to expand and innovate, Benton developed another radio program for the university, "The Human Adventure," that dramatized current research efforts and became a highly respected public service program. It was through my involvement in these two programs that I first became associated with Benton—an association that became much more complicated, as well as more intense, when, in 1943, he became proprietor of the Encyclopaedia Britannica company and I fell in love with his secretary. My association with him at Britannica continued without interruption until his death in 1973; my relationship with his secretary was terminated after three tempestuous years that brought me to the verge of divorce and to the threat of dismissal from the university for behavior which was then regarded as intolerable by the academy.

Less than six months after Benton assumed the management of the encyclopaedia company, he was ready and eager to propose a new publishing venture. The idea occurred to him when he became annoyed by his inability to purchase the assigned reading for the University Club great books class of which he had become a member. Paperback editions of the classics did not then exist. (The only editions available in the United States at that time were to be found in the Modern Library

series, the Everyman's Library series, and the Oxford Press series of
World Classics, but during wartime many of these had been allowed to
go out of print. In any case, they included only a fraction of the titles
that comprised *Great Books of the Western World*.) Under these conditions, it was a most natural move on the part of a person of Benton's
inclinations and temperament to propose that he should publish these
works himself. What better way to solve the problem of getting his
hands on them? It did not occur to him that it might take years to
complete the proposed publishing project.

In June 1943, Benton brought Powell, the president of the Britannica
company, and Yust, the editor of the encyclopaedia, to meet with Bob
Hutchins and me to discuss the possibility of our editing a set of great
books. Bob's immediate reaction was adverse. He said that he had no
doubt that the encyclopaedia salesmen would be able to sell another set
of books in the same way that they sold *Britannica,* but he for one had
no interest in providing American homes with books that would be put
on the shelf as colorful furniture. Without the kind of instruction provided by great books discussion groups (to whose members the sale
could obviously not be limited), what would induce the purchaser of a
set of great books to take them off the shelf and use them to furnish his
mind rather than his home?

That first meeting broke up with the project tabled until either Bob
or I could come up with some device that might make the set an instrument of self-education that would be effective without the intervention
of a teacher or the support of a discussion group—something that would
be not only helpful but also seductive in a way that would get the books
opened up and used. During the summer of 1943, while I was writing
How To Think About War and Peace, I kept thinking about the problem. Curiously enough, that apparently unrelated occupation popped
the solution into my mind.

In the course of writing the book, I had gone to the great books to
find out what had been thought about war and peace in the 2,500 years
of the Western tradition. To my astonishment, I came upon some extraordinary insights for the first time on pages that I had read many
times before, and on which other passages were marked, not, however,
the particular passage that now jumped out at me. How could I have
missed these passages on prior readings? The answer, obviously, was
that on those prior readings, I had not been thinking about war and
peace, and so I had not read the books under the activating push of the
question. What did Homer, Plato, Thucydides, Virgil, Hobbes, Locke,
Kant, or Tolstoi think about war and peace?

Once I grasped this, it occurred to me that the only way the great
books could be thoroughly mined involved reading them again and
again, each time with a different specific question in mind. That would

require reading them an extraordinarily large number of times in order
to ferret out the views they express on an equally large number of important subjects. It did not occur to me at the time, though it did some
years later, that the project I was then contemplating might be a study
preparatory to the construction of a *Summa Dialectica*—something I
had first envisioned while writing *Dialectic* in 1927. But what did occur
to me at once was that I had discovered the device that Bob Hutchins
insisted we had to invent to make publishing the great books a worthwhile educational, and not just a commercial, venture.

Why not construct an index to the great books which would, for
each idea of basic importance, assemble the references to relevant
passages in the books? Such an index would provide a map or chart of
the conversation about fundamental subjects in which the authors of
the great books engaged with one another across the centuries. It would
enable the owner of a set of great books to use it as a reference library,
in which he could look up the discussion of any subject in which he had
a special interest. That, in turn, might lead him into taking the books
off the shelf and starting to read them. What he found might further
entice him to read more comprehensively an author whose views and
style attracted him. I agreed with Bob that it would be illusory to expect the purchaser of a set of great books to read them through in
chronological order from Homer to the terminal author in the series.
However, if he could be persuaded to read *in* some of the great books
on subjects of initial interest to him before he had read *through* all of
them, that very process might go a long way toward turning him into
an habitual reader of them. It would certainly provide him with intellectual guidance that might serve him in place of the help a discussion group or a teacher could give.

At the end of that summer in 1943, I drafted a memorandum that
proposed the construction of an idea-index for the great books, and also
answered a number of other questions about the composition of the
set and about its editorial policies. Using various great books lists—
those drawn up at Columbia, the one Hutchins and I had adopted in
Chicago, the list of the Committee on the Liberal Arts, the St. John's
reading list—I submitted an initial, tentative recommendation of
82 authors. It included a number of authors who did not get into the
set (for example, Cicero, Erasmus, Calvin, Molière, Schopenhauer,
Nietzsche, Ibsen, Mark Twain); it also failed to include a number of
authors that we later selected (some of the natural scientists and mathematicians on the St. John's list).

I recommended that, wherever possible, our set should distinguish
itself from previous collections, such as the *Harvard Classics,* not only
publishing whole works rather than excerpts, but also by including the
great classics of mathematics and the natural sciences as well as the

great works of imaginative literature, history, theology, and philosophy. On the negative side, I urged that no scholarly prefaces be included and that scholarly apparatus should be kept to the minimum, so that the authors might address themselves to the reader without the intervention of lesser minds. To provide some guidance for the reader, a volume of essays introducing the set as a whole, and an idea-index the shape and utility of which I had outlined, would accompany the set.

Bob Hutchins immediately approved my suggestion of an idea-index. In subsequent conferences that September and October with Bill Benton and Britannica officers, I was commissioned to undertake the task of constructing the proposed index, for which a budget of $60,000 was set up, the work to be done in approximately two years. The task actually took seven years and cost nearly one million dollars. Bill Benton never forgot, and never quite forgave, the enormous discrepancy between the original estimate and the final cost. When, in later years, I submitted budgets and schedules for other editorial projects, he would hark back to how grievously I had misled him about the index project.

My other initial recommendations were also adopted in principle. To reach a final list of works to be included, Bob Hutchins formed an advisory board of editors and asked Scott Buchanan, Winkie Barr, and Mark Van Doren to become members; two professors at the University of Chicago—Joseph Schwab, a scientist, and Clarence Faust, dean of the college—were also drawn into the group. It was completed by the addition of John Erskine, who had introduced me to the great books at Columbia, and, lastly, by Alexander Meiklejohn, who had been Scott's teacher at Amherst College. Bob became editor in chief of the set; some years later, after acting as chairman of the meetings of the Advisory Board when Hutchins could not attend them, I was appointed associate editor. It was also tentatively decided that the volume of introductory essays, which would attempt to delineate the unity and continuity of the Western tradition from different perspectives, would consist of pieces written by Hutchins, Buchanan, Barr, Van Doren, and me. For a variety of reasons that decision was finally set aside, even though first drafts of some of the essays had been completed. In place of the introductory volume as originally conceived, the set as a whole was introduced by a single essay, written by Hutchins, entitled "The Great Conversation."

Hutchins was rarely able to be present when the Advisory Board met, which it did at fairly regular intervals for more than two years. I chaired most of the meetings and relayed to him the results of our deliberations, carrying back to our next meeting his comments or recommendations. In the course of approximately ten meetings, we drew up various lists of authors to be included, ranging from as few as 69 to as many as 110. The longer lists would have required the publication of about 75 or 80 volumes and over 45,000 pages. This, we were told, vastly exceeded what the publishers could afford to produce or could expect to sell at a marketable price. To cut back from our longer lists, we divided the authors into first- and second-string candidates. Our 34 first-string candidates remained constant: they appeared on all the lists we drew up; they had also appeared on all prior lists that had been drawn up, beginning with Erskine's original list.

The authors about whom there was little or no question were the monumental makers of the Western tradition from Homer down to the end of the seventeenth century. We had no differences of opinion about which Greeks to include and only a few about Roman, Hellenistic, and mediaeval writers. Our disagreements became more numerous as well as more acerbic when we considered modern authors from the seventeenth century on. The nearer we approached our own day, the more difficult it became for us to agree on candidates for inclusion, and from this sprang our decision to end the set with William James and Sigmund Freud, who straddled the end of the nineteenth century and the beginning of the twentieth.

The semifinal list of authors and works to be included still exceeded the number of volumes and pages that we were allowed. Cutting it down to size required some last-minute pruning of authors and titles by Hutchins and me, resulting in 443 works by 74 authors, in a set of 54 volumes and 32,000 pages, of which one volume would be reserved for Hutchins's essay and two for the idea-index that would ultimately be called "The Great Ideas, a Syntopicon." I will presently explain why we replaced the word *index* with that made-up word.

Two criteria were appealed to as the basis of our selection. Scott Buchanan took the stand that we should include the books we thought indispensable to anyone's liberal education. I suggested that we should also try to choose works we deemed indispensable for the broadest and deepest exploration of the great ideas, lists of which I had begun to construct during the early years of work on the Syntopicon. By these or any other criteria, the attempt to draw up a definitive list of great books must necessarily fall short of the ideal—unanimous agreement on the part of all who are competent to make such judgments. I think we did as well as could be expected.

In the years since *Great Books of the Western World* was published in 1952, I have asked a large number of competent judges which authors they would wish to see added or subtracted. Among judges who disagreed with one another, I have found not more than seven or eight suggestions for addition or subtraction. That amounts to about 10 percent of the 74 authors in the set, which means that general agreement prevails with regard to the other 90 percent of the set's composition. In my own reflections about the set in the years since it was published,

I regret most of all our failure to include Cicero, Calvin, Leibniz, and Molière.

The other chief defect in *Great Books of the Western World,* as I now see it twenty-five years later, is the absence of great works written in the twentieth century, books representing the significant contributions that clearly distinguish this century from its predecessors. In the forties, when we were editing the set, we were right not to attempt making such a selection. It was too early in the century for us to have perspective for that task. But now that we are approaching the end of the century, it is possible to nominate, if not definitively to select, the great works of our time.

Some of us have already taken steps in that direction. In 1965, Clifton Fadiman and I wrote a pair of articles on how the next century might assess the major contributions of the present one. Limiting myself to works in history, philosophy, and the natural and the social sciences, I nominated the following twelve: Henri Bergson, John Dewey, Alfred North Whitehead, Jacques Maritain, Jean-Paul Sartre, Max Planck, Albert Einstein, Niels Bohr, Werner Heisenberg, John Maynard Keynes, Arnold Toynbee, and Pierre Teilhard de Chardin. Fadiman, taking imaginative literature as his domain, nominated nine: George Bernard Shaw, Joseph Conrad, Marcel Proust, Thomas Mann, James Joyce, Franz Kafka, D. H. Lawrence, T. S. Eliot, and William Faulkner; to which he added three poets: William Butler Yeats, Robert Frost, and Rainer Maria Rilke. In the 1969 issue of *The Great Ideas Today* (an annual supplement to *Great Books of the Western World*), Mark Van Doren drew up his own list of imaginative writers. While concurring with most of Fadiman's nominations, Van Doren added Sholom Aleichem, Camus, Orwell, and Aleksandr Solzhenitsyn; to the list of lyric poets, he added Emily Dickinson and Thomas Hardy. He also proposed the inclusion of short-story writers, such as Conan Doyle, Ernest Hemingway, Isak Dinesen, Ring Lardner, and James Thurber. To my own list of historians, philosophers, and scientists, others might wish to add Martin Buber, Martin Heidegger, Edmund Husserl, Carl Gustav Jung, Nicolai Lenin, T. H. Morgan, John von Neumann, José Ortega y Gasset, Bertrand Russell, George Santayana, R. H. Tawney, Miguel de Unamuno, Max Weber, and Ludwig Wittgenstein.

Making up a list of the great ideas was a task somewhat like that of deciding which authors to include in the great books set. It took nearly two years to sift through a provisional enumeration of about 700 terms culled from dictionaries of all sorts and to cut it down to size by dividing the terms into those which expressed truly basic concepts and those which expressed subordinate ones. At the end of two years we had agreed upon 105 fundamental ideas, and these, with further work, we reduced to 102, each a constellation comprising an orderly set of subordinate notions. As the work of indexing proceeded, the number of subordinate terms that fell into focus within the framework of a great idea increased. It reached almost two thousand when we finally constructed an alphabetical inventory of terms to help a user of the Syntopicon locate a particular subject in the context of one or more of 102 great ideas.

It gradually became clear to us that a great idea was not a simple concept, but a complex and comprehensive one, having an inner structure of related notions and a pattern of topics, problems, or issues. Each has a life of its own and a unique historical development; each is a center from which radiate lines of connection with other great ideas. The more thoroughly we examined the discussion of any one of the great ideas, the more convinced we became that lines of relationships can be drawn from each to all the others. That decided us against attempting to group the great ideas; instead, we adopted an alphabetical enumeration as being the least tendentious and the most neutral ordering. Here it is:

Angel	God	Mind
Animal	Good and Evil	Monarchy
Aristocracy	Government	Nature
Art	Habit	Necessity and
Astronomy	Happiness	Contingency
Beauty	History	Oligarchy
Being	Honor	One and Many
Cause	Hypothesis	Opinion
Chance	Idea	Opposition
Change	Immortality	Philosophy
Citizen	Induction	Physics
Constitution	Infinity	Pleasure and Pain
Courage	Judgment	Poetry
Custom and	Justice	Principle
Convention	Knowledge	Progress
Definition	Labor	Prophecy
Democracy	Language	Prudence
Desire	Law	Punishment
Dialectic	Liberty	Quality
Duty	Life and Death	Quantity
Education	Logic	Reasoning
Element	Love	Relation
Emotion	Man	Religion
Eternity	Mathematics	Revolution
Evolution	Matter	Rhetoric
Experience	Mechanics	Same and Other
Family	Medicine	Science
Fate	Memory and Imagination	Sense
Form	Metaphysics	Sign and Symbol

Sin	Theology	Virtue and Vice
Slavery	Time	War and Peace
Soul	Truth	Wealth
Space	Tyranny	Will
State	Universal and	Wisdom
Temperance	Particular	World

This enumeration of great ideas elicited a variety of reactions from persons who were informed about the enterprise of indexing the great books by reference to basic categories. I remember a dinner party at my house at which Bill Benton, Bee Ruml, and Dick McKeon were present. In the course of conversation, Dick and I advanced the opinion that, in 2,500 years of recorded Western history, a relatively small number of great ideas had emerged, adding that the emergence of a new great idea would be an event of momentous historical importance. Benton hotly challenged this view. New ideas, he said, were "a dime a dozen." He referred to his experience as head of an advertising agency, where the staff had to come up with a hundred ideas before one worth using was adopted. It took the better part of that evening, and much laboring of the point, before Dick and I succeeded in getting Benton to see that what was meant by an idea in an advertising agency or in business differed from what we meant by an idea that had been the focus of thought and discussion for over twenty centuries. Later, when I had sent Bill Benton a list of the great ideas, he did not get past the A's, from Angel through Astronomy, without expostulating, "But where's Adultery?" When I told him that he would find a topic about adultery under the idea of Family, he asked, "What's it doing there?"

Early in 1948, when work on the idea-index was still two years from completion, *Look* and *Life* magazines ran picture stories about the indexing project. The *Look* story carried the heading "There are only 102 Great Ideas, and they are all pictured here"; *Life*'s heading, "The 102 Great Ideas: Scholars complete a monumental catalogue," accompanied a double-page spread that consisted of a photograph of 102 boxes of index cards, one for each of the great ideas, around and behind which stood or sat the members of the staff engaged in the work.

During the interviews with the reporters from *Life* and *Look,* I tried to explain that there was nothing magical or sacrosanct about the number 102. If, for example, it had been more convenient to let the idea of Government include Aristocracy, Democracy, Monarchy, Oligarchy, and Tyranny, and similarly, the idea of Virtue and Vice include specific virtues (Courage, Temperance, Prudence, Wisdom), the number would have turned out to be fewer than 102. That was inconvenient simply because the amount of discussion to be covered would be too voluminous if it were concentrated under one great idea instead of distributed among four or five. In the opposite direction, the number might have been increased, had such ideas as Power (in the political sense), Property, and Equality been given primary, instead of subordinate, status. But, while these three ideas certainly deserve primary status if one were considering the discussion of them since the beginning of the nineteenth century, and especially in the twentieth century, their claim to such treatment is much more questionable if one considers the whole tradition of Western thought from classical antiquity to the end of the nineteenth century.

Constructing a tentative list of great ideas and then refining it was by far the easiest part of the task of producing an idea-index to the great books. That it occupied seven to eight years of my life in more strenuous intellectual effort than anything in which I had ever engaged before; that it required the collaboration of a scholarly staff of over thirty men and women, supported by a clerical staff of almost twice that size; that it involved over 400,000 man hours of reading by this staff, and, on my part, thirty months of writing and revising 102 essays —these facts may provide some measure of the magnitude of the project but not of its intrinsic difficulty. At one point, I would have said its "impossibility" rather than its "difficulty," because at the end of the first two years I had little hope that what I had in mind could be accomplished. I was prepared to tell Hutchins and Benton that we would have to call the whole thing off.

Thousands upon thousands of indices have been constructed, either by the writers of books, by their editors, or by collaborators assigned this special task. But never had anyone attempted indexing the works of two or more authors by reference to a single set of terms or categories. Here we were going to deal with 74 authors and 443 distinct works. In addition, *Great Books of the Western World* would include poetry and imaginative literature, as well as great works of history, and not just philosophical and theological treatises, and mathematical and scientific expositions. To my knowledge, no one had ever before attempted to index the intellectual or ideational content of epic and dramatic poetry, of novels and plays, or of historical narratives; and doing it in a way that would relate the indexed passages in such works to comparable passages in expository treatises.

From my own experience as an indexer, beginning with John Stuart Mill's *Autobiography* in my early years at Columbia, and then later my own books, I knew that an indispensable step is to discover the words or terms that express the author's conceptual apparatus. But when the task is to index a large number of authors and of works, as different in character as Homer's *Iliad,* Dante's *Divine Comedy,* Shakespeare's plays and sonnets, Gibbon's *Decline and Fall of the Roman Empire,* and Dostoevsky's *Brothers Karamazov,* on the one hand, and Plato's *Dialogues,* Euclid's *Elements of Geometry,* Locke's *Essay on Human Un-*

derstanding, Adam Smith's *Wealth of Nations,* and Darwin's *Origin of Species,* on the other, the selection of a set of terms, under which to make page references to relevant passages, will simply not work. Different authors often use different terms to name the same subject that they are thinking about; and just as often they use the same term to name quite different objects of thought. Even a single author's vocabulary will change in the course of writing a succession of works over a number of years.

If I had been more cautious, I would probably have taken such obstacles into account before jauntily proposing to Hutchins and Benton that the great books set should have an idea-index. But if I had done that, I might not have accepted a budget and a schedule for doing the job, the one too small, the other too short. As it turned out, it was better that I blithely accepted the assignment, only to learn in the course of the first two years of work why it looked impossible. With failure staring me in the face, I was compelled to find a solution. I have had similar experiences since then, most recently with the task of constructing a topical table of contents for the 15th edition of the *Encyclopaedia Britannica.* By taking on apparently impossible tasks one is forced to invent or discover the means of accomplishing them, however difficult that may be.

The breakthrough occurred in January 1945. The work of indexing had begun in November 1943, with the construction of what I called the "Greek index." We began with the Greeks because they were the only authors we all agreed should be included in the set. The indexing was done by two teams, one headed by Milton Mayer in Chicago, the other by William Gorman at St. John's College in Annapolis. Milton, who had been associated with Bob Hutchins and me in teaching the great books, assembled a group of needy friends to do the job. The indexers were paid two dollars an hour; Milton's group included Saul Bellow, an aspiring but as yet unknown novelist. Bill Gorman, who had been a tutor in the Trivium course at Chicago and subsequently joined the faculty of St. John's College, enlisted some of his students to do the job, among whom was Peter Wolff, who later became an assistant editor when Gorman became my top associate on the Syntopicon.

By the summer of 1944, we had accumulated about five thousand index cards. Each of these recorded an indexer's judgment that a particular passage discussed a certain idea as expressed by one of the principal or subordinate terms that we had provisionally drawn up. It also contained a brief comment by the indexer concerning the relevance of the passage cited. We called these comments "tag lines."

I remember spending a good part of August playing solitaire with those cards, throwing them out into different piles on the bed, reshuffling them, and trying another play. With the cards divided into a large number of small sets, I devoted most of the autumn to typing up the Greek index, while the two groups of indexers carried on with other books that we were pretty sure would be included in the set. While doing this work, I hit upon the solution to our problem, though I did not know it at the time. Using the indexers' tag lines, I could put a given reference under the idea of Art and could also place it under a briefly worded topic, such as "The origin of the arts," "General theory of art," "Political censorship of the arts," or "The relation of art to nature."

At the end of four months of typing, the Greek index filled a fat binder. I brought it to a meeting with Bill Gorman and Milton Mayer in Washington, at which we tried to decide how we would proceed with the work from that point on. Our examination of the Greek index gave us the clue. Ordinary indices can use single terms—the very words that the author himself uses—to refer to particular passages. But no set of terms is common to 74 authors and 443 works, spread out in time from Homer to Freud. The index heading could not be a single word or term, but had to be a carefully worded topic—something like the topics I had formulated while typing up the Greek index. That one insight—the necessity of substituting *indexing by topics* for *indexing by words or terms*—turned the trick. In the future, we decided, the indexer would assign a passage to one or another of the topics that belonged to the structure of a great idea.

We had solved the problem of how to index a whole set of books, but in principle only. We still had to construct an outline of topics for each of the 102 ideas. I undertook to do this by writing a series of memoranda to the staff. For each idea, I wrote a brief introduction to explain its main points of interest, following it by a breakdown of the idea into a set of topics representing themes, problems, or issues that have been dealt with in the discussion of the idea. I also added a set of cross-references, calling attention to related topics under other great ideas.

Of these efforts, the most important—and, to me, the most absorbing —was the task of constructing analytical outlines of topics for each of the great ideas. My elementary schooling at a public school in New York City—P.S. 186—included instruction in the art of making outlines, just as it included exercises in syntax that involved diagramming the structure of a sentence. Outlining fascinated me from the very beginning, for by compelling one to determine which matters were coordinate, which supraordinate or subordinate, and how all together should be ordered, it exposed the skeletal structure of one's thought.

In the outlining work I undertook for the Syntopicon, the novel feature was the substitution of topics for sentences. A topic, from the phrasing of which the assertive "is" or "is not" must always be excluded, asserts nothing; it lays down a theme, a problem, or an issue concerning which diverse points of view can be expressed. For that reason it ideally served our purpose—providing a place where passages from the great books might be assembled in order to exhibit the variety of their authors' opinions about a subject to which their thought was, in varying degrees and in different ways, relevant.

It might be interesting to the reader to see how an outline is structured and how topics are phrased. Here is the Outline of Topics for the idea of Family.

1. The nature and necessity of the family
2. The family and the state
    2a. Comparison of the domestic and political community in origin, structure, and function
    2b. Comparison of the domestic and political community in manner of government
    2c. The place and rights of the family in the state: the control and education of children
3. The economics of the family
    3a. The wealth of families: the maintenance of the domestic economy
    3b. The effects of political economy: the family in the industrial system
4. The institution of marriage: its nature and purpose
    4a. Monogamy and polygamy
    4b. The religious views of marriage: the sacrament of matrimony
    4c. Matrimony and celibacy
    4d. The laws and customs regulating marriage: adultery, incest
    4e. Divorce
5. The position of women
    5a. The role of women in the family: the relation of husband and wife in domestic government
    5b. The status of women in the state: the right to citizenship, property, education
    5c. Women in relation to war
6. Parents and children: fatherhood, motherhood
    6a. The desire for offspring
    6b. Eugenics: control of breeding; birth control
    6c. The condition of immaturity
    6d. The care and government of children: the rights and duties of the child; parental despotism and tyranny
    6e. The initiation of children into adult life
7. The life of the family

7a. Marriage and love: romantic, conjugal, and illicit love

7b. The continuity of the family: the veneration of ancestors; family pride, feuds, curses

7c. Patterns of friendship in the family: man and wife; parents and children; brothers and sisters

7d. The emotional impact of family life upon the child: the domestic triangle; the symbolic roles of father and mother

8. Historical observations on the institution of marriage and the family

The above outline was the last of many drafts in a series of revisions that responded to the demands of the indexers representing different authors in the great books. As guardians of their authors' rights to be accommodated without distortion or prejudice, the indexers called for additional or expanded topics, and for rephrasings that were more appropriate to their authors' thought. The final versions of the 102 outlines reflected a vast amount of reading and rereading of the great books. Far from being imposed upon the discussion of the great ideas that is contained in the great books, the outlines were drawn out of the great books by our knowledge and understanding of the themes which they discuss.

In the course of redoing the 102 Outlines of Topics, I became increasingly adept at the business of making outlines and of formulating topics. My preoccupation with the finesse of these tasks resulted in the writing of a long essay which I added to the Syntopicon as an appendix, entitled "The Principles and Methods of Syntopical Construction." I am probably the only person who ever read that essay through; and certainly the only one who ever enjoyed reading it.

By December 1945, I had completed memoranda only as far as ideas that began with the letter N. It would take me another six months to reach the W's. Not to lose momentum, Gorman took a leave of absence from St. John's, moved to an office in New York City, and undertook to file the 20,000 index cards by then available in 102 boxes, one for each of the great ideas, each box subdivided by tab cards for the various topics that constituted the inner structure of the idea. By the summer of 1946 we began to see what the finished work would look like. Each of the 102 chapters would be divided into five parts. It would begin with an introductory essay to guide the reader. This would involve rewriting the memos I had prepared to guide the indexers. The introductory essay would be followed by an Outline of Topics, expanding and refining the outline I had written for the indexing staff. Then each chapter would have a section consisting, topic by topic, of references to passages in the great books relevant to that topic, arranged in chronological order. This, in turn, would be followed by a set of cross-references to related topics in chapters about other great ideas; and finally the chapter would conclude with a set of recommended readings, listing important relevant works not included in the set of great books.

We realized that the index staff had to be greatly enlarged and that most of the indexing would have to be reexamined and probably redone. We could no longer operate with one small staff at St. John's College and another in a basement room of the Social Science Building at the University of Chicago. A three-story building on the university campus was appropriated for an enlarged staff. It came to be called "Index House." An ex-student of mine, Herman Bernick, just released from military service, helped us to fill the desks at Index House, hiring indexers by testing their knowledge of certain authors and their competence as analytical readers of their works. In this way, we developed an index staff of young men and women, each of whom became responsible for indexing two or three authors. A staff of about 25 could thus handle the indexing of 74 authors. To support the work of the indexers, a clerical staff of more than twice that size had to be assembled. As the work proceeded, it was necessary for each indexer to have a record of all prior indexing. Each was given a purple ditto of a typed-out version of the index cards, organized topic by topic. At one stage, when the number of index citations had grown from 30,000 to over 150,000, this purple ditto filled 120 large black binders. Each indexer also needed a visible file that enabled him to flip from one of the 102 outlines of topics to any other; he could hardly be expected to remember the phrasing of almost 3,000 topics.

It became clear that I could not direct the work of this enlarged staff and also write 102 essays on the great ideas while continuing as an active member of the University of Chicago faculty. At my request, I was granted a leave of absence beginning in the academic year 1946–1947. By that time, I had been teaching undergraduates for almost twenty-five years, and I was quite content to give it up. I must confess that I have never felt any pangs of remorse or deprivation about departing from the undergraduate classroom. Twenty-five years of that experience is quite enough for a single lifetime. I could not, however, entirely give up teaching and lecturing without a profound sense of loss. No matter how occupied I was with producing the Syntopicon (a word that we coined to replace the word *index*, built from two Greek roots meaning "a collection of topics"), I could not give up conducting great books seminars for adults. Throughout those overburdened years between 1946 and 1950, I continued with the University Club great books class, and I undertook to give an annual series of six or eight lectures on the great ideas for participants in great books discussion groups throughout the metropolitan area. I found that when one is heavily taxed with one job, taking on a somewhat different task provides a kind of relaxation and refreshment that is much more therapeutic than a vacation.

In the summer of 1946, Bill Gorman and I revised all 102 Outlines of Topics, so that the enlarged staff which began its first round of refined indexing would have them to work with. That staff went through three successive rounds of indexing: a first round lasting six months, proceeding at the rate of four ideas a week, in which they attempted to correct errors of commission and which resulted in the reduction of 80,000 references to 30,000; a second round, of the same duration and proceeding at the same rate, in which they attempted to correct errors of omission and which resulted in the expansion of 30,000 references to nearly 150,000; and a third round, lasting 15 weeks, at the increased pace of seven ideas a week, which aimed at a critical review of all the outlines of topics and all the index references under them. There was to be a fourth round, running only three months, which would involve making a final judgment on the relevance of each of the passages referred to, topic by topic. That fourth round did not take place as planned for the index staff as a whole. Why it did not, I will relate presently.

During each of these three rounds, a biweekly staff conference was held, at which I tried to give the staff specific directions for indexing the authors they represented by discussing the outline of topics for the ideas coming up for consideration. The members of the staff then called my attention to defects in the outlines of topics, requesting revisions or additions to accommodate their authors without strain or distortion. The indexer representing Aristotle and Aquinas would ask for a certain topic or a new phrasing, and he would be countered by the indexer representing Immanual Kant or Karl Marx or the Bible, or Shakespeare or Tolstoi, who would claim that the topic or phrasing called for by that Aristotelian fellow failed to accommodate the authors he represented. So it would go, back and forth, until I could finally hit upon a set of topics and refinements in phrasing that satisfied the whole staff. As a result, the outlines of topics went through many stages of revision, often fifteen or twenty drafts.

While these three rounds of staff work were in process, I spent what time I had left writing the introductory essays that were to open each of the chapters of the Syntopicon. Writing 102 essays was like writing 102 books. Each had to be adapted to the unique idea it dealt with. Each was a fresh start. In addition, I thought it imperative that these essays be written with dialectical objectivity—that they should be point-of-viewless while suggesting the diverse points of view in the great books about a given idea. It was not until I reached the ideas which began with L that I finally achieved the requisite style for writing these introductory essays, a style that involved generous quotations from the great books, so that the conflicting opinions of the authors could be expressed in their own words.

What was I to do now—go back to the A's and start rewriting the first 43 of the 102 essays or go on to finish the remaining 59 before revising them all? My quandary was resolved by the willingness of Otto Bird, who had been a student of mine, to undertake the task of revising the first 43 while I went on with writing the rest. Between September 1947 and February 1948, he redrafted the 43 essays and also made suggestions for the revision of the remaining 59. When I completed my own first drafts of all 102, I had on file not only Otto's recommendations for revision, but also suggestions from Bob Hutchins, Milton Mayer, and Bill Gorman.

The final revision of all 102 essays took another year to complete. To cap the climax, one further step of revision became necessary when the essays were set in type. The introductory essay together with the Outline of Topics in each chapter had to end on one page, or at least fill three-quarters of it, so that the Reference Section could begin at the top of the next. The makeup man dummied the pages of the Syntopicon in my office and, chapter after chapter, he would ask me to cut out or add a number of lines to each essay so that it would fit the page. By this time I was so fatigued that cutting out 54 words or adding 28 to a tightly written composition became extraordinarily irksome.

As if the magnitude of the tasks to be performed and the exacting time schedule were not challenge enough, other obstacles had to be overcome. Bob Hutchins was twice approached with pleas to discontinue the enterprise, one from Scott Buchanan, who was then in the throes of trying to set up another version of St. John's College in Massachusetts, and another from John U. Nef, chairman of the Committee on Social Thought at the University of Chicago. Scott wrote Bob a letter which Bob showed me and which I still find it difficult to forgive him for writing, though I can now perceive that what may have motivated his emotional attack on the Syntopicon was the fact that my involvement with it prevented me from considering his invitation to join him in establishing the new college. That reason did not, of course, appear on the surface of his letter. Instead, he indicted the effort to index the idea content of the great books on the grounds that I would foist my own philosophical doctrines on readers of the great books and not carry out the policy that we, as editors, should not in any way stand between the mind of the reader of a great book and the mind of its author.

Bob, more intimately acquainted with the indexing project than Scott, knew that what we were engaged in doing was meticulously calculated to avoid the result that Scott was imagining and deploring.

No one's philosophical doctrines, least of all my own, would be given perferential treatment in the introductory essays or in the outlines of topics. "Dialectical neutrality" was, in fact, our daily watchword. If used with diligence and care, the Syntopicon would never tell a reader what to think; it would merely give him the relevant materials to think about on any one of the three thousand themes; it would save him many hours of digging to find the passages to think about. It was only the digging that we had done for him, not the thinking.

The letter from John Nef came after a dinner party at John's house, to which members of the Committee of Social Thought were invited to learn what I was doing across the campus at Index House. Among those present was Daniel Boorstin, then a young professor of American history and now Librarian of Congress. Dan, like many historians who think that ideas can be studied only in their historical context, condemned the Syntopicon project as inherently impossible because the authors being indexed were centuries and cultures apart. In his view, as in the similar views of R. G. Collingwood, Karl Mannheim, and others, our conception of the great conversation as a discussion of ideas by authors who, though spread across twenty-five hundred years of Western history, were talking to one another as if they were contemporaries, had to be dismissed as a fantastic illusion.

When someone challenges you on the ground that what you are trying to do is impossible, the only effective rebuttal is to do it. To believe that it could be done, in advance of the actual accomplishment, took faith on Bob Hutchins's part. He dismissed Nef's and Boorstin's objections. Any user of the Syntopicon can judge the extent to which the impossible was in fact achieved.

I would not claim that the achievement perfectly demonstrated that the discussion of ideas can be completely disengaged from historical contexts. To claim that would be to claim too much, just as the opposite claim that no disengagement at all is possible claims too much and is the fallacy of historicism. I tried to state a balanced position that lies between these two extremes in my essay on Syntopical construction. I wrote:

> To collapse thirty centuries of imagination and thought into a single historical moment would seem to be unhistorical or, worse, anti-historical. Yet the Introductions have just been described as doing exactly this, since they treat the authors of the great books as if they were contemporaries, and use the present tense in reporting their discussion of ideas.
>
> Mill and Aristotle, for example, may be reported as taking one side of an issue, on which they are opposed by Plato and Hobbes. Lucretius may be said to be more in agreement with Freud on certain matters than he is with anyone in antiquity. As far as possible the authors are associated with one another in terms of their thought, not their times. They are

opposed to one another in the same way. The centuries can be as readily bridged by genuine agreements as they can be divided by disagreements, apparent or genuine. Neither the agreement nor the disagreement is a necessary function of simultaneity or succession in time.

Yet sometimes a certain point of view is characteristic of a period or phase of Western civilization. Sometimes the political, economic, and cultural conditions of a time are more than the background of thinking or the environment to which the thought refers; they are conditions of the thought itself, and therefore of its intelligibility. It is unquestionable that some men originate ideas which others borrow and often change. There is little doubt that the thought of one whole period influences the thought of a later period, either to react against it or to alter it for assimilation. Certainly, then, the succession of the centuries, the location of minds in time, the relation of thought and imagery to the culture of a period, the influence of one mind upon another and one period upon another—certainly all these things are significant features of the great conversation as it develops in time. The very word "tradition" connotes a passing from age to age—both a heritage and an inheritance. To consider the tradition of Western thought is, therefore, to deal with the history of ideas.

Both sides of the picture contain a portion of the truth—the temporal and the non-temporal, the historical and the unhistorical. Thought transcends time to a certain extent, and to a certain extent time conditions thought. Ideas have a career in time and, therefore, a history; but they also have an inner logic which transcends history. To some extent, therefore, all minds dealing with the same ideas are contemporary; they are together in the same logical, if not historical, moment by virtue of their agreements and disagreements. To deny this is to commit the error of historicism. But in some measure minds dealing with the same ideas cannot deal with them in the same way at different historical moments. To neglect or ignore this fact is to commit an opposite error which might be labelled transcendentalism.

The Introductions try to avoid the fallacies of both extremes by combining the historical with the logical treatment of ideas. But they do not try to do equal justice to both aspects of the matter, and in consequence do not preserve a perfect balance between the two approaches. The primary aim of the Introductions is not historical, as it is not semantic. It is dialectical. The Introductions do not carry verbal clarification further than is necessary to prevent language from obscuring the logical realities—the issues, the agreements, the disagreements, and the arguments. For the same reason, the Introductions do not engage in the history of ideas for its own sake. They remain unhistorical wherever possible, and become historical only to indicate places where the history of ideas is itself part of the dialectic of ideas.

The passage just quoted served to explain and justify the work on the Syntopicon and laid the foundation for an even larger and more ambitious project to which the Syntopicon gave rise—the work of the Institute for Philosophical Research.

Intellectual opposition was not the only hurdle that had to be surmounted before the Syntopicon was finished. We were almost put out of business by two financial crises. The first occurred in the fall of 1947, when the Encyclopaedia Britannica company found itself in serious financial straits. Its bankers questioned the advisability of continuing to spend huge sums on the publication of the great books and the production of the Syntopicon. By that time, about $750,000 had already been invested in the project, and the salary roll at Index House came to about $26,000 a month. Under pressure from the bankers, Harry Houghton, then president of the company, ordered me to give the Syntopicon staff two weeks' notice and close the shop without completing the job. He was not to be dissuaded by my telling him that this spelled utter disaster. If the staff were dispersed, it would probably never be assembled again, with the result that all the work done and money expended would bear no fruit. Yet, Houghton reiterated, the company simply could not afford to sustain a $26,000 monthly disbursement for the next four or five months to complete the job.

It was much easier for Houghton to make this decision than it was for me to accept it. In fact, I refused to do so. I telephoned Bill Benton, who was attending a meeting of UNESCO in Mexico City. When my call succeeded in dragging him out of the conference, I told him that I refused to accept the cease-work order and that Bob Hutchins and I would somehow raise the money to complete the work, so that the Syntopicon would finally be published with the great books set. I cannot now remember whether I had his blessing or his reluctant acquiescence, but as things turned out I should have been given the equivalent of a medal infrequently awarded to officers in the imperial army of Austria-Hungary—the Maria Theresa Medal for Successful Disobedience.

Bob Hutchins persuaded the First National Bank of Chicago to allow the company to spend $21,000 more immediately; that, together with another $4,500 that he dug out of his own university budget, financed the completion of the clerical and indexing work of Round III. Obtaining these emergency funds only partly solved the problem. In addition to the difficult and painful task of dismissing a large staff of extraordinarily faithful and well-trained workers, I had to develop some financially feasible scheme for completing Round IV. I finally proposed doing the work of Round IV in two years—the whole of 1948 and 1949—instead of completing it in four months, from January through April of 1948. The work would be done with a staff reduced to four of my closest associates, Bill Gorman, Herman Bernick, Peter Wolff, and Otto Bird, on a budget reduced from $26,000 to $6,000 a month. Though the total investment would be larger, bringing the cost of the Syntopicon to nearly one million dollars before printing, the reduced monthly cash flow made the expenditure acceptable, even to the bankers.

Surmounting that financial obstacle proved to be a blessing in disguise. Instead of a large staff judging the appropriateness of 165,000 references, four men, who worked very closely together, would do it. We set up a schedule that required each man to read and judge a cited passage at the rate of one every four minutes in what turned out to be a seven-day work week over a period of two years, with the exception of the three or four days each month that we met to discuss the judgments we thought were questionable. We finished Round IV on schedule in January 1950.

When the mechanical work of setting 54 volumes in type had been completed, we encountered another financial obstacle. Money was not available to pay for the paper, printing, and binding of even the small number of sets that would have to be produced for experimental efforts to sell them. There was talk of selling the plates to some other company, or just putting them on the shelf in the hope that the necessary funds might become available. Neither alternative pleased Bob Hutchins or me. In desperation, I went to Bill Benton and Harry Houghton with a plan for raising $250,000 to defray the cost of printing and binding 2,500 sets. It involved selling a numbered edition of 500 sets at $500 a set to individuals who would be listed as patrons of the enterprise. With Benton and Houghton's approval, I drafted a letter to be sent out over Bob's signature or my own to persons we thought would lend their support to the project. The letter reminded them of publications in the past that needed such patronage. It suggested that, by helping us to publish *Great Books of the Western World,* they would join the company of Alexander the Great, Augustus Caesar, Maecenas, the Earl of Essex, and the Earl of Shaftesbury, the patrons of Aristotle, Virgil, Horace, Francis Bacon, and John Locke. In the course of telling them how Samuel Johnson depended on charter subscribers to bring out the first edition of his famous dictionary, I even reminded them that he had defined a patron as "a wretch who supports with influence and is paid with flattery."

Bob and I signed about 1,000 copies of this letter, and within a few weeks, we received back nearly 250 subscriptions, each accompanied by a check for $500. However extraordinary this 25 percent return on a solicitation by mail, our amazing success left us with the goal only half-achieved. We had to get another 250 subscriptions, and that task fell to me. I spent a good part of the next six months making personal solicitations, by long-distance telephone or long-distance travel.

There was the gratifying moment when I succeeded in persuading Paul Mellon to purchase ten sets for distribution to colleges and libraries. Harold Linder took another ten; Eugene Meyer, of the *Wash-*

ington Post, fifteen. The high spot in my adventures as a salesman came
one Friday afternoon in the office of Earl Puckett, chairman of the
board of Allied Stores, an organization that included about eighty-five
department stores across the country. I was admitted to Mr. Puckett's
office at 4:00 P.M. He was about to leave for the weekend and obviously
impatient. I knew I had to make the sale quickly. I took five minutes
to show him the list of great books and another five to lay before him
the page proofs of one chapter of the Syntopicon, with a list of the
great ideas. Without indicating whether this turned him on or off, he
asked me what I wanted him to do. "Purchase one set of books for each
of your department stores," I replied, "and have them, as a public relations gesture, make a gift of the set to the public library or to an educational institution in the city in which they do business." Without a
word of comment, he buzzed for his secretary and asked her for the list
of department stores in his organization. Glancing at the list, he sat
there quietly as he put a check mark against the name of this or that
department store. Before fifteen minutes had elapsed, he got up from
his desk to leave, saying, "We'll take forty-five sets." That, I have been
told, was one of the largest book sales ever made, and in the shortest
time. Bob Hutchins did better on one later occasion, though it was not
actually a sale, when he persuaded the Old Dominion Foundation to
make a grant for the purchase of 1,600 sets of *Great Books of the Western World,* by then in its second printing, to be given to that number
of public libraries.

As we neared our goal of 500, getting subscriptions became harder
and harder. Toward the end of this arduous campaign, I found myself,
through the helpful intervention of Clare Luce, in Dallas, in the office
of H. L. Hunt, reputedly one of the richest men in Texas. At that
time, Mr. Hunt was putting money into what he called "educational
enterprises," really ill-concealed efforts at propaganda. I had two sessions with him, devoted mainly to discussing his schemes for combating
the "liberalism" he hated and sought to check. On the second day, he
served me lunch laid out on a newspaper on his desk; it consisted of
barbecued beef sandwiches and cartons of milk, supplemented by an
apple and a little parcel of carrots he had brought from home. Finally,
I managed to show him the list of the authors included in the set. I
left his office without making the sale and, on the way out, passed
Winthrop Aldrich, chairman of the board of the Chase Manhattan
Bank, and a group of New York bankers whom Hunt had kept waiting
for more than an hour. Two days later in Chicago, I encountered my
friend General Wood, chairman of Sears Roebuck. "Mortimer," he
asked, "were you in Texas recently?" "Yes," I replied, "why?" The
general then told me he had just had a phone call from Hunt, asking
whether or not I was a Communist, his reason for thinking so being

the presence of Karl Marx and *The Communist Manifesto* in the great books set.

I failed with Hunt but I succeeded with others in Texas and elsewhere, including a drawing room on the 20th Century Limited where Bob Hutchins and I managed to corner Conrad Hilton and add him to our list. We tried but failed to get him to buy one set for each of his hotels. Finally, the 500 subscriptions were in hand and the presses started turning. Subscribers had been promised delivery of their numbered and inscribed sets six months after we closed the subscription list. It took about twice that time; but the day came when the Founders Edition of *Great Books of the Western World,* in a special buckram binding, was formally presented to its subscribers at a celebration banquet held in the Grand Ballroom of the Waldorf-Astoria Hotel in New York—April 15, 1952. Among those present were Alfred Vanderbilt, Gilbert Chapman, Nelson and David Rockefeller, Thomas Watson, Jr., Paul Hoffman, Conrad Hilton, John Mott, Walter Paepcke, Raymond Rubicam, John Cowles, Will Hays, Russell Davenport, John S. Knight, Alicia Patterson, M. Lincoln Schuster, Lester Markel, John K. Jessup, Joseph L. Mankiewicz, Jacques Barzun, Father Theodore Hesburgh, Leo Rosten, and Henry Anatole Grunwald.

In addition to Bob Hutchins and me (who had to be allowed to say our pieces for the occasion), the speakers of the evening included Jacques Maritain, then professor of philosophy at Princeton, and my old friend Clifton Fadiman, who had been in my first great books class at Columbia. J. Robert Oppenheimer was compelled to cancel at the last moment. Lawrence Kimpton, who had succeeded Hutchins as chancellor of the university, presided, and Bill Benton made the formal presentation of the set to the subscribers.

The eloquence displayed matched the excellence of the food and wine that the Waldorf served. Jacques Maritain, speaking as a European remarked that "the notion of tradition, in its living and genuine sense, is now being rehabilitated, and the task of saving and promoting the best of this tradition is now being taken over by the pioneering spirit of America." He concluded:

> At the core of the work undertaken in publishing *Great Books of the Western World,* there is abiding faith in the dignity of the mind and the virtue of knowledge. Such a work is inspired by what might be called humanist generosity. Those who struggle for the liberties of the human mind have first to believe in the dignity of the human mind and to trust in its natural energies.

Kip Fadiman paid Bill Benton the tribute he fully deserved. "Nine years passed," he said, "before the walls of Troy fell to the hands of the Greeks."

And nine years passed in battle and turmoil before these fifty-four volumes could be delivered into your hands. During the darkest days of those nine years (around 1947, I think it was), some of the more cautious of Senator Benton's business associates wearied of the strife, and understandably so. They paled with a pallor quite properly known as editorial pallor at the vast expenses piling up. They paled and then quailed at the seeming impossibility of ever selling these books, even if they should ever get published. During those days, it was Bill Benton who said, "Damn the budget; full steam ahead."

Fadiman went on to speak of what reading the great books might do "for those millions of Americans who have triumphantly escaped illiteracy without ever achieving cultivation." Reading them, he said, had helped him "to reduce the yawning gap stretching between the analphabetic and the educated man."

I stand here as a kind of walking testimonial . . . to endorse the patent medicine compounded by seventy-four pharmacists, from Homer to Freud. I hereby state that this medicine, while no panacea, has made me feel like a new man. My mental backaches are much relieved. I no longer suffer from pains in the dialectic, and when I get up at night it is only for the purpose of consulting the Syntopicon.

Serious for a moment, he spoke of the great books as that "magic wand whose touch has broken for me that trance of the transient in which so many of us are frozen. They are also a magic wand to bear me away from the doldrums of despair. . . . For me, therefore, these books, often apparently so dry or so difficult, become, when studied to the point and very edge of love, a mighty fortress against the invasion of the barbarians."

During the first year after publication, the set received lengthy and enthusiastic notices in all the major critical journals. The *Saturday Review* published a symposium of comments by eleven scholars, opening with a piece by Professor Joad entitled "Guide to Parnassus." The reviews were uniformly enthusiastic about both the set and the Syntopicon, with the one exception of a hatchet job delivered by Dwight MacDonald in the *New Yorker*.

It took much longer for the sale of the set to get off the ground, but that finally happened toward the end of the fifties when an incredibly expert sales executive, Kenneth Hardin, who organized and managed a national sales force, increased sales from year to year, reaching a peak of 49,000 sets sold in a single year. From that point on, sales declined, but in the quarter century that has elapsed since publication, the number of sets sold in the United States and in foreign markets, both English-speaking and otherwise, comes to almost a million. For a while, the sale appeared to be profitable to the Britannica company, but, in the last decade, with increased manufacturing, advertising, and selling costs, it turned from profit to loss. I have listened to heated arguments about whether or not the company ever made money on its initial investment of more than two and a half million dollars, but there can be no question that over the years many of the sales executives did. Kip Fadiman, when invited to address a meeting of the Great Books sales force at Phoenix in 1965, kidded them about their earnings from the sale of great books as compared with the earnings of the men who wrote them.

> All these fellows, from Homer to Freud, took hold of the wrong end of the stick. Now you and I know—seriously speaking—that the world is better off because they did. But that's not the point I am emphasizing in this convivial meeting. It is *you* who have taken hold of the *right* end of the stick. I've got to hand it to you.

At one point, it looked as if the work I did on the set and the Syntopicon might reap a reward that would take care of my family and me in the years ahead. Bill Benton, in a moment of enthusiasm and generosity, talked about a royalty payment which, if it had been no more than 1 percent of the sales price, might have added up to a small fortune in the last twenty-five years. I reminded him, on several occasions, of what he had said, only to learn the difference between a passing remark and a serious promise. Nine years of work on the set and the Syntopicon turned out in the end to be what it was at the beginning—a labor of love. Perhaps, if I had been in a position to refuse to do all that work for an editorial salary from Britannica, which was several times larger than my university salary, I might have been able to insist upon a royalty instead, however speculative its future earnings might be. As it was, I had no reserves to draw on for the support of my family in the intervening years. One has to have a cushion of wealth in order to take the risks, and enjoy the advantages, of an entrepreneur.

Chapter 13

Separation from Academia

Bob Hutchins left the University of Chicago in 1951 to become vice-president of the Ford Foundation, where he would work in close collaboration with Paul Hoffman, its first president. He had spent more than twenty-five years in academic life, more than twenty of them in important administrative positions. My departure from academic life followed, in 1952, after more than thirty years, ten at Columbia University and twenty-two at the University of Chicago.

Neither of us regarded our separation from the academy as an abandonment of the intellectual life. On the contrary, we made that move in order to initiate and carry on intellectual undertakings that had little chance of prospering within the confines of a university. As émigrés from academic life, we looked forward to doing things we had not been able either to do at all or to do with sufficient freedom. In retrospect, twenty-five years later, I think I can speak for Bob as well as for myself in saying that we have never regretted the move. The adventures and the opportunities that opened up more than compensated for the loss of the sheltered security of university tenure.

I felt that I was following in the footsteps of the idol of my youth. John Stuart Mill earned his living as a clerk in the East India Company while writing the books that made him one of the most respected of British thinkers in the nineteenth century. Experimental scientists and humanistic scholars may need the resources of a university for their researches, but the decay of intellectual community and the obstacles to communication or collaboration that characterize the contemporary university, especially with regard to the discussion of ideas, make it desirable for a philosopher to try to find a more congenial and more supportive environment.

While I was still working on the Syntopicon, I laid the groundwork for three intellectual pursuits that have occupied a major portion of my time and energy in the last twenty-five years. One was a revival of my youthful vision of a *Summa Dialectica*, which might be a twentieth-century counterpart of the *Summa Theologica* constructed in the thirteenth—as different, of course, as the twentieth century is different from the thirteenth. As early as 1946, seeing in the development of the Syntopicon an organization of materials that might facilitate a dialectical summation, I wrote a memorandum to Bob Hutchins urging him to find funds to set up this project at the university. He postponed action on it in order to establish what was more urgent in the year after the explosion of the first atomic bombs—the Committee to Frame a World Constitution. However, with a grant-in-aid from the Old Dominion Foundation, we did organize a Program of Syntopical Research in 1951. It was carried on for two years by a small group who had worked together on the Syntopicon, but it did not really become operative until Bob went to the Ford Foundation and arranged for a substantial grant that established, in 1952, the Institute for Philosophical Research, separate from and independent of universities.

A second and equally absorbing intellectual pursuit began with a memorandum Bill Gorman and I submitted in 1948 to the Board of Editors of the *Encylopaedia Britannica,* urging that the encyclopaedia be made more than a reference book. We suggested that it might become, as well, an instrument of liberal education through the addition of a device that would function for users of an encyclopaedia as the Syntopicon would for readers of the great books. Eventually, this led to plans for producing the new fifteenth edition of the *Britannica.* Work on this, and especially on the Outline of Knowledge that is the encyclopaedic analogue of the Syntopicon, occupied eight years of my life, beginning in 1966.

The third intellectual venture might not have occurred had Walter and Elizabeth Paepcke not been members of the University Club great books class from its beginning in 1942–1943. Our association through the great books group prompted Walter to talk to me about his dreams for Aspen, following the striking success of the Goethe Festival which had been held there during the summer of 1949. Our conversations in the following year eventually led to the establishment of the Aspen Institute for Humanistic Studies, with which I have been intimately affiliated ever since.

Of these three nonacademic pursuits, the last represents my abiding interest in the continued learning of adults, and the one form of teaching that has never lost its fascination for me. In my judgment, the Executive Seminars at Aspen provide the consummate experience in adult learning for all concerned—the moderator as well as the participants. The work of the Institute for Philosophical Research and editorial work for the Encyclopaedia Britannica company represent my passion for outlining and organizing vast amounts of material as well as my passion for very large projects, a touch of megalomania on my part.

1. ASPEN

Taking a back road to Denver from their ranch near Colorado Springs, Walter and Elizabeth Paepcke came upon the sleepy, almost deserted, mining town of Aspen in 1945. Walter's practiced eye noted the angle from which sunlight fell upon Aspen Mountain, rising from the valley floor to over 11,000 feet, and decided that the slope might provide excellent facilities for skiing. The decaying Hotel Jerome was renovated in the style of the 1890s; a corporation was formed to build and operate ski runs and lifts; and Aspen, like Sun Valley, soon became a ski resort years before skiing achieved the popularity it enjoys today.

It might have remained no more than that had it not been for Professor Borgese's determination that the 200th anniversary, in 1949, of Goethe's birth should be appropriately celebrated in this country, not only for its own sake but also to renew the cultural bonds between the United States and Germany that had been weakened by the war. Together with Arnold Bergstrasser, professor of Germanic language and literature at the University of Chicago, he persuaded Hutchins that the university should celebrate the Goethe bicentennial. It occurred to Bob that Walter Paepcke, who was a trustee of the university and was devoted to Goethe (he was given to reciting passages from *Faust* in mellifluous German), might be interested in staging the event at Aspen.

Invitations were sent to Goethe scholars in this country and abroad. Bob and Walter engaged in a strenuous campaign to raise the funds needed to finance a Goethe Festival at Aspen. Announcements were placed in the public prints, and reservations for attendance were solicited. But what finally created nationwide excitement and made the event so great a success that the program of lectures and concerts had to be repeated a second time that summer of 1949 was the announcement that Albert Schweitzer would come from Africa to deliver a talk. A gift of $5,000 to his hospital in Lambaréné played no small part in persuading him. Even so, he might not have made the long journey— extremely arduous at that time—but for his mistaken impression that Aspen was a suburb of Chicago, not another 1,000 miles or more further west and across the Continental Divide.

In the autumn following the Goethe Festival, Walter Paepcke telephoned to ask me to have lunch with him at the Container Corporation of America, of which he was chief executive. Friendship with the

Paepckes had ripened out of many common interests and activities: Walter was a director of Encyclopaedia Britannica, Inc., and had supported the work to produce *Great Books of the Western World* and the Syntopicon; Elizabeth was a member of the board of the Great Books Foundation and had been a staunch ally in the effort to promote great books discussion groups for adults. After lunch, Walter posed the problem that bothered him. The success of the Goethe Festival the previous summer had made him realize that Aspen should not be used exclusively for skiing in the wintertime. Why not arrange an annual cultural festival for the Aspen summers, combining, as the Goethe bicentennial did, concerts, lectures, and discussions? As Walter probably anticipated, I responded with a proposal that came bouncing off the tip of my tongue. How about lectures on the great ideas and discussions of the great books? Walter immediately agreed and asked me to help him make plans for the next summer's program; he and Elizabeth would take care of arranging for the concerts to complete the picture.

My first trip to Aspen occurred in the company of Elizabeth, in April 1950. I cannot remember what I expected it to look like, but I do remember how appalled I was by the sea of mud that, in the spring thaw, filled all of Aspen's unpaved streets and almost prevented me from appreciating the beauty of the mountains and the clarity of the atmosphere. After a number of sessions with the Paepckes in the little cottage that adjoined their Aspen residence (called the Schweitzer Cottage because he had stayed there), plans for lectures and discussions took shape. I put myself down for the opening lecture, on the nature of man, which I thought an appropriate topic for an institution dedicated to humanistic studies. With Walter's approval, I drew up a list of other lecturers to follow and nominated associates to help conduct great books seminars, including my old friends Clifton Fadiman and Mark Van Doren, Bill Gorman, my right-hand man on the Syntopicon, and Clarence Faust, Champion Ward, and Meredith Wilson, with whom I had been closely connected in curricular reforms at the University of Chicago.

During the Aspen summers of 1950 and 1951, the lectures were delivered in the morning in the tent that Eero Saarinen had constructed for the Goethe Festival, and in the evening in the hastily renovated auditorium of the old Opera House. A succession of distinguished speakers offered an extraordinarily varied intellectual fare. All of them had the common trait of being interested in ideas—the prime prerequisite from Walter Paepcke's point of view. Gracing the platform, in addition to Bob Hutchins and those I have already mentioned, were Jacques Barzun, Norman Cousins, Alexander Meiklejohn, Scott Buchanan, Reinhold Niebuhr, Father John Courtney Murray, Charles Malik, Edward Weeks, Jr., Judge Charles Wyzanski, and Paul Weiss.

To adapt the seminars to the constantly changing summer population, we found it necessary to conduct the discussions with a small panel of selected persons who had read the book assigned for a particular occasion, attended by a larger group who came to the meeting without having read the book. This worked the night that Bill Gorman and I conducted a discussion of Thomas Aquinas's Treatise on Law with a panel of two bright and beautiful women—Clare Luce at one end of the table and Elizabeth Paepcke at the other. For a variety of reasons, the spectators found that a fascinating performance. But for the most part these panel discussions failed to be genuinely intelligible to an audience that had not read the book. It would be an understatement to say that they did not serve the educational objectives we had in mind. We abandoned them and found a substitute for them, largely as a result of the intervention of Harry Luce, who accompanied Clare to Aspen that summer in 1950.

Luce and Paepcke had been classmates at Yale and were friends of long standing. After being at Aspen for several weeks and observing the performances and audiences in the Opera House, Luce told Walter that he thought the Aspen program was missing the boat. The audiences at these great books discussions, he said, were mainly made up of schoolteachers, librarians, lawyers, and other professional people. He thought that what they got from these Aspen sessions, they could get at home. Anyway, he went on, these are not the people who need the mental stimulation most. You have forgotten, he chided Walter, the great intellectually unwashed group in this country—American businessmen. Get them to come to Aspen for readings and discussions, and you will really be doing something worthwhile.

From that conversation was born the Aspen Executive Program. It started with a small group in the summer of 1951, with a hastily improvised set of readings, and with extremely informal discussions led by Meyer Kestnbaum, president of Hart, Schaffner and Marx, and me. We met on the porch of the Four Seasons Club near a little mountain lake. The following summer, better planning and recruitment resulted in the organization of four or five executive seminars, each running two weeks, with six two-hour sessions a week. The readings were mainly drawn from *The People Shall Judge,* a two-volume compilation that the staff of the social science general course at the University of Chicago had produced. The selections were both historically and currently germane to the consideration of the problems and issues that confront the citizens of an industrial, free-enterprise, capitalistic democracy, and especially citizens who also are executives of large corporations.

Adopting the format of great books discussion groups, the Executive Seminars were moderated by two leaders. To support them and enrich the discussions, Walter added three or four resource persons drawn from government, labor unions, the press, and the learned professions. Meredith Wilson and Champion Ward conducted two of the Executive Seminars that took place in 1951; Clarence Faust and I, another two. Of all the persons involved in the early years of the Aspen executive program, either as moderators or resource persons, I think I am the only one who, with one or two exceptions, has repeated the experience annually since 1951, more than twenty-five years.

What I have learned as a moderator has certainly contributed to my own education—refining insights, honing arguments, and enlarging theories that went into my own preparation for the seminars and came out of them greatly improved. No less important has been my friendship with the Paepckes, from whom I learned a great deal about the arts to which they were devoted—music, painting, sculpture, and graphic design. As much from their personal contacts with Walter and Elizabeth Paepcke as from the seminar discussions, participants in the Aspen experience were awakened to a realization that, in the scale of values, the Platonic triad of the true, the good, and the beautiful takes precedence over the Machiavellian triad of money, fame, and power.

The stated educational and cultural aims of the Aspen Institute for Humanistic Studies drew their vitality in no small part from the kind and quality of life that the Paepckes themselves lived. During Walter's lifetime, the Aspen Institute, as a nonprofit corporation, always labored under a burden of debt that he helped to defray from his own pocket or by passing the hat among his friends. Summer after summer, facing the fact that the gate receipts for the chair lift up Aspen Mountain exceeded the income from admissions to all the concerts, lectures, and seminars, he would wryly repeat his favorite quotation from Plato: "What is honored in a country will be cultivated there." Unfortunately, he did not live to see Aspen achieve the international recognition it has won in recent years, or the more stable financing that his successors have marshalled for its educational and other programs. His successors, by the way, have all been products of the Aspen Executive Seminars. Robert O. Anderson, who had been a student of Bob Hutchins's and mine at the University of Chicago and a member of my Aspen seminar in 1955, succeeded Walter, by the latter's wise choice, in the chairmanship of the Aspen Institute. Under Bob Anderson's chairmanship, William Stevenson, Alvin Eurich, and Joseph Slater, who have served successively as presidents of the institute, either moderated seminars in the early days or, as in Slater's case, participated in them.

Under Joe Slater's presidency, the Aspen Institute has embarked on a large number of research and discussion projects, many of which operate throughout the year in other parts of this country and abroad, and come to focus in Aspen during the summer months. Though I have taken some part in these other activities of the Aspen Institute, the

Executive Seminar remains for me the heart of the matter, not only because of my commitment to Walter Paepcke's vision of its objectives, but also because it has served so effectively as a vigorous forum for the airing and clarifying of ideas. Since I always prepared especially for the occasion with attention to some idea or theory that related to problems or issues under discussion in the Executive Seminars, the more than two score of lectures that I have delivered at Aspen in the last twenty-five years have often been preliminary skirmishes that cleared the underbrush and opened the road for writing the books and essays that I have produced during that time.

It was not until 1956 that I was able to construct a reading list for the Executive Seminar that ideally suited the purposes Walter and I had in mind. With a few modifications, I have used that list ever since, as has my friend Jacques Barzun. I have steadfastly refused to adopt alterations suggested by the administrators of the Aspen Institute since Walter Paepcke's death or alternative reading lists drawn up by other moderators, working as committees to revise the Aspen readings. A good reading list, like a work of art, cannot be constructed by a committee, each member of which has some favorite selection he wishes to include or some book or author he wishes to eliminate. That necessarily results in an incoherent hodgepodge. For the purposes of an Executive Seminar, the readings must be organized so that issues are illuminated by the expression of opposing points of view at each session, and so that, in the course of two weeks, the discussion moves forward cumulatively and progressively, systematically broadening the scope of the discussion while at the same time retaining clarifications already achieved.

To the readings that were originally drawn from *The People Shall Judge,* I added selections from Plato, Aristotle, Machiavelli, Locke, Rousseau, Tocqueville, J. S. Mill, and Karl Marx. I have profited from the repeated use of this reading list for more than twenty years now, not only because it is, for me, inexhaustibly rereadable, but also because the discussions that the same readings provoke differ time after time as the participants in the seminars differ in their backgrounds and convictions. My notes and resumés record the variations and accretions of each new Executive Seminar. I must confess that, though I have tried, I have not been able to persuade other moderators either to adopt my reading list or my pedagogical style, which requires that the discussions be controlled by a very close reading of the texts assigned and that the participants be subject to the discipline of answering questions and facing issues arising from the texts.

Be that as it may, I can happily report that my method of conducting Aspen Executive Seminars has seemed rewarding to most of the participants. It is true that they are restive under its discipline during the first few sessions, but they end up after two weeks with the joy of feeling that their minds have been pried wide open—and even changed for the better. Some have returned to Aspen for a second go at the same readings. Some have organized groups to carry on the Aspen type of seminar at home, and some have returned to their organizations with missionary zeal to form corporate seminars; for example, those conducted for the Industrial Indemnity Insurance Company in San Francisco, the seminars at the Inland Steel Company in Chicago, and the Executive Seminars that were held under the auspices of the Institute for Philosophical Research. Perhaps the most interesting and unusual of all these offshoots of Aspen were the seminars organized by the International Pressmen's Union for its own labor leaders. These ran for four or five years following the attendance at Aspen of two of its top executives in 1956.

I cannot close this account of the Aspen experience without telling two stories. One concerns a lecture on natural law by Father Walter Farrell, with whom I had once collaborated in writing a series of essays on the theory of democracy. In the question period that followed Father Farrell's talk, a fallen-away Catholic in the audience thought he would stump the priest-philosopher by asking for his view of celibacy according to the natural law. Quick as a flash, Father Farrell replied, "That's easy. Celibacy, according to the natural law, is sheer idiocy."

The other story is about another question period that followed a lecture in which I presented arguments to support the thesis that man differs essentially in kind from apes and other higher mammals by virtue of possessing the power of conceptual thought and of syntactical speech. Walter Orr Roberts, the astronomer and climatologist, a resource person in my Executive Seminar, posed the following question: "What would you say, Dr. Adler, if an anthropoid ape who had been hiding behind a screen during your lecture now came forth and said to you. 'Dr. Adler, I disagree with your thesis.'" Not as quick as Father Farrell, I paused for a moment, and then replied, "I would tell him that he is either a liar or a fool."

2. INSTITUTE FOR PHILOSOPHICAL RESEARCH

The Institute for Philosophical Research celebrates its twenty-fifth anniversary in 1977. It came into existence with a single and singular objective—to produce a *Summa Dialectica* of Western thought. That objective, as the reader knows from an earlier chapter, had its origin in a fantasy of mine when, at the age of twenty-five, I wrote my first book—*Dialectic*—and concluded it by projecting the possibility of a philosophical summation for the twentieth century somewhat analogous to the great theological summations in the thirteenth. Twenty years later I revived the idea in a memorandum I wrote Bob Hutchins. My conception of that project had been radically transformed by the construction of the Syntopicon. Instead of trying to deal with oppositions among conflicting systems of philosophy, which had been my earlier conception of the project, I now conceived the task as one of dealing with the philosophical controversies that have arisen in the sphere of each of the great ideas. The completed Syntopicon, I had come to realize, would provide a first, tentative, and incomplete approximation to a chart of the fundamental issues on which philosophers divide.

One other thing, which I had forgotten in 1927 and remembered in 1945, altered and matured my conception of the project. That was an address delivered in 1916 to the American Philosophical Association by Prof. A. O. Lovejoy, "On Some Conditions of Progress in Philosophical Inquiry." While I was still an undergraduate at Columbia, I had been deeply impressed by Lovejoy's critique of the failure of philosophers to join issue and engage in well-conducted disputation. I was also inspired by his vision of the advances that might be made in philosophical thought if philosophers were to work cooperatively, not to settle their differences, but to agree about the points on which they differed, to formulate issues with precision and clarity, and to marshall the arguments pro and con. The *Summa Dialectica* would lay the groundwork for progress in philosophical thought. The title of the institute was, therefore, a serious misnomer. It would not be engaged in philosophical thought but rather in thinking about philosophical thought, past and present, so that philosophical thinking in the future might make new strides in the pursuit of truth. Instead of calling it an Institute for Philosophical Research, I should have called it an Institute for the Dialectical Clarification of Fundamental Ideas, or an Institute for Realizing the Indispensable Conditions of Progress in Philosophy. Either would have been an exact but clumsy title.

When the institute opened its doors in San Francisco in 1952, I was repeatedly asked in press interviews for a statement of its purpose. A full explanation, I knew, would be both too lengthy and too intricate, so I managed to forge a brief statement that ran as follows: "The Institute will be engaged in an effort to take stock of Western thought on subjects which have been of continuing philosophical interest from the advent of philosophy in ancient Greece to the present day; and in this process, it hopes to discover the extent and kinds of agreement that exist among men who disagree about what is true." The subjects I had in mind were to be drawn from the Syntopicon—the great ideas. The agreements I had in mind were those that must exist if disagreement is to be real rather than merely apparent.

It has been repeatedly said, until it has become wearisome, that philosophers disagree on almost every subject that they consider and discuss. But the conditions prerequisite to real, as contrasted with apparent, disagreement are more difficult to fulfill than is generally supposed. In order to disagree, two men must, first of all, agree with precision about the subject under consideration. They must have an identical object of thought before their minds. Secondly, they must, with regard to that subject, be engaged in responding to one and the same question, formulated as precisely as possible. These two prerequisites are so difficult that they are rarely satisfied by the thinkers themselves, with the result that they seldom really disagree but only appear to do so. It also frequently happens that philosophers who do not appear to disagree really do when matters are carefully examined.

Until real disagreements, or genuine issues, are discovered and formulated, philosophical controversy cannot begin; and until controversies can be constructed in which philosophers, who join issue, advance arguments in well-conducted disputes, there is little or no hope of ever resolving those issues. If, as Lovejoy so ably contended, the history of philosophy so far, as well as current philosophical thought, reveals how few fundamental issues are clearly joined and thoroughly disputed, then the task of constructing controversies by formulating issues and setting up disputes should be undertaken by a group of collaborative workers who would eschew being philosophers themselves in order to serve philosophers in the future. They would eschew being philosophers in that they would not themselves be engaged in trying to discover the true doctrine about any basic subject. Instead of such doctrinal truth, the only truth they might, if successful, achieve would be dialectical truth—truth about the issues and disputes exhibited in a correctly constructed controversy. The dialectical summation that the institute was established to achieve would be a comprehensive summation of such dialectical truths.

So conceived, a *Summa Dialectica* will, I fear, never be completed. In the twenty-five years of its existence, the institute has been able to do the work required in the sphere of only a small number of ideas, and it has done it comprehensively with regard to only one idea. The work done on the idea of freedom represents the kind of work—in method and in scope—that the institute originally set out to do in the sphere of every basic idea. The reading that a sizeable staff of researchers did, their discussions, and the successive drafts through which the writing went, in order to produce the 1,500 pages of the two volumes of *The Idea of Freedom*, took eight full years. The bibliography of books and articles referred to or examined is in excess of 1,300 titles by about 800 authors, ranging across twenty-five centuries of Western thought.

In the years that led up to the establishment of the institute, or even during the first eight or ten years of its existence, I did not realize the unfeasibility of completing a *Summa Dialectica*. From 1945 on, though preoccupied with the Syntopicon, I took every occasion to promote the project of constructing one. A letter from Bill Benton in 1946 begged me "not to leave the Great Books in the lurch too soon for your 'Summa Dialectica.' " An address on the nature of philosophical work, which I gave at the University of Chicago in 1947, concluded with a statement about the need for a *Summa Dialectica*. It contained the following optimistic estimate.

> It might take twenty or thirty years to draft the first outlines of a Summa Dialectica, but if that work were done in the right way in its initial stage, no matter how inadequately or tentatively, it would be the basis for a continually growing expansion and rectification as the work continued indefinitely into the future.

In 1951, Bob Hutchins persuaded the Old Dominion Foundation to make a grant to the university to support the formation of a "Program of Syntopical Research"; and in his farewell address to the trustees and faculty, before departing for the Ford Foundation, he praised the Syntopicon as something that had been done at the university and declared that the university should look beyond the Syntopicon to the construction of a *Summa Dialectica*. Bill Gorman, Herman Bernick, Peter Wolff, and I collaborated for two years in the Program of Syntopical Research at Chicago; we made a first stab at a dialectical construction of the controversy about the idea of induction, its logic and methodology.

Whether the work would have gone on and developed further at the university if Hutchins had remained president, I do not know. But I think it is reasonably certain that the Institute for Philosophical Research would not have come into existence had Bob not left the university for the Ford Foundation, and had he not made it possible for me to leave the university by obtaining funds to support the one job that I wanted most to do. Between the time Bob moved to Pasadena, where Paul Hoffman had set up the Ford Foundation, and the time funds were made available to establish the institute, I became a consultant of the foundation. In that capacity I prepared three elaborate outlines, each as a basis for conducting a conference for directors and staff of the foundation and other guests—one a conference on the conditions of peace, a subject dear to Paul Hoffman's heart; a second, on the issues concerning freedom, which dealt, in part, with civil liberties and civil rights and which laid the groundwork for the Fund for the Republic that Bob Hutchins subsequently converted into the Center for the Study of Democratic Institutions at Santa Barbara; and a third on the basic issues concerning education in a democratic society. The last—a three-day conference in Philadelphia attended by all the directors and officers of the Fund for the Advancement of Education and the Fund for Adult Education—occurred in January 1952, just a few months before the April board meeting of the Fund for the Advancement of Education, of which Clarence Faust was president. To support his request for funds, I gave Clarence a copy of Professor Lovejoy's paper, together with a passage from Prof. Edmund Husserl's introduction to his *Cartesian Meditations,* in which he pointed out that "there are plenty of philosophical meetings, but it is the philosophers who meet, not their philosophies." I also gave Clarence a statement about the *Summa Dialectica* made by Jacques Maritain, at the banquet at the Waldorf when *Great Books of the Western World* and the Syntopicon were first unveiled, as well as a letter from Prof. Etienne Gilson of the Collège de France, who wrote:

> My global impression is that the Syntopicon will provide a useful starting point, or base, for a Summa Dialectica. . . . It was a herculean task to do it, and the amount of intelligence it has taken to lick so much ideological matter into shape deserves unqualified admiration. Moreover, I beg to suggest that I consider the Syntopicon a typically "American" masterpiece; and, believe me, there is no trace of irony in the epithet.

Like Gilson, Maritain also praised the Syntopicon as a product of "the American mind and American zeal," and went on to say that it should be regarded "as a starting point. Let us hope," he added, "that the next step will be a summing up—what Mortimer Adler calls a *Summa Dialectica*—if not of the principles and theoretical certainties unanimously agreed upon by the Western intellect, at least of the crucial issues with which we are faced and of the conflicting answers which have been or may be offered." A *Time* cover story, in March 1952, on the production of the Syntopican quoted me as referring to the *Summa Dialectica* as the next big job to be undertaken. Toward the end of April, the Fund for the Advancement of Education, together with the Old Dominion Foundation, made a grant which provided $200,000 a year for three years and some additional funds to equip the institute with furniture, a library, and other facilities.

Had I suspected that, at the end of three years, the Fund for the Advancement of Education would give the institute a terminal grant for one more year and then push it off to sink or swim, I might have husbanded our resources more thriftily. I did not do that. Instead of starting slowly and feeling my way, I used the available funds to engage as large a staff as the money would support.

The nucleus of the institute's staff was drawn from the Syntopicon and the Program of Syntopical Research—I as director, Bill Gorman as associate director, and Bernick and Wolff as assistants to the director. We quickly recruited fifteen young men, students and teachers of philosophy or scholars in related humanistic disciplines. Jacques Maritain, Richard McKeon, and Paul Weiss, then professor of philosophy at Yale, became consultants, as did two other old friends—Otto Bird, who had worked with me on the Syntopicon, and Arthur Rubin.

Arthur had been *agent provocateur,* if not instigator, of the *Summa*

Dialectica in the germinal fantasy of it back in the twenties when we were both at Columbia. During the years that I was preoccupied with the Syntopicon, he and I spent little time together, but with the establishment of the institute to develop what Arthur regarded as "his baby," he and I once again resumed, until his death in 1973, a steady collaboration, one that involved intense and often acrimonious interchanges. It would be difficult to overstate the debt I owe him for a lifelong friendship, for his practical guidance in moments of crisis, and most of all for his unremitting insistence on intellectual integrity, precision, and clarity. On that last count, all those who, through the institute, became associated with him are similarly in his debt.

As far as I was concerned, the question of where the newly established institute should be located had only one answer—San Francisco. My first brief visit in 1934 instilled in me the desire to live there, a desire intensified by the week that I spent there in the early forties giving a series of public lectures on God, freedom, and immortality. The only obstacle was Paul Hoffman's hope that, by locating the institute in Pasadena, I might be in closer contact with the operations of the Ford Foundation. To settle this matter, I met Paul in Chicago. At that time, he was busily engaged in an effort to get General Eisenhower nominated by the Republican party. The little time he had to spare for a conversation with me found us together in a taxicab driving from Midway Airport to the Chicago Club. When Paul proposed that I move to Pasadena, I countered by suggesting that San Francisco had the advantage of proximity to three large universities with splendid libraries and that the speed of air travel would allow me to fly to Pasadena as often as necessary. Preoccupied with more important matters, Paul gave his assent, and I quickly changed the subject to the problem of getting Eisenhower nominated and elected. That settled it.

San Francisco proved to be not only an exciting place to live, but also a city that took pride in the work the institute was trying to do. When the institute encountered difficulties keeping afloat, the friends it had made in San Francisco rallied to its support. I took every occasion offered me to explain why I regarded San Francisco as an ideal habitat for intellectual work, even quoting, in a speech before the Chamber of Commerce, the passages from Aristotle's *Politics* in which he describes the physical features of the ideal city, many of which San Francisco possesses to a high degree. At a dinner to celebrate the installation of the institute in a magnificent old mansion on Pacific Heights, a dinner attended by San Francisco members of the institute's board, by Bob Hutchins and Clarence Faust, and by Earl Warren, who was then governor of California, I related two anecdotes that expressed my delight with San Francisco. One reported a telephone call to the institute which asked whether this was "The Institute for Popsolipsical Research." The other was a greeting from a handsome black gripman on the cable car that ran in front of the institute's doors. I was coming out of the building as the cable car passed by. He leaned over the rear railing of the car and cried out, "Hi, Dr. Adler, how goes philosophical research?"

One other thing that happened at that dinner I cannot refrain from relating. Bill Gorman, who was present as associate director of the institute, read the text of a little essay that had been written by my son Mark to record his impressions of the evening in March 1952 when I awaited a telephone call from Clarence Faust telling me whether the board of the Fund for the Advancement of Education had approved a grant to support the project of constructing a *Summa Dialectica*. Mark had observed the anxiety and impatience with which I paced up and down my study for the several hours during which the anticipated phone call did not come. He was obviously impressed by the world-shaking importance of the event that hung in the balance—whether or not the making of a *Summa Dialectica* would be undertaken. Here is the opening paragraph of his account of that occasion (with all misspellings retained):

The founding of the Summa Diealectia.

The project of a century lies in the hands of 14 men. On it depends the entire future of a man who has waited 7 years for this great event. Will it come true? Probely he did not get a good day of work done. His nerves are calm as a ocean on a breesless day, or at least he seemes so on the outside. After making numberous phone calls during the day, he comes home exhausted. He immeadeately sits down and makes more phone calls. Time is running short.—either he has a lifetime of the kind of work he wantes to do—or he will be forced to give up his lifetime ambition.

Work started in September 1952. As in the case of the Syntopicon, it took at least two years, with many false starts and discarded trials, to discover the right track to pursue. It took more time to develop methods for collaborative intellectual work, and even more time to organize the results as well as to devise an effective style for presenting our formulations. Before I could begin writing *The Idea of Freedom,* I wrote three drafts, each book length—one in February 1953, based on no more than six weeks of research, the criticism of which helped to get us on the right track; one late in 1954 that culminated eighteen months of research and discussion which had been directed by what proved to be the correct dialectical hypothesis; and one in 1956 that became the first approximation or draft of Book I of *The Idea of Freedom.*

The first mistake we made, when the work began in September 1952, was the selection of Man as the initial subject to treat dialectically. We outlined a number of dialectical schemes for catching and clarifying the philosophical issues that revolved around Man, but they proved to be too numerous and too complicated for us to handle. After pre-liminary sallies with some of the subordinate subjects, such as human origins and human rights, we decided to concentrate on human freedom, a subject on which I had already done some ground-clearing in a lengthy paper for a Ford Foundation seminar.

The second mistake was wholly mine—a willingness, even an eager-ness, to prepare a document for discussion at a conference scheduled in Princeton on March 6, 1953. The purpose of the conference was to explore the possibility of setting up what Bob Hutchins referred to as "the Academy"—an assemblage of the world's leading minds in all fields to discuss the most important issues of our time. The conferees included Robert Oppenheimer, Paul Tillich, Etienne Gilson, Jacques Maritain, Walter Lippmann, Paul Weiss, and Charles Malik. I should have told Bob that I would come to the conference but that I would not be able to bring with me any materials, produced by the institute, which might give the conferees a taste of what participation in the academy would be like. Instead, for six weeks, I drove the institute staff into a frenzy of hurried research on human freedom and then, in less than four weeks, I drafted a document entitled "The Controversy Concerning Human Freedom," to which was attached a very extensive bibliography. I finished writing it just in time to carry with me to Princeton enough copies of the document for all the conferees. Of course, they had no time even to glance through it before Bob introduced it, in the opening session, as material to be discussed the next day. The subsequent dis-cussion paid little attention to the unread example of what the Institute for Philosophical Research might do for the luminaries of the pro-spective academy. In the very middle of the one effort I made to gain some attention for the institute's work, I was called to the telephone to learn that my mother, who had recently undergone an operation for cancer, had suddenly died in San Francisco, where six years earlier after the death of my father she had gone to live near my sister. I drove into New York and flew to San Francisco for her funeral. When I returned to Princeton, I found the conference a shambles, and the institute's first trial effort completely discarded. That was hardly an auspicious be-ginning, but our own discovery, after the Princeton conference, of all the ways in which that first effort went wrong helped to put us on the right track.

Another conference held in London in May was a second attempt to explore the possibilities of realizing Bob Hutchins's dream of an academy. Its roster included R. H. Tawney, Isaiah Berlin, Werner Heisenberg, Niels Bohr, Michael Polanyi, Arthur Goodhart, Sir Richard Livingstone, and Herbert Butterfield. Though I took part, I did not make the mistake of exposing to it premature formulations from the institute. Bob learned from this conference that his vision of the

In the bar at Hotel Jerome, Aspen, Colorado, in the summer of 1951;
from left to right: William Gomberg, now a trustee of the Aspen
Institute for Humanistic Studies; Raymond Moley; Elizabeth Paepcke;
Robert Hutchins, and Walter Paepcke.

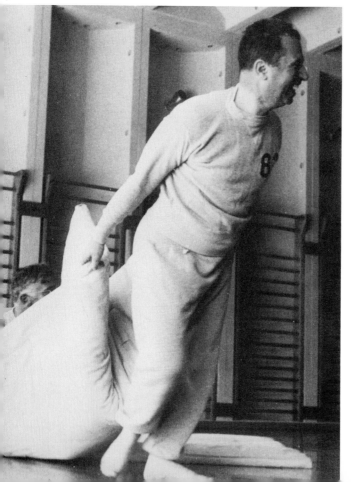

ABOVE Adler conducting an executive seminar in Aspen in the late 1950s. BELOW Having overcome his aversion to physical exercise, Adler romps in the Health Center at Aspen.

With the family in Aspen. ABOVE With
wife Caroline and family friend Rosemary
Barnes; in front, Philip and Douglas. BELOW
With his wife, Douglas, and Philip.

ABOVE With William F. Buckley, Jr., on Kup's Show, Chicago, 1967.
BELOW With Hugh Downs on the Today Show, 1967, at the time of the
publication of *The Difference of Man and The Difference It Makes.*

Clifton Fadiman.

Arthur A. Houghton, Jr.

Mark Van Doren.

Arthur Rubin.
(*Mrs. Arthur L.H. Rubin*)

esident Stringfellow Barr and
an Scott Buchanan at St.
n's College, Annapolis,
ryland.

With Richard Weigle, president of St. John's College,
Santa Fe, New Mexico.

Board of Editors of Encyclopaedia Britannica, 1968, photographed in front of the Swan Hotel at the time of the celebration of the Encyclopaedia Britannica's two-hundredth anniversary.

From left to right. Sir Geoffrey Crowther, vice chairman, editorial board, Encyclopaedia Britannica, Inc.; Warren Everote, president, Encyclopaedia Britannica Educational Corp.; Alexis Ladas, vice president/international, Encyclopaedia Britannica, Inc.; Thomas Park, professor emeritus, University of Chicago; Christopher H.W. Kent, deputy editor, Encyclopaedia Britannica, Ltd., London; David Owen, co-administrator, U.N. Development Programme, London; Clifton Fadiman, author and critic; Warren E. Preece, general editor, *Encyclopaedia Britannica;* Edward H. Levi, president, University of Chicago; Robert M. Hutchins, president, Center for the Study of Democratic Institutions; Sir George Weidenfeld, publisher, Weidenfeld & Nicolson, London; John S. Robling, vice president, advertising/public relations; Philip Gove, editor in chief, Merriam-Webster, *Third New International Dictionary;* Sir William Haley, editor in chief, *Encyclopaedia Britannica;* Charles E. Swanson, president, Encyclopaedia Britannica, Inc.; Howard L. Goodkind, executive vice president/editorial, Encyclopaedia Britannica, Inc.; Mortimer J. Adler, chairman, editorial planning committee; George N. Shuster, assistant to the president of University of Notre Dame.

With William Benton, chairman of the board of Encyclopaedia Britannica, Inc., at a press conference for *The Annals of America,* 1969. The man on the left is Henry Dorman, president, Library of Presidential Papers, New York.

Adler alongside one of his favorite English philosophers, John Locke (painting by John Greenhill), London, 1974. (*Time-Life Picture Agency*)

At 10 Downing Street at the time of the presentation of *Britannica 3*. From left to right: Philip Kaiser, chairman of the board of Encyclopaedia Britannica, Ltd., London; Adler; Prime Minister Harold Wilson; Howard L. Goodkind, president, Encyclopaedia Britannica, Ltd., London.

Adler with Caroline and Clifton Fadiman at the entrance to 10 Downing Street at the occasion of a reception celebrating Britannica's two-hundredth anniversary.

Board of Editors after Robert Hutchins relinquished the
chairmanship to Adler, 1975. Standing from left to right:
John S. Robling, vice president, advertising/public relations,
Encyclopaedia Britannica, Inc.; Ross Sackett, president, Encyclopaedia Britannica Educational Corp.; Warren E. Preece,
vice chairman, board of editors; Frank Gibney, vice president/
planning and development, Encyclopaedia Britannica, Inc.;
Charles Swanson, president, Encyclopaedia Britannica, Inc.;
Dr. Walter Perry, vice-chancellor, The Open University, England; Clifton Fadiman, author and critic.
Seated from left to right: Clare Boothe Luce, playwright and
former U.S. congresswoman; Adler, chairman, board of editors;
Margaret Sutton, secretary, board of editors.
Absent from picture: Howard L. Goodkind, chairman, Encyclopaedia Britannica, Ltd., London; Maurice B. Mitchell,
chancellor, University of Denver; Thomas Park, professor
emeritus, University of Chicago; Charles Van Doren, vice
president/editorial, Encyclopaedia Britannica, Inc.; Lord
George Weidenfeld, publisher, Weidenfeld & Nicolson,
London.

PHILOSOPHY IS NO DAMN GOOD

Addressing an audience in Melbourne, Australia, 1962.

Adler with his sons Douglas
and Philip looking at *Britannica 3* at the time of its
publication.

Outside their townhouse in London, 1975, Adler poses with his wife Caroline and his sons Douglas, 11, and Philip, 9. (*Time-Life Picture Agency*)

Adler at the desk where he wrote his autobiography.

academy was more visionary than practicable; like Plato, whose *Laws* delineate a state that is second-best to the ideal state of his *Republic,* Bob some years later set up the Center for the Study of Democratic Institutions as a practicable second-best to his ideal academy. I learned from the London conference how undisciplined are even the very best minds in the world when they turn from the solitary tasks of thinking and writing to the collaborative task of discussion. In the critique of the London Conference I wrote for Bob Hutchins and Clarence Faust, I pointed out that its dismal performance reconfirmed our sense of the contribution the institute might make to the meeting of minds and the carrying on of controversy.

Still another conference, held in New York City, was organized by the institute for the purpose of learning from a highly diversified group what opinions were generally held, outside of philosophical circles, on the subject of human freedom. Meyer Kestnbaum of the institute's Board of Directors sent out the invitations and chaired the sessions. The participants included Arthur A. Houghton, Jr., president of Steuben Glass; Ralph S. Damon, president of Trans-World Airlines; Judge Charles E. Clark of the federal appellate bench; President John Dickey of Dartmouth College; Dr. Gregory Zilboorg, an eminent psychoanalyst; and Dr. Karl Menninger, an eminent psychiatrist. From the institute's point of view, this was the only conference, of the three held that year, which made any contribution to its work. By the time it was held, a brief memorandum, which I labelled "A Brainstorm," led to the precise identification of the three distinct objects, all called freedom, which were the pivots of three quite separate controversies in the sphere of that great idea. In addition, the nonacademic mentalities of its highly intelligent participants permitted a wide-ranging discussion not paralyzed by rigid doctrinal commitments that each participant thought had to be defended to the hilt. The New York conference was also momentous in its consequences, both for the institute and for me personally, because it was there that I first met and came to admire Arthur Houghton, who has been a steadfast friend of mine and of the institute ever since.

As the work on freedom advanced, other conferences were held, some at the institute's quarters in San Francisco and some in Europe. The former were attended by philosophers from the universities in the Bay area. Dick McKeon, who arranged and conducted the conferences in Europe, addressed their attention to the results so far achieved with respect to freedom, as well as to the dialectical objectives of the institute and the program of constructing a *Summa Dialectica*. These European meetings were held in the summer of 1954, in London, Zurich, Paris, and at a castle near Darmstadt in Germany; they drew participants from the leading universities in Great Britain and on the Continent. Dick reported on each of the conferences and added a final summarizing view of them.

> The interest in the problems on which the Institute is working is almost universal—not in the sense that philosophers are already working on these problems or in the sense that they acknowledge an interest when the problems are first described in general terms, but in the sense that they became absorbed in the problems once they had been led by discussion into the issues raised. The participants in the conferences were usually enthusiastic about the level and quality of the philosophical discussions that resulted from considering these issues. . . . I am convinced, after the experience of conducting these four conferences, of the great importance of the work of the Institute.

In my biennial report to the institute's Board of Directors, for the years 1952–1954, I called attention to several activities I had undertaken to make the institute's work known beyond the academic audience. One of these was a series of public lectures in the Bay area dealing with basic issues that needed clarification. The other was a series of half-hour television programs on the great ideas. These began with broadcasts by a local television station and developed into the production of fifty-two films on the great ideas, made for the national educational television network. I told the board that I thought "the experience gained from talking about fundamental ideas and issues to a fairly large audience may afford some help in developing an effective non-technical style for expounding the Institute's results to the intelligent layman."

The television films aroused the enthusiasm of an officer of the William Morris Agency, Jerry Stagg, who thought they should reach a still larger audience by being broadcast as a public service feature on one of the commercial networks. I was in his office in Los Angeles when he telephoned a vice-president of NBC to arrange a viewing of some of my films in New York. Stagg was obviously getting a cool reception of his proposal, for I heard him say, "You don't know who Mortimer Adler is?" A short pause followed, and then, in true Hollywood fashion, he said, "Why, he is the highest-paid philosopher in the world," to which the executive in New York immediately responded with "Send him in!" Some of my films were viewed and thought well of, but they were never broadcast by NBC, because Warren Weaver, who had to give his approval to the project, did know who Mortimer Adler was and did not like him. Weaver, a disciple of John Dewey and a proponent of pragmatism, had developed an unusually strong prejudice against the great books and the great ideas. As for my being the highest-paid philosopher, I suppose that may have been true, considering the scale of academic salaries at the time.

The work on the idea of freedom was just beginning to jell in 1955 when the rug was pulled out from under us. An upheaval in the Ford

Foundation brought Paul Hoffman and Bob Hutchins to the end of their tenure as president and vice-president. Although my good friend Clarence Faust continued for some time as president of the Fund for the Advancement of Education, he could not succeed in getting his board to renew the original grant to the institute for another three years. A small terminal grant for one more year required a drastic reduction in staff. While the reading and analysis of the vast literature on freedom had been almost completed, and our staff conferences had amply confirmed the soundness of our dialectical hypothesis concerning the major controversies about freedom, the job of writing them up still remained to be done. My guess is that Clarence failed to obtain further support because of a policy common to most of the big foundations—to initiate a project and then expect it to survive by raising funds from other sources. I also suspect that Clarence failed because two board members upon whom he relied for enthusiastic support of the institute—Walter Lippmann and Mr. Justice Roberts—failed to come through in the pinch.

Why, I will never fully understand. Mr. Justice Roberts spent a week at the institute several months before the critical board meeting. My impression of his reactions to our staff conferences left me with considerable hope of his making an affirmative recommendation. Walter Lippmann and I had been friends ever since Bob Hutchins invited him to give some lectures at the University of Chicago. We had corresponded over the years about philosophical matters. During the summer of 1955, I spent considerable time going over the manuscript of his latest book, *The Public Philosophy,* and at his request sent him lengthy commentaries on it suggesting corrections and expansions, chapter by chapter. That may have been one cause of the disaffection, for I found Walter's style of writing, however good it was for newspaper columns, inadequate for the task of handling difficult points in political philosophy. Another may have been his not having understood the dialectical objectives of the institute when he first gave it his support, and his disappointment when he realized that the institute's approach to the problems of freedom was not the one he had hoped for.

In the years immediately following the terminal grant from the Ford Foundation, I divided my efforts between writing the first volume of *The Idea of Freedom* and raising money to finance the continued existence of the institute. At this juncture, friends of the institute in San Francisco formed a group to raise some of the money needed. However, without the major contributions that came from Paul Mellon and Arthur Houghton, I doubt that the institute would have been able to carry on for long. The Old Dominion Foundation, of which Paul Mellon was chairman and Ernest Brooks was president during those years, continued to make three-year grants from 1956 on to 1969, when the

Old Dominion was merged into the Mellon Foundation. My associates and I owe Paul Mellon a debt of gratitude that we inadequately discharged by dedicating the first volume of *The Idea of Freedom* to him and to Arthur O. Lovejoy. The dedication of the second volume to Arthur Houghton and Adolph Schmidt, a member of the Old Dominion board, insufficiently expressed the gratitude we owed to these two good friends who, like Paul Mellon, understood what the institute was trying to accomplish for philosophy and the world of ideas. They were firm in their belief that our work should be supported because the objectives of the institute were not being served by any other agency in our society, least of all by the universities. They even shared our hope that the institute's program might exert an influence on liberal education in this country, as well as restore confidence in the intellect's ability to deal rationally with matters about which reasonable men hold conflicting views.

The institute's debt to Arthur Houghton for his unceasing support does not compare with my own debt to him for his influence on my life during the last twenty-five years. I have spent more hours of sustained, vigorous—and sometimes overexcited—conversations about ideas with him than with anyone else, at his homes in New York and Florida, at his estate in Maryland, where he overlooks the work of his Wye Institute, or on trips abroad that my wife and I have taken with him. There is no matter of intellectual substance in which Arthur, once acquainted with it, does not become actively interested. Once, when he visited me in San Francisco, I mentioned my fascination with the theological doctrine of angels. Conversation after conversation about the nature and properties of angels led Arthur to invite me to New York to deliver a lecture on angelology before the assembled artists of Steuben Glass, with the possibility in mind that glass angels might be designed. A bas-relief in glass of the archangel Raphael was created for the Kennedy Foundation, but for technical reasons glass angels in the round never took their place alongside the animals in Steuben's crystal zoo. Because of the extraordinary range of his intellectual interests, Arthur Houghton has been able to turn every activity in which he engages into a leisure pursuit, in the true sense of that word which means learning and the cultivation of the mind and spirit, not play, recreation, or amusement. Because learning is as amusing to him as play is for most men, he has never had to kill time or fill it with light diversions. He has never been bored and he never will be. He comes as near as anyone I know to being the ideal amateur philosopher that everyone should wish to be.

One regrettable consequence of the pressing need to raise money to keep the institute going was the decision we felt compelled to make to publish the first volume of *The Idea of Freedom* before the second could be completed and published. The first volume was widely and favorably reviewed; the acclaim it received was more than I had hoped for. The most gratifying accolade came from Prof. Brand Blanshard of Yale, who declared that "the impartiality . . . is judicial and almost regal. Mr. Adler never chides and never raises voice or eyebrow." In his review in the *New York Times,* Blanshard said that the book

> threads its way through a maze of heads and subheads with admirable patience, thoroughness, and lucidity. . . . If one wants a general clarification of the problems of freedom, there is nothing in English to compare with this book.

Professor Hale, in the *Columbia Law Review,* confirmed Blanshard's judgment that the author of the book and his associates had "adhered to the goal of impartiality which they set before themselves."

The separate publication of the second volume three years after the first prevented most reviewers from appraising the work as a whole. The two volumes were integrally related, the first containing material strictly preparatory for the analysis of the controversies in the second. Most reviewers did not bother to examine the second volume in the light of the first, or to reassess the first in relation to the second. However, a few did; and one had this to say about the two volumes viewed as parts of one whole. In the *Philosophical Quarterly,* Prof. C. A. Campbell wrote:

> In reviewing Vol. I of this work I qualified my general commendation of it by confessing to a mild doubt whether its value was quite commensurate with the enormous labour its production had obviously entailed. After reading Vol. II I find that my doubts have largely vanished. The work is, of course, one to consult rather than to read straight through. But as so used—and, despite its bulk, good craftsmanship has made it surprisingly easy to consult—its comprehensive, orderly, lucid pinpointing of the really vital questions should be of signal service to philosophy. If philosophers concerned with freedom avail themselves of the guidance here offered, controversies in this sphere should in future be a great deal less conspicuous for confusion and misunderstandings than they unfortunately are today.

From 1956 to the present, the institute has operated with a reduced budget and a reduced staff, but in that time, in addition to my two volumes of *The Idea of Freedom,* my associates have worked on and produced books about four other great ideas—the ideas of Justice, Love, Progress, and Happiness. They are currently at work on still other ideas—Equality, Good, Art, Religion, and Beauty. The treatments of Justice, Love, Progress, and Happiness could not be as comprehensive as the treatment of Freedom. Nevertheless, like *The Idea of Freedom,* the books about these other subjects resulted from collaborative work, and were dialectical clarifications of issues and dialectical constructions of disputes about those issues.

While supervising these institute efforts, I also wrote seven books of my own. The first two, both published in 1958, the year that the first volume of *The Idea of Freedom* appeared, had little connection with the institute's work, though one, *The Revolution in Education* (written in collaboration with Milton Mayer), was based on the papers that I had submitted as the basis for a discussion of education at the Ford Foundation seminar on education in the early fifties; and the other, *The Capitalist Manifesto,* was written with Louis Kelso, with whom I became acquainted through his interest in the institute and who subsequently became a member of its Board of Directors. The remaining five profited from collaboration with my associates at the institute; and, while not strictly a dialectical construction, each dealt with basic philosophical issues.

It was Jacques Maritain who persuaded me not to devote all my energies to merely dialectical work for the sake of philosophical advances to be made by others. He thought that such devotion was too self-sacrificing and that, while carrying on the work of the institute, for which his enthusiasm never waned, I should write books that expressed my own understanding of philosophical doctrines that I could defend as true. Pulling against Maritain was Arthur Rubin, for whom the pursuit of dialectical, as opposed to doctrinal, truth was paramount. Arthur never wearied under the restraints of the dialectical task, as I must confess I did. That, I think, ultimately won me over to Maritain's side of the argument.

I still think that the fulfillment of the institute's ideal—a dialectical summation of Western thought in the sphere of every one of its great ideas—would make an invaluable contribution to progress in philosophy, perhaps not in the present generation, but in the longer future. My initial conviction that the work the institute set out to do was needed for the sake of genuine advances in philosophical thought was confirmed by the results of the dialectical work we did on Freedom. In the concluding pages of the second volume of *The Idea of Freedom,* I was compelled to make the following rather dismal appraisal of the whole of Western thought so far on the subject of freedom.

> There may be considerable difference of opinion about whether the state of the controversies about freedom is what might have been expected in view of the nature of the philosophical enterprise as a whole, and the generally recognized defects of discussion when it deals with difficult subjects. But if the idea of rational debate is appropriate to the philosophical enterprise, as we think it is, then it would be hard to gainsay the fact that what has been accomplished in twenty-five centuries of Western thought about freedom is a very poor performance, indeed.
>
> Individual thinkers have presented us with elaborate theories and have told us, with clarity and cogency, the reasons for the conclusions they have reached about freedom. There has been no dearth of theoretical in-

sights, no lack of originality or variety. Century after century, great intellectual resources have been lavished on the discussion of freedom. The signal contributions of individual genius have started new ways of thinking about the subject and enriched or deepened others. Yet the fact remains that the profound disagreements which have emerged from all this intellectual effort have not become well-disputed issues in a sustained and rationally conducted series of controversies about freedom.

I do not think this estimate is exaggerated. If I am right, there can be little hope for much progress in philosophical thought—about freedom, or any other fundamental idea—unless the project of a *Summa Dialectica* is somehow completed, if not by the Institute for Philosophical Research, then by some other agency.

3. Britannica 3

After living in New York City the first twenty-seven years of my life, then moving to Chicago and living there for the next twenty-two years, I might have expected, when I made my next move westward, to settle on San Francisco as my permanent home. That, however, was not the way things turned out. I lived there only ten years. In 1963, the Institute for Philosophical Research, which had opened its doors in San Francisco in 1952, was relocated in Chicago, where I have been living ever since.

The move back to Chicago might not have occurred had not Senator Benton wished me to play a more active part in the affairs of the Encyclopaedia Britannica company. When he wanted something, Bill knew how to be persuasive. I could not resist his offer, which permitted me to wear three hats. It not only allowed me to continue as director of the Institute for Philosophical Research while serving as a consultant to Britannica, but it also involved the establishment of a Britannica Lectureship at the University of Chicago, with me as the first incumbent. I had delayed writing a number of philosophical books for which I had been making notes over the years. The Britannica Lectureship required my meeting certain deadlines, and so the writing of these books would take precedence over more urgent, though less important, demands on my time. Without such external checks, it is difficult to avoid giving priority to the urgent rather than to the important. That alone might have decided me in favor of the move back to Chicago, but the invitation became irresistible when Bill Benton offered me a contract that gave me financial security for the rest of my life.

I have not yet told the whole story, I must confess. During the ten years I lived in San Francisco, I continued my connections with Encyclopaedia Britannica, Inc. Having sold the first 500 sets of *Great Books of the Western World* in order to launch its publication, I became interested in doing whatever I could to promote the sale of subsequent printings and to help the sales effort after a Great Books sales force had been organized. I enjoyed talking at sales meetings on the art of salesmanship, presenting a compact summary of Aristotle's formulation of the three basic factors operative in persuading anyone to do anything— *ethos, pathos,* and *logos.* (Once, when I explained to an audience of advertising men in San Francisco the meaning of those three terms in Aristotle's *Rhetoric,* the bookstores of the city reported an extraordinary—and to them quite puzzling—demand for copies of the book.) In addition to making myself useful in this way, Bob Hutchins and I edited, with the help of Clifton Fadiman and Charles Van Doren, another set of books—a collection of shorter classics, assembled in ten volumes under the title *Gateway to the Great Books* (published in 1963); while still in San Francisco, I worked out the plans for an annual publication to be sold to purchasers of the Great Books—*The Great Ideas Today.* It first appeared in 1961, with Bob Hutchins and me as its co-editors, and it has been issued every year since then.

I mention these things in order to say that I might have responded to Bill Benton's urging me to return to Chicago by pointing out what I had been doing for his Encyclopaedia Britannica company while living in San Francisco. I was already wearing two hats in San Francisco. I could even discharge my obligations under the Britannica Lectureship at the University of Chicago by commuting to the Middle West to deliver the lectures on schedule. I might have been able to counter Bill Benton's persuasive efforts by trying to persuade him to substitute San Francisco for Chicago in the contract he was offering me. But when Bill first suggested the move back to Chicago, I was not only open to the suggestion, I jumped at it.

Without knowing it, Bill had approached me at a time when the opportunity to start a new life in another city was more attractive than all the other elements in his offer. A love affair, which resulted in my separation and divorce from Helen, had come to a disastrous climax. A year and a half later, with both of these things behind me, I fell in love with Caroline Pring, my editorial assistant on *Gateway to the Great Books.* In the very months that Bill began talking to me about Chicago, I nurtured secret hopes of persuading Caroline to marry me. Things worked out perfectly. Caroline and I were married in February 1963; the contract with Britannica was signed in March; Caroline and I took up residence in Chicago in April, and the institute moved there in June.

Between 1963 and 1966, while carrying on the work of the institute and delivering the first and second series of Britannica Lectures at the University of Chicago (which resulted in the publication of *The Conditions of Philosophy* and *The Difference of Man and The Difference*

It Makes), I somehow managed to find enough time to work on a number of editorial projects for Britannica, as well as serve the company as a consultant. Charles Van Doren, who moved to Chicago from New York to join me in both institute and Britannica work, made these accomplishments feasible. Together, abetted by an able staff, we edited three sets of books—*The Annals of America,* in 20 volumes, published in 1968; *The Negro in American History,* in 3 volumes, published in 1969; and *The Makers of America,* in 10 volumes, published in 1971. All three sets consisted of documentary materials, not just state papers or official records, but letters, editorials, speeches, poems, songs, etc. Adapting the principles underlying the Syntopicon and employing the same methods, we produced, to accompany *The Annals of America,* a two-volume Conspectus, "Great Issues in American Life." This consisted of 25 chapters, modelled on the Syntopicon's 102 chapters on the great ideas. It was designed to help a reader find, among the documentary materials contained in the *Annals,* the passages relevant to a particular issue and even a particular topic connected with that issue.

If I were to include the 30 volumes of the new 15th edition of *Britannica,* and the more than a dozen volumes of *The Great Ideas Today,* the editorial products I have worked on since the Syntopicon began in 1943 add up to well over 140 volumes. Of all of these, the one that I always regarded as out of my territory—the one I did not think of becoming involved in when I returned to Chicago in 1963—was the encyclopaedia itself. Yet, from 1966 until 1974, that turned out to be my major editorial assignment for the magnitude and difficulty of which eight years of work on the Syntopicon provided some preparation. In fact, the Syntopicon did more than prepare me for planning a brand-new edition of *Britannica,* reconceived, reconstructed, and rewritten; it led me into doing it.

In 1948, as work on the Syntopicon neared completion, the memorandum that Bill Gorman and I wrote to the Board of Editors of Britannica pointed out that an alphabetical order of articles, together with an alphabetical index of their contents, may serve the purpose of those who go to an encyclopaedia to look something up—some particular fact or item of information, or even the knowledge available about a particular subject. But it impedes the effort of those who try to use this compendium of knowledge to study systematically and thoroughly a whole field of subject matter. In the discussion of our memorandum, Bob Hutchins remarked that a topically organized encyclopaedia could perform the educational function much better than an alphabetically organized one, but he also conceded that, even with an alphabetical index, a topical encyclopaedia might be less useful as a reference work. On the assumption that the encyclopaedia would remain alphabetical in organization (an assumption confirmed by Bill Benton's strong opposition to converting *Britannica* into a topical encyclopaedia), Gorman and I proposed the construction of an introductory volume that would serve the encyclopaedia as the Syntopicon was designed to serve the set of great books—giving the reader an overview of the contents in terms of systematically organized categories and topics.

After discussing the idea at several meetings of the Board of Editors, the matter was dropped. More than ten years elapsed before we again focussed our attention on how to improve the encyclopaedia by reconstructing it instead of merely revising its contents. The renewed discussion of this problem in 1961 was occasioned by the imminence, in 1968, of the 200th anniversary of the *Britannica*'s first publication. I wrote a memorandum in 1961 entitled "The Restructuring of EB," and followed this up in 1963 with another that revived, with a new twist, the earlier proposal of an introductory volume to survey the organization of knowledge contained in the encyclopaedia.

> We should construct for EB an orderly and intelligible Table of Contents, which would set forth the basic structure of the encyclopaedia as a systematic report of what is known in all major fields of art and science.

This Table of Contents "would put the leading articles and their subordinate parts into an intelligible order, while at the same time leaving them in their alphabetical arrangement in the encyclopaedia itself." This memorandum also suggested restructuring the encyclopaedia, something the Board of Editors had been considering for a number of years: separating the leading articles on major subjects from short entries providing readily accessible information about a much larger number of minor or subordinate subjects.

These suggestions were not acted on in time to produce that new edition for the 200th anniversary of the *Britannica* in 1968. The Board of Editors continued to debate the alternatives of alphabetical and topical organization; the revision of major articles continued; but by 1965 no steps had been taken to break away from the traditional structure of the encyclopaedia and the traditional methods of editing and revising it. Nevertheless, as the 200th anniversary approached, both Bill Benton and Bob Hutchins resolved that every effort should be made, and no expense spared, to produce a reconstructed encyclopaedia. In March 1965, I wrote Maurice Mitchell, then president of Britannica, a memorandum outlining the steps to be taken to produce a new encyclopaedia within the next ten years. A second memorandum urged that the initial indispensable step must be the construction of a systematic, topical table of contents for an encyclopaedia that still retained an alphabetical organization of its major and minor articles. This would resolve the apparently irresolvable conflict between the alphabetical and topical principles of organization by combining in one encyclopaedia the virtues of both.

Things nows began to move. By the end of April, Warren Preece, the editor in chief, and his editorial associates were asked to draw up budgets for the work to be done in accordance with "Plan B"—the name given to the scheme outlined in my various memoranda. My old friend Kip Fadiman and I put our heads together to consider what was involved in constructing a topical table of contents for an alphabetically organized encyclopaedia. We soon realized that the task was much larger and more difficult than we at first supposed. What it called for was a comprehensive and systematic outline of the knowledge to be covered in a general encyclopaedia. That would require the labors of a fairly large staff of competent editors and academic consultants; in addition, in order to get that work started, we needed a provisional scheme for developing the outline. It looked at first as if an ordering of fields of subject matter might appear to grade them in importance or to relate them according to some arbitrarily selected set of principles. Because of this, I even suggested, at one point, the construction of "a pluralistic table of contents"—a set of alternative outlines, each organized on different principles.

Another whole year of false starts and troubled discussions went by before we finally came to grips with the job to be done. In June 1966, I was made chairman of the Editorial Planning Committee and assigned the task of outlining the knowledge to be covered in our projected new edition of the *Encyclopaedia Britannica*. For a while, we referred to this outline as a "Table of Contents," even though that was obviously a misnomer, since the articles which would comprise the contents were not yet written, or even solicited from contributors. The definitive table of contents for a book is usually drawn up after a book is written, not before it is started. This is especially true of a detailed, analytical table of contents. Here we were trying to draw up that kind of table of contents for a multivolumed work before a single word of it was written.

What we were doing, of course, was constructing a Table of Intents, not a Table of Contents. When completed, it would provide us with the basis for determining the subjects of the articles to be written, for specifying what should be covered in those articles, for treating similar subjects in similar fashion, and for putting articles about related subjects into relation with one another. It would give the editorial staff a detailed blueprint for commissioning articles and editing them. After all the articles were in hand and edited, the Table of Intents could be converted into a Table of Contents, by accommodating it to the actual substance of the articles in the encyclopaedia.

The work of constructing the Table of Intents took the Editorial Planning Committee from July 1966 to June 1968, and was completed on schedule. During that time, the committee met several times a week. The meetings were attended by all the administrative and principal editors and usually included one or more consultants who were specialists in various departments of knowledge. The outline of knowledge went through innumerable drafts and revisions, based not only on the criticisms or recommendations of the Planning Committee, but also upon criticisms or recommendations solicited from the encyclopaedia's academic consultants and advisors all over the world.

The insight that the various parts in the outline of knowledge might be ordered in a circular, rather than a rectilinear, fashion solved the problem of appearing to give one branch of knowledge precedence over another. A finite straight line has a beginning point and an end point, but a circle, though finite, has no beginning or end. To conceive the various parts as being related to one another as segments in a circle of learning has, in addition, a certain aptness; the Greek roots of the word *encyclopaedia* literally mean "circle of learning," or "circle of knowledge." However, it was still necessary for purpose of reference to number the ten parts, even though Part One was not first in any preferential order, nor Part Ten last. To the ten parts that we finally settled on, we gave the following titles:

Part One:	Matter and Energy
Part Two:	The Earth
Part Three:	Life on Earth
Part Four:	Human Life
Part Five:	Human Society
Part Six:	The Arts
Part Seven:	Technology
Part Eight:	Religion
Part Nine:	The History of Mankind
Part Ten:	The Branches of Knowledge

We broke each of the ten parts into a number of divisions, and each of the divisions into a number of subordinate sections. It was only after we passed to the next level that we began to formulate and order the subjects that would be covered in each section of the whole. Weeks of frustrated effort went by before we understood the distinction between titles or headings and the subjects to be covered under them. That distinction occurred to me in a moment of despair, when I was about ready to say the job could not be done. It reminded me of the early days of work on the Syntopicon, before I thought of an elaborately phrased topic rather than the single word as the unit of indexing. In both cases, the insight came as a result of putting down on paper all the reasons why the undertaking appeared to be an impossible one. The mind under rigorous constraint develops the energy and ingenuity needed to break out of the box. This is the Houdini formula on the intellectual plane.

As in the case of the Syntopicon, the work of the Editorial Planning Committee permitted me to give almost unlimited vent to my passion for outlining. To draw up the 102 outlines of topics in the Syntopicon, Bill Gorman and I could rely on our own knowledge of the contents of the great books and their discussion of the great ideas. But when it came to outlining the whole range of knowledge to be covered in a comprehensive general encyclopaedia, it was necessary to rely on the work of editors or consultants who were specialists in the various fields to be treated. Few of my associates in this effort possessed the skill requisite for outlining. Some, including eminent scholars, were embarrassingly inept at the task, even to the point of not knowing how to number or arrange matters that were supraordinate, coordinate, or subordinate. Obviously, the art of outlining is no longer an ingredient in general or liberal schooling, with unfortunate consequences for much that is currently written and published.

Just about midway in the development of the outline of knowledge, an intervention by Bill Benton threatened the whole project. It occurred in the summer of 1967. Caroline and I and our two boys were in Aspen, where I was conducting an Executive Seminar in which Bill participated. At the end of the seminar, I drove him to the airport. As he boarded the flight to Denver, he told me that he was thinking of inviting Sir William Haley to become editor in chief of the new encyclopaedia, replacing Warren Preece. My immediate reaction was negative. Haley had been editor of the *Manchester Guardian,* then director-general of the BBC, and now was editor of *The Times* of London. We had met earlier that year, in May when he visited Chicago and sat through a whole day's exposition, by Warren Preece and me, of our plan for the new encyclopaedia. My impression of him raised serious doubts in my mind whether the plan would ever be carried out by him as editor, a fear I expressed in a letter to the president of the company at the time.

After Benton's plane took off, I drove home and went immediately to my typewriter to pound out an angry four-page letter to the Senator, reiterating in even stronger language what I had written Mitchell in May. If we were simply revising *Britannica,* Haley's editorial skills would undoubtedly be useful to us. He would certainly set a high standard of literary excellence to be met by our contributors and he would use his editorial blue pencil with great skill to help achieve the level of writing he sought. But we were constructing a new encyclopaedia, on a plan that had been approved by the Board of Editors, and for that purpose the control of the work should be in the hands of those who had formulated the plan and understood it. Preece and I working together formed a team that Haley could not replace without disastrous consequences. I urged Benton to rescind his invitation, telling him that he was making an expensive mistake, one that would turn out to be costly to us in time as well as money.

My protests did not deter Benton from gratifying his wish to have an English knight as editor in chief. He compounded what I believed to be his initial mistake by giving Haley the authority to review the editorial principles and policies of Plan B and to decide whether he would carry them out or substitute instead some other plan of his own. The fact that Haley requested such authority as a condition of his acceptance of the invitation made me respect him; but it also should have warned Benton, and everyone else concerned, that Haley already had serious reservations about Plan B. Remarks he made revealed that his encyclopaedic ideal was the 11th edition of *Britannica,* published in 1910. He seemed to be quite satisfied to produce an updated, revised, and rewritten 11th edition. It soon became apparent that he had little sympathy for the reasons why we thought it necessary to restructure the encyclopaedia.

When Sir William Haley became editor in chief in January of 1968, I stated plainly that I would be willing to work *with* him on the same basis that I had worked with Warren Preece, with equal authority for carrying out Plan B, but that I would not work *for* him, especially if he contemplated any departure from the plan. I completed the semifinal draft of the Table of Intents. Having delivered to Sir William the basic blueprint, I withdrew to the sidelines, but I kept in touch with what was going on. Warren Preece and other former associates kept me informed of the direction Sir William seemed to be taking. I wrote countless letters during the next nine months, many to Haley in a vain effort to defend this or that aspect of Plan B, and others to Bob Hutchins, Bill Benton, and Charles Swanson (who had succeeded Maurice Mitchell as president of the company)—letters that were Cassandra-like predictions of impending doom and increasingly angry protests against the scuttling of Plan B.

In November 1968, the 200th anniversary of *Encyclopaedia Britannica* was celebrated by a grand dinner at the Guild Hall in London, attended by almost a thousand persons, the vast majority of whom were contributors from the United Kingdom. Speaking on that occasion, Sir William made it patently clear that, faced with the alternatives of carrying on an ancient tradition or instituting innovations, he definitely favored tradition over innovation. As he uttered that sentiment from the rostrum, he looked directly at me.

I got the message, but Benton and Hutchins were not yet disposed to read it loud and clear. What finally brought them around to my way of thinking occurred by indirection. Haley, at a meeting of the Board of Editors, submitted specifications for the new encyclopaedia which called for 47, instead of 41, million words. When, under question from management during the early months of 1969, Sir William persisted in defending his specifications, it gradually became clear to everyone concerned that Haley's conception of the new encyclopaedia departed from certain principles essential to Plan B and would result in the production of an encyclopaedia probably too expensive for the market. The latter fact might well have been sufficient to end Haley's occupancy of his office; but the issue over editorial principles finally came to a head. At a Board of Editors' meeting in April 1969, Sir William's negative reply to the question whether, if given absolutely free rein, he would have adopted all the provisions of Plan B, preceded by only a few hours his letter of resignation as editor in chief.

Warren Preece was restored to his post as top editor; I became his closest associate as director of editorial planning. I also acted as chairman of an Editorial Executive Committee, in which was vested the ultimate authority for critical editorial decisions. From May 1969 until the end of the job, the heavy burden of editing over 40 million words fell on the shoulders of Warren Preece and his very able executive editor, Tom Goetz. That was the toughest job of all. Warren and Tom had more to manage than they could handle easily; their whole editorial group was just one of many interlocking elements in the picture. To solve the problem of fitting all the elements together so that they meshed smoothly in an incredibly complicated schedule and met inexorably demanding deadlines, Charles Swanson asked me to assume the post of project manager, with the responsibility of ensuring that the 15th edition would be printed, bound, and ready for distribution on time. No one else who knew enough about the project was available to take that responsibility; in addition, I had a record of meeting publication deadlines without fail and a reputation for driving my co-workers beyond what they regarded as their normal limits.

I served as project manager from January 1971 until publication day in February 1974. During that time, the publication date had to be moved, first from January 1973 to April 1973 (because we had not been able to make up for editorial delays), and then to January 1974 (because we lost about nine months as a result of our failure with computer typesetting). The last eighteen months was a period of greater tension than I had ever before experienced. There were daily meetings of the managers of the various departments that represented all the elements in the production picture, getting reports each day of quotas made or missed, compensating for failures by setting new and more onerous quotas, shifting or adjusting deadlines, and overcoming each day's crises only to have new ones emerge the following day.

For twenty-six consecutive months, in order to meet our deadlines, we sent between 400,000 and 500,000 words of edited, copy-edited, proofread, and illustrated manuscript to the printer each week. Weekly news-

290 PHILOSOPHER AT LARGE

magazines, such as *Time* and *Newsweek,* with very large staffs, deliver to their printers about 75,000 to 80,000 words a week, words produced in their own shops. Ours had to come in on schedule each week from contributors all over the world, in many cases in foreign languages that had to be translated into English; in addition, professors, who constituted the majority of our learned contributors, can be amazingly light-hearted about meeting deadlines.

One other fact increased the tension I felt in discharging my responsibilities as project manager. In the publication of trade books, the failure to meet a publication date may be serious, but it is not a disaster. With the *Encyclopaedia Britannica,* as with other expensive sets of books, the case is different. Consumers have never developed the habit of buying sets of books in bookstores. They have to be called on to be sold. A direct-to-consumer sales force is indispensable for distribution in sufficient quantity to be profitable. Of course, a sales force must have the books to sell. Here was the problem that confronted us. The 1973 printing of *Encyclopaedia Britannica* would be sold out by the end of that year. If the new *Britannica* were not ready for sale early in 1974— if we were late by as much as four months—the sales force would have no sets to deliver. This could conceivably result in the company's bankruptcy. A catastrophe thus loomed before us, and the responsibility for avoiding it fell on my shoulders with increasing pressure every day. Fortunately, I had a number of devoted colleagues who were as concerned as I, and as determined that we should come out on time. We made it. The 15th edition of *Encyclopaedia Britannica,* called "Britannica 3," was presented to a press conference in New York on January 15, 1974, and to another press conference the very next morning in London, to which Warren Preece and I flew overnight.

We called the 15th edition "Britannica 3" in order to draw everyone's attention to the three-part structure of the new encyclopaedia. Before the Syntopicon was published, I thought it necessary to coin a word to name our invention of an idea-index. So here I thought it advisable to coin words to name the three parts of the new encyclopaedia. There was considerable reluctance to adopt these coined words, but they finally appeared on the spines and title pages of the volumes. We called the Outline of Knowledge a "Propaedia," which, Englishing the Greek roots, means an introduction to learning or knowledge; we called the nineteen volumes of long, scholarly essays on major subjects a "Macropaedia," which means large units of learning or knowledge; we called the ten volumes of short entries on minor subjects a "Micropaedia," which means small units of learning or knowledge. It did not take long for these names to become familiar and accepted—by reviewers, by the public, and even by the advertising copywriters and the sales force.

Before publication day, Warren Preece and I would gladly have settled for an even break on the critical appraisals of the set by competent scholars—half favorable and half unfavorable. With almost all of the critical notices now in, many of them painstaking and extensive reviews of the new *Britannica*, the pleasing fact is that only a very small fraction have been adverse. Of those only a few have pointed out defects that we can and will correct, defects not so much in the plan itself as in our execution of it.

The painful truth is that the work of an encyclopaedist is never finished, because facts change and knowledge expands, and because there is always room for improvement. *Britannica 3* will undoubtedly be improved in the years ahead. In my judgment, the principles that underlie its structuring and editing are sufficiently sound and the execution of those principles is sufficiently good to justify the perpetuation of the 15th edition until well into the next century, when someone may devise a different plan for a new edition.

Chapter 14

Philosopher at Large

The ancient garden where most men
Step daintily, in specimen dust,
He bulldozes; plows deep;
Moves earth; says someone must,
If truth is ever to be found
That so long since went underground.

What truth? Why down? He shakes his head.
He does not know. But roots and rocks
Go tumbling, tearing, as his blade,
Shivering from its own shocks,
Bites farther, and upturns pure clay
He does not pause to smooth away.

And horrifies those men, by hedge
And dust plot, whom the top sufficed.
They thought the garden theirs. And still
It is; but the dead air is spiced
With damp new things dug up. Or old,
He says; like God, like buried gold.

The poem written by Mark Van Doren and dedicated to me bears the same title as this chapter. I am far from sure that I know what Mark had in mind when he used the words *at large* to qualify *philosopher*. Two possible meanings have occurred to me: a philosopher *at large* is one who is not confined within academic walls; he is also a generalist in philosophy, not a specialist in ethics or aesthetics, the philosophy of science or the theory of knowledge. The poem epitomizes a seldom-recognized characteristic of Aristotle, both as a philosopher and in relation to his predecessors—the Aristotle who said, it is necessary to call into council the views of our predecessors, in order that we may profit by whatever is sound in their thought and avoid their errors;

because he realized that

the investigation of the truth is in one way hard, in another easy. An indication of this is found in the fact that no one is able to attain the truth adequately, while, on the other hand, we do not collectively fail.

If I were to label myself an Aristotelian, I would mean not only that I have tried to philosophize in Aristotle's manner and with his temper, but also that my search for philosophical truth has always reached bedrock only when it succeeded in digging down to the foundations that Aristotle laid—foundations too often ignored in our day because they are now so far underground.

I have done many things with my life, but the single thread running through it that ties it together is the desire that impelled me, as a boy, to give up journalism for college—the desire to imitate Socrates by following the leads opened up by the kind of difficult questions he asked, the desire to use my mind reflectively in the pursuit of the most fundamental truths, in short, the desire to be a philosopher. Plato presided over my initiation into this career. His dialogues raised many, if not all, the questions that any philosopher must ponder. But I soon discovered in the treatises of Aristotle the clues to where and how the answers might be found. It was my inestimable good fortune that Professor Woodbridge not only displayed unusual eloquence in his exposition of Aristotle, but also convincingly communicated his judgment that the high point in the whole history of philosohy had been reached very early—in the work of Aristotle.

I believe I can say, without inaccuracy or exaggeration, that almost all of the philosophical truths that I have come to know and understand I have learned from Aristotle, or from Thomas Aquinas as a student of Aristotle, or from Jacques Maritain as a student of both Aristotle and Aquinas. I have admiration for a few modern philosophers—two in particular I have read with delight and sympathy, John Locke and John Stuart Mill. But I cannot attribute to them the origin of a single truth that I cherish, with the possible exception of the truth that democracy is the only perfectly just form of government. It is mainly in the field of political philosophy that the thought of the ancients is both erroneous and defective and needs correcting and enlarging in the light of insights developed in modern times. Even here, I find it necessary to add that modern advances are unfortunately accompanied by the fiction that civil society came into being as the result of a contract entered into by men living anarchically in the state of nature. Aristotle and Aquinas would not have had to employ that fiction in order to explain the truth that modern thinkers such as Hobbes, Locke, and Rousseau were reaching for—the truth that the state, or political community, is both natural and conventional, natural in the sense that it is needed for a good human life (or at least a better one than men could live in a hypothetical state of nature), and conventional in the sense that it is voluntarily instituted and constituted, not the product of instinctive determination as is the beehive or the anthill.

To say, as I have said, that I have not learned a single fundamental truth from the writings of modern philosophers is not to say that I have learned nothing at all from them. With the exception of Hegel and other post-Kantian German philosophers, I have read their works with both pleasure and profit. The pleasure has come from the perception of errors the serious consequences of which tend to reinforce my hold on the truths I have learned from Aristotle and Aquinas. The profit has come from the perception of new but genuine problems, not the pseudo-problems, perplexities, and puzzlements invented by therapeutic positivism and by linguistic or analytical philosophy in our own century.

The genuine problems to which I am referring are questions that have been generated under the cultural circumstances characteristic of modern times, especially the effect on philosophy of its gradually recognized distinction from investigative science and from dogmatic theology, as well as the effect on it of certain developments in modern science and certain revolutionary changes in the institutions of modern society.

The profit to be derived from the perception of these problems (of which Aristotle and Aquinas were not aware or were only dimly aware) is the stimulus it gives us to try to extend their thought in response to them. I have always found that I could solve such problems within the general framework and in the light of the basic principles of their thought. They may not have faced the questions that we are obliged to answer, but they nevertheless do provide us with the clues or leads needed for discovering the answers.

Many years ago, in our early days together at the University of Chicago, my friend Dick McKeon once quipped that the difference between the members of the American Philosophical Association and the members of the American Catholic Philosophical Association was that philosophers in our secular universities specialized in very good and novel questions, to which the scholastic philosophers did not yet have the answers, whereas the scholastics had a rich supply of true principles and conclusions but usually failed to be aware of many important questions to the answering of which they could be applied. My own experience has confirmed the wisdom as well as the wit of that observation. Let me illustrate the point by one example drawn from some work that I have been doing recently in political and economic philosophy, which concerns the relation of liberty and of equality to justice.

The following questions have, in various forms, pervaded the thinking of the last hundred and fifty years about liberty and equality. Of these two goods, the circumstantial freedom of individuals in society and the equality of conditions under which individuals may live in society, which is the supreme or sovereign value? Should individual freedom be encroached upon to establish a complete equality of conditions? Should inequalities of condition be allowed to remain if that is necessary to maximize individual freedom? Is there some way of reconciling liberty and equality so that the ideal that each represents can be served without sacrificing the other?

As far as I know, these questions do not appear in ancient or mediaeval thought, certainly not with the clarity and explicitness with which modern thinkers have posed them. I must also say that, as far as I know, sound answers to these questions cannot be found in modern thought. Quite the contrary! Such answers as can be found there are, upon close examination, unsatisfactory—inadequate and untenable. However, recourse to the wisdom of Aristotelian and Thomistic thought provides us with two crucial insights which hold the key that will solve these modern problems. The first is that neither liberty nor equality is a supreme or sovereign value. Justice is sovereign; the pursuit of both liberty and equality must be regulated by criteria of justice. When they are so regulated, there is no irreconcilable conflict between efforts to maximize liberty on the one hand and efforts to maximize equality on the other, for neither should be maximized beyond a limit appointed by justice. We should not seek more liberty than justice allows, for beyond this limit lies not liberty, but license—actions that injure other individuals or the community as a whole. We should not seek more equality than justice requires, an equality with respect to all the external goods or conditions to which everyone has a natural and, therefore, an equal right. Within these limits, both equality and liberty can be maximized without conflict.

In the eyes of my contemporaries, the label "Aristotelian" has dyslogistic connotations: it has had such connotations since the beginning of modern times. To call a man an Aristotelian carries with it highly derogatory implications. It suggests that his is a closed mind, in such slavish subjection to the thought of one philosopher as to be impervious to the insights or arguments of others. However, it is certainly possible to be an Aristotelian—or the devoted disciple of some other philosopher—without also being a blind and slavish adherent of his views, declaring with misplaced piety that he is right in everything he says, never in error, or that he has cornered the market on truth and is in no respect deficient or defective.

Such a declaration would be so preposterous that only a fool would affirm it. Foolish Aristotelians there must have been among the decadent scholastics who taught philosophy in the universities of the sixteenth and seventeenth centuries. They probably account for the vehemence of the reaction against Aristotle, as well as the flagrant misapprehension or ignorance of his thought, that is to be found in Thomas Hobbes and Francis Bacon, in Descartes, Spinoza, and Leibniz. The folly is not the peculiar affliction of Aristotelians. Cases of it can certainly be found, in the last century, among those who gladly called themselves Kantians or Hegelians; and in our own day, among those who take pride in being disciples of John Dewey or Ludwig Wittgenstein. But if it is possible to be a follower of one of the modern thinkers without going to an extreme that is foolish, it is no less possible to be an Aristotelian who rejects his errors and deficiencies while embracing the truths he is able to teach.

I think the published record will support my claim to being an enlightened Aristotelian. I have written articles and books that focussed on deficiencies or errors in the thought of Aristotle and Aquinas: for example, their erroneous position with respect to natural slavery; their inadequacies and mistakes in political theory; their failure to resolve their own inconsistencies with regard to the specific forms of life; their claim to have demonstrated the existence of God.

I will presently relate the stubborn opposition I encountered from colleagues who regarded themselves as Aristotelians and Thomists when I published such criticisms of Aristotle and Aquinas. There were moments when I thought I knew how it felt to be an excommunicated heretic, or how it felt to be thrown out of the Party for being a Marxist revisionist. I mention these experiences here to substantiate two points, not one—the point that there are doctrinaire adherents of doctrines which have considerable truth in them, and the point that I am not one of them.

Even granting that it is possible to be an Aristotelian without being doctrinaire about it, it remains the case that being an Aristotelian is somehow less respectable in recent centuries and in our time than being a Kantian or a Hegelian, an existentialist, a utilitarian, a pragmatist, or some other "ist" or "ian." I know, for example, that many of my contemporaries were outraged by my statement that Aristotle's *Ethics* is

a unique book in the Western tradition of moral philosophy . . . the only ethics that is sound, practical, and undogmatic, offering what little normative wisdom there is for all men to be guided by, but refraining from laying down rules of conduct to cover the multifarious and contingent circumstances of human life. In the history of Western moral thought, it is the only book centrally concerned and concerned throughout with the goodness of a whole human life . . . and with putting the parts together in the right order and proportion.

That statement occurs in my Postscript to *The Time of Our Lives: The Ethics of Common Sense.* It is immediately followed by another statement to the effect that

> this book of mine contains formulations, analytical distinctions, arguments, and elaborations that cannot be found in the *Ethics;* in addition, the conceptions and insights taken from Aristotle are not simply adopted without modification, but adapted to fit together into a theoretical framework that is somewhat different from Aristotle's. . . . Much of what is new or altered in my formulation of the ethics of common sense results from my effort to defend its wisdom against philosophical objections that were unknown to Aristotle, or to correct misconceptions, misunderstandings, and ignorances that have dominated the scene in the last few hundred years.

If similar statements were made by a disciple of Kant or John Stuart Mill in a book that expounded and defended the Kantian or utilitarian position in moral philosophy, they would be received without raised eyebrows or shaking heads. For example, in this century, it has been said again and again, and gone unchallenged, that Bertrand Russell's theory of descriptions has been crucially pivotal in the philosophy of language; but it simply will not do for me to make exactly the same statement about the Aristotelian theory of signs (adding that it puts Russell's theory of descriptions into better perspective than the current view of it does).

Why is this so? My only answer is that it must be believed that, because Aristotle and Aquinas did their thinking so long ago, they cannot reasonably be supposed to have been right in matters about which those who came later were wrong. Much must have happened in the realm of philosophical thought during the last three or four hundred years that requires an open-minded person to abandon their teachings for something more recent and, therefore, supposedly better. My response to that view is negative. I have found faults in the writings of Aristotle and Aquinas, but it has not been my reading of modern philosophical works that has called my attention to these faults, or helped me to correct them. On the contrary, it has been my understanding of the underlying principles and the formative insights that govern the thought of Aristotle and Aquinas that has provided the basis for amending or amplifying their views where they are fallacious or defective.

The negative answer given above needs a few words of explanation if it is to be palatable. The explanation involves, first of all, a conception of philosophy itself that helps us to understand how an ancient or mediaeval philosopher can be superior to his modern successors; and,

second, a view of the history of philosophy in modern times that helps
us to understand why modern thinkers failed signally to improve upon
their predecessors.

The various conceptions of philosophy with which I first became acquainted left me very uncomfortable about my choice of philosophy as
a career. In one way or another they downgraded philosophy to a second-
rate enterprise, making it much less respectable than science as a pursuit of truth, either turning it into a handmaiden of science, or relegat-
ing it to the role of commentator on other primary disciplines, or,
even worse, conceding that it was more like personal opinion or a work
of the imagination than like certifiable and testable knowledge. Of all
the intellectual debts I owe Jacques Maritain, and they are many, the
greatest is for a conception of philosophy, especially in relation to the
empirical sciences, that gave it dignity and made it respectable as an
undertaking to which one might devote one's life.

That conception was elaborately set forth in Maritain's *Les Degrés du
Savoir,* published in 1932, but I first ran across it in his *Introduction to
Philosophy* (1930), and it became for me a vivid and controlling insight
after I heard him expound it in one of the first lectures he gave at the
University of Chicago. My efforts to assimilate it and develop all its implications have taken many years, during which I produced successively
more detailed, and I hope sounder and more mature, statements of the
view that philosophy, like science, is a body of knowledge, not a set of
opinions, knowledge of the world in which we live, of the nature of
things, of man and of society. As such it does not compete or conflict
with science.

My earliest statement, an *Analysis of the Kinds of Knowledge,* was
prepared in 1935 for students at the University of Chicago and exists
only in mimeographed form. That was soon followed, in 1937, by a
chapter on knowledge and opinion in *Art and Prudence* and by an extensive series of notes which I appended to my lectures on psychoanalysis, also published in 1937 under the title *What Man Has Made of Man.*
Those notes, together with an epilogue to the book considering the consequences of this view of philosophy for an interpretation of its history,
became the basis for two lectures that I gave, one entitled "Modern
Science and Ancient Wisdom," the other, "The Questions Science
Cannot Answer." But it was not until the early sixties that I finally
achieved a fully satisfactory exposition of the conception of philosophy
that had been germinating in my mind for almost thirty years. I presented it in the first series of Britannica Lectures at the University of
Chicago, which I turned into a book entitled *The Conditions of Philosophy,* published in 1965.

Once the likeness between philosophy and science is understood, it is
the difference between them which explains why philosophers who lived

hundreds or thousands of years ago were able to discover truths that still command our assent, whereas few if any scientific formulations of such ancient vintage do. Philosophy and science are alike in that both are justified in claiming to be knowledge rather than opinion. However the line is drawn between mere opinion, held as a matter of predilection, and valid knowledge that consists of certifiable and corrigible truths, philosophy no less than science belongs on the side of knowledge rather than opinion. As knowledge, they are further alike in that their conclusions, reached in the light of experience, are capable not only of being confirmed by experience, but also of being falsified or corrected by experience. To this extent philosophy is no less empirical than science. The difference between them emerges when we become more precise about the way in which each is empirical. The difference lies in the kind of experience to which each appeals and on which it relies.

The simplest way to express this difference is to say that science is investigative whereas philosophy, like mathematics, is not. The experience upon which the scientist relies is the product of his deliberate efforts to make observations under the control of definite questions and carried out by instruments or devices contrived for the purpose. To call the data of scientific investigation "special experience" is to say that it is *not* the experience men have in the course of their daily lives and that it would not exist but for the special investigative efforts of scientists. In contrast, what can be called "common or ordinary experience" is the experience that all of us have at every moment of our waking lives, without any special effort on our part to make observations, without any attempt on our part to answer definitely formulated questions, and without the employment of any instruments of observation or other special devices.

It is upon such common experience that philosophy as a noninvestigative mode of inquiry relies. Philosophical questions are questions that can be answered in the light of such experience, and therefore do not require investigation to answer. They are questions that investigation cannot be employed to answer, just as other questions, which do require investigation, cannot be answered by philosophers, but only by scientists. It is precisely because science and philosophy are different modes of empirical inquiry that each is limited to a set of questions appropriate to its method and inappropriate for the method of the other; and since they are concerned with answering different sets of questions, each is relatively autonomous, or independent of the other. Neither is in a position to challenge or invalidate the conclusions reached by the other when each stays within the domain of its own questions and proceeds by its own method.

Most important of all, scientific knowledge changes, grows, improves, expands as a result of refinements in and accretions to the special ex-

perience—the observational data—on which science as an investigative
mode of inquiry must rely. Philosophical knowledge is not subject to
the same conditions of change or growth. Common experience, or, more
precisely, the general lineaments of common experience which suffice
for the philosopher, remain relatively constant over the ages. Descartes
and Spinoza in the seventeenth century, or Alfred North Whitehead
and Martin Heidegger in the twentieth, enjoy no greater advantages
in this respect than Plato and Aristotle in antiquity, or than Thomas
Aquinas and Roger Bacon in the Middle Ages.

The great advantage (and a most important one) that the moderns
have over their predecessors stems from the fact that the line of de-
marcation between science and philosophy has been more clearly drawn
for them, and so they are safeguarded from venturing into territory
that is not theirs. But when ancient or mediaeval philosophers stayed
within their own domain (as sometimes they did not), when they were
concerned with those purely philosophical questions which science
cannot answer and to the answering of which the most advanced scientific knowledge is totally without relevance, their position in time in no
way affects the soundness or durability of the answers they formulated.

There are a certain number of mixed questions that cannot be answered solely by philosophical analysis or reflection, but require taking
into account the best scientific knowledge available. Here science op-
erates as a check on the answers philosophers propose. An example is
the question about the difference between man and other animals, or
between the human mind and the artificial intelligence of computers
or automata. I addressed myself to this type of mixed question in the
second series of Britannica Lectures at the University of Chicago, which
subsequently became *The Difference of Man and The Difference It
Makes*, published in 1967. The central thesis of that book—that man
differs in kind, not degree, from other animals—is one that Aristotle
affirmed more than two thousand years ago, and for which Aquinas
marshalled impressive arguments more than seven hundred years ago.
Nevertheless, new paleoanthropological evidence, scientific findings
about human and animal behavior, and technological achievements in
the field of computers required me to reformulate distinctions, to consider novel hypotheses, and to construct new arguments in order to re-
affirm a conclusion that Aristotle and Aquinas found easier to defend.

Since *The Difference of Man and The Difference It Makes* was published, scientific investigations have turned up additional evidence relevant to the problem—observations of linguistic performances on the
part of chimpanzees. That man, with the power of syntactical speech
and conceptual thought, differs in kind from all nonlinguistic animals
remains as clear and certain as before. As for the recent chimpanzee
studies, I still think it can be shown that their vocabularies, the way in

which they acquire the use of symbols, and the way in which they use them, are so radically different from human speech, even in the case of the human infant, that a difference in kind remains. I presented arguments to this effect in an article I wrote for *The Great Ideas Today* in 1975, but I was also careful to point out that further scientific research might turn up evidence to the contrary.

In contrast to theoretical questions, or questions of fact, some of which are purely philosophical questions and some mixed questions involving the consideration of the findings of science, all normative questions—all questions about good and evil, or about right and wrong—are purely philosophical. However, there is a difference between problems in moral and in political philosophy comparable to the difference between purely philosophical and mixed questions concerning matters of fact. In the sphere of ethics, my third series of Britannica Lectures (published under the title *The Time of Our Lives*) presented a modern version of Aristotle's *Ethics*—a version that was modern not in any of its essential insights, but only in the manner in which they were reformulated and in the arguments that had to be constructed against objections of recent origin. When, however, in my fourth series of Britannica Lectures, I came to deal with problems in political philosophy, the resulting book—*The Common Sense of Politics*—repudiated certain positions taken by Aristotle and Aquinas. In addition, it had to introduce considerations that derived from the writings of Locke, Rousseau, J. S. Mill, and Karl Marx, and it had to take account of institutional innovations and revolutionary changes that have occurred in the last few hundred years.

Having indicated the respects in which modern thought can improve upon the wisdom of the past, I must say once more that, with regard to purely philosophical questions in speculative philosophy—in metaphysics, in the theory of knowledge, in the philosophy of mind—few if any advances have been made in modern times. On the contrary, much has been lost as the result of errors that might have been avoided if ancient truths had been preserved in the modern period instead of being ignored. Why this happened needs to be explained.

Modern philosophy, as I see it, got off to a very bad start—with Hobbes and Locke in England, and with Descartes, Spinoza, and Leibniz on the Continent. Each of these thinkers acted as if he had no predecessors worth consulting, as if he were starting with a clean slate, to construct for the first time the whole of philosophical knowledge. We cannot find in their writings the slightest evidence of their sharing Aristotle's insight that no man by himself is able to attain the truth adequately, though collectively men do not fail to amass a considerable amount; nor do they ever manifest the slightest trace of a willingness to call into council the views of their predecessors in order to profit from whatever is sound in their thought and to avoid their errors. On the contrary, without anything like a careful, critical examination of the views of their predecessors, these modern thinkers issue blanket repudiations of the past as a repository of errors. The discovery of philosophical truth begins with themselves.

Proceeding, therefore, in ignorance or misunderstanding of truths that could have been found in the funded tradition of almost 2,000 years of Western thought, these modern philosophers made crucial mistakes, both in their points of departure and in their initial postulates— little errors in the beginning which, as Aristotle pointed out, usually lead to disastrous consequences in the end. The commission of these consequential errors can be explained in part by antagonism toward the past, and even contempt for it. The explanation of the antagonism lies in the character of the teachers under whom these modern philosophers studied in their youth. Instead of passing on the philosophical tradition as a living thing by recourse to the writings of the great philosophers of the past; instead of reading and commenting on the works of Aristotle, for example, as the great teachers of the thirteenth century did, the decadent scholastics who occupied teaching posts in the universities of the sixteenth and seventeenth centuries fossilized the tradition by presenting it in a deadly, dogmatic fashion, using a jargon that concealed, rather than conveyed, the insights it contained. Their lectures must have been as wooden and uninspiring as most textbooks or manuals are; their examinations must have called for a verbal parroting of the letter of ancient doctrines rather than for an understanding of their spirit.

It is no wonder that early modern thinkers, thus mistaught, recoiled. Their repugnance, though certainly explicable, may not be wholly pardonable, for they could have repaired the damage by turning to the texts of Aristotle or Aquinas in their mature years and by reading them perceptively and critically. That they did not do this can be ascertained from an examination of their major works and from their intellectual biographies. When they reject certain points of doctrine inherited from the past, it is perfectly clear that they do not properly understand them; in addition, they make mistakes that arise from ignorance of distinctions and insights highly relevant to problems they attempt to solve.

With very few exceptions, such misunderstanding and ignorance of philosophical achievements prior to the sixteenth century have been the besetting sin of modern thought. Its effects are not confined to philosophers of the seventeenth and eighteenth centuries. They are evident in the work of nineteenth-century philosophers and in the writings of our own day. We can find them, for example, in the works of Ludwig Wittgenstein who, for all his native brilliance and philosophical fervor, stumbles in the dark in dealing with problems on which his premodern predecessors, unknown to him, have thrown great light.

In the centuries that followed the opening period of modern thought, thinkers who adopted some of the premises of Descartes or Locke while reacting against other elements in their thought compounded the initial errors which they made. Judging the consequences to which the adopted premises led to be unacceptable, these subsequent thinkers should have recognized that these consequences followed from errors that could have been corrected. This they did not do. Instead, in order to avoid consequences they regarded as repugnant, they struck out in other directions and fell into more grievous errors.

Locke, like Descartes, made the initial error of declaring that ideas are the objects of the mind when it thinks. (This stands in sharp contrast to the view held by Aquinas that ideas, far from being the objects we apprehend, are that by which we apprehend objects of perception, memory, imagination, and thought.) Locke also failed to distinguish the cognitive power of the intellect from the cognitive power of the senses. These two mistakes, uncorrected by Locke's immediate successors in English thought, produced the subjective idealism of Bishop Berkeley and the skepticism of David Hume. Carrying Locke's premises to their logical conclusions drove Hume to a position that he himself regarded as practically absurd—unlivable if not unthinkable.

Hume's skepticism and his phenomenalism were unacceptable to Immanuel Kant, even though, as he tells us, they woke him from his dogmatic slumbers. But in his reaction to Hume, Kant did not go back to Hume's starting points to see if the conclusions he found repugnant had their origin in errors that could be corrected. Instead of looking for the little errors in the beginning that accounted for Hume's untenable conclusions, Kant constructed a vast piece of intellectual machinery designed to produce conclusions of an opposite tenor. The intricacy of the apparatus and the ingenuity of the design cannot help evoking admiration, even from those who are suspicious of the sanity of the whole enterprise, but they do not help us to get at the truth, which can be found only by correcting Hume's initial errors, and those of Locke and Descartes, and by starting afresh from correct premises that lead to conclusions quite different from those of either Hume or Kant.

These observations about Kant in relation to Hume apply also to the whole tradition of British empirical philosophy following Locke and Hume. All of the philosophical puzzles, paradoxes, and pseudoproblems that linguistic or analytical philosophy and therapeutic positivism have focussed their attention on in this century, and have tried to eliminate by inventing philosophical devices designed for that purpose, would never have arisen in the first place if the little errors in the beginning, made by Locke and Hume, had not gone unnoticed, but had been explicitly rejected.

Modern philosophy has never recovered from its false start. Like men floundering in quicksand who compound their difficulties by struggling to extricate themselves, Kant and his successors have multiplied the difficulties and perplexities of modern philosophy by the very strenuousness—and even ingenuity—of their efforts to extricate themselves from the muddle left in their path by Descartes, Locke, and Hume. To make a fresh start, it is only necessary to open the great philosophical books of the past (especially those written by Aristotle and in his tradition) and to read them with the effort of understanding that they deserve. The recovery of basic truths, long hidden from view, would eradicate errors that have had such disastrous consequences in modern times.

The errors to which I have called attention fall mainly in the theory of knowledge, which has occupied so large a place in modern thought. Modern thought is plagued by equally serious errors in the sphere of moral philosophy. For example, the view that ethics must be noncognitive (that normative propositions, asserting what ought or ought not to be done, cannot be either true or false) might never have arisen if attention had been paid to Aristotle's distinction between two kinds of truth—descriptive truth and normative truth. Another example is the modern misconception of happiness in psychological terms as a state of contentment arising from the satisfaction of whatever desires the individual happens to have developed—a view held by many in ignorance of the ancient conception of happiness in purely ethical terms as the quality of a whole life enriched by all the real goods that a man should seek. This latter view would, of course, require the understanding of still other distinctions ignored by modern thought—the distinction between real and apparent goods and the correlative distinction between natural desires, or needs, and individually acquired desires, or wants. I have dealt in detail with these matters in parts 2 and 3 of *The Time of Our Lives*.

Dissatisfaction with modern philosophy took hold of my mind in the middle thirties in a form that was, perhaps, less articulate and less definite than the terms in which I have just expressed it. Under its influence, I was inclined to turn toward contemporaries who were thinkers of Aristotelian or Thomistic persuasion—most, if not all, of them teachers of philosophy in Catholic universities. The intellectual community that I could not find in my colleagues in secular universities, certainly not at the University of Chicago, I looked for in the circles of the American Catholic Philosophical Association, the leading members of which at that time, as is no longer the case, acknowledged themselves to be disciples of Aristotle and Thomas Aquinas. Just as a certain period in the work of a painter is designated by reference to a color or style that characterizes his canvases over a number of years, so I think it appropriate to speak of the philosophical essays and books that I wrote in the the ten years between 1935 and 1945 as the work of my "Thomistic period."

These books and essays were written in a style and in a manner that made their contents relatively inaccessible to anyone who was not in neo-scholastic circles. They were heavily footnoted with references to the texts of Aristotle, Aquinas, and other writers in the tradition of their thought. They were couched in a technical jargon that made sense only to others already accustomed to its use. At that time I was firmly persuaded of the thesis that I presented at a meeting of the American Catholic Philosophical Association in 1937—a paper entitled "Tradition and Communication." In it I argued that the effort to communicate thought is effective only within the framework and against the background of a common tradition. While I still think that thesis sound, I no longer think it should determine the tenor or direction of one's philosophical writing.

A philosopher should try to communicate his thought in a style that makes it accessible to the intelligent layman. To do so, he should eschew every trace of technical jargon. Though I learned a great deal from the efforts of my Thomistic period, I now regard the books and essays written then as mainly incidents in my own philosophical education, not as philosophical works on which I would like my reputation to rest. In the latter category are the books I have written since 1963, twenty years after I ceased to delight in addressing myself only to an audience of fellow Thomists. How that change occurred, I shall now relate.

As the reader may recall, my fascination with Aquinas dates from my Columbia days when I first procured an English translation of the *Summa Theologica,* which Scott Buchanan, Arthur Rubin, and I read aloud on Saturday mornings. From then on, my growing interest in the thought of Aquinas stemmed from the help he gave me in my efforts to understand Aristotle. Just as, for Aquinas, Aristotle was "the Philosopher" and Averroës was "the Commentator" on Aristotle, so for me, to whom Averroës was unavailable, Aquinas was the commentator—the disciple of Aristotle who uncovered truths hard to ferret out of the latter's difficult texts. In addition, I could not help admiring the magnitude, scope, and style of the *Summa Theologica,* both as a philosophical enterprise and as a work in dogmatic theology.

In the early thirties, Scott Buchanan organized a series of theology lectures at the University of Virginia. When he invited me to give a number of them on especially difficult topics, such as the angelic hierarchy, or the resurrection of the body and the end of the world, I studied parts of the *Summa* that I might never have ventured into in pursuit of philosophical truth. However, even in treating such purely theological questions, Aquinas often introduced a distinction or developed an analysis that, taken out of its theological context, had relevance to philosophical problems with which I was concerned. My excursions into dogmatic (that is, sacred not natural) theology instilled in me great respect for that subject as an intellectual discipline, as rigorous in its way as mathematics is in its. In my judgment, the two subjects most attractive to anyone who enjoys intellectual exercise for its own sake are theoretical physics and dogmatic theology—the one for those with a mathematical turn of mind, the other for those with a passion for making distinctions.

The rumor spread far and wide that a young professor at the University of Chicago was reading the *Summa Theologica* with his undergraduate students. As far as I know, this was unusual to the point of being unique, not only in secular universities but in Catholic institutions as well. When, in addition, at the invitation of the Calvert Club at the University of Chicago, I delivered a lecture on theology as the queen of the sciences, I became something of a legend in Catholic circles.

I can remember the effect of a lecture I gave in the early thirties at a meeting of the Men's Forum of a synagogue in Detroit. The lecture, called "The Misapplications of Psychology," criticized current trends in so-called scientific psychology, such as behaviorism and psychoanalysis, in the light of the philosophical psychology to be found in Aristotle and Aquinas. A professor of philosophy from the Jesuit University of Detroit, Father René Belleperche, was in the audience, and immediately after the lecture, he invited me to come to the University of Detroit to repeat it before his students. They had never heard such things said, he explained, by anyone not wearing a Roman collar. Hearing them from me might help to persuade his students that commitment to these propositions could be something other than strict adherence to a party line.

Events of this sort led to my being invited to deliver the Annual Association Address at the meeting of the American Catholic Philosophical Association in 1934. I chose as my subject "The New Scholastic Philosophy and the Secular University," and took this occasion to question the meaning of the word *scholastic* as applied to philosophy. If philosophy consists of such wisdom as can be distilled by the reflective operation of the intellect upon the materials of common experience, and if scholastic philosophy is philosophy in this sense, then the word *scholastic* signifies only that philosophy

> is not the work of a single man, but the work of a school of men preserving and adding to traditional human wisdom. It is only in modern times that philosophy is not scholastic in this sense, because each thinker insists upon the novelty of his system and hence necessarily discards the tradition.

I questioned the advisability of referring to a "new" scholasticism. Granting that philosophy should address itself to contemporary problems and that, to this extent, it is necessary to rethink Aristotelianism and Thomism, would it not be better, I asked, to refer to such efforts as a revival of philosophy rather than as a new scholasticism?

> . . . this revived philosophy is no more essentially Catholic than it is Greek. It can be called Greek if we wish to refer to the accident of its origin; it can be called Catholic if we wish to refer to the accident of its adoption by the Church. But as perennial wisdom, the only proper qualification of philosophy is as *human*.

In subsequent years, I delivered other papers at meetings of the American Catholic Philosophical Association. One of these entitled "The Demonstration of Democracy," delivered in 1939, marked the beginning of my troubles in Thomistic, or "neo-scholastic" circles.

Aquinas, in his short treatise *The Governance of Rulers*, repeats a sixfold classification of the forms of government that is to be found in Book III of Aristotle's *Politics*, according to which monarchy is the best of the good forms of government, as tyranny is the worst of the bad forms. In this sixfold classification, democracy appears in the company of oligarchy and tyranny as one of three bad forms of government. My own study of Aristotle's *Politics* had persuaded me that the sixfold classification of good and bad forms given in Book III did not represent Aristotle's own deeper insights about the kinds of government and about the criteria of justice in government.

As I interpreted Book I, Aristotle's basic distinction in kinds of government was between constitutional regimes, in which the citizens are free men and equals and in which they rule and are ruled in turn, and all forms of despotism, whether tyrannical or benevolent, in which the ruled are nonparticipating subjects of a government by men, not constituents of or participants in a government of laws. Furthermore, Books IV and VI of Aristotle's *Politics* treat democracy and oligarchy as the two major forms of constitutional government. In the former, free men are citizens even if they have little property; in the latter, only the wealthy are admitted to citizenship.

Clearly, Aristotle, defending the institution of slavery and disfranchisement of artisans, was not an exponent of democracy in John Stuart Mill's sense of that term—constitutional government with universal suffrage, with no political pariahs. Nevertheless, by one of Aristotle's own principles—that man is by nature a political animal—I thought I could prove that Aristotle and, following him, Aquinas were wrong in their adverse views on democracy.

The paper I delivered in 1939 attempted to show that the sixfold classification of the forms of government presented in Book III of Aristotle's *Politics*, as adopted by Aquinas and as enshrined by contemporary

Thomists, should be discarded as egregiously superficial; it also presented arguments which I thought demonstrated, by Aristotelian and Thomistic principles, that democracy was the only completely just form of government and that monarchy (in the sense of benevolent despotism) was the least just of the good forms—just only to the extent that the absolute ruler exercised his power for the common good of the political community, not for his private interests.

My "Demonstration of Democracy" was received in stunned silence, soon broken by letters that defended the words of Aquinas as if they were sacrosanct, and later by articles in the journals that paid little attention to my analysis of the texts in Aristotle or to the argument that I had developed from them, and simply reiterated that the only criterion of justice in government consisted in its being for the common good. To my astonishment, here in the twentieth century, some of my fellow Thomists, appealing to this one criterion, were still stubbornly holding on to the obviously false view that monarchy was the best form of government.

A short time later, I suffered a second shock. My continued study of Aristotle and Aquinas had uncovered what for me were a number of unresolved difficulties. It seemed to me that it would be a highly useful undertaking to write a series of articles about these difficulties under the title "Problems for Thomists." The first in this projected series consisted of a number of articles about the problem of species, published in successive issues of the *Thomist* in the years 1938 and 1939. These articles pointed out that in the writings of Aristotle and Aquinas could be found two quite different views of the specific forms of life. According to one view, supported by a large number of texts, there were only three species of living organisms—vegetative, brute animal, and human life. According to the other view, supported by an equally large number of texts, there were a very large number of species of both plants and animals. Which of these views should prevail? Could they be reconciled by making distinctions not actually made by either Aquinas or Aristotle?

The appearance of these articles raised a storm of protest that blew up at the meeting of the American Catholic Philosophical Association in 1939, fueled by an angry blast, delivered on that occasion, against the impudence of my trying to be a "Thomist revisionist." Jacques Maritain, and one or two others, came to my defense. In fact, when the *Thomist* articles were subsequently published in 1940 in book form, Maritain wrote a foreword to the volume in which he said:

> In striving to establish a *problematic* of Thomism, Mortimer Adler shows us that Thomism is a continuously unfolding philosophy. . . . [He] has not left medieval scholasticism behind in order to meet up with modern thought and to attempt an *adaptation* of the one to the other. If this is what the word "neo-Thomism" means, he is not a "neo-Thomist." He

prefers to be a modern Thomist, engaged above all in the current of modern thought, while yet adhering to the truth of Aristotelian and Thomistic principles.

Maritain concluded his foreword by stating the hope "that *The Problem of Species* and the works to follow will excite many readers to a wealth of reflections which will assist them in examining and clarifying their own conceptions."

The "works to follow" never saw the light of day. I decided that calling attention to unresolved difficulties in the thought of Aristotle and Aquinas was just about as unwelcome among my contemporaries who declared themselves adherents of these two philosophers, as similar revisionism was unwelcome in the party founded by Marx and Engels. Nevertheless, I published, in 1941, an essay entitled "Solution of the Problem of Species," which distinguished between the meaning of the term *species* as used in Aristotle's metaphysics and its meaning as used in his biological treatises and by modern biological scientists, especially those concerned with theories about the origin of species. In my judgment, the "Solution" all but demonstrated that, according to the metaphysical conception of species, there could be no more than three species of living organisms. The missing link needed to complete the demonstration, I finally was able to provide in a paper delivered at a meeting of the Metaphysical Society at Yale, entitled "The Hierarchy of Essences," published in the *Review of Metaphysics* in 1952.

Though I decided not to write any more articles in the projected series of "Problems for Thomists," I continued my efforts to extend the thought of Aristotle and Aquinas or to rectify it where it seemed to me indeterminate, deficient, or, in some cases, definitely in error. Just as I followed up *The Problem of Species* with subsequent articles resolving the difficulty on which it focussed, so I followed up "The Demonstration of Democracy" with a long series of articles written with Father Walter Farrell, a professor of theology in the Dominican House of Studies in Washington, D.C. These were published in the *Thomist* in successive issues during 1941–1943. To my regret, Father Farrell's untimely death, after wartime service as a naval chaplain, prevented the completion of the series. With the addition to the nine published articles of three more that Father Farrell and I had planned, the whole series might have seen wider circulation in book form.

In 1945, both Father Farrell and I delivered addresses at a meeting of the American Catholic Philosophical Association, in which we took the position that the superiority of democracy to all other forms of government could no longer be questioned by philosophers who regarded themselves as Aristotelians or Thomists, even though Aristotle and Aquinas could not be quoted in support of that thesis. At the opening of my address, I reminded the audience of the murmurings and mutterings which spread through the philosophical corridors after ["The Demonstration of Democracy"] was delivered, voices of dissent from so radical a thesis, voices of doubt about the steps of the proof, and last but not least, voices of disapproval over the fact that the author of the paper had said—not by implication, but explicitly, and without apology—that the political philosophy of Aristotle and St. Thomas fell short of the whole truth, both by reason of serious inadequacies and because of grave errors.

To this I added that there was nothing extraordinary about these failures on their part, because "political philosophers must suffer the blindnesses of their limited historical perspectives. Aristotle did well enough for a Greek, and St. Thomas well enough for a thirteenth-century man, but neither could do well enough for all time." No one can.

A third episode, the one which finally persuaded me to abandon my efforts to write books or articles addressed solely to an audience of contemporary Thomists, occurred at about the same time. Jacques Maritain celebrated his fiftieth birthday in 1943, and the editors of the *Thomist* decided to publish a special *festschrift* volume in his honor, to which they invited me to contribute. I did so with an essay entitled "The Demonstration of God's Existence." Still not fully convinced that it was impossible to win an open-minded reception to criticisms of established Thomistic doctrines, I tried to show that the famous "five ways" in which Aquinas presents the arguments for God's existence in Question 3 of Part One of the *Summa Theologica* do not succeed as valid demonstrations of the proposition to be proved. I also tried to explain that this was so largely because critical considerations introduced by Aquinas much later in the *Summa* invalidated the arguments advanced in its opening pages. Question 3—the question whether God's existence can be demonstrated—came much too early for Aquinas to be able to bring to bear all the considerations that weighed heavily in a full handling of the question. Marshalling these considerations, I concluded with the construction of a proof that was Thomistic in principle even though it was never actually formulated by Aquinas in the way in which I presented it. The demonstration, I admitted, left a number of difficulties still to be resolved. This amounted to saying that, although God's existence might be demonstrated in the future, it had not yet been accomplished, as far as I could see.

After the editors of the *Thomist* received my manuscript, I received a frantic phone call from Father Slavin, urging me to withdraw the piece. Otherwise, he said, the *Thomist,* under the restraints of ecclesiastical censorship, would be compelled to reject it on the grounds that the Church had officially declared, as a matter of faith, that God's existence can be proved by reason without any appeal to faith. I told

Father Slavin that he and the other editors must be overexcited and consequently somewhat confused. My essay had not asserted that God's existence *cannot* be proved by reason; it only asserted that a completely satisfactory proof *had not been offered by Aquinas, and was not yet available.* The Church, I pointed out, could not declare as a dogma of faith the truth of a purely historical proposition, namely, that Aquinas had in fact demonstrated God's existence in the five ways set forth in his *Summa Theologica.* Since it was only that historical proposition which I denied, my article did not fall under the prohibitions of ecclesiastical censorship.

After some consultation with his follow editors, Father Slavin phoned back to say that the *Thomist* would publish my article in the Maritain volume. That, however, was not the end of the story. Its publication elicited a barrage of adverse reactions, some quite extreme in their denunciation of my essay. Convinced that my approach to the problem was essentially sound, I could not let the matter drop. I composed an elaborate reply to the criticisms. It ran to some 140 pages of single-spaced copy, which I circulated under the title "Rough Draft of a Second Article on the Demonstration of God's Existence." It did not succeed, any more than the first article did, in getting the kind of hearing which I felt my analysis and argument deserved. My greatest disappointment occurred when I learned that I had even failed to make any headway in changing Maritain's mind on the subject. From then on, I lost my zeal for trying to reform Thomism, though I did not give up on the problem of God's existence. During the fifties and the sixties, I returned to the problem, revising and refining a lecture that I delivered on numerous occasions, learning a great deal each time from the questions raised by the audience. I hope some day to return to that lecture and expand it into a book.

To complete this account of the "Thomistic period" in my philosophical career, I must mention two other attempts I made to think through problems in accordance with the controlling principles of Thomistic thought but without subscribing to the letter of Aquinas's doctrine, as that is encoded in the textbooks of scholastic philosophy. One was an essay, "A Question About Law," that I contributed to a volume called *Essays in Thomism,* published in 1941. When I first started to teach the philosophy of law at the University of Chicago, I floundered until I discovered the Treatise on Law in the *Summa Theologica,* which put the subject into perspective for me. In subsequent years, I reread the treatise again and again, each time finding new insights and new details in Aquinas's analysis of the nature, kinds, and properties of law. But I also found difficulties that had not been apparent on earlier readings.

Does the term *law* have an identical meaning when we speak of the

Divine positive law, such as the Ten Commandments, of the natural moral law, and the man-made law of the state? If not, the definition of law that Aquinas gives in the opening pages of his treatise does not apply univocally to all the kinds of law that he distinguishes. It then becomes necessary to ask whether the different kinds of law are alike analogically or whether the word *law* is being used equivocally or ambiguously when we pass from the consideration of one kind of law to another. That is the question I propounded in "A Question About Law." My answer pointed out that the meaning of "law" clearly did change in its various applications, but the character of the changes that took place was not so clear. I had not yet adequately grasped Aquinas's threefold division of word usage into the univocal, the equivocal, and the analogical, or his further subdivisions of both equivocal and analogical speech.

My efforts to improve my understanding of these distinctions became a major undertaking. Dissatisfied with the existing interpretation of them, exemplified in Father Gerald Phelan's *St. Thomas and Analogy,* a book I was given to review about this time, I began to study the relevant texts in Aquinas and Aristotle, as well as some of the commentaries. What started out as a review turned gradually into plans for writing a book, and those plans expanded into the projection of a three-volume work to be entitled *Semantics and Metaphysics.*

I spent a great deal of time on this project in the years 1941–1943, but I had completed only the first twelve chapters, about 800 pages, when the increasing pressure of work on the Syntopicon prevented me from finishing even that first volume, which I planned to call "Aristotle's Theory of Ambiguity and Analogy." Nor did I ever get further than making notes for the second volume, which would have dealt with Aquinas's theory of the modes of signification of the names that we apply to God and to his creatures. Notes, outlines, and partially completed manuscript went into a file box, where they remained until very recently.

In 1974, when I was asked to contribute an essay to an issue of *The New Scholasticism* devoted to honoring St. Thomas on the 700th anniversary of his death, I decided to summarize the focal points in my analysis of equivocation and analogy. The essay I wrote, "The Equivocal Use of the Word 'Analogical,' " was as plainly a departure from views long prevalent and generally accepted as anything I had written in the late thirties or early forties on the theory of democracy, the problem of species, or the demonstration of God's existence. But in the intervening years, many changes had taken place in the intellectual temper and attitude of the American Catholic Philosophical Association. My proposal of a revision of Thomistic doctrine no longer elicited the outraged responses that similar proposals drew thirty years earlier. On the contrary! In 1976, at the annual meeting of the association, I received the Aquinas Medal in recognition of my contributions to the study of St. Thomas's philosophy. The pleasure of that occasion was not diminished by the fact that I had long since emerged from my "Thomistic period."

Since 1946, when I revived the project of producing a *Summa Dialectica,* my conception of the philosopher's task has undergone a radical alteration. In my opinion, philosophers should not be engaged in writing books or essays intended solely for other philosophers to read, as mathematicians, theoretical physicists, or even social scientists do for an audience of fellow professionals. Philosophy prospers only when it strives to be the least professional, the least academic of all the academic disciplines. Philosophy is everyone's business. The task of the philosopher is to shape his thought and to express it in such a way that it is accessible to anyone who will make the effort to think about the matters under consideration.

While I did not fully and explicitly formulate this view until I came to writing *The Conditions of Philosophy* in 1963, earlier writings moved in that direction—an essay entitled "The Philosopher" which was published in 1947 in an anthology entitled *The Works of the Mind;* a paper entitled "The Next Twenty-five Years in Philosophy" which was my contribution to an issue of *The New Scholasticism* that celebrated its own twenty-fifth anniversary in 1951; and the Annual Association Address that I delivered at the 1965 meeting of the American Catholic Philosophical Association, under the title "Controversy in the Life and Teaching of Philosophy." All of these, in varying degrees, reflected my understanding of the way in which the dialectical clarification of basic issues in philosophy might serve philosophers in their effort to work as they should work—cooperatively, not in the isolation that is proper for poets, painters, or musicians—to advance the ascertainment of truth beyond what has so far been attained.

One book that goes back to the early years of my "Thomistic period" contains some intimations of these later views of philosophical work. In 1938, I was invited by the Aristotelian Society of Marquette University to give the annual Aquinas Lecture. I can still remember the agony I suffered in trying to formulate an appropriate message for that occasion. Days and weeks went by, notes accumulated, but no vision of an overall theme emerged. As the date of the lecture approached, Father Gerard Smith telephoned, asking me to submit the manuscript of my lecture two days later. I shuffled through all my notes and made new ones, with the intention of sitting down at my typewriter early the next morning. I did so, and I sat there staring at a blank paper for about an hour, but nothing came—no title, no first sentence. Exhausted by the effort, I lay down on the couch in my study and promptly fell asleep.

Awakening, two hours later, I dashed some cold water on my face and once more sat down at the typewriter. Almost immediately I had the title I wanted—"St. Thomas and the Gentiles"—a title that drew reflected light from Aquinas's *Summa Contra Gentiles.* A moment later out came the first sentence and then, without pause, thirty pages rolled out of my typewriter, right down to the final full stop, without a single x-ing out of infelicities, without a single pencilling in of additions or emendations. I had never before had that experience in writing and I have never had it again.

In *St. Thomas and the Gentiles,* I appealed to exponents of the philosophy of St. Thomas to address themselves not to fellow Thomists, but to philosophers generally. It was accompanied by a series of admonitions about how they should conduct themselves in relation to those who did not initially share their admiration of Aquinas—how they should sympathetically approach problems that Aquinas had not himself considered, problems that had arisen since his day, yet problems to the solution of which his thought, if creatively extended, might contribute. My admonitions fell on deaf ears, including, I must confess, my own; for during the next five or six years, I made little or no effort to follow my own advice.

I cannot leave this account of my "Thomistic period" without discussing the question of my relation not just to the thought of St. Thomas Aquinas, but to his religion. That question arose early on. It was quite natural for many people to assume that anyone who publicly espoused the main tenets of St. Thomas's philosophy must also be a communicant in his religion. It never occurred to them that another, and equally apt interpretation, might be that anyone who felt as I did about the style and content of Aristotle's philosophizing would also be inclined to feel the same way about the style and content of Aquinas's. Neglecting that interpretation, and not clearly understanding the separation of Aquinas's philosophical thought from his work as a theologian, they could not understand how commitment to certain philosophical doctrines did not inexorably lead to the adoption of certain theological dogmas.

This whole matter was unduly complicated at the University of Chicago by the conversion to Roman Catholicism of a number of students who had been introduced to the *Summa Theologica* in the great books class that Bob Hutchins and I taught, or in the Trivium course I taught with Malcolm Sharp. This apparently confirmed the suspicions then rampant, though, of course, we had nothing to do with these conversions. I was no more responsible for them than I was for some of my students becoming Marxists after studying the *Communist Manifesto* and *Capital* in one of my classes. That fact went unnoticed or unbelieved, even though a moment's thought should have made anyone realize how improper it would be for a non-Catholic deliberately to convert others to Catholicism. But, of course, they did not believe that I was a non-Catholic. Rumors of all sorts were rife at the University of Chicago—that Bob Hutchins and I had been secretly baptized, that we had been seen on our knees at the altar rail of the Catholic church near the university campus, and so on.

During the ten years between 1935 and 1945, and even for some time after that, such rumors spread, and the question of my religion or lack of religion was debated in a variety of quarters. The question agitated me. I realized that I was causing scandal in circles that were shocked by even the slightest intimation of a tendency on my part to become a Roman Catholic as well as in circles that were shocked by the fact that I had not taken a step in that direction. I must also confess that for a number of years, I tried to face up to the question that I was repeatedly asked by my intimates, by my Catholic friends and associates, by friendly colleagues at the university and by others not so friendly, even by strangers who came up at the end of a lecture begging permission to ask me what they called a "personal question." Was I a Roman Catholic? My negative answer elicited the further question, Why not?

In retrospect, I realize that the answers I gave to others—at least to those who, in my judgment, deserved an answer to a question so personal and so searching—usually fitted the occasion and the character of my interlocutor. None, I think, really got down to the subterranean truth about myself. During the years between 1935 and 1939 when I agonized over the question, the reason I gave myself as well as others was the wish not to offend my parents who were still alive, my wife, Helen, who had strong feelings on the subject, and such friends as Arthur Rubin and Scott Buchanan with whom I frequently discussed the matter and who strongly opposed my becoming a Catholic. But that was certainly not a good reason for deciding against a move on which one's happiness—and, perhaps, one's salvation—might depend.

Nor was the reason I gave some years later to Clare Luce either a good or a thoroughly honest explanation. Clare herself had recently become a Catholic convert. In view of my admiration and affection for Aquinas and for his philosophy, it was natural and proper for her to ask me why I had not become a convert also. I replied by telling her of the distinction that Aquinas makes between dead and living faith. Dead faith consists in faith without charity—a purely philosophical state of mind in which the dogmas of the Church are viewed as comprehensible, as reasonable, and as believable. What is lacking to make the believable actually believed as a living creed is charity—the love of God and the will to live in accordance with that love. My state of mind, I told Clare, bore some resemblance to what Aquinas described as dead, rather than living, faith.

That answer came nearer to the truth than any other I had come up with earlier, but it fell short by virtue of the still unanswered question, Why did I not take the steps needed to close the gap between dead and living faith? Even though faith, according to dogmatic theology, is a supernatural virtue (one that cannot be acquired by voluntary effort but rather is received as a gift of God's grace), the individual still has the option to dispose himself by his own acts for its reception. By prayer and other actions equally within his power, he can do the things that by themselves do not suffice, but nevertheless do express an active openness and striving on his part.

I think I now know the answer to that crucial question, though I did not grasp it at the time. It lies in the state of one's will, not in the state of one's mind. The individual who is born a Jew or a Christian, a Catholic or a Protestant, can know himself to be such, however loosely or feebly, without having to live as a truly religious Jew or Christian should live. But the case of the convert to Judaism or Christianity is quite different. The only reason to *adopt* a religion is that one wishes and intends to live henceforth in accordance with its precepts, forswearing conduct and habits that are incompatible. For me to become a Roman Catholic—or, for that matter, an Anglo-Catholic or Episcopalian—would require a radical change in my way of life, a basic alteration in the direction of my day-to-day choices as well as in the ultimate objectives to be sought or hoped for. I have too clear and too detailed an understanding of moral theology to fool myself on that score. The simple truth of the matter is that I did not wish to live up to being a genuinely religious person. I could not bring myself to will what I ought to will for my whole future if I were to resolve my will, at a particular moment, with regard to religious conversion.

With the approach of my seventy-fifth birthday, it is, perhaps, appropriate to take stock of a lifelong dedication to philosophical thought, though one that was frequently interrupted, often for long intervals, by other undertakings. I would like my reputation as a philosopher to rest on the books I have written since 1963—four out of the five of them based on Britannica Lectures that I delivered at the University of Chicago, all of them written in the light of discussions with my associates at the Institute for Philosophical Research. There is one other thing to be said about all five of these books. They draw on much earlier work— lectures given, the manuscripts of unpublished books or articles, and books or articles published in earlier years, some going all the way back to my Columbia days and to my first five years at Chicago.

If one aspect of being a philosopher at large is being a generalist in philosophy, the work I have accomplished so far can be regarded as a fair approximation to the range of philosophical subjects to be covered: the theory of knowledge and of truth, in *The Conditions of Philosophy;* the philosophy of man, or philosophical anthropology, in *The Differ-*

ence of Man and The Difference It Makes; ethics, or the theory of the good life, in *The Time of Our Lives;* politics, or the theory of the good society, in *The Common Sense of Politics;* and the philosophy of mind, or philosophical psychology, in *Some Questions About Language.* Filling out the picture on the periphery of the central themes are books, essays, or unpublished lectures on the philosophy of education, the philosophy of art, the philosophy of law, and the philosophy of logic.

In the years ahead, if by good fortune they should turn out to be sufficient for the purpose, I would like to complete the picture by writing a book dealing with some of the most difficult, and most central, of philosophical problems—the problems of metaphysics, questions about being and becoming, about the modes of being, about existence and nonexistence, and about the existence of God. Whether or not I shall ever be able to resolve the difficulties I have encountered in all earlier attempts to construct a valid proof of God's existence, the best judgment I can reach about the matter would, in my opinion, be a fitting close not only to that book, which remains to be written, but also to my philosophical career.

Chapter 15

Three Birthday Parties

M Y SIXTIETH BIRTHDAY approached in an atmosphere of gloom so enveloping that I could not bring myself to think of the approaching event. Once before in my life I had reached what I thought at the time was bottom. The circumstances were somewhat similar. A protracted love affair had for several years occupied a major part of my time and attention and had emptied my mind of its usual concerns. Then as later, I felt as if my mind had almost ceased to function except in the service of my emotions. In both instances a love affair had come to a sudden end, the emotions that had been so thought-consuming vanished, leaving a void in a life drained of all interest and purpose.

In December 1944, I wrote a birthday note to myself, a personal inventory on two sheets of yellow paper. Under the headings "University situation," "Extra-university work," and "Domestic situation," I recorded my lack of status at the university, my dissatisfaction with teaching, my feeling of not being a member of the academic community, my failure to find a receptive audience for my philosophical writings outside the university, my inability to establish good relations with my two adopted sons, and my despair about saving my marriage after the irreparable damage I had inflicted on it.

The second sheet also had three headings—"assets," "liabilities," and "possibilities." Under assets, I listed intelligence, education, energy, a few friends, and some good habits which, though recently in abeyance, might be restored. Under liabilities, I cited bad habits of two years' standing, stagnation as the result of a two-year vacation from my normal work routines, lack of drive, lack of any clear objectives. It all added up to three possible courses of action: quit the University of Chicago and go to St. John's College in Annapolis; get out of academic life and find another way to earn a living; suicide. Divorce was not listed among the possibilities; I felt responsible for my part in the rearing of our two children, still quite young. I did not foresee the recuperative effect that immersion in work on the Syntopicon would have on my intellectual energies and interests. That not only restored my zest for living, but also reinstated a pattern of life and work which made me feel at home with myself.

I did not draw up a similar balance sheet in 1962. If I had, it might have been even more unbalanced on the side of liabilities and failures, with even fewer options still open, except for my personal life. The love affair that I had hoped would end in remarriage had already brought about my separation and divorce from Helen.

My contemplation of a second marriage envisioned starting a new life, one that was domestically more attractive and more comfortable, one that involved new professional interests and new diversions. This was abruptly ended by a sudden discovery that my trust as well as my hopes had been betrayed. I had invested all my psychic resources in an account that was now bankrupt. I could not at once recoup them or redirect my libido to other objects.

By the summer of 1962 I felt as if I were living in both an emotional and an intellectual vacuum. My despondency derived from the loneliness of living alone without any emotional attachments and from what I felt was the withering of my intellectual resources. I drew no satisfaction from past achievements—books written, work done. The future could not have looked blanker or bleaker.

One evening in September, I went out to dinner with Robert Hazo, then associate director of the Institute for Philosophical Research. I owe him an immense debt of gratitude for almost constant companionship during the year leading up to that September. Evening after evening, he listened patiently and sympathetically to tiresomely reiterated complaints about my life, to self-deprecatory assessments of what I had done, and to my obstinate refusals to concede that the future might hold anything in store. On this particular occasion, our conversation started out with the same tune and in the same tone, but it was brought to an abrupt halt by Robert's attempt to cheer me up and give me something to look forward to by letting me in on a secret. He told me that Kip Fadiman and Bob Hutchins were planning a surprise sixtieth birthday party for me—to be held in Santa Barbara on December 28. They were aware of my dejected state of mind and hoped the birthday party might be a therapeutic, heart warming gesture. Their plans included putting together a large album of congratulatory letters written to me by numerous friends and associates.

As he told me about laudatory remarks in some of the letters which had already come in, I could stand it no longer. I choked up, my eyes

filled, and I found it impossible to suppress my tears. We were seated
at a center table in the crowded dining room of a San Francisco restau-
rant, and, as my convulsive sobbing increased, we naturally became the
center of attention. Robert tried his best to help me quiet down, but I
was inconsolable. I had to bury my head in my arms and cry it out
until my eyes dried and my chest stopped heaving. Only then could I
try to explain my feelings to Robert and beg him to ask Kip and Bob
to call the whole thing off. That, he replied, was out of the question;
invitations had gone out; letters were coming in. I would either have
to alter my mood before the party occurred or in the next two months
steel myself for the ordeal of going through with it.

My mood did change. That evening at La Bourgogne was certainly
the low point of my despair. Some time before that event I had met
Caroline Pring, who had come to work with me as editorial assistant on
a ten-volume set, *Gateway to the Great Books,* which Britannica planned
to publish. During that autumn we saw each other almost as frequently
out of the office as in it. When Charles Van Doren came to San Francisco in early November to work with Caroline and me on *Gateway,* he
brought his wife Geraldine with him, and the four of us dined together
every night for a week. By then my feelings showed. Our evenings together left Charles and Gerry in little doubt about what my intentions
were. But they were far from sure whether Caroline would be willing to
marry me. I was even less sure than they until one evening when something prompted me to unburden myself to Caroline about the events of
the preceding year and the depression that followed in their wake.

I told her the story of the dinner when I had uncontrollably broken
down. As I finished relating the episode in all its grim details, Caroline
asked me under what circumstances I would look forward to the birthday party with pleasure and enjoy the congratulations of my friends.
If I were happily married, or about to be married, I replied, and if I
were back on the main track of my life (from which recent events had
derailed me)—writing or planning to write the philosophical books that
I had postponed or put aside during the long years of work on the
Syntopicon and the equally long years occupied with the dialectical
projects of the Institute for Philosophical Research.

Caroline's smile at that reply and one or two little comments she made
encouraged me to think that a favorable resolution might be nearer
than I had dared to hope. One evening later that month, after the two
of us dined with her father, who was visiting San Francisco, I asked her
to marry me. We discussed the difference in our ages—more than thirty
years—and all the risks that might involve, as well as the reaction of
her friends and mine. The conversation did not conclude with a decision.

I was scheduled to fly to Australia a few days later for two weeks of lecturing at universities there. Before my departure, Caroline gave me a letter that I was to open after takeoff. The answer I was hoping for was almost there. I tried to overcome the benumbing distance between Australia and California, which under normal circumstances seems like more than half a planet away, by daily letters and by frequent telephone calls which, before a cable existed, did not go through loud and clear. My words may have been garbled in radio transmission, but my emotions came through plainly enough, and when Caroline met me in Los Angeles on my return, the answer was yes.

Less than a month now remained before my sixtieth birthday party on December 28. Caroline had to break the news to her parents, who lived in Fayetteville, New York, just outside of Syracuse. I had met her mother and father earlier that fall, after a lecture that I gave in Syracuse, and liked them both. I felt that they liked me—but in some capacity other than that of son-in-law. How they would take to that neither Caroline nor I could guess, though her trepidation about telling them betrayed her fears. She flew to Fayetteville the week before Christmas. I waited in San Francisco for a telephone call from her after she had spoken to her parents; in fact, I waited in the company of my sister, Carolyn, to whom I had just reported the step I was about to take. When the call finally came through, Caroline told me that it had been heavy going at first but that all was well and that George and Eleanor Pring invited me to spend Christmas with them in Fayetteville.

Being gentle and gracious human beings, George and Eleanor made me welcome in their home. Caroline told me that her father was much less reconciled to the decision than her mother, but I only learned later the extent to which they, and others, had sombre reservations. On the day of our wedding in February, her parents, my sister, and some of my closest friends, discussing the event after the departure of the bride and groom, were very apprehensive about the success and the durability of the marriage. On both counts, I am glad to say and they are now equally glad to concede, they were wrong. My sister soon discovered one reason—and it was only one of many—why their lugubrious predictions turned out to be wrong. She told me how struck she was by Caroline's remarkable agelessness—the complete ease and naturalness with which she adapted herself to persons of my age as well as to persons of her own.

The birthday party turned out to be a very joyous affair. The assemblage included my sister and her husband, Leon Lewis, Bill Benton, Scott Buchanan, Robert Hazo, and, of course, Bob and Vesta Hutchins and Kip and Analee Fadiman. Since the good news about Caroline and me was not yet public knowledge, she did not attend, but she was there at least in the minds of Kip Fadiman, Bob Hutchins, and Robert Hazo, in whom I confided. In the short speech that I made after the usual round of toasts, I remarked on how different was my state of mind from what it had been several months earlier, adding that on this, my sixtieth birthday, I felt as if I had a future full of promise.

I could now read the letters that Kip and Bob had assembled in the birthday album they presented to me, without the anguish I had anticipated several months earlier. Plaudits and eulogies, even when they succeed in avoiding flattery, cause discomfort and embarrassment, which I tried to reduce by saying that I hoped what I might be able to accomplish in the next ten or fifteen years would deserve some of the comments in the letters. The unalloyed pleasure that album of letters gave me came simply from the names of the persons who had written them, old friends and close associates who had been unable to come to Santa Barbara for the party. There were letters from Arthur Rubin, Mark Van Doren, Charles Van Doren, Jacques Barzun, Saul Bellow, Bill Douglas, Clarence Faust, Paul Mellon, Arthur Houghton, Paul Weiss, Franz Alexander, Richard McKeon, Jerry McGill, Dean Rusk, Norman Cousins, Geoffrey Crowther, Paul Hoffman, Charles Malik, Milton Mayer, Bill Gorman, Otto Bird, Stringfellow Barr, Elizabeth Mann Borgese, Edward Levi, Adolph Schmidt, Max Schuster, Henry Anatole Grunwald, Father John Courtney Murray, Father John Cavanaugh, Father Theodore Hesburgh, and Malcolm Sharp; and from those who either were then or were later to become members of the Board of Directors of the Institute for Philosophical Research— Mortimer Fleishhacker, Jr., Harold Linder, Prentis Hale, Robert Gwinn, Louis Kelso, Ralph Tyler, Daggett Harvey, Hermon Dunlap Smith, and Elizabeth Paepcke.

I have not mentioned one incident connected with the party that augured well for the promise I had implicitly made to Caroline when we contemplated getting married. Bob Hutchins, still unaware that the birthday party planned for the evening of December 28 was not going to be a surprise, asked me to come to Santa Barbara that day to conduct a conference at his Center for the Study of Democratic Institutions. I agreed and proposed as the theme for a day's discussion the conditions under which philosophy might once again become a respectable and self-respecting enterprise, equal to scientific investigation, historical research, and humanistic scholarship in the esteem it deserved from the community, as well as in the self-esteem of its practitioners. My paper and the discussion it generated were initial steps toward the writing of *The Conditions of Philosophy*—the first in the series of books that I had promised Caroline I would write after we were married. When that book was completed a year or so later, I dedicated it to her with the words *"primae inter causas secundas"*—To Caroline, first among second causes, as she most certainly was. The same dedication might have been inscribed in each of the next four books that were completed in the first ten years of our marriage.

The mood that attended the celebration of my sixty-fifth and seventieth birthdays confirmed the feeling that I expressed on my six-tieth birthday—that the future looked bright. By the time my sixty-fifth birthday came around, I not only had completed two of the five books projected, but I was also halfway through the two-year stint of planning the new *Britannica*.

My memory of the party is of an evening devoted to eating, drinking, and dancing rather than to speech-making. In fact, the only speech was a brief toast by Charles Van Doren, who paid an eloquent tribute to Caroline for my youthfulness at sixty-five. I must confess that I felt younger then—more energetic and with more things to look forward to—than I had five years earlier. It was not only that my wife was many years younger than I, but also that we were blessed with two handsome little boys. Douglas and Philip were at this time respectively three and one. Walking the floor with them when, as infants, they suf-fered discomfort at night; getting down on the floor to play with them and their toys as they started to crawl and walk; sharing their feelings as they tried to assert and communicate their individuality—these and the countless other pleasures and pains in rearing children seemed to slow up senescence.

Another result, in my case, was the sobering realization that, of all human undertakings, the rearing of children is the most difficult. In the last ten years I have made some of the same mistakes with Douglas and Philip that I made thirty years earlier with Mark and Michael. The reason, perhaps, is that the mistakes flow from defects in one's character, defects so deep that the best resolutions fail to eradicate them. I have watched Mark and Michael with their own children, observing them repeat mistakes that I wished I had not made. If I live long enough to be a grandfather a second time around with the offspring of Douglas and Philip, the same thing will probably be true in their case. Fortunately, most of the mistakes that parents make, unless they are grievously injurious, only impede but do not prevent the child from developing the individuality of character that is strikingly manifested in his or her behavior even as an infant.. The same child with other parents making other mistakes would probably turn out very much the same.

A seventieth birthday party is, I suppose, an appropriate time and place to consider what comes next. Elizabeth Paepcke reported her dream of a celestial dialogue in which St. Peter examined my credentials for admission. Things were not going well until a beautiful angel in-tervened, introducing herself as Saint Caroline and saying: "I can vouch for this man. I know him well. He sometimes becomes confused in his priorities, but in the end he always straightens up. He may never have learned how to swim, but he knows how to write a book and he knows that love conquers all—even me." Charles Van Doren read two telegrams, one from St. Thomas Aquinas and the other from Aristotle, coming from opposite directions, each concerned with the possibility of my joining them in their final abode. Aristotle was the more persuasive in making a case for the attractiveness of his companions and environment.

For me, the occasion seemed appropriate for retrospection. I had long ago learned from Aristotle that no life can be judged happy or unhappy until it has been completed. That judgment about a man's life should be made after he is dead, by friends who knew him well. The criteria for making the judgment are summed up in two succinct statements—one by St. Augustine (Happy is the man who in the course of his days has achieved all that he desires, "provided that he desire nothing amiss"), the other by Aristotle (Happiness is the quality of a life that has been "lived in accordance with virtue"). The second statement dovetails with the first, because moral virtue consists in the habitual disposition to desire nothing amiss.

There is one further factor which Aristotle mentions. The goods that enrich a man's life are acquired either by choice or by chance. Whether he chooses correctly depends upon a man's virtue, which prevents him from seeking things that only appear to be good, but are not really good for him. But some of the real goods that contribute to the happiness of a human life are gifts of fortune. Virtue, though indispensable, does not by itself suffice.

What could I say about my life from the vantage point of seventy years? Though not yet completed, it might be possible to say "So far, so good," and to express the hope that it would go on to the end in a similar vein. If, looking back over the road one has travelled, one is tempted to congratulate one's self, discretion counsels that one should not take credit for one's good luck—the fortunate circumstances and the benign accidents that lie beyond one's power.

In a brief speech at my seventieth birthday party, I counted my blessings. Concerning some of them the reader is already well informed—especially the persons who became my lifelong friends but who came into my life through fortunate coincidences for which I am everlastingly thankful. However, these do not go back further than my twentieth year. To go all the way back, I explained why I was grateful for the accidents of birth itself—the genes inherited through my parents, the country and century in which I was born, and a father and mother who tempered loving care with discipline that was not too restrictive, yet exacting enough to form sturdy habits.

It was my good fortune, I said, to have had a father who worked very hard, did not make much money doing it, but never regarded his failure in that respect as a cause for complaint. Making a lot of money was never held up to me as identical with getting ahead in the world. Nor was going into his business, which was silverware and jewelry, ever proposed or, for that matter, was there any thought of a business career. My father had left Germany before he was twenty in order to evade two years of service in the kaiser's army. Finding hospitality with some cousins in Montgomery, Alabama, he subsequently moved northward to Norfolk, Virginia, and then to New York City. The employment he found there with a large wholesale jeweler on Maiden Lane brought him into contact with one of my mother's brothers, my uncle Henry; and when the firm for which they both worked went out of business, my uncle and my father (now married to my mother) decided to join forces and go into the jewelry business for themselves. Though my uncle Henry's son did enter the business, it was never suggested that I do so. Even after I dropped out of high school, I was allowed to follow my own bent toward journalism rather than toward jewelry.

It was equally my good fortune to have a mother who was a teacher. One of seven children—five boys and two girls, one of whom had died in her youth—my mother graduated from Hunter College in New York City and, before marriage, taught at the elementary level in the public schools. About the same time that I went to work, she returned to teaching to supplement my father's income; and she continued teaching English to foreigners all during my college years to make up for the fact that I had moved from the credit to the debit side of the family ledger. Her willingness to do this so that I could go to college, even though the burden of doing it grew heavier from year to year, sprang from a determination to put the education of her children first and everything else second. When my younger sister, Carolyn, and I were in grade school, she spent hour upon hour with us as we did our homework. Both she and my father could see no reason why our monthly report cards should not be invariably marked with three A's—for achievement, effort, and conduct. Once when a single B plus slipped in among the A's, I brought the report card home with great trepidation, after vainly trying to think of some way of forging my father's signature so that I did not have to show him that card. My sister never slipped up—or, perhaps, I should say down—even once.

It was not only in the matter of grades that my father and mother expected compliance with their standards. As I look back, the demands they made upon their children were thoroughly reasonable even though, in some particulars, they were severe or exacting. We were expected to be polite or well-spoken in the manner in which we addressed our elders; we took second place at the family board and were permitted to speak only when the conversation lapsed. During most of the years I lived at home, there were usually six or seven adults seated around the dining room table at the evening meal; my mother and father, my sister, and I formed the nucleus of a family that included my grandmother, my grandmother's two sisters, and one of my mother's unmarried brothers. I think my sister and I benefited from the discipline this imposed upon us, the two youngest members of the family circle. In fact, I count it among the blessings of good fortune that permissiveness, which tends to breed waywardness, self-indulgence, and even sloppiness, had not yet come into vogue, just as I also count it a blessing that the meager means of my parents required me to fend for myself and earn my way instead of having the things I wanted handed to me. In this last respect I regard my own children as being less fortunate than I; and I sometimes fear it may also be true that, although they have enjoyed more advantages in their childhood than I ever had, they will in years to come be less grateful for what they have received than I now am for what my parents did for me.

I do not wish to give the impression that I was always docile or obedient. My own memory of infractions and punishments has become faint and fragmentary, but I have it on the testimony of my sister that I was a difficult child, especially during the troublesome period of adolescence. I think things might have been better if I had left home when I went to college at seventeen, but my scholarship covered only tuition and my family could not afford more than a few dollars a week of pocket money for books, subway fares, and lunches. The major run-in I had with my father during those years arose from his demand that I return home before midnight. After a number of angry scenes occasioned by my delinquency, he laid down the principle that I could do as I pleased only after I was supporting myself, but that I would have to comply with his requests as long as he was paying the bills. I capitulated. It seemed to me then, as it does now, that he had reason on his side.

My sister's memory of our childhood together, which I am sure is much more reliable than my own, makes me out to have been somewhat imperious in the demands I made on my family, as well as somewhat overbearing toward her. Carolyn was four years younger than I, more docile and more studious. Musical, she learned to play the piano by watching me take piano lessons. They were entirely wasted on me, but she became an accomplished musician. Her academic career, unlike mine, involved no irregularities; she went from one level to another, all the way up to a Ph.D. in anthropology, getting diplomas and degrees with honors at all the appointed intervals on the way.

Carolyn recollects my early obsession with putting and keeping things in order. After I began to collect books, I would become furious if their arrangement were in the least respect disturbed. I would leave notes on the door of my room warning anyone who attempted to clean it that the papers on my desk were not to be touched. She tells me that I would often shut the door of that room, not only on my family, but also on my friends, saying, "Go away, I'm thinking." She and her friends patiently submitted to my trial efforts at being a teacher and a lecturer. Perhaps I discovered fairly early that trying to transmit what one has just learned is a good way to understand it better. One story that she tells, I hope is apocryphal. While we were both still of a tender age, I undertook to explain the facts of life to her in evolutionary terms, saying, "First there are fish, then come monkeys, and then little girls. Mother will tell you the rest."

My parents, my sister, and the rest of my family put up with all these oddities. It might have been better for me if they had been a little less tolerant; some of my excesses might have been tempered, especially one that my wife and various secretaries have complained about—compulsive orderliness. Nevertheless, I regard the circumstances of my childhood and youth as beneficent, and for most of the blessings conferred upon my early years, I am grateful to my parents.

Looking back on my life since I left home, I count myself unusually fortunate that, during more than fifty years of earning a living, almost all the work I have elected to do has consisted of tasks that I would gladly have taken on even if I had had an independent income. If leisure work, as opposed to drudgery, comprises all those activities in which one would engage for reasons of intrinsic reward and without need of extrinsic compensation, then most of my paid employments have been largely leisure pursuits. Drudgery consists of tasks that no one would perform unless he could not earn his subsistence in any other way. In between the extremes of subsistence work that is drudgery and leisure work for which one is paid, there lies a spectrum of occupations in which both aspects of work are found in varying degrees of admixture. My good fortune has been that I have had the opportunity to choose the occupations of my life so that they would be predominantly filled with leisure.

Adding this to all the other blessings that I have mentioned, I should say that the external conditions of my life have, in the main, facilitated, rather than impeded, the pursuit of happiness—the effort to make a good human life for one's self. The extent to which an individual succeeds or fails depends on how he takes advantage of the conditions of his life to control what is wholly within his power—his desires and choices, the use of his talents, the direction of his energies, and the employment of his mind. The conditions of my life being so favorable, my failures are entirely my own fault.

According to a story told by Plutarch, Plato, when asked to enumerate the circumstances for which he was grateful, mentioned just two—that he was born a Greek rather than a barbarian, and in the time of Socrates rather than at any other time. Among the elements of good fortune in my life, I would certainly include being born in the United States and being born in this century. In many critical respects, the environment, both physical and social, has changed drastically in my lifetime. However, as far as I can tell, the direction of my life has not been altered by the changing scene. I have lived through two world wars and many smaller ones, two or three serious economic depressions, the atomic bomb, mounting inflation, the ever-increasing rapidity of technological change, the so-called knowledge explosion, some personal experiences of environmental pollution. I have suffered serious distress, but not despair, with regard to Vietnam, the continuing injustice to the blacks, the manifest discontent on the part of the young, and the corruption associated with the name of Watergate. I have also grown increasingly aware of the threats to the future raised by the deterioration of the environment, population growth, the depletion of energy and other resources, the shortage of food, and the failures of schooling. Throughout all this, I have not found it necessary to adopt different principles or to reorder my priorities.

Some of my contemporaries, including close friends, have been strongly affected by current crises and disorders and even frustrated by their intractability. To use the current jargon, many of my contemporaries have suffered alienation, future shock, an identity crisis, loss of faith, or a shift in values. Yet, in all honesty, I must confess that I have not found life more difficult, more complicated, more dehumanized, more uncomfortable, more fearful. However difficult it may be to lead a good human life at any time, I doubt that it is any more difficult to make a good life for one's self today than it was at any earlier moment in human history.

Not even the knowledge explosion has affected me adversely, though this, of all external changes, perhaps impinges most directly upon the kind of work I have done. The knowledge explosion imposes heavier and heavier burdens on the specialist—narrowing the field of his specialty and making communication with other specialists more difficult. But it does not affect the generalist. It is no more difficult for the generalist to survey the whole of human knowledge than it was at the beginning of this century. More than two thousand years ago, Aristotle, in addition to being a generalist able to survey the whole of human knowledge, was also a specialist in almost every field. That is no longer possible for anyone; but one can still be a generalist without being a specialist in more than one field.

On the occasion of a lecture that I gave at Aspen in 1974, I asked myself and the audience a series of questions, all couched in the same rhetorical form, and all aiming to discover whether the external changes through which we have lived have caused us to change our minds in any fundamental commitment. The questions follow:

1. If we ever did think that having some grasp of the truth about the world, about man, and about society is worth having, have we any reason not to think so still?

2. If we ever did think that having our life enriched by genuine human friendships and loves is an indispensable good, have we any reason to change our mind on that score?

3. If we ever did think that being reasonable in dealing with other human beings and being prudent in the conduct of our own affairs are desirable forms of conduct, do we not still think so?

4. If we ever did think that health, in both body and mind, and longevity are conditions contributing to our happiness, have we changed our mind on this score?

5. If we ever did think that having enough free time to engage in the pursuits of leisure is needed in order to live a good human life, do we not still think so?

6. If we ever did think that a good life requires a moderate possession of worldly goods and that either too much or too little wealth can be a serious disadvantage, have we any reason to think otherwise now?

7. If we ever did think that having a good moral character or being morally mature is indispensable to living well (or, in other words, being temperate and having fortitude instead of yielding to childish indulgences and childish fears), are we not still of the same mind?

8. If we ever did think that civil peace and social justice are factors which facilitate the individual's pursuit of happiness, have we any reason now for thinking the opposite?

9. If we ever did think that the reign of law, not of force, and a government of laws which secures and protects natural rights based on natural needs, creates a society that enhances human life, are we still of the same opinion?

10. If we ever did think that everyone should have as much freedom as he can use justly, without harming other individuals or the community as a whole, do we not still think so?

How has the changing scene affected our answers to these questions? I must say that no changes that have occurred around me have altered my affirmation of the fundamental values to which these questions call attention. Nothing that has happened challenges them or raises any disturbing doubts about them. But on one score, and I think only one, a great change has taken place, and that is in my attitude toward the future. The future no longer seems benign to me, as it once did. I am concerned about the circumstances under which my children will live and the kind of lives they will be able to lead. I am concerned about the human prospect.

Bibliography of Mortimer J. Adler

Compiled by Otto A. Bird and Marlys G. Allen

BOOKS

1927

Dialectic, London, Kegan Paul, Trench Trubner & Co., Ltd., and New York, Harcourt, Brace and Company, Inc., 1927.

1929

Music Appreciation: An Experimental Approach to its Measurement, New York, *Archives of Psychology,* No. 110, 1929 (Ph.D. dissertation).

1931

(with Jerome Michael) *The Nature of Judicial Proof. An Inquiry into the Logical, Legal, and Empirical Aspects of the Law of Evidence,* New York, Columbia University Law School, 1931.

1933

(with Jerome Michael) *Crime, Law and Social Science,* London, Kegan Paul, Trench Trubner & Co., Ltd., and New York, Harcourt, Brace and Company, 1933; reprinted with Introduction by Gilbert Geis, Montclair, N.J., Patterson Smith, 1971.

1935

(with Maude Phelps Hutchins) *Diagrammatics,* New York, Random House, Inc., 1935.

1937

Art and Prudence: A Study in Practical Philosophy, New York and Toronto, Longmans, Green and Co., 1937; Chapters 1–5; 12, reprinted with Introduction by Samuel Hazo as *Poetry and Politics,* Pittsburgh, Pa., Duquesne University Press, 1965.

What Man Has Made of Man: A Study of the Consequences of Platonism and Positivism in Psychology, Introduction by Dr. Franz Alexander, New York and Toronto, Longmans, Green and Co., 1937, reprinted New York, Frederick Ungar Publishing Co., 1957.

1938

Saint Thomas and the Gentiles (The Aquinas Lecture), Milwaukee, Wis., Marquette University Press, 1938.

1940

Problems for Thomists: The Problem of Species, New York, Sheed & Ward, 1940.

The Philosophy and Science of Man: A Collection of Texts as a Foundation for Ethics and Politics, The University of Chicago Bookstore, 1940 (mimeograph).

How To Read A Book: The Art of Getting a Liberal Education, New York, Simon and Schuster, Inc., 1940.

1941

A Dialectic of Morals, Towards the Foundations of Political Philosophy, Notre Dame, Ind., University of Notre Dame Press, 1941, reprinted New York, Frederick Ungar Publishing Co., 1958.

1944

How To Think About War and Peace, New York, Simon and Schuster, Inc., 1944.

1954

Research on Freedom, 2 vols., San Francisco, Institute for Philosophical Research, 1954.

1958

(with Milton Mayer) *The Revolution in Education,* Introduction by Clarence Faust, Chicago, The University of Chicago Press, 1958.

(with Louis O. Kelso) *The Capitalist Manifesto,* New York, Random House, Inc., 1958, reprinted Westport, Conn., Greenwood Press, Publishers, 1973.

The Idea of Freedom: A Dialectical Examination of the Conceptions of Freedom, Volume I, Garden City, N.Y., Doubleday & Company, Inc., 1958, reprinted Westport, Conn., Greenwood Press, Publishers, 1973.

1961

(with Louis O. Kelso) *The New Capitalists: A Proposal to Free Economic Growth from the Slavery of Savings,* New York, Random House, Inc., 1961, reprinted Westport, Conn., Greenwood Press, Publishers, 1975.

The Idea of Freedom: A Dialectical Examination of the Controversies about Freedom, Volume II, Garden City, N.Y., Doubleday & Company, Inc., 1961, reprinted Westport, Conn., Greenwood Press, Publishers, 1973.

1965

The Conditions of Philosophy: Its Checkered Past, Its Present Disorder, and Its Future Promise (based on the Encyclopaedia Britannica Lectures delivered at the University of Chicago, 1964), New York, Atheneum Publishers, 1965.

1967

The Difference of Man and The Difference It Makes (based on the Encyclopaedia Britannica Lectures delivered at the University of Chicago, 1966), New York, Holt, Rinehart and Winston, Inc., 1967.

1970

The Time of Our Lives: The Ethics of Common Sense, New York, Holt, Rinehart and Winston, Inc., 1970.

1971

The Common Sense of Politics, New York, Holt, Rinehart and Winston, Inc., 1971.

1972

(with Charles Van Doren) *How To Read A Book: The Classic Guide to Intelligent Reading,* Revised and Updated Edition, New York, Simon and Schuster, Inc., 1972.

1975

(with William Gorman) *The American Testament,* New York, Praeger Publishers, Inc., 1975.

1976

Some Questions About Language: A Theory of Human Discourse and Its Objects, La Salle, Ill., Open Court Publishing Co., 1976.

ARTICLES

1927

"The Human Equation in Dialectic," *Psyche,* 28 (April 1927), 68–82 (consisting of pp. 102–122 of *Dialectic*).

"Spengler, The Spenglerites, and Spenglerism," *Psyche,* 29 (July 1927), 73–84.

1931

"Legal Certainty," in "Law and the Modern Mind: A Symposium," *Columbia Law Review,* XXXI (January 1931), 91–108.

1933

"A Determination of Useful Observables," in "A Symposium on the Observability of Social Phenomena with Respect to Statistical Analysis," *Sociologus,* 9 (March 1933), 38–44.

1934

(with Jerome Michael) "The Trial of an Issue of Fact," *Columbia Law Review,* XXXIV (November–December 1934), 1–115.

"Art and Aesthetics," *Comment,* The University of Chicago Literary and Critical Quarterly, 2 (Winter 1934), 1–2.

1935

"Creation and Imitation: An Analysis of *Poiesis,*" *Proceedings of the American Catholic Philosophical Association,* December 1935, 153–174.

1937

"Tradition and Communication," *Proceedings of the American Catholic Philosophical Association,* December 1937, 101–131.

1938

"Reading," *The University of Chicago Magazine,* June 1938, 10–13.

1939

"A Christian Educator," *Orate Fratres,* XIII (January 22, 1939), 123–129.

"Parties and the Common Good," *The Review of Politics,* 1 (January 1939), 51–83.

"The Crisis in Contemporary Education," *The Social Frontier,* V (February 1939), 140–145.

"Are the Schools Doing Their Job?", *Town Meeting,* Columbia University Press, 4 (March 6, 1939), 11–16.

"Education and Democracy," *The Commonweal,* XXIX (March 17, 1939), 581–583.

"Can Catholic Education Be Criticized?", *The Commonweal,* XXIX (April 14, 1939), 680–683.

"Hierarchy," *Saint Mary's Chimes,* XLVIII (June 1939), 111–116, reprinted *Catholic Digest,* 4 (October 1940), 39–43.

"Tradition and Novelty in Education," *Better Schools,* 1 (June 1939), 104; 108.

"Liberalism and Liberal Education," *The Educational Record,* July 1939, 422–436.

"Lesson in Criticism," *The Commonweal,* XXX (October 13, 1939), 548–551.

"The Demonstration of Democracy," *Proceedings of the American Catholic Philosophical Association,* December 1939, 1–44.

1940

"The Great Books: 1," *The University of Chicago Magazine,* February 1940, 10–11; 26–28.

"The Great Books: 2," *The University of Chicago Magazine,* March 1940, 8–10; 25–26.

"Education in Contemporary America," *Better Schools,* 2 (March–April 1940), 76–80.

"Docility and Authority," *The Commonweal,* XXXI (April 5, 1940), 504–507.

"Docility and History," *The Commonweal,* XXXII (April 26, 1940), 4–8.

"To the College Graduate—June, 1940," *The Commonweal,* XXXII (June 28, 1940), 201–203.

"How to Mark a Book," *The Saturday Review of Literature,* July 6, 1940, 11–12.

"The Use and Abuse of Dictionaries," *Good Housekeeping,* September 1940, 160–161.

"How to Answer Questions," *Good Housekeeping,* October 1940, 73; 201–202.

"This Pre-War Generation," *Harper's Magazine,* October 1940, 524–534.

"God and the Professors" (An address given at the Conference of Science, Philosophy and Religion in New York City in September 1940), Huntington, Ind., Our Sunday Visitor Press, December 1, 1940.

"Before You Read A Book," *Good Housekeeping,* December 1940, 32–33.

"How To Keep Awake While Reading," *Good Housekeeping,* June 1940, 62.

1941

"Invitation to the Pain of Learning," *The Journal of Educational Sociology,* 14 (February 1941), 358–363.

"What Is Basic About English?" *College English,* 2 (April 1941), 653–675.

"The Demonstrability of Democracy: A Reply to Dr. [Charles] O'Neil," *The New Scholasticism,* XV (April 1941), 162–168.

"Solution of the Problem of Species," *The Thomist,* III (April 1941), 279–379.

(with Walter Farrell, O.P.) "The Theory of Democracy," *The Thomist,* III (July 1941), 397–449.

"Are There Absolute and Universal Principles on Which Education Should Be Founded?" (A debate in which Adler takes Pro view and Paul A. Schilpp takes Con), *Educational Trends,* Northwestern University, IX (July–August 1941), 11–18. [Adler's portion]

"The Order of Learning," *The Moraga Quarterly,* Autumn 1941, 3–25.

"The Chicago School," *Harper's Magazine,* September 1941, 377–388.

"Progressive Education? No!" *The Rotarian,* September 1941, 29–30; 56–57.

(with Walter Farrell, O.P.) "The Theory of Democracy—Part II," *The Thomist,* III (October 1941), 588–652.

"How to Read a Dictionary," *The Saturday Review of Literature,* December 13, 1941, 3–4; 18–20.

"A Question About Law," *Essays in Thomism,* edited by R. E. Brennan, New York, Sheed & Ward, 1941, 207–236.

"Introduction" to *Thomistic Psychology,* by R. E. Brennan, New York, Macmillan, Inc., 1941, vii–xiv.

1942

(with Walter Farrell, O.P.) "The Theory of Democracy—Part III," *The Thomist,* IV (January 1942), 121–181.

"What Every Schoolboy Doesn't Know," *Pulse,* March 1942, 7–9; 32.

(with Walter Farrell, O.P.) "The Theory of Democracy—Part III (Continued)," *The Thomist,* IV (April 1942), 286–354.

(with Walter Farrell, O.P.) "The Theory of Democracy—Part IV," *The Thomist,* IV (July 1942), 446–522.

(with Walter Farrell, O.P.) "The Theory of Democracy—Part IV (Continued)," *The Thomist,* IV (October 1942), 692–761.

"In Defense of the Philosophy of Education," *Philosophies of Education,* Forty-first Yearbook, Part I, 1942, 197–249.

1943

"The Demonstration of God's Existence," *The Thomist,* V (January 1943), 188–218.

(with Walter Farrell, O.P.) "The Theory of Democracy—Part IV (Continued)," *The Thomist,* VI (April 1943), 49–118.

(with Walter Farrell, O.P.) "The Theory of Democracy—Part IV (Continued)," *The Thomist,* VI (July 1943), 251–277.

(with Walter Farrell, O.P.) "The Theory of Democracy—Part V," *The Thomist,* VI (October 1943), 367–407.

1944

"Thinking Straight on War and Peace," *Vogue,* January 15, 1944, 61–62.

"What Every Schoolboy Doesn't Know," *Coronet,* January 1944, 87–91.

"The Fetish of Internationalism," *Common Sense,* XIII (January 1944), 15–19.

(with Walter Farrell, O.P.) "The Theory of Democracy—Part V (Continued)," *The Thomist,* VII (January 1944), 80–131.

"Can Adults Think?", *Ladies Home Journal,* April 1944, 24; 188.

"How to Talk Sense in Company," *Esquire,* June 1944, 59; 171–176.

"War and the Rule of Law," *War and the Law,* edited by Ernst W. Puttkammer, Chicago, The University of Chicago Press, 1944, 178–198.

1945

"Liberal Education—Theory and Practice," *The University of Chicago Magazine,* 37 (March 1945), 10–11, reprinted in the *Vassar Alumnae Magazine,* November 15, 1945.

"The State of the Nation's Higher Education—Two Views of Benjamin Fine's New Book [*Democratic Education: A Report on the Colleges*]," *Saturday Review,* December 29, 1945, 7–8; 31. [Adler's view]

"The Future of Democracy," *Proceedings of the American Catholic Philosophical Association,* 1945, 3–24.

1947

"The Philosopher," *The Works of the Mind,* edited by Robert B. Heywood, Chicago and London, The University of Chicago Press, 1947, 215–246.

"The Doctrine of Natural Law in Philosophy," *Natural Law Institute Proceedings,* 1947, University of Notre Dame, 1 (1949), 65–84.

1951

"The Next Twenty-five Years in Philosophy," *The New Scholasticism,* XXV (January 1951), 81–110.

"Labor, Leisure, and Liberal Education," *The Journal of General Education,* VI (October 1951), 35–45.

1952

"Adult Education," *Journal of Higher Education,* XXIII (February 1952), 59–68.

(with Jerome Michael) "Real Proof: I," *Vanderbilt Law Review,* 5 (April 1952), 344–384.

"Doctor and Disciple," *Journal of Higher Education,* XXIII (April 1952), 173–180.

"The Hierarchy of Essences," *The Review of Metaphysics,* VI (September 1952), 3–30.

(with Philip F. Mulhern, O.P.) "Footnote to *The Theory of Democracy,*" in *From an Abundant Spring,* The Walter Farrell Memorial Volume of *The Thomist,* edited by The Staff, New York: P. J. Kenedy & Sons, 1952, 137–151.

1953

"Jerome Michael," *Columbia Law Review,* 53 (March 1953), 310–311.

1956

"Controversy in the Life and Teaching of Philosophy," *Proceedings of the American Catholic Philosophical Association,* 1956, 3–22.

1957

"The Questions Science Cannot Answer," *Bulletin of the Atomic Scientists,* XIII (April 1957), 120–125.

1958

"Freedom: A Study of the Development of the Concept in the English and American Traditions of Philosophy," *The Review of Metaphysics,* XI (March 1958), 380–410.

"What Is an Idea?", *Saturday Review,* November 22, 1958, 13; 40–41.

"Leisure and Retirement," *Eagle,* November 1958, 12–13.

"Hard Reading Made Easy," *Mayfair* (Montreal), November 1958, condensed in *Reader's Digest,* December 1958, 81–83.

1959

"The Professor or the Dialogue?", *The Owl,* Santa Clara University, 1959, 10–19.

1963

"Challenges of Philosophies in Communication," *Journalism Quarterly,* University of Washington, June 14, 1962, Special Summer Supplement 1963, 449–459.

"How to Read a Book Superficially," *Playboy,* December 1963, 115; 122; 196; 199.

"Never Say 'Retire,' " *The Journal of the American Society of Chartered Life Underwriters,* XVII (Winter 1963), 5–14.

1964

"The Future of Democracy: A Swan Song," *Humanistic Education and Western Civilization: Essays for Robert M. Hutchins,* edited by Arthur A. Cohen, New York, Holt, Rinehart and Winston, Inc., 1964, 30–43.

1966

"The Great Books of 2066," *Playboy,* January 1966, 137; 224–226; 228.

"Contributions of the West," *The Barat Review,* 1 (June 1966), 91–97.

"God and Modern Man," *The Critic,* XXV (October–November 1966), 18–23.

1967

"Intentionality and Immateriality," *The New Scholasticism,* XLI (Summer 1967), 312–344.

"The Immateriality of Conceptual Thought," *The New Scholasticism,* XLI (Autumn 1967), 489–497.

1968

"Sense Cognition: Aristotle vs. Aquinas," *The New Scholasticism,* XLII (Autumn 1968), 578–591.

"The Challenge to the Computer," *Proceedings of the American Catholic Philosophical Association*, 1968, 20–27 (taken from Chapter 14 of *The Difference of Man and The Difference It Makes*).

1974

"Little Errors in the Beginning," *The Thomist*, XXXVIII (January 1974), 27–48.

"The Equivocal Use of the Word 'Analogical,'" *The New Scholasticism*, XLVIII (Winter 1974), 4–18.

"The Joy of Learning," *Know: The [Encyclopaedia] Britannica Magazine*, I (1974), 18–21.

1976

"Education and the Pursuit of Happiness," Commencement Address, University of Denver, May 29, 1976.

"Declaration v. Manifesto," *The Center Magazine*, IX (September–October, 1976), 38–48.

"Teaching and Learning," *From Parnassus: Essays in Honor of Jacques Barzun*, edited by William R. Keylor and Dora B. Weiner, New York, Harper & Row, Publishers, 1976.

"The Schooling of a People," *The Americans: 1976*, Critical Choices for Americans, Volume II, edited by Irving Kristol and Paul H. Weaver, Lexington, Mass., D. C. Heath and Company, 1976, 131–149.

"The Bodyguards of Truth," *Proceedings of the American Catholic Philosophical Association*, L, 1976.

EDITED WORKS

Great Books of the Western World (52 vols.), Chicago, Encyclopaedia Britannica, Inc., 1952.

The Great Ideas, A Syntopicon of Great Books of the Western World (2 vols.), Chicago, Encyclopaedia Britannica, Inc., 1952.

(with Robert M. Hutchins) *The Great Ideas Today*, Chicago, Encyclopaedia Britannica, Inc., 1961– .

(with Robert M. Hutchins) *Gateway to the Great Books* (10 vols.), Chicago, Encyclopaedia Britannica, Inc., 1963.

The Annals of America (20 vols.), Chicago, Encyclopaedia Britannica, Inc., 1968.

Propaedia: Outline of Knowledge and Guide to the Britannica, The New Encyclopaedia Britannica (30 vols.), 15th Edition, Chicago, Encyclopaedia Britannica, Inc., 1974.

Index